Papa Doc & the Tonton Macoutes

This book is dedicated to the Haitian people who, tired of being merely spectators of their fate and without resorting to armed force, gave the world a lesson by uprooting the Duvalier dictatorship in its 29th year. They made possible the publication of this book, previously banned in Haiti.

It is hoped that understanding the errors of the past may aid the people in not repeating those errors. There is much to be "dechouke"—poverty, misery, macoutism, dishonesty, greed and graft. Most vital is the changing of the attitude that made such a dictatorship possible. All Haitians must be vigilant and understand the egotism and hunger for power and wealth that drive some people to such excess. It is time for Haiti to enjoy a government at the service of its people—not a people at the service of its president, his family and his friends.

Papa Doc & the Tonton Macoutes

BERNARD DIEDERICH
and AL BURT

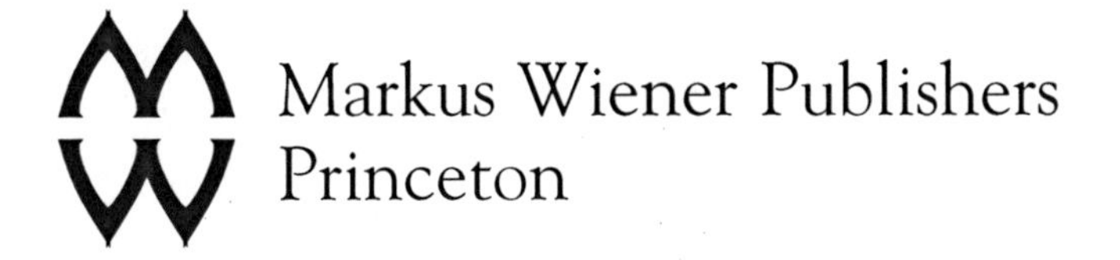
Markus Wiener Publishers
Princeton

Third printing, 2009

First Markus Wiener Publishers Edition, 2005

Originally published under the title *Papa Doc: Haiti and Its Dictator*

Cover design by J. B. Diederich

For information write to:
Markus Wiener Publishers
231 Nassau Street
Princeton, NJ 08542 USA
www.markuswiener.com

Library of Congress Cataloging-in-Publication Data
Diederich, Bernard.
Papa Doc & the Tonton Macoutes / Bernard Diederich and Al Burt.
Includes index.
ISBN-13: 978-1-55876-290-9 (alk. paper)
ISBN-10: 1-55876-290-6 (alk. paper)
1. Duvalier, François, 1907-1971. 2. Haiti—History—1934-1986.
I. Burt, Al. II. Title.
F1928.D86D5 2005
972.94'06'092—dc22
[B]

2005043954

Markus Wiener Publishers books are printed in the United States of America on acid-free paper, and meet the guidelines for permanence and durability of the Committee on Production Guidelines for Book Longevity of the Council on Library Resources.

Contents

Preface

In a world racked by seemingly larger issues of global terrorism and nuclear threat, it is easy to overlook the less-sensational geopolitical crises that abound. Yet none is more wrenching—and demanding of international attention—than the tragedy of Haiti.

As the French colony of St. Domingue, the Caribbean land was populated by African slaves who made it the major center of transatlantic trade, providing Europe with sugar, coffee, tobacco, and precious hardwoods, among other products. However, this Creole-speaking nation, which won its independence from France in 1804 after a long and bloody slave revolt, stands today as a Dante-esque example of the human devastation that can be wrought by a despotic ruler's megalomania, greed, and murderous brutality. This book is about one of those tyrants, François (Papa Doc) Duvalier, whose barbaric, authoritarian legacy continues to plague Haiti today.

Nearly four decades ago, a journalist colleague and I, with the publication of this book, *Papa Doc*, endeavored to sound an alarm about the dire plight of the people of Haiti under the Duvalier dictatorship. Though he died in 1971 of natural causes, his ghost haunted Haitians for another fifteen years under the less repressive, yet only slightly less terrifying and exploitive, regime of his son and successor, Jean-Claude (Baby Doc) Duvalier.

By the time Jean-Claude Duvalier was ousted in 1986, the nearly 30-year-long Duvalier dynasty had, in the name of absolute power, destroyed the nation's social, political, and juridical fabric, establishing in its stead a new order: a predatory, kleptocratic state, sustained by state terrorism.

Jean-Claude Duvalier was followed by a succession of military interim regimes rocked by instability and violence, but in the late 1980s a glimmer of hope appeared on the horizon—in the form of a young, politically ambitious Roman Catholic priest named Jean-Bertrand Aristide. Casting himself as the people's Messiah—Papa Doc also played on the people's faith—the volatile cleric won their confidence, and they gave him their overwhelming majority vote in Haiti's first truly democratic balloting in 1990. His downtrodden followers had cried out for "Justice!" but for Aristide the pull of traditional despotism was too great to resist. In 2004 it proved to be his downfall. Faced with a popular rebellion led by students and members of the former Haitian army, Aristide and his family fled Haiti on February 29, 2004. He now resides in South Africa.

Like Papa Doc, Aristide blended a benign façade with cold-blooded terror, charting a violent course and flouting the constitutional confines of parliamentary democracy. (The reason why so many Haitian chiefs of state have been overthrown or met untimely deaths has been their reluctance to relinquish power.) For concerned Haitians who had survived Papa Doc's brutal rule, the great fear all along was that history would repeat itself. Unfortunately, Aristide's demagogic outbursts and Machiavellian tactics harked back to Papa Doc's darkest days. As early as 1986, Aristide, as the little priest serving Port-au-Prince's St. Jean Bosco church, preached "*dechouhaj*" (literally, "uprooting") and no mercy for Tonton Macoutes.

That same year, when this book was finally published in Haiti, I gave a copy of the French-language edition to Father Aristide. He had just delivered his fiery trademark sermon, as usual more political than theological. The Foreword to that Haitian edition of *Papa Doc* contained a plea for Haitians to beware another devastating dictatorship and one-man rule; to be vigilant and understand the egotism and hunger for power and wealth that drives people to such excesses.

Alas, as president, Aristide, if he ever read it, ignored my message. Under his rule, Papa Doc's Tonton Macoutes (literally, "bogeymen"; i.e., enforcers and killers) morphed into Aristide's *Chimeres*.

Two decades of dashed hopes after the rise of Aristide, the Haitian people are still mired in the most pitiful misery imaginable, endeavoring to survive without the most basic requirements of human life and amid daily violence. Most have no potable water, not even rudimentary health services, and schools are out of reach for most children. Haitians grow poorer by the hour. At this writing, in the Spring of 2005, they still face the law of the gun, as gangs continue to operate with impunity. Some Haitians desperately attempt to flee by makeshift boat—to the Bahamas, to the Turks & Caicos Islands, to Florida, anywhere—only to be returned to their homeland while others drown in the attempt.

Today, though United Nations peacekeepers are on hand, violence is unabated. Sporadic attacks by marauding gunmen continue on security forces, aimed, officials say, at destabilizing the country ahead of scheduled Fall elections.

Whatever happens in those elections, and afterward, several indisputable facts concerning Haiti are starkly clear: Haiti does not need a self-styled messianic savior, but instead a sincere, level-headed reformer, a unifier who will govern based not only on popular mandate but also on respect for all Haitians. One who will not have, as his or her sole objective, the sheer retention of power, but instead that of serving the authentic best interests of the country and its people; one who will forego the traditional self-serving nepotism of rewarding only relatives and cronies, and instead will instill the values and disciplines of truly representative democracy and constructive meritocracy—the only workable foundations of a modern nation-state.

Otherwise, Haiti will only continue its descent into the social chaos of a failed state—the eight million people inhabiting its crowded confines becoming more desperate by the day; its exploited and depleted natural resources representing a worsening ecological disaster; its human exodus to foreign shores becoming a growing concern for Haiti's hemispheric neighbors.

For Haiti to survive as a viable geopolitical entity, it will require continued, long-term international assistance. However, notwithstanding their current misery, and even though the roots of their country's decades-long contemporary crisis lie in the dark legacy of one man—Papa Doc Duvalier—in the end only Haitians themselves, as a collectivity and a political culture, can rescue their society from the abyss. They must do so by demanding from their future leaders, not a prophet's promised miracles, but, instead, statesmanlike performance. And above all a government that serves the people, not one that exploits even the poor to gain power and wealth.

Bernard Diederich, Port-au-Prince, Haiti, April 2005

Foreword

No one alive (and the dead cannot speak from their unknown graves except to Papa Doc) is better qualified than Bernard Diederich to tell the horrifying story of Haiti under the rule of Dr François Duvalier. Diederich lived in Haiti for fourteen years and he had personal experience not only of the early Duvalier days but of what seems now by contrast to have been the golden period of Magloire's rule; he is married to a Haitian and after his arrest and expulsion by Papa Doc he followed the fortunes of his adopted country from across the border in Santo Domingo. What a story it is: tragic, terrifying, bizarre, even at times comic. Papa Doc sits in his bath wearing his top hat for meditating: the head of his enemy Philogènes stands on his desk: the hearse carrying another enemy's body is stolen by the Tonton Macoutes at the church door: the writer Alexis is stoned to death. There is material here for a Suetonius: Diederich is not a Suetonius, but his book is better documented.

There is something peculiarly Roman in the air of Haiti: Roman in its cruelty, in its corruption and in its heroism. You will not walk far in any Haitian town without seeing the names of Brutus and Cato, perhaps over a baker's shop or a garage. The auguries are still told in the entrails of beasts, and a Senator will sometime take his life in his hands by a declaration against tyranny, like Moreau who spoke up in the Senate against the special powers demanded by Duvalier and paid the extreme penalty (so far as anyone knows). We are nearer to the Europe of Nero and Tiberius than to the Africa of Nkrumah.

That is why Haiti is irrelevant in any discussion of black power. Haiti is the scene of a classical tragedy and not like many emerging states of a black comedy farce in the contemporary manner. We feel sometimes that we are witnessing a tragedy by Racine played by coloured actors – or at the worst moments *Titus Andronicus*.

> On the orders of the President, Lieutenant Abel Jérome cut Philogènes's head off and placed it in a pail of ice. Duvalier dispatched a special Air Force fighter to fetch the head. Why did Duvalier want the head delivered to him at the palace? Weird stories circulated around Port-au-Prince which told of Duvalier sitting alone with the head for hours, trying to communicate with it.

We would not be surprised to see Lavinia enter on the same stage, 'her hands cut off, and her tongue cut out'. Or a messenger bearing two heads and a hand.

This is a very full account of Duvalier's reign which will be indispensable to future historians. I would suggest that the best way to make a track through the thick jungle of savagery, incompetence, greed and superstition is to consider Duvalier's reign in stages. During the first stage it might have been possible to hope that Papa Doc, as he chose to call himself, would not prove a much worse ruler than many others in Haiti's cruel history, but that hope was ended in the carnage of the first bizarre attempt to overthrow him made by two sheriffs of Dade County, Florida, in 1958. The two sheriffs and six men, only three of whom were Haitian, succeeded in seizing the army barracks just behind the National Palace. Not one survived, but they came within an ace of success.

The second stage, perhaps accelerated by fear and insecurity, saw the final establishment of the police state, when Duvalier, unable any longer to trust the army, built up the militia, the palace guard and the Tonton Macoutes at their expense. Then began his long and clever blackmail of the United States. In the OAS and the United Nations Haiti had a vote which the United States needed, equal in importance to any other power, and Duvalier saw to it that they paid cash and credit for that vote. In the absurd world organization with which we have been saddled since the Hitler war, the unscrupulous ruler of even so tiny a state as Haiti can exact protection money like a Chicago gangster from the rich. This second stage ended with the shooting of his old hatchet man Clément Barbot. Barbot, who had been in touch with the American military mission, had attempted to kidnap Duvalier's children. If Duvalier was to be overthrown he seems to have been the American choice as Duvalier's successor, though it is doubtful whether Haiti would have benefited much from the change of tyrant.

After the attempt on Duvalier's children followed the third stage, the stage of terror unlimited and of ineffective guerrilla risings which have continued till today, when half the revenue of the country was spent on the personal security of the President, when American aid was stopped and the American Ambassador withdrawn, when Dominican troops were poised on the frontier and Duvalier threatened a blood-bath in Port-au-Prince and only a rash man would have bet a Haitian *gourde* on his survival. But the guerrillas failed, President Bosch of Santo Domingo was overthrown, and President Johnson gave in to blackmail, sending back to Haiti an Ambassador as timorous as his name, Benson Timmons III, whom Duvalier kept waiting five weeks for an audience and then lectured on how an ambassador should behave, a lecture which he took to heart.

Now we have reached the final stage of tyranny (or so one dares to hope), the stage of megalomania marked politically by Papa Doc's 'election' as President for Life. Now Duvalier has begun to speak of himself as a great writer, he announces (in *Jours de France*) the publication of his collected works, he compares himself with Trotsky, with Mao Tse-tung and with General de Gaulle, and in one remarkable passage in *Le Catéchisme de la révolution* with one higher even than these.

> Our Doc who art in the National Palace for life, hallowed be Thy name by present and future generations. Thy will be done in Port-au-Prince and in the provinces. Give us this day our new Haiti and never forgive the trespasses of the anti-patriots . . .

Surely the end cannot long be delayed. Classical tragedy demands that the pendulum shall swing when it has reached the furthest point of its arc.

When the pendulum does descend I share the authors' hope that Haiti will be allowed to work out her own salvation, without interference from her great neighbour. The Marines were ready to bring Barbot to power in Haiti as they brought Trujillo to power in Santo Domingo. But after the rule of the tyrant, Haiti ought to be given the chance to be ruled by heroes. Heroes are produced by tyranny, and they have not been lacking in her recent history: the Deputy Séraphin, the Senator Moreau, Alexis the writer, the young man Riobé who kept the army and the Tonton at bay from a cave above Kenscoff and shot himself with his last bullet, the thirteen members of the organization *Jeune Haiti* who held out in the mountains of the south-west for three months and died to the last man.

Graham Greene

Introduction

The authors of this book are journalists, not historians or sociologists. They do not pretend to present any kind of dogmatic or scientific picture of Haiti under Dr François Duvalier, Papa Doc. They are not moralists; they do not have a political, a social, an economic or a racial axe to grind. They have attempted to tell the story of a decade under his rule as witnessed by Bernard Diederich, who lived nearly fourteen years in Haiti until his arrest by Tonton Macoutes on 27 April 1963 and his deportation two days later. Al Burt has travelled often to Haiti and has contributed the informed outsider's point of view, so important in interpreting events and their repercussions both inside and outside Haiti.

So as not to implicate Haitians, the authors touched cautiously on certain events because any indiscretion could bring reprisals from one of history's bloodiest tyrants. *The authors wish to point out that no Haitian has co-operated on this book or even seen the manuscript.*

This book is dedicated to the people of Haiti in the hope that once Duvalier goes, they *alone* may find their way to the better life which they so deserve. It was written without any intention of maligning Haiti or the Haitian people. A sincere effort was made to avoid sensationalism.

We feel we must insist on one point: this book is intended as a frank account of the Papa Doc years. If Haitians see in it the fault of their system, the disease that has made Papa Doc possible, then so much the better. They will have to be watchful and selfless in the future and fight courageously and intelligently against this sickness to establish a healthy, enduring regime. It is our hope that the Haitian people will establish a democracy which will bring the peasant into the twentieth century and halt the exploitation of Haitians by Haitians.

There are persistent reports of contingency plans for United States and hemisphere troops to land in Haiti when the dictator goes – plans to which some Latin-American nations are supposed to have subscribed. Allegedly the intervention would be made in the name of peace, to avoid chaos, bloodshed, to safeguard lives of foreign citizens. Yet chaos and bloodshed have been officially sanctioned by hemisphere countries in Haiti for most of the past decade. The authors hope that President Nixon, no stranger to Haiti (cf. Chapter Seven), will not repeat his predecessor's military adventures next door in the Dominican Republic (cf. Chapter Seventeen) by unleashing the Marines on Haiti again. Furthermore, the authors believe that Haitians should be permitted to find their own solutions, that another occupation would only frustrate the application of Haitian solutions to Haitian problems.

Bernard Diederich
Al Burt

1
Election Day

A siren sounded at 6 a.m. that Sunday morning. Election day had begun. The risen sun was just appearing over the mountains and Port-au-Prince was fresh and cool. A few churchgoers hurried to early mass, but most of the capital was gathered at the voting bureaus where Haitians of all colours and social strata stood in lengthening lines. For the first time in 153 years of independence all Haitians over twenty-one were being allowed to vote. Some were anxious to get the job over and done with before either the day or tempers heated up, for this was the third attempt to hold general elections in nine months. During that period of political ferment the country had tried, and abandoned, six provisional forms of government which it had borrowed from its nineteenth-century history. The vacillation and manoeuvring from one form to the other left many dead and many more sorrowing. Families were split; overnight, lifelong friends became mortal enemies. For one brief day there had been civil war.

This 22 September 1957 appeared as a new opportunity of finally ending the political turmoil that had begun the preceding December when a general strike forced strong-man Paul E. Magloire into exile. The choice that confronted the people was deceptively simple – almost one in terms of black and white. Or black versus white, because in colour-conscious Haiti, where 90 per cent of the population is black and the other 10 per cent differs only by shades, the degree of pigmentation is both subtle and vitally important.

One of the Presidential candidates was Dr François Duvalier, an owlish, soft-spoken, strange little black man, son of a justice of the peace. He looked at the world through thick-lensed glasses and spoke in correct, Academy-approved

French about honesty in government and a fair deal for the masses. He talked about his work in a US health programme to eliminate yaws and described himself as a country doctor who had won the support of rural Haiti and US aid technicians.

The contrasting choice was Louis Déjoie, ten years a senator, one of the café-au-lait mulatto elite, a prestigious, starchy-clean type. He claimed the office as a birthright passed down from his ancestor, President Fabre Nicolas Geffrard. Déjoie boasted that he had more US support than Duvalier, including the favour of US business interests as well as the American Embassy.

The question seemed to be whether Haitians preferred a self-styled black idealist or a haughty mulatto patrician. They waited in line to answer, clutching ballots passed to them by partisans, occasionally scrambling and grabbing in playful attempts to substitute their own favourite's papers. There were no official ballots. The parties furnished them. A voter had only to accept one and drop it into a tin box ten inches wide and long and eighteen inches deep. Most would not be able to read the name of the candidate they deposited. For those who could write and had ideas about a candidate of their own, blank paper was furnished. In addition to the President, twenty-one senators and thirty-seven deputies were being elected – an entire new government at once.

Crudely painted campaign signs still decorated the streets. *Votez* and/or *à bas Duvalier/Déjoie* alternated. After months of radio harangues, exploding bombs, and daily gunfire, the capital was strangely quiet. Barking dogs and crowing roosters had it all to themselves. Despite regulations, a few passers-by still wore the blue-peaked 'Duvalier' cloth caps and lettered T-shirts, or the buttons and native straw hats emblazoned with 'Déjoie'. Loosely observed election-day laws forbade active campaigning, equally prohibited sale of alcoholic beverages, travel between communes, and allowed only the military to bear arms. This time the ruling military junta had promised Haiti an orderly election process.

Déjoie partisans shuttled back and forth in their cars between the voting bureaus, casting their own votes and then persuading servants and workers to agree with them. The military favoured Duvalier because he was obviously a harmless little fellow who could be manipulated. To people who believed this, Duvalier would only smile his mysterious half-smile and say nothing; Déjoie said much too much. He threatened sanctions against the military if there was any tampering with the electoral process.

From Cap-Haïtien in the north to Jacmel in the south-west, to the island of Gonave, washed by the blue Caribbean between the jaws of Haiti's upper and lower peninsulas, there were 1,400 polling places, or bureaus. Each of these was limited to accepting 1,500 votes. This was believed adequate to handle the 1.5 million Haitians of voting age listed in the 1950 census.

Even though Haiti's first President, Alexandre Pétion, established voting rights in the Constitution of 1816, this was the first time they were actually being put into practice. Pétion's constitution allowed 'universal suffrage – except for women, criminals, idiots, and menials'. Which gave the vote to about 3 per cent of the population. The ballot was traditionally reserved for the elite and the soldiers who protected its interests. Because Presidential appointees counted the ballots, it was not unusual to discover great unity of opinion in the country. Although by 1950 Congress no longer elected the President, the military had a hand in tabulating the final returns. It was they who announced that Colonel Paul E. Magloire had decisively won. After Magloire's ouster, warring political factions and the reigning military junta agreed on universal suffrage for all Haitians over twenty-one.

Four major candidates had entered the 1957 campaign. They were: Daniel Fignolé, Clément Jumelle, Louis Déjoie, and François Duvalier. During the nine long months of Haiti's political gestation period they elbowed one another for position, threatened, cajoled, and promised. Each strove to control the local magistrates who counted votes and, protected by the army, established and enforced procedure at the polls.

Daniel Fignolé, the recently-appointed compromise President pro tem, was the first to go.

On the night of 16 June enlisted men at the Casernes Dessalines, the main barracks, were allowed to attend a double-feature cowboy movie. On the pretext that some impressionable soldier at a stirring moment might pick up his gun and shoot the screen villain, the soldiers were ordered to leave their weapons at the door. At the end of the second feature the still-unarmed soldiers were driven far out into the boon-docks while a group of officers toting sub machine guns burst into a cabinet meeting, arrested provisional President Fig-nolé, and, detaining his colleagues at gun point, kidnapped him. General Antonio Th. Kébreau, who that night became head of the junta ruling Haiti, explained that he had uncovered a plot to subvert the elections: Fignolé wanted to promote many soldiers and, most suspicious of all, was trying to up the enlisted man's pay. Fignolé was packed off to exile in the United States. It was a turning point of the election.

One of the three dark-complexioned candidates, Fignolé was the darling of the masses in Port-au-Prince. He spoke a pungent, richly descriptive Creole and, when he wished to, could fill the streets of the capital with thousands of stirred-up demonstrators. Fignolé called his oratorical technique 'pressing the button' and, once pressed, his 'steam roller' flattened everything in sight, usually lamp-posts. Since not even he could be sure of controlling the steam roller once it gathered momen-tum, Fignolé used 'the button' as a very effective reserve weapon whenever the campaign appeared to be taking an unusually violent turn. It was his ultimate deterrent. But the cowboy movies left his citadel undefended, and Fignolé was gone before he could open his mouth.

The next black candidate to drop out was Clément Jumelle, a handsome, US-trained economist who was popular with the technicians and the middle class from which Duvalier also derived. However, he had been Minister of Finance during the spendthrift Magloire regime – a serious taint in a land with a more than passing familiarity with starvation. Two days be-fore the elections Jumelle quit the race. He accused the army of arranging for Duvalier's victory and tried to warn Déjoie of the fix. Déjoie ignored him. The only black candidate left was François Duvalier.

Twice during the campaign he and the other two blacks had forgotten their differences when it appeared that Déjoie, the mulatto, might gain control of the country. The second time Fignolé gave his co-operation in exchange for the provisional presidency, a post he held exactly nineteen days. Through all this the military remained the real power, linking one provisional government with the next, eliminating one after the other as the winds of favour blew.

When election day finally came, the tension mounted to a fever pitch. In long lines people sweated and waited for their turn to feed the tin ballot box. There was no registration system. The voter gave his name, which was recorded beside a number in a book. Once his ballot was deposited, the voter went through two processes designed to prevent him voting a second time. An election official clipped the nail off the little finger of his right hand, then another dipped that finger into a bowl of red indelible ink. Floors of the bureaus soon became splattered with red ink and fingernails.

Near the Hôtel de Ville, where pools of water had collected in the street, urchins eager for one more vote knelt and scrubbed off the red ink. More serious double voters stuffed dirt or soap under their fingernails to keep them from being trimmed very short. Later they pushed back the cuticle where the ink had collected; with a thorough wash, their nails could pass muster again.

In the old coffee port of Jacmel, Déjoists discovered the army substituting ballots. One man was killed in the ensuing fracas. In Port-au-Prince four Déjoists were arrested on the charge of vote buying. In all, election day proved a fitting end to a campaign that had seen both candidates literally stoned when they tried to enter the other's most loyal sections.

Traditionally, politicians consider that there are two separate Haitian republics, the republic of the capital and that of the provinces. The republic of Port-au-Prince, where Déjoie was strongest, had never been beaten in any of Haiti's elections, no matter what kind. And over at Duvalier's headquarters concern was growing. François Duvalier sat behind a desk in the study of his house and talked quietly. He was flanked by two bodyguards and against the wall behind him stood a portrait of Jean-Jacques Dessalines in a bicornered hat. Dessalines, Haitian hero of the independence movement, the slave who became renowned as a relentless warrior, was Duvalier's hero. Fighting the French in 1802–4 and the mulattoes in 1805–6, Dessalines's cry had been, 'Cut off their heads; burn down their houses.' Altogether, he was a strange idol for a mild-mannered, soft-spoken, naïve little country doctor to venerate. Or so it seemed at the time.

The din outside Duvalier's house grew with the heat of the day. Sound trucks blared out illegal election slogans; partisans trampled through his small garden. Duvalier could hardly make himself heard above the din. 'The people', he said, 'present the sad spectacle of black misery in the heart of riches. This nation has sufficient wealth, but it is not properly distributed. It is the wretched condition of the masses which drove Dr Duvalier into politics to begin with.' (He frequently refers to himself in the third person.) Duvalier went on to compliment the army and called it a symbol of vigilance. He spoke of honesty and integrity. Then he addressed himself to the topic of voudou whose folkloric importance he acknowledged even while insisting that Haiti should be liberated from the grip of superstition. 'Voudou should be rationalized, like Buddhism and other religions. . . .' This was more of the same low-key persuasiveness that Duvalier had used quite effectively throughout the nine-month campaign. But no matter how enlightened he seemed, the little doctor was always on the alert for treachery (or sorcery).

An election-day crisis developed when an aide walked around the desk between Duvalier and the portrait of Dessalines and leaned over and whispered into Duvalier's ear. The stare through those thick glasses never faltered; the stolid expression never changed. Duvalier rose calmly, climbed a wooden staircase to the second floor, and walked out on to the balcony overlooking the garden. He raised his right arm and pointed toward the water-front slum of La Saline. His followers awaited his words.

It was a startlingly different Duvalier who finally spoke. There issued from this quiet little man the loud, threatening shout of a zealot. 'We are winning in the west. We are winning in the north,' he yelled. 'But here they are buying the vote. They are trying to steal our election from us.' His arm stabbed again and again toward La Saline, where votes were going for two *gourdes* (40 cents United States) each. 'Watch them! Stop them!' Duvalier stormed. As he flailed his arms, his coat flapped open, revealing a pistol tucked into the belt.

This was his first, but not his last, public tirade. This was the Duvalier of whom the little country doctor had spoken in the third person with such admiration. This was the other Duvalier, the one who not only read of Dessalines's head-chopping and house-burning, but who was to imitate him as well.

Duvalier's followers stormed out of the garden, into the trucks, and down the street. Had not the army stopped them, there would have been fighting in the streets which might have sabotaged yet another attempt at a general election.

The next morning the first spectacular election results came in from across the bay. The Isle of Gonave's return, its vote tabulated while Port-au-Prince was still busy counting, was reported in crisp military fashion by Major Gérard Constant, later to become Duvalier's fourth commander of the armed forces: Duvalier, 18,841; Déjoie, 463. The count contrasted somewhat with a 1950 census report which gave the roadless island a voting population of 13,302.

Many charges of irregularities followed. Déjoists claimed that the magistrates rigged the vote, and that the military had pressured for Duvalier. They complained that the distribution of polling booths was arranged so that in some populous areas the number of booths – each allowed only 1,500 votes –

was not sufficient. Only in Port-au-Prince, where Déjoie won, did they concede an honest count.

Officially, Duvalier received 679,884 votes to Déjoie's 266,993. Duvalierists swept the Senate, including Déjoie's own Senate seat, and the Déjoie party won only two seats in the House.

In the battle of the two republics, Port-au-Prince had lost to the provinces for the first time in history. Haiti had held its first election by universal suffrage and, with the army's decisive prodding, 'chosen' Dr François Duvalier.

2
History

When Duvalier moved into Haiti's gleaming white presidential palace in 1957 there was some hope in the tiny land that had always felt itself to be the orphan of the Americas. Seldom has a leader been confronted by a greater historic challenge or a greater opportunity to change the course of history.

Duvalier had the basis for strong support. He was black and he had both the prestige of being an MD plus the sure attraction of knowing and understanding voudou. He campaigned on the platform of Dumarsais Estimé, a grass-roots social reformer; he swore that he would advance the revolution Estimé had begun. But for Haiti, rich only in Haitians – 90 per cent of them peasant – it is a historic truth that politicians always promise the peasant the most and deliver him the least. Soon after he assumed office it became painfully clear that Duvalier was bound by the same unhappy traditions he had promised to change. Nine years after he took over, Haitians knew that Papa Doc was only different from his predecessors in the volume of his brutality and greed. Under him Haiti became the horror of the hemisphere, a land where, in human terms, conditions were far worse than under the more widely publicized and condemned Communist regime of Fidel Castro.

Ironically, Haiti had once been the jewel of the Caribbees, the single richest colony in the world, and 'rich as a Creole' had once been a common expression. But that was in the days when Haiti (the western third of the Island of Hispaniola; Santo Domingo, the Dominican Republic, occupying the other two-thirds) was a lush French plantation worked by African slaves.

Slavery came to Hispaniola just eighteen years after Columbus discovered the New World. It was necessary to import blacks from Africa since the Spaniards had already worked most of the island's native Arawak Indians to death in a search for gold.

The French did not arrive until early in the seventeenth century when a few wanderers settled on the Isle of Tortuga, six miles off Hispaniola's north coast. They raided the mainland for Spanish cattle which ran wild. Their custom of curing meat over green-wood fires on spits or grills called *boucans* earned them the name *boucaniers,* later anglicized to buccaneers.

Although Spain retained firm control of the rest of the island, the French gradually infiltrated the westernmost segment and established legal claim to it through the Treaty of Ryswick in 1697. During the next hundred years this territory with its slaves and sugar cane became the envy of all the world's other colony-seeking nations. In fact, the total trade of what is now known as Haiti was once estimated as greater than all of England's thirteen North American colonies put together. Shock waves sent out by the French Revolution in 1789 changed all this, however.

The white aristocracy then numbered about 36,000 with some 28,000 *affranchis* or freedmen, mostly mulatto, and one-half million black slaves. The first great revolt began on 14 August 1791, at a secret gathering of slave foremen at Bois Caïman or Alligator Woods. The meeting, held on a night made eerie by a tropical storm, was presided over by a giant slave named Boukman, famed far and wide as a voudou priest or *houngan*.

Boukman and his followers swore to 'live free or die'. They sealed their call to revolution with the blood of a sacrificed pig. In a matter of days former slaves ran wild; flames shot hundreds of feet into the air; the sky turned blood red. Although Boukman himself died fighting, the oath he extracted was to unleash centuries of still-unslaked fury as other leaders emerged.

The greatest of these, Toussaint Louverture, was about fifty when the revolt began. A coachman in his slave days, he had taught himself to read and write at the age of forty. He was small, ugly, smart, and strong. His excellent horsemanship earned him the nickname *centaure de la Savanne* or The Savannah Centaur. With his knowledge of the written word and his innate military skill, he commanded the attention of the Spanish and soon they made him leader of the amorphous bands of former slaves who had come over to their side in the struggle against France.

But Toussaint Louverture was more than a military genius, he also proved himself a statesman, for during this period he envisioned – and later carried out – a dream to free Haiti while retaining an attachment to France through dominion status, thus providing a sure market for Haiti's sugar and rum. In 1794 Toussaint, persuaded that the newly liberated Haitians would gain more with the French Republic than under the Spanish king, took his army of 4,000 blacks and defected from Spain. He then fought the Spanish and the British under the French *tricolore*.

When he had the situation well in hand, Toussaint replaced the French governor as his first step towards acquiring independent dominion status. The French Directoire, worried by Toussaint's disquieting aims, quickly appointed a new governor who, by flattering the mulatto leader Rigaud, managed to pit him against Toussaint. But the black general merely deported this new governor to France and seized the reins of the government as Rigaud revolted. For the first time in Haiti's bloody history, mulatto–versus–black antagonism flared up.

In 1800, after a year of warfare, the beaten Rigaud left for France with his second-in-command, Pétion, and several other mulatto officers. The following year Toussaint marched east and seized the capital city, Santo Domingo, from the Spanish. With all Hispaniola under his rule, it appeared as though prosperity might again be in the offing for the lush little island. But then Napoleon sent a force of 43,000 veteran troops under his brother-in-law, Leclerc, to depose 'that gilded African', as he called Toussaint, and restore slavery. Leclerc landed in 1802 at Cap-Haïtien.

As Leclerc's troops pushed inland, Toussaint instigated a scorched-earth policy. Towns were burned, and the first to go was Cap-Français (now Cap-Haïtien), the pride of the colony. Everywhere they went, the French found smouldering ruins and charred crops. Henry Christophe, the English-speaking ex-slave who had been a member of a contingent that included some eight hundred Haitian 'volunteers' against the British in the American War of Independence, and who had fought alongside Washington in the 1778 siege of Savannah, put the torch to his own residence in Cap-Français. Dessalines followed by setting his own palatial residence at Petite Rivière de l'Artibonite ablaze. Everywhere the French encountered stiff resistance, and several of Napoleon's veteran regiments were soundly defeated. On both sides bitterness grew.

Yet Toussaint still believed that his country would prosper most as a trading partner with France and his failure to raise a cry for complete and total independence caused confusion among his followers. The former slaves were not inspired to the heights of fanatical bravery that would have decisively turned the war in their favour.

Eventually Christophe went over to Leclerc, who already had in his ranks such brilliant Haitians as Pétion, Rigaud, and many other officers of wide local prestige and influence. With Christophe gone, the French defeated the black army in the Artibonite Valley and Toussaint and Dessalines surrendered to generous, and insincere, promises. The French wanted to restore slavery, something they had already done in Martinique.

Toussaint was kidnapped and sent to France, where he died in a dungeon. But as the Haitians understood what the French were really after, the insurrection began anew. Pétion joined Dessalines and blacks and mulattoes made common cause.

The French also faced another deadly enemy, yellow fever. Leclerc died and was replaced by one of the most brutal of French generals, Rochambeau, who imported dogs from Cuba to pursue and attack the blacks.

The rallying cry became independence from France. The Haitian army won its last decisive battle at Vertières and the surviving French, numbering about 8,000, surrendered to the English fleet rather than face *les sublimes va-nu-pieds* ('the ragtail army') under Dessalines.

On 1 January 1804 Dessalines officially named the former colony Haiti (an old Arawak name) and proclaimed its independence. It was the first Negro republic and second free republic in the Western Hemisphere.

Boisrond Tonnère, a fiery lieutenant of Dessalines, was chosen to write the Act of Independence and Dessalines's inauguration speech because he had explained dramatically and emotionally: 'To write this Act of Independence we must have a white man's skin for parchment, his skull for an inkwell, his blood for ink, and a bayonet as pen.'

After the ruthless total war tactics of Dessalines no foreigner came to Haiti in the role of master for more than a hundred years until the U S Marines landed.

When the slaves began their fight for freedom, Haiti was rich, but years of battle and land-misuse soon impoverished it. Irrigation systems, built by the French to serve their great plantations, were destroyed by men who, above all else, wanted to forget what plantation life had meant. What escaped damage by the revolution was buffeted by the frequent tropical storms.

The former slaves wanted their own land and a chance to lead their own lives, and so the plantations were chopped up and parcelled out as small farms. The majority of the recently liberated population drifted away from the plains and into the hills and mountains where nature was kinder and coffee a relatively easier crop to grow than sugar cane. From one generation to the next land holdings were divided and subdivided. Small farming was pursued with hoe, grub hook, and often just hands.

At the beginning of independence there were only half a million Haitians and the land was still fertile. The new joys of freedom, however, did not always entail an understanding of responsibilities to the land. During periods of drought layers of soil recently claimed from the jungle blew away. When storms came, water crashed down the mountains, eroding stream beds into gullies and gullies into crevices, carrying more topsoil down to the sea. Each cycle of rain and drought punished the people and the land more severely, and the beautiful cloud-capped mountains turned from green to brown.

The mulattoes, because they had become literate and skilled under French rule, began to occupy key posts in the various new administrations. In 1805 Dessalines declared himself emperor, like Napoleon, and in 1806 he was assassinated. His successor was Henry Christophe. To prevent Christophe from having the absolute powers enjoyed by Dessalines, a new constitution was drawn up, but Christophe refused its limitations. He seized the north, declared himself King Henry I. After unsuccessful tries at forcing union, he gave up the south to the mulattoes under Pétion.

These early black rulers, fearing both each other and further French attempts at reconquest, lavished much of their manpower on fortifications. Christophe not only built the opulent Sans-Souci Palace, but also the towering mountain-top fortress, Citadelle Laferrière, as mighty an undertaking for his people as the pyramids were for the Egyptians.

Haiti remained divided between Christophe's north and Pétion's south until 1820 when Christophe, paralysed by a stroke which prevented him from mounting his horse, committed suicide as his enemies hammered at the Sans-Souci Palace gates. Legend says that he shot himself with a silver bullet. In the south, Jean-Pierre Boyer had succeeded Pétion in 1818. After Christophe's death, Boyer united Haiti again.

When the eastern Spanish-speaking part of the island (the Dominican Republic) revolted against Spain, Boyer answered the Dominican call and the Spanish were beaten. Boyer brought all the isle of Hispaniola under his rule for the next twenty-two years.

Along with all its other problems, Haiti was heavily in debt. To win recognition from France, Boyer had agreed to pay 150 million francs in gold as indemnity for French property lost during the rebellion. This figure eventually was reduced to 60 million, but the infant nation still staggered under its weight.

In 1843 a civil war overturned Boyer and the Dominicans

took advantage of it to rebel and establish their own freedom. From that year until the US Marines landed in 1915 the country suffered almost constant tyranny and disorder. Repeated revolutions shook Haiti as twenty-two dictators came and went. The masses, as always, bore the brunt of their misrule. The mulatto elite, superior in training as well as being established in the business of governing, carefully manipulated the country under a succession of black tyrants. The colour gap widened. The elite became a tighter circle and the blacks a more bitter majority.

The world at large, dependent upon slave manpower, looked uneasily at the bad example a free Negro country could set. Haiti had difficulty getting recognition and foreign trade. Among the newly liberated nations of Latin America Haiti did not fare well.

Even the Great Liberator himself, Sìmón Bolívar, was not able to help at the first formal meeting, the Congress of Panama in 1826, to promote an Inter-American system. Bolívar at that time was leader of the multination Gran Colombia. In 1816, after two defeats by the Spanish, Bolívar had gone to Haiti, where Pétion equipped him for a third assault on Venezuela. This, too, failed, but the next year success was his and he liberated a succession of countries to form Gran Colombia.

While the Congress of Panama did not accept Haiti, recognition did not come from the United States either, despite favourable trade relations, until 1862, when Abraham Lincoln was President and the United States itself was gripped by a civil war in which slavery had become the central issue in the public mind.

It was little wonder that Haiti felt itself to be an outcast in the Americas. Revolutions destroyed its wealth, bad agricultural practices peeled away its beauty, and its violent racism made neighbour nations shy away.

3
The Country

The true flavour of Haiti, like its language and folklore, is indigenous. Although the language, Creole, borrows heavily from seventeenth-century French and slightly from Spanish and English, it can only be described as Haitian.[1] Some of its descriptive words are created out of sounds whose impact is so aptly illustrative that Haitians hearing them for the first time know exactly what they mean. They possess a certain native truth that makes them right and proper. Daniel Fignolé, the presidential candidate undone by the cowboy movies, was so brilliant in Creole that he could invent words in the middle of a speech and his coinages added to, rather than detracted from, his audience's understanding.

In a hemisphere where mostly Spanish or English is spoken, the uniqueness of the Haitian tongue – as with Haiti's other main cultural attributes – sets it attractively apart in some ways and in others merely isolates it. In its voudou, its blackness, its extraordinary problems brought on by the inheritance of a system of small farms, lie both a freshness and a despair. A Haitian proverb has it that *if work were a good thing, the rich would have grabbed it for themselves long ago.* Another says: *Stupidity doesn't kill you, but it makes you sweat.*

Water has always been a problem. About 80 per cent of Haiti's 10,714 square miles is mountainous and there are three general climate zones – the north, where it rains lightly but often; the centre and south, where heavy rains are often fol-

1. Generally, the dialects spoken in the Louisiana bayous and in Martinique are about as akin to the 'Haitian tongue' as Schweitzerdeutsch is to High German.

lowed by seasons of drought. Ninety per cent of Haiti's farming is devoted to raising enough food merely to subsist on. Drought still means starvation. Families still have to walk five miles or more to find water, and most of it is still reserved for drinking because there is not enough to spare for baths or for the crops, which aggravates health problems.

Through it all the peasant remains essentially a man trying to be happy with his lot. Perhaps because neither he nor his grandparents have known very much better, he accepts suffering as his fate. '*Bon Dieu bon,*' he mutters. 'God is good.' If someone asks how he is, he nearly always replies with a certain dignity, '*Pa pi mal, merci*'; 'Not too bad, thanks.' Emaciated adults hide from strangers as though starving were sinful. Few in the countryside prior to Duvalier would beg, in striking contrast to the city. On a mountain trail the peasant greeting is 'Honour'. You are expected to reply 'Respect'. A greeting from a Haitian shuffling along the trail might be a philosophical 'Courage, godfather of my son'. A man calculates his age by remembering who was President when he was born. Since Haiti has had so many Presidents, the method is surprisingly accurate.

The land system, while it racks Haiti in many ways, makes it rich in others. It creates a society of landowners. The people have their own identity, and out of it stems the unique Haitian culture, nurtured in tight little circles. One result is that nearly all Haitians are, in some way or another, given to expressing themselves in art, and voudou is the heart and soul of it. Strange, unfettered expressions abound in dances, music, writing, painting, weaving, and woodcarving. These are the products of a land where zombies are more powerful to most people than the Pope and a voudou god more real than an astronaut. The painting of voudou *vévés*, or symbols, has developed into a widely acclaimed primitive art. A voudou priest, Hector Hyppolite, became a major discovery in the outside world. Completely self-taught, using chicken feathers as brushes, he began his career by decorating a roadside bar near Port-au-Prince with incredibly painted birds and flowers.

Hyppolite's first painting went for eight dollars, but so rapidly did this strange, gaunt man's fame spread that, in no time at all, his work was commanding thousands. Draped in a bizarre robe of his own making, wearing his hair long enough to reach his shoulders, speaking in parables of strange visions, Hyppolite became in pre-hippy days a true celebrity. He is indeed singular, but is by no means unique. Many is the worker who returns to his *caille* after a long day to daub paint on animal hides or dried-mud walls with chicken feathers. Sometimes masterpieces are produced. The result is always lively.

The peasant's creativity is perhaps furthered by the widespread custom of polygamy, since each wife acts as the business manager of her household, thus freeing her husband for more spiritual tasks. Originally, the custom was regarded as economically desirable – communities began where a man built his thatched-roof *caille* and, as wives and offspring multiplied, a cluster of other huts grew up around it, the complex eventually becoming known as a *lakou*.

There are several types of *cailles*, all with handmade wooden frames and tamped earth floors. Some have walls made of mud and lime plastered over a latticework of twigs; some walls are straw thatch, or painted plaster. The lime imparts a clean, whitewashed look that tourists find picturesque. Inside the hut there are mats made of banana-tree branches. These are slept on. Chickens and pigs – if the peasant is a man of substance and can afford them – roam in the yard. A palm-frond lean-to covers the cooking area, which consists of three stones and a fire that assumes the status of an eternal flame. If it goes out, a long, slow walk to a neighbouring *lakou* ensues, followed by a hurried return with live coals or a burning brand. These open fires are a hazard to small children playing nearby.

All in all, the peasant's existence is nasty, brutish, and short. (Life expectancy is something less than forty years.) A balance of labour and authority is worked out between the man and his women, whose common-law marriages are called *plaçages*. Besides his artistic endeavours, the husband does all the heavy work: he digs, plants, builds, and repairs the various *cailles* he and his wives own; fetches wood for fuel, clay for pottery; weaves palm or latanier baskets; buys and cares for the livestock, and – truly a backbreaking labour – cuts the sisal and the sugar cane.

The woman is the organizer. She cooks, washes, rears the children, handles the finances, and makes all purchases, excepting the animals. She lugs the produce to the nearest market or sells it to a middleman speculator who in turn peddles it in the city. On market day she can be seen striding along the jungle paths to market, balancing a basket of produce on her head as regally as a queen with an outsize crown.

Sometimes, in later years, if he can afford it, a man might marry one of his wives as a reward for a lifetime of work and childbearing. The wedding party, made as stylish as possible, is known as a *bamboche*. An unwritten law prohibits a man giving money acquired from one wife's labours to another wife.

A conch shell's throaty bleat echoing through the mountains or the blast of a bamboo trumpet begins the day in a typical *coumbite* or co-operative, which may include several thatch-roofed villages. These *coumbites* are responsible for providing labour at planting and harvest times, and in some areas they develop into *sociétés*, adopting their own distinctive flags. But their nexus is religious – care and maintenance of the local *houmfort* or voudou temple.

After a dawn breakfast of sweetened coffee and, in flush times, a biscuit, the women of the *coumbite* face the task of getting water. As soon as a girl can walk, she learns how to balance baskets and water tins on her head. The women leave home early each morning and trek miles over hogbacks and gullies to springs or streams. Hours later they return, balancing their sloshing burdens on their heads. Children who do not go out after water are called on to crush corn or coffee with a mortar and pestle.

Early in the evening rising trails of blue smoke mark the locations of the various little villages in the mountains. At that time families eat their main, and all too often only, meal;

then they sit around the fire and scare one another with stories. At night the fires glow like bright measles across the hills and valleys.

The Haitian peasant has evolved a folklore rich in exaggeration. Out of it springs an ardent belief in the supernatural which, embroidered by generations of African-born superstition and coated with a smattering of Christian hagiography, approximates that phenomenon known as voudou, which will be investigated more exhaustively in Chapter Twenty. Here suffice it to say that the flickering fire, the rank tropical night, and the incessant throbbing of drums contribute to some highly imaginative evenings. *Cric,* goes the storyteller; if the group responds *crac,* the tales begin, and zombies, werewolves, and demons galore begin populating the darkness just beyond the fire's perimeter.

Bogeyman tales centre around a terrible giant who strides from mountaintop to mountaintop, stuffing bad little boys and girls into his *macoute* or knapsack. This is 'Uncle Knapsack' or Tonton Macoute – under Duvalier's regime a name to be reckoned with, for it is by this eponym that Duvalier's officially sanctioned thugs are known. And mere mention of them strikes terror into the hearts of adults as well as children.

The peasant is born into the world under the shadow of death, and it never seems to leave him. If a baby survives tetanus, prevalent because the umbilical cord is often cut with unsanitary instruments such as a machete or a broken piece of glass, he later faces the weakening effects of malnutrition and parasites. These undermine his stamina and make him prey to such diseases as malaria and tuberculosis.

Perhaps because his entire life is built on a gamble against nature, the Haitian loves games of chance, like the dice game *zo,* or cards. Cockfights are the single biggest attraction. However beset an area might be by drought or other problems, on Sundays the cockfights draw a crowd of the relatively affluent. A human wall forms around the pit, and vendors hawk cassava bread and candied peanuts. There are sharp cries at the gambling tables and a quick turnover of pennies and *gourdes* (the

Haitian money unit worth twenty United States cents). The love of gambling is one facet of the *esprit magique,* the plunge of a fatalist, who feels life cannot get worse and therefore God *must* change his luck.

If the peasant's luck does not change, he probably will pay the voudou priest, the *houngan,* or the more sinister witch doctor, the *bocor,* to provide a charm against the evil eye which is plaguing him. The same procedure is used to remove evil spirits from a sick member of the family. The peasant fears sudden illness or misfortune as a godly vengeance being visited on him for something he has done or has failed to do. By consulting the spirits, the voudou priest is supposed to be able to determine the cause of the bad fortune and correct it with an offering to the gods or with a conglomerate of magical practices and recipes.

The peasant's biggest moment is death. In anticipation of that day, he might mortgage his farm to ensure a proper wake, where his personal god, or *loa,* will be removed from his body by the *houngan* via elaborate ceremonies. Some Haitians believe that their souls return to their ancestral home, the mystical Guinea.

Because life and counsel from his parents have convinced the Haitian that supernatural enemies are lurking about, he believes that the dead need extra protection. This, too, comes from the *houngan,* and is designed to save the corpse from becoming the zombie slave of an enemy. There also is a voudou ceremony, the 'last prayers', nine days after the funeral to keep the body settled.

So death, too, is just one more burden on the family. The deceased's land is subdivided among heirs. Sometimes part of it has to be sold to pay for the funeral. The lawyer takes one fifth of the land in question as a payment. To avoid this, heirs sometimes don't divide the land legally, which later usually leads to quarrels and lawsuits. When an illiterate peasant's land title is challenged, he faces the alternative either of losing the challenge or paying the legal fees with a portion of the land in disput. In this manner peasants become sharecroppers, dividing and subdividing what already had barely been sufficient. A feudal system builds up, its structure made of the near absolute power employed by the rural chieftains or *Chefs de Section.* From revolutionary times to Duvalier, the number of Haitians has increased eightfold or more. The struggle for independence forged a land of small farmers; the elements and human predators have tended to reverse the process.

The peasant has few links to the city and, for the most part, fears them. The first is the middleman, or speculator, who buys surplus crops cheaply at local markets and sells them in Port-au-Prince. The most important man is the *Chef de Section,* who represents the government in all its functions, from tax collector to policeman. He has to be consulted on all matters. It is not uncommon for him to require the paying of tribute in settling land squabbles. His word is final. The man literally has the power of life and death. To the peasant he is the government. Once when a new Haitian President visited a village, the peasant *gros nèg,* headman in the community, was so taken with his guest that he expressed a wish that the President might one day rise to the station of *Chef de Section.*

The republic of the provinces, where 90 per cent of Haiti still lives, produces 90 per cent of what the country exports. Of the imports that these goods buy, 90 per cent remain in Port-au-Prince. Although income tax rarely produces as much as 10 per cent, the government traditionally taxes agriculture severely enough to draw some 60 per cent or more of its revenue from it. The life of Haiti flows from the country to the city, and little comes back in return.

One of the few white influences that reach the peasant is the Mon Père, the Catholic priest or Protestant missionary. For many, the *blanc* or white man is synonymous with the US Marines, who occupied Haiti from 1915 to 1934 to put down peasant uprisings and maintain law and order. Although Roman Catholicism arrived with Columbus, it has never deeply influenced the masses. Its saints, much in the same way that French was given an African syntax and gradually converted into Creole, were simply transferred bodily into voudou legends.

Catholicism is often called the dominant religion, but voudou is what the Haitian really puts his trust in. Recently Protestantism has been making inroads. With their social work, distribution of food, setting up of schools and clinics, some sects have gained large followings. But occasionally missionaries have insisted that the peasant relinquish voudou and all its trappings, including the drum. The resulting emotional conflict has been a barrier to conversion. The peasant is reluctant to abandon the symbols of culture passed to him by his father and grandfather. Without voudou he might become a rootless creature deprived of the sustaining influences that spring from his land. Under Duvalier, the Church was severely persecuted and crippled as an institution, and even voudou has come in for heavy taxation.

In the city, where the other 10 per cent of Haiti lives, there exists a class system along lines of colour, wealth, and position. Although the Duvalier government stresses *Négritude,* a pride in blackness and the African heritage, marrying a person of lighter colour is still one way to achieve social status. Duvalier himself did this. However, money and power achieve the same thing. The old motto that *a poor mulatto is a Negro; a rich Negro is a mulatto* has become a truism. Urban Haiti always was dominated by the mulatto descendants of the *affranchis,* the skilled freedmen whose talents put them in positions of influence after the 1804 revolution.

Traditionally, the mulatto elite has looked down on the *moune-mornes* or country folk, and even when a black President was in the palace, it has managed to control the country's government and commerce. In the 1920s an incipient tide of nationalism and black middle-class self-awareness began to challenge the system. But up until 1957, when Duvalier took over, it had hardly changed. However, while Papa Doc has emphasized blackness, he has punished his own class as harshly as he has all others.

If the countryside *houmforts* provide the nation with its soul, Port-au-Prince sets the pace of Haiti's heartbeat. Like all Latin-American capitals, it is a study in extremes. There is a fantastic range between the squalor of La Saline on the waterfront, the old gingerbread-Victorian-style houses of the middle class, and the modern villas and imposing resort hotels in the cool mountains. (While Port-au-Prince swelters the year round, just thirty minutes away on the mountainside towards the Kenscoff Market sweaters are being worn.) Tourists out of another world leave jet airplanes for a city which, although decades in advance of what is found in the countryside, boasts a telephone system that rarely functions, a power-supply system that even patriots term erratic, and a waterworks totally inadequate to minimum sanitary standards.

Most of the country's industry is centred in Port-au-Prince. Sugar and sisal are the biggest single products, but there are textile factories, rum distilleries, tanneries, corn and rice mills, and a handicraft industry where skilled artisans do intricate woodcarving and weaving.

To be a member of the urban lower classes means to live in a slum like La Saline and to work in either one of these industries or, if female and lucky, as a domestic in a rich mulatto's household. It is also to dream the dream of becoming the friend of a politician or – most impossible of all – of becoming President oneself. Haitian governments have always been governments of men, not of institutions. Contacts are all-important. Since all spoils go to the President and his friends, it is impossible to be apolitical. Indeed, any popular army officer, shrewd businessman, or influential teacher automatically becomes a power factor. Traditionally, politics has been the fastest and sometimes the only way up the socio-economic ladder.

François Duvalier came to power promising to help the black masses out of their misery. The time has come, he told the peasants, for you to get a share of the nation's bounty (and booty). That was in 1957. In the ensuing years the peasant's life has become even more problematical; that his urban counterpart lives in just as straitened and even more dangerous circumstances makes for cold comfort.

4

Duvalier – The Early Years

For most Haitians Duvalier's origins are a mystery and there are conflicting versions as to his background. Certainly he grew up within sight and sound of key moments in his country's modern history; these include both the birth of Communism and the US Marine occupation. The early years of this century were tumultuous and, for the ambitious, the epoch offered object lessons in the tactics of survival – namely that any premature show of force was fatal and that in Haiti's tangled political thickets power succeeded only when absolute.

In 1907, the year of Duvalier's birth, Port-au-Prince was a city of unpaved streets bordered with open drainage ditches that doubled as sewers. Small, lean horses dragged buggies about town, leaving deep ruts in the mud behind them. On the Bord de Mer merchants built their stores with rock and mortar and barred them with heavy iron doors to withstand the violence of frequent revolutions.

It was a time of economic depression and political scandal. The director of the National Bank was accused of fleecing the treasury of over a million dollars, and three former cabinet ministers were his alleged accomplices. Each one of the latter eventually became President of the republio.

Haiti was bullied by foreigners, French, German, and American, whose countries' gunboats reinforced their claims in financial disputes. Influential Germans made fortunes by underwriting revolutions – double their money back if their side won – which was usually the case, until the next revolution, for the poorly paid government army (fifty US cents per month) rarely put up much of a fight. Backed by good financing, self-proclaimed generals raised mercenary armies of peasants, called *cacos*, and frequently came down out of the north to force a change of faces in the palace and the Chamber of Deputies. Germans also owned most of the important public utilities, and German shipping carried the bulk of Haiti's trade. The French, however, remained the little island nation's best customers and chief creditors. Because of this markedly international state of Haitian affairs, concern grew in Washington, where interventionist aspirations, nourished by the Monroe Doctrine, were in full bloom among some influential congressmen and newspaper publishers.

The young François Duvalier's life (about which so little is known and into which few people today are brave enough to delve) must have been intimately connected with the socio-economic and serio-comic day-to-day events of pungent Port-au-Prince life.

He was born a few blocks from the National Palace during the military dictatorship of Nord Alexis, the son of Duval Duvalier, a primary schoolteacher, and Uritia Abraham, a barefoot bakery employee. When he was one year old General Antoine Simon overthrew Alexis. He was four when a revolution ousted Simon and five when an explosion reduced the old wooden Palais National and President Cincinnatus Leconte along with it to splinters. Duvalier was six when President Tancrède Auguste was poisoned; his funeral was interrupted when two generals began fighting over his succession. . . . One Michel Oreste got the job, but he was overthrown the following year by a man named Zamor, who in turn fell a year later to Davilmar Théodore.

Whatever effect these events may have had on the little François, they were costly to Haiti. Its loans, principally from France, were over-extended, and the various revolutions brought a clamour of claims from the Americans, British, Germans, and Italians, as well as the French. In 1910, with a Haitian government loan, American, French, and German bankers established the Banque Nationale, a privately owned institution which acted as the government treasury, and had custody over all government funds. United States interests held 40 per cent of the stock. In 1914, to help straighten out a financial tangle, the bank began pressing the United States to take control of Haitian customs, as it had done in the Dominican Republic in 1905.

The 1910 agreement between the Haitian government and an American firm to build a twenty-one-section railroad from Port-au-Prince to Cap-Haïtien led to another serious problem. The company finished three sections, and billed the government for $3,600,000. After making a few interest payments in 1913 the government stopped all payment on the grounds that the company had not finished the railroad and therefore had not fulfilled its contract. The railroad replied that the country's chronic instability had prevented its completion, and that therefore it could not be held responsible. The United States exerted pressure on behalf of the railroad.

The year 1914, dawn of the first great war, brought increasing pressures on Haiti from foreign interests and resulted in US occupation the following year. During revolutionary disturbances in January, British, German, French, and US warships called briefly on Haitian ports in demonstrations of support for their respective interests, then withdrew. In August, after the Banque Nationale refused his government financial help, President Zamor accepted German loans at what were described as ruinous terms. This further aroused fear of German financial control and the possible establishment of a German naval base. In November Zamor was ousted by Théodore, who inherited all the financial problems. He tried by force to seize state funds in the bank (part of the 1910 loan) placed there to redeem paper currency. Because this was a violation of the terms of the loan, and because the bank had already asked the United States for financial control of Haitian customs, now the bank called for US protection. On 17 December 1914 the US cruiser *Machais* landed a detachment of sixty-five Marines armed with billy clubs and revolvers. They escorted $500,000 in gold from the bank to the ship, which took it back to New York. The Haitians considered this an affront and protested angrily. The money remained the property of the Banque Nationale and collected two per cent interest in a New York bank.

In January 1915 a *caco* army under Vilbrun Guillaume Sam

marched out of the north and seized control of the government. Admiral William B. Caperton, aboard the USS *Washington,* with other US warships in the area, persuaded Sam not to wreck the towns of Gonaïves and St Marc on his way to Port-au-Prince. By March, with Sam in control, the situation had quieted down and the US warships withdrew. However, peace was short-lived. Another revolution was being fomented in northern Haiti by Rosalvo Bobo, who was recruiting mercenaries and making the foreigners uneasy. On 19 June the French cruiser *Descartes* landed fifty men at Cap-Haïtien as protection against threatened attacks on political refugees sheltered in its consulate. The United States immediately sent back Admiral Caperton, who thanked the French and relieved them. As Bobo's revolution progressed, Admiral Caperton, after conferring with foreign consuls, advised the contending factions that he would allow no fighting in Cap-Haïtien, but whoever won the battle outside would be allowed to take the city if it was done in orderly fashion. On 27 July an uprising in Port-au-Prince sent the Admiral and the *Washington* steaming to the capital. He left the USS *Eagle* to watch Cap-Haïtien.

At the outset of fighting in Port-au-Prince President Sam rounded up 167 political opponents and jailed them. He ordered the prison commander to kill them if the revolt succeeded. As the revolt drove Sam from the palace to take asylum in the French Embassy, all but five of the 167 prisoners, most from well-known Port-au-Prince families, were slaughtered. Blood ran in the streets, and families searched through a courtyard of corpses to claim the bodies. The next morning, 28 July, after a feverish night of grave-digging, funeral processions wound their way through Port-au-Prince to the cemetery. At 10.30 a.m. the USS *Washington* arrived. Rumours spread through the crowd that the warships were there to protect Sam. The processions turned into angry mobs that marched on the French Embassy. They broke in, dragged out Sam (one report said he was hiding in the bathroom, another that he was under a bed), and impaled his body on the spikes of the embassy's iron fence. Then he was torn to pieces.

That afternoon two companies of US Marines and three companies of sailors landed and took control of the city. They were later reinforced, and an occupation that was to last nineteen years had begun. By forced treaty (first for ten years, then renewed for another ten), the United States took over everything but the departments of Justice, Education, and the Post Office. As a boy of eight, Duvalier had a front-row seat to it all.

On 30 August, when the US Marines reached Léogane, the first important town west of the capital, they ran into Charlemagne Péralte, an obstinate, tall, moustached commander of the arrondissement who refused to hand over his office, arms, and flag. He refused to budge until he was formally dismissed by the new president, Sudre Dartiguenave. Péralte withdrew to his family farm near Hinche, a town in the central plateau not far from the Haitian-Dominican border. On 11 October 1917 Péralte was falsely accused of having taken part in an attack on Hinche by a group of *cacos* led by an officer named Gabriel. He was arrested in Hinche and later sent to a prison at Ouanaminthe.

In January 1918 a marine court-martial condemned Péralte and his brother Saul to five years' forced labour. They had the job of sweeping the dusty streets of the little border town. In August, while sweeping the streets of Cap-Haïtien, where he had been transferred, Péralte escaped.

Gathering a group of friends, he attacked Hinche in October 1918. In 1919 the Marines re-established the *corvée*, forced labour to maintain roads. Péralte raised an army of unhappy peasants who fought a guerrilla war against the Marines. For those times it was a rare instance of a peasant revolt and guerrilla warfare. It was often a case of the peasant with a hoe in his hands during the day and at night a Krag rifle lifted to his shoulder.

The Marines enlisted the help of a Haitian, Jean Conzé, who was promised a $2,000 reward to capture or kill Péralte. On 1 November 1919 Captain Herman Heneken of the US Marines, his face blackened, led a patrol into Péralte's mountain headquarters. Conzé pointed Péralte out as the man wearing a silk vest, peering over the campfire at the new arrivals. Heneken shot and killed Péralte. For this the US government awarded him the Congressional Medal of Honor and his picture and a brief story appeared in advertisements for war bonds in the mid-1950s. The almost naked body of Péralte was tied to a door, with feet in the mud, and exposed at the general headquarters of the gendarmerie in Cap-Haïtien. Conzé was also honoured, receiving the Haitian decoration 'Honour and Merit'.

The peasant uprising was short-lived. When Duvalier was twelve, *caco* forces twice tried suicidal attacks on the 2,000-man Marine force stationed in the capital. Each time they were driven off with heavy losses. The bodies in the streets, the acrid smoke of burning wooden homes, must have left an indelible mark on the young boy.

During the Marine occupation, despite *caco* leader Bobo's popular following, Sudre Dartiguenave, the head of the Senate, was installed as the new President. Under his administration (1915–22) François's father, Duval Duvalier, earning four dollars a month, was dismissed from his job teaching primary school because, born in Martinique, he was considered a foreigner. In 1916 the Marines also began outright occupation of the Dominican Republic, thus obtaining control of the entire island.

Old-timers around Port-au-Prince remember François as a quiet, introverted boy who did not play games, liked to be alone, and wore clothes tailored by his grandfather. He attended primary and secondary school at Lycée Alexandre Pétion. The ancient, tin-roofed, sunbaked lycée in the Bel Air section overlooked the capital and is a state-owned institution founded in 1816 by Pétion, the first mulatto president. From the school one had a clear view of the harbour and palace where such a violent political panorama unfolded. Among Duvalier's high-school professors were Dr Jean Price Mars and Dumarsais Estimé. The year Duvalier graduated, Dr Price Mars, Haiti's leading ethnologist, published *Ainsi Parla l'Oncle*, 'Thus Spoke the Uncle' (1928). The book was a milestone in Haitian literature. Dumarsais Estimé, a lean young black man of peasant stock from the Artibonite Valley, was later to lead the revival of the revolution of the black middle class. Duvalier's teachers were all members of an organization that called for an end to the Marine occupation.

As poverty-stricken and as backward as the schools like the one young François attended may have seemed to Americans, they were a source of pride to the people of Haiti. The teachers were all Haitian, although the United States attempted to insert American advisers, and the curriculum was modelled on the French. The Haitian elite followed the aristocratic prejudice of honouring literary and professional work and despising manual labour. Hard physical work was linked in their minds with slavery and regarded as the prerogative of the ignorant and the poor. They feared that American influence might direct their educational system away from French cultural traditions and towards more materialistic goals. The general exclusion of agricultural and industrial education, the failure to emphasize the dignity of labour, hurt the country. It shaped an educated class who sought the professions of law, medicine, and politics, and little else.

If burning nationalistic passions consumed him, as they did others, Duvalier managed to keep the fires well banked. At a time when poets and writers stressed the notion that Haiti was the godchild of Guinea, no one can say for sure whether the adolescent was proud of his African heritage or not.

After the lycée, Duvalier entered a medical school which Americans had reorganized over the bitter objections of Haitian doctors. He enrolled without the requirement of an entrance examination.

Within a year Duvalier's former classmates spearheaded an opposition movement to the occupation and its second puppet President, Louis Borno (1922–30). Friends of Duvalier's father had persuaded this administration to restore Duval to his teaching job. In November 1929 a strike began among students. In a short time most of the country was aroused. Young writers stirred the people further by reciting impassioned nationalistic poems in public places. Duvalier, then twenty-two, remained on the fringe, not directly involved, but he was already meeting with Lorimer Denis, twenty-four, a mystic who studied voudou and was said to exert a strong influence on Duvalier, to discuss the new nationalist ideas. The pressures of the strike and its aftermath forced Borno out of office and focused attention on the Haitians chafing under the occupation. Upon the recommendation of the Forbes Commission, which had studied the Haitian question, US President Herbert Hoover inaugurated a five-year plan for an orderly withdrawal of the Marines.

Riding a wave of nationalism, the mulatto former mayor of Port-au-Prince, Sténio Vincent, was picked for the Presidency by a fifty-seven-member Congress which had been chosen in a nationwide election supervised by the Marines. The effectiveness of the student strike and Vincent's rise to the office of President (1930–36) were vivid illustrations of power tactics new to Haitians.

Duvalier at this point began to emerge as an individual with some talent and a sense of personal direction. It reflected on his father, who was named justice of the peace at Grand-Bos, a rural community near the Haitian-Dominican border. François himself was now involved with the budding *Négritude* movement. His constant companion was the mystic Lorimer Denis. The first article under Duvalier's signature appeared in *Le Petit Impartial* on 10 January 1931. In 1933, the year before he graduated from medical school, Duvalier was co-author with Denis and Arthur Bonhomme of a booklet called *Les Tendances d'une Génération*, 'Trends of a Generation', echoing the call for a truly Haitian literature.

In 1934 the withdrawal of the Marines was completed. President Franklin D. Roosevelt formalized it in a ceremony at Cap-Haïtien. He was the first US President even to visit Haiti while in office.

The Marines left behind signs of material progress and considerable resentment. Highways were built, sanitation and water-supply systems improved, an automatic telephone system installed; private, commercial, and passenger transportation improved tremendously; wharves and docks, hospitals, schools, and bridges were completed, public health and agricultural services fostered, and a professional gendarmerie trained and developed. In addition, a sound currency was established as well as an orderly process for handling the country's financial problems.

The same year that the Marines departed, 1934, Duvalier received his medical diploma, one of fifteen graduates, and began his internship at the Hospice Saint François-de-Sales. An instructor at the medical school told a story which revealed something of the young intern's character. Duvalier shared a room at a boarding-house with another medical student. He heard from the houseboy that his room-mate had spoken unfavourably about him. Without questioning the gossip Duvalier moved out and never spoke to the room-mate again. The doctor commented on his pupil-president: 'He feels that nobody less educated than he could ever deceive him, so he believes them.' As President, Duvalier later followed this belief in choosing associates he could trust, no matter how ignorant they were.

His growing interest in *Négritude* was tied not so much to the fiery nationalistic poets who stated their position so clearly and passionately as to the group who looked for mystic ties with the past and expressed their ideas and nationalism in booklets less easily understandable.

During that year, 1934, Duvalier was a contributor to the Nationalist daily *Action Nationale*. He wrote his column under the pen name Abderrahman, the French phonetic spelling of Abd-al-Rahman, eighth emir and first Caliph (A.D. 912–961), who founded the medical school of Cordova. He covered many subjects: literature, ethics, politics, eulogizing the contemporary or popular Haitian authors of the time. In many ways his style is typical of the period – flowery, replete with voudou terms, ardently patriotic. He stigmatizes the occupation, severely criticizes the elite for their selfishness and lack of interest in the masses whose sorry lot and abject state 'enrage' him when 'compared to that of a useless elite, bloated with pride, stupid, and imbecile' (*Action Nationale*, 13 July 1934).

These articles in *Action Nationale* often lift a corner of the curtain covering young Duvalier's soul. He speaks in admiration for such leaders of Haitian thought as Dr J. C. Dorsainville and agrees wholeheartedly with the writings of some of his contemporaries – Stephen Alexis *et al.* He also 'interrogates history at the light of a smoky lamp' to try to find solutions to the problems of his motherland. In some of his pieces Duvalier bitterly attacked Léon Laleau who criticized the generation of 'after 1915' for not cultivating 'art for art's sake', but who, instead, used its pen as an arm for patriotism and as a weapon against social injustice.

Answers Duvalier:

> Well! when like me, Abderrahman, one is in this category of youth called bastard, thrown into contempt and hate, because it emerged from the darkness of the true country, like me, Abderrahman, repelled toward the anonymous flock of the homeless and breadless, one goes side by side every day with abysses of distress, and one is splashed over every day by the impudent morgue of the Boeotians, the insulting luxury of the neo-arrivists ... [*Action Nationale,* 25 July 1934]

Abderrahman also expresses great bitterness and discouragement about Haiti's fate. 'Everywhere and for everything, the great mediocres, the famous pimps are preferred to the interesting ones who, on their own, emerged from darkness. And for a century and more they only spit in the faces of the true children of this immortal motherland' (12 July 1934). But he also expresses hope that 'a man will come' to correct injustice and set things right ...

As the Marines left, the inevitable political manoeuvring began. Port-au-Prince masses, encouraged by President Vincent, went on a binge of wild and unreasoning reaction against the occupation. In a blind fury they tore up bridges and telephone installations which the country badly needed. Vincent responded by declaring martial law, suspending the constitution, and ousting opposition members of Congress. By this neat process he became the first post-occupation dictator.

5

The Formative Years

Nineteen thirty-seven proved to be one of the most tragic years in modern Haitian history. The US Depression seriously affected Haiti's economy. The export of agricultural products – the backbone of the island's economy – brought in little money. More Haitians than usual left to become sugar-cane cutters in the neighbouring Dominican Republic or, just across the Windward Passage, in Cuba. The dictators of those two countries, Rafael Trujillo of the Dominican Republic and Fulgencio Batista of Cuba, feeling the pinch of poor sugar prices, became concerned about this migration and the legion of Haitian cane cutters they had on their territories.

Cutting cane is a backbreaking job and living in the sugar *bateys*[1] almost subhuman, but the Haitian peasants, who had more and more difficulty making little patches of land feed growing families, welcomed the work. They left with the hope of returning home with a little cash to purchase livestock and rebuild their *cailles* or expand their land holdings. Most returned but many stayed on from one season to another. The Dominican and the Cuban shunned the sugar-cutting jobs. Not even Trujillo could force his own people to work under the broiling sun in the cane fields, fighting off giant ants. It was a job for the lowly Haitian, they said. The Haitians were more than willing and, when sugar prices were right, more than welcome.

But in the mid-thirties most sugar mills in Cuba and in the Dominican Republic were forced to close and many Haitians who had migrated there sought work in other fields of labour. Batista was the first to react by ordering the expulsion of

1. Workers' compounds.

Haitian cane cutters. If this was a harsh solution, it compared favourably with what Trujillo did.

When it became necessary to take more drastic measures to remove Haitians from Dominican soil, Trujillo conceived of 'Operación Perejil', literally 'Operation Parsley'. Creole-speaking Haitians were known to have difficulty pronouncing the word parsley in Spanish, and this was the only feature that distinguished Haitian from Dominican. Thus, Trujillo's troops, garbed in peasant clothes, ranged up and down the border carrying sprigs of parsley. 'What is it?' they would ask the peasant whose nationality they were not sure of. If the reply was 'pelegil' instead of the Spanish 'perejil', the man was marked for death.

For about a month the world was unaware of the Dominican dictator's incredible blood-letting. Then the procession of wounded, mutilated by machete and bayonet, who staggered into the hospital at Cap-Haïtien broke the story. The slaughter of Haitians began in September 1937. At first Haitians along the northern section of the border were killed as cattle thieves. But the climax came the night of 2 October in Dajabon, a Dominican town on the banks of the aptly named Massacre River that marks the border, after a personal visit by Generalissimo Trujillo. Wholesale slaughter of Haitian peasants began that night and spread to other cities in the Dominican Republic. The terror sent Haitians of all ages scrambling across the Massacre River. Within thirty-six hours the number of dead soared to over twenty thousand.

Trujillo, who was known to resent his Haitian ancestry, was believed motivated by the desire to preserve what he considered the 'whiteness' of his people. Like numerous members of the Dominican upper class of partly European ancestry, the Dominican dictator feared, he privately told intimates, 'a weakening of the national blood' by the more populous next-door neighbours. He called Haitians the 'despised Negro aliens whose voudou, cattle rustling, and presence on Dominican soil was the ruin of a good life for Dominicans.' There was little but world public opinion to deter him. In the short period he had assumed control of the country he had already built up a personal military force of 30,000, one of the largest in Latin America. Haiti at the time had only a 2,500-man force trained by US Marines mostly for police duties.

To 'protect' his country from Haitians in the years after the massacre, the Dominican dictator created a sort of 'sanitary strip', an area along the border where churches and villages with electricity and water, were built mostly for Spanish, Japanese, and Hungarian immigrants.

Dr Price Mars, Haitian Ambassador to the Dominican Republic in the years after the massacre, reported that he was told by a Dominican official: 'We Dominicans accept responsibility in this most regrettable affair but what you do not know, Mr Ambassador, is that we have authentic information attesting to the formal, although indirect, participation of eminent Haitian officials in the preparation of the drama.'

In the shocking aftermath of the massacre President Vincent was forced to seek a settlement with Trujillo. He asked for United States, Mexican, and Cuban mediation. An indemnity of $750,000 – about thirty-eight dollars per head – was finally arranged, of which Trujillo paid only $500,000. When the Dominican agent made what became the last instalment in Port-au-Prince he also handed out $25,000 in ten- and twenty-dollar bills to politicians and political leaders as a good-will gesture. How much, if any, of the indemnity went to the peasants is not known. Within a year Haitian peasants were sneaking back across the border.

The criminal incident fired up Trujillo's anxiety to export his influence into Haiti. In this way he could close up an escape route for his regime's enemies. He had been trying for several years to get a man of his choice into the Haitian Presidency. The dictator had things pretty well under control in his own country and had organized one of the largest secret-service systems in Latin America. He especially sought to influence politics in all the countries lapped by the Caribbean Sea.

Late in 1933 Elie Lescot, who as Haiti's Minister of Interior controlled the vital internal security and secret-police operations, met with Trujillo for the first time during a conference at the border between the Dominican dictator and the Haitian

President Sténio Vincent. The meeting blossomed into a long friendship between Trujillo and Lescot and was instrumental in getting the Haitian elected to the Presidency nine years later.

Trujillo made a state visit to Port-au-Prince in 1934, and among the many honours bestowed upon him was a banquet given by Colonel Démosthènes Calixte, commander of the Haitian army. Another long friendship, beneficial to the Haitien, developed.

President Vincent returned the state visit to Santo Domingo in 1936 and, on a trip to Montecristi on the border, was entertained by Trujillo at the home of Isabel Mayer, a courtesan who frequently serviced the Dominican dictator. It was at the Mayer home, indeed, on the night of 2 October 1937, that Trujillo learned of the disappearance and arrest of a number of his agents working in Port-au-Prince to overthrow Sténio Vincent and seat Colonel Calixte.

The plot called for the machine-gunning of police chief Colonel Durcé Armand and a brother officer. The plotters hoped that this would lure President Vincent out of the National Palace either to visit Armand in the hospital or to attend his funeral. Colonel Calixte would then seize the palace.

But the plot was called off when Calixte's mistress, a *mambo* or voudou priestess, declared that the moment was not propitious for him. Vincent, apprised of the plot, fired Calixte from his army command, and Arthur Bonhomme, who had collaborated with Duvalier in the writing of an anthropological essay, was one of the plotters who wound up in jail for his efforts. So strife-torn were the late thirties that a friend remarked in later years that 'François was the only one of his generation who never knew the inside of a prison.'

When Duvalier began his internship at Saint François-de-Sales hospital he was as much concerned with the ideas of a small group of intellectuals to which he belonged as he was with medicine. *Les Griots,* a Guinean word meaning bards, was slowly evolving into a literary circle that regarded black nationalism and voudou as the essential sources of Haitian art and literature. In 1938, with the financial assistance of a member's father who was then mayor of Port-au-Prince, the magazine bearing the group's name was launched. *Les Griots'* purpose, as defined by one of its founders, was 'to put back in honour the *assotor* and the *asson* [the voudou ceremonial drum and gourd].'

> Our nostalgic glances turn toward painful and maternal Africa. The abolished splendours of the Sudanese civilizations make our hearts bleed. Manly and gloriously, also perhaps childishly, we swear to make our motherland the Negro miracle, as Hellas was the white miracle....

Upon completing his internship, Dr Duvalier was appointed government consultant at the Clinique Emilie Séguineau, an old-age home ten miles south of Port-au-Prince. His duties entailed visiting the home several times a month, but he could usually be found at Le Globe, the clinic-pharmacy of his protector, Dr Félix Coicou, which stood almost within earshot, and certainly within gunshot, of the National Palace.

A fellow doctor described Duvalier at this time as too introverted to develop a successful private practice, which – in addition to a winning personality or bedside manner – took money and enough social standing to surmount the barriers facing a black man. Duvalier's job assured him of a government cheque until 1943 and allowed him considerable time to devote to *Les Griots*, where he confined himself to anthropological and 'scientific' matters. Never once did he define his politics.

In 1939 friends of Duvalier decided that it was time for him to marry. They introduced him to a nurse named Simone Ovide, taller than he, but with a childhood and retiring personality similar in many ways to his. Her father was a mulatto merchant named Jules Faine, and her mother one of the maids in his household. At an early age Simone had been placed in an orphanage, run by a Frenchwoman and supported by the elite. Under the urging of friends, the match was made. Two days after Christmas François and Simone exchanged vows in the St Pierre Church of Pétionville, the town in the hills above Port-au-Prince.

In 1941 pressures were building up for President Vincent to retire, and he was agreeable. The old bachelor was suffering from eye trouble which was later to cause blindness. The stigma of the 1937 massacre had worn heavily upon him. He went abroad for treatment of his eyes, and the Congress picked another mulatto, Elie Lescot, to replace him.

The high-living Lescot had become Ambassador to the Dominican Republic in June 1934. During his four-year stay in Santo Domingo he joined the elite circle of court favourites surrounding Trujillo. Even while Lescot was Ambassador to Washington, Trujillo financed his extracurricular activities in the US capital. It was Trujillo's money and power that got Lescot the Presidency after Vincent stepped down, but the friendship waned and finally, in 1943, Trujillo and Lescot had a falling out.

In October 1944 Trujillo offered $30,000 and weapons to fifteen Haitians to kill Lescot. The plot failed and the arms turned out to be US lend-lease equipment sent to the Dominicans.

Lescot cancelled the elections scheduled for 1945 in a bid to retain power. But Trujillo helped administer him the death blow by making public all their correspondence between 1937 and 1945. The correspondence pictured Lescot as a Trujillo puppet, a man who literally 'sold his own country's interests and an embezzler who "borrowed" money from the Dominican dictator to cover government funds he had misused in Washington.'

Lescot had no political finesse. During his Presidency the privileged position of the elite became more pronounced and drew increasing resentment. Inept members of the upper class held choice government jobs, while the social barriers kept ambitious blacks from making progress on merit. To his sons Lescot farmed out cabinet posts, and his friends fared well. It was Lescot who helped ambitious Paul E. Magloire up another rung of the ladder to power. He had appointed him first chief of police and two years later head of the palace guard.

With Lescot's blessing, the Church began a campaign against voudou. Drums, gourds and other ceremonial symbols were destroyed in solemn *auto-da-fé* by parish priests. Alfred Métraux, a French anthropologist visiting Haiti at the time, became alarmed at the possibility of a disappearing folk culture. He urged Jacques Roumain, a young writer, to record the story of voudou. Together they toured the countryside. As a result of their association, Roumain founded the Bureau of Ethnology, with Dr Price Mars as director. Roumain saved important voudou collections from the church fires and undertook research into little-known aspects of the cult.

One of the first members of the Bureau of Ethnology was Lorimer Denis, who in September 1942 became assistant director. The Bureau offered Haitian intellectuals a new platform, and Duvalier joined. The *Négritude* movement fostered by *Les Griots* was furthered by the Bureau.

Denis came from a poor Cap-Haïtien family. In his youth he won a scholarship to study in Port-au-Prince and never returned home. He developed into a grim-lipped, humourless man and assumed the magisterial air of the voudou priests he studied so closely. Denis and later Duvalier himself were considered full-fledged *houngans* (priests) because of their study of voudou.[2]

2. As an example of the Denis–Duvalier preoccupations at the time which, for want of a better word, might be termed 'mystic', here is an excerpt from a declaration they signed in an early edition of *Les Griots*:

'What are the essential points of *Les Griots*' doctrine? Since a dogma of racial inferiority is attached to one of the ethnic components of the Haitian, we have questioned history, anthropology, ethnography, to lay out all the scientific data concerning the problem. And we have also taken into account the Alpine–Armenian influence. The historical study of the colonial milieu has permitted us to follow the evolution of the African element in its new human and physical milieu. The Haitian who was born of *métissage* [miscegenation] has contracted the defects coming from the social psychology. It is thus the main task of educators to modify our mentality.

'Since our whole effort from independence to date has been toward the systematic suppression of our African heritage, in the literary field, as well as on the politico-social plane, our action should lead us to demand the valorization of this raciological factor.... The Haitian problem seems to us a cultural problem above all. Its solution can only be found in a complete reform of Haitian mentality.'

Les Griots carried poetry, short stories, discussions of international politics, economics, psychiatry and voudou, all viewed from the perspective of black thought and heritage. Five issues appeared between 1938 and 1940. In a country used to mediocre newspapers and pamphlets, the review went largely unnoticed.

In his early forties Lorimer Denis became a professor at the Collège de Port-au-Prince, a private school attended mostly by sons of the elite. He was an erect and imposing man who wore his hat and carried his *cocomacaque* (cane) continuously, even indoors. Students considered him both a comic and a mystic. But his influence on Duvalier was considerable. It was he who introduced Duvalier to his fellow professor Daniel Fignolé and in 1946 got Duvalier to join Fignolé's political party, the MOP,[3] of which Denis was a founding member. Duvalier appeared most of the time incapable of writing on his own; most of the articles he co-authored were the work of Denis. One Haitian who knew them describes the Denis–Duvalier relationship as follows: 'Duvalier was like the female egg that needs a male to make it produce. In this case Denis was the male.'

In January 1942, at the Conference of Foreign Ministers of the American States held in Rio de Janeiro, the United States offered to become a partner in the development of public health services to any nation that would request assistance. Haiti accepted, along with seventeen other countries. This step was to bring Duvalier close to the Americans and a step closer to the palace.

The Inter-American Affairs Commission authorized the spending of $150,000 to expand existing health and sanitation programmes in Haiti, including a programme to control the spreading of yaws, a non-venereal contagious disease that maims patients and causes open infectious lesions. It does not kill but attacks the vital organs and dooms its victims to living torment. It can shrink and twist limbs to uselessness, eat away facial features, or cripple by ulcerating the soles of the feet. It is caused by a spirochete similar to that of syphilis (ironically each disease immunizes the victim against the other). It is transmitted by contact and flourishes particularly in tropical areas where people go barefoot and do not bathe often. Conditions in Haiti favoured its spread. It was second only to

3. Mouvement des Ouvriers et Paysans.

malaria as the country's major health problem, particularly among children.

Haiti first began to fight yaws in 1918. In 1924 a study by the Rockefeller Foundation showed that out of 2,500 persons surveyed 78 per cent were infected. It was then attacked with shots of arsenic and bismuth, but this did not prove satisfactory because too many victims would accept the initial relief and never finish the full three-month treatment necessary for cure. After 1942 this gave way to the more effective and rapid shots of penicillin. But for the first few years penicillin in large quantities was too expensive for the health mission.

The Inter-American Affairs Commission sought a specialist in dermatology and syphilology to handle the programme. In January 1943 Dr James Dwinelle of Rye, New York, arrived in Haiti with a commission in the US Army and an appointment to direct the yaws-control project.

There was a limited number of doctors in Haiti. Duvalier was available, applied for a job, and was one of the first three hired. Dwinelle spoke no Creole and very little French. Duvalier spoke more English than the other doctors, quickly boned up on it, and soon became Dwinelle's interpreter.

Records of the Service National d'Hygiène showed that yaws was more prevalent around Gressier, some fifteen miles southwest of Port-au-Prince, than in any other part of Haiti. It was decided to concentrate anti-yaws work in one region at a time, thus a central clinic was set up at Gressier to train Haitian physicians and medical assistants in the diagnosis, treatment, and follow-up care of the disease. At the same time, surveys in other parts of the country and investigations about the efficiency of various treatments were made. Gressier was not far from the Séguineau clinic where Duvalier had served on his first job as government consultant.

The clinic was popular; it grew from twenty-five patients per week to as many as 1,000 on a single day. Although Duvalier later boasted to foreign newsmen that the shots he administered to the sick at Gressier won him that region's support, the area was, and remains, strongly pro-Fignolé in politics.

Actually, Duvalier and other doctors did not administer the shots. Aides assisted in this. Haitians flocked by the thousands to the little white building under a giant mapou tree, on donkey and on foot, their yaws-infected bodies forcing them to come like crabs, slowly down the hills on the sides of their feet.

By June that year the Gressier Clinic could not handle them all. Meanwhile Haitian physicians had completed training and were ready to start operating in other areas. The programme began to branch out. Duvalier became chief of the Gressier training centre. In August 1943 Dwinelle established a clinic at Cayes-Jacmel. Despite the popularity of both clinics, it soon became apparent that to make the campaign truly effective there would have to be mobile clinics for the mountain districts and a follow-up public health programme to aid in the prevention of a resurgence of the disease.

In August 1944 Duvalier was chosen, along with twenty Haitian doctors, by the Inter-American Affairs Commission to study in the graduate school of public health at the University of Michigan. He went to Michigan for two semesters, and then rejoined Dwinelle at the Gressier Clinic.

Dwinelle remembers Duvalier as a placid, near-sighted assistant who rarely spoke unless spoken to. He regarded him as a poor administrator because he rarely refused a request even if it disrupted established procedure. Dwinelle, years later, said he had no inkling that Duvalier was interested in politics or even voudou. Duvalier and Dr Aurèle Joseph who worked with him at Gressier, and later succeeded him as director, were nicknamed the 'dumb twins' by their fellow workers. In Haiti, where the love of humour and gossip is legendary, Haitians interpreted their silence as meaning they had nothing to contribute.

These were the years of the Second World War. Under pressure from the United States for help, President Lescot had accepted a US loan to form the Haitian-American Society for Agricultural Development (SHADA is its French acronym). It was an autonomous corporation accountable to the Haitian government. Under the law of eminent domain it took over thousands of plots of choice peasant land. It cut down trees, including the fruit-bearing ones (mangoes, breadfruit, etc.) so important in the peasant diet, to plant an experimental shrub, erypotosegia. The shrub was expected to yield rubber but proved a failure and eventually had to be uprooted. A grass root, vetiver, was cultivated for the production of essential oils to make up for the loss of production centres in the Pacific because of the war.

Demands of the war and SHADA money made the economy relatively prosperous. Some businessmen made fortunes dealing in the black market on goods that were in short supply because of war needs. But the year 1945 marked the beginning of the end for Lescot. He asked the United States for a new loan and was refused. Bitter, he attacked the United States publicly, complaining particularly about SHADA.

Late in 1945 Lescot announced the extension of his Presidency to 1951. Historically, such an act, especially when coupled with public quarrels with the United States and with Trujillo, had been unwise. In the case of Lescot, they set the stage for his fall and opened the way for the closest thing Haiti had to a revolution since the war of independence. They also propelled Duvalier headlong into politics.

6
Birth of a Politician

The Second World War had ended. Under Elie Lescot's inept and autocratic administration Haiti cried out for social reform, social justice. Nineteen forty-six marked the turning point in the struggle between the urban social classes – the entrenched mulatto and the rising black – for control of the government. *Power to the black man* became the new slogan in Port-au-Prince; as usual it did not refer to the peasants.

Since the disgust with Lescot had become general, the inevitable revolt came in January. High-school and university students spearheaded a general strike; it started as a protest over the closing of the newspaper, *La Ruche* ('The Beehive'), that catered to the young intellectuals. On the advice of the US Legation (later upped to embassy status), US businesses supported the strike. Word was passed to the army that the United States would sanction Lescot's ouster. The army was ready and waiting.

After Lescot was deposed, a three-man military junta was set up. Colonel Paul E. Magloire, who, as commander of the palace guard, was well acquainted with the intricacies of and the intrigues behind power, assumed the dual portfolios of the Ministry of the Interior and the Ministry of National Defence. General elections were scheduled for August 1946.

Wartime inflation had ground the urban masses ever further down, and they were ready to welcome a champion. He appeared in the form of a twenty-six-year-old mathematics teacher named Daniel Fignolé.

In the wake of the 1946 revolution, Fignolé formed one of the rare political parties in Haitian history. He called it the Mouvement des Ouvriers et Paysans (MOP) or the Worker-Farmer Movement. It attracted François Duvalier the medical doctor and anthro-socio-voudougraph. Duvalier the intellectual lent a certain lustre to party headquarters, and Fignolé made the taciturn little doctor Secretary-General of the MOP.

The political ideology of the MOP might have been a trifle vague at first, but Fignolé with his golden voice and amazing command of language came over loud and clear. He preached to the black man against the mulatto elite. In no time at all he had won extraordinary popularity with Port-au-Prince's poor and put the spark to a powder barrel of cumulative hatred for the urban rich.

Being too young for the Presidency himself, Fignolé advanced the tall, thin, humdrum Colonel Démosthènes Pétrus Calixte who, in 1937, had very nearly instigated a *coup* against Sténio Vincent. He was court-martialled for his trouble and then, inexplicably, sent abroad by Vincent to a diplomatic post – at which he had no sooner arrived than he learned that he had been sentenced *in absentia* to death for treason. For the next few years Calixte lived off the bounty of his good friend, Rafael Trujillo, who gave him a commission in the Dominican army and, at one time, posted him to the Haitian border in order to annoy Vincent. In 1946 Trujillo backed Calixte's candidacy.

But all was not well between Colonel Calixte and Daniel Fignolé. Fignolé was addressing the urban masses, the workers and the domestic help for the first time in their political lives. With innocent fervour they took his rhetoric literally and believed that when his front-man Calixte came to power they would begin enjoying the lovely homes, mistresses, and big cars of their mulatto employers. Colonel Calixte professed embarrassment at Fignolé's wild campaigning. Nevertheless, the streets of the capital resounded with the cry: *Vive, Calixte, vive, Fignolé: à bas la misère!*

In addition to the MOP, two Marxist parties emerged in 1946: the Popular Socialist party and the Haitian Communist party. Edgar Néré Numas, a black intellectual pegged as puppet, ran for the Popular Socialists; surprisingly, he was the choice of both the mulatto elite and the American Embassy. The elite controlled the National Assembly and its building became an embattled islet in a sea of social-reform storms in the days prior to the August election. Fignolé had his steam roller moving and the streets churned with demonstrators doing their best to pressure the Assembly into voting for Calixte and the MOP. A number of severe injuries resulted.

Rouleau dehors – 'the steam roller is outside' – became a cry that resulted in the hasty barring of doors and closing of shops. The beleaguered Assembly denounced Fignolé's movement as Fascist. After several days of being steam-rollered, the Assembly, not to be intimidated, elected Dumarsais Estimé, a lean black man from the Artibonite Valley peasantry, President of Haiti on the second ballot. Port-au-Prince went wild.

Furious Fignolists vented their wrath on the electric bulbs of the street lamps which provided the principal, and, in many cases, the sole, source of lighting for many of the city's districts. This was to prove the first time the urban mob expressed its fury in so vehement a fashion, but hardly the last. As the news circulated, a state of shock descended upon the country at large. Dumarsais Estimé was an able enough parliamentarian (and former coffee speculator, lycée instructor, and Minister of Education in 1937), but who exactly was he? No one seemed to know. In damp triumph the next day he toured a silent Port-au-Prince while armoured cars patrolled the downtown areas. Word was passed that neither the United States nor Trujillo was happy with Haiti's new President.

But Estimé was canny enough to ride the emotional tide the campaign had engendered. He formed a coalition cabinet in which all contending factions received some representation. To Fignolé he handed the portfolio of the Ministry of Education and to unsuccessful Senate candidate Georges E. Rigaud, a prominent mulatto member of the Popular Socialist Party, that of the Ministry of Commerce.

He permitted them to talk freely to the press and radio as though the election campaign had not ended. Fignolé continued to address his partisans and attack whomever he wished, even his fellow cabinet ministers. He singled out Dr Rigaud for a particularly violent attack which brought about a cabinet crisis caused by Rigaud's resignation when Estimé refused to curb Fignolé. Estimé's move was to raise the pay of non-commissioned officers and enlisted men in Garde d'Haiti to ensure their support. Then he let the cabinet fall. He thus out-manoeuvred some of his early opponents.

Because of his position in the MOP, Duvalier was named Director of Public Health. With his fattened government pay cheque he moved his family, now numbering four, into the Ruelle Roy house, which he continued to occupy until he became President. It was located in a middle-class neighbourhood. The Duvaliers continued to live modestly; in fact they did not even own a refrigerator and borrowed ice from the neighbours. The doctor sometimes even stored medicines which needed refrigeration in a neighbour's icebox.

When Fignolé left the government after sixty-five days in the Ministry of Education, Duvalier turned his back on the MOP for good. He found himself not only in a government of his liking but with one foot already on the rung of the ladder to the National Palace.

Duvalier was not very close to Estimé, who regarded him as a questionable new ally because of his former associations. But Duvalier kept quiet, which was a virtue in Haitian politics. In 1948 he was appointed Under-Minister of Labour and the following year achieved cabinet status as Minister of Public Health and Labour. Contemporaries recall no particular programme he pushed, and said he simply seemed to be sitting out the job. This had been, and would continue to be, a successful tactic in many phases of his career. They recalled that he was 'very secretive' about his work. At a medical convention some were surprised to see that his only contribution was to exhibit a few pictures of yaws patients. He aroused few enmities and made few strong impressions on anyone.

There was a brief row with the Church, which complained of a group of intellectuals involved in voudou, among them Duvalier. Catholic priests charged that some of the ethnological studies had gone so far that it was difficult to determine the difference between those who called themselves scientific students of voudou and those who practised it. During this period

Les Griots reappeared, this time published by a government printing press. The magazine was circulated weekly for a year, with Duvalier's name on the masthead as a co-founder.

Estimé was committed to the black man but gave another nod to practical politics by maintaining some mulattoes in leading positions, where both he and they profited from their experience. This produced an odd situation. The blacks concentrated on politics but failed to expand their power by developing outside business connections. They simply enriched themselves in opportunistic fashion by their mismanagement of public funds during a favourable economic period, emerging as a sort of 'black elite', thus challenging the mulatto establishment which had a broader base of power.

Estimé began a programme of reforms aimed at consolidating the movement he started. He increased the minimum daily wage for workers from thirty to seventy cents; called for legislation that amounted to Haiti's first social security programme; tried to create favourable conditions for Haitian business while encouraging foreign investment; boosted tourism by financing new hotels and building the $6,000,000 bicentennial exposition (International Fair) of 1949–50, a process which cleaned out sixty acres of ugly city slums; cooperated with international organizations in cultural and economic development; paid off the US loan of 1922, thus freeing the Central Bank of foreign control. His was a black man's movement trying to reform the country, but within the same old structure.

Another Estimé project was the rebuilding of the border town of Belladère opposite Elías Piña, the town Trujillo had rebuilt on the Dominican side of the border. Belladère was on the main road from Port-au-Prince to the Dominican Republic. At a cost of $600,000 Estimé paved the main street, put in a new hotel and new homes, supplied them with electricity and drinking water. It apparently made Trujillo unhappy to see such progress next door. In opposition, he rerouted Dominican traffic through the town of Jimaní, a more southern border exit, and Belladère was left isolated.

Despite this setback, a boom began in Port-au-Prince. The new exposition site improved the look along the waterfront, and postwar tourists responded to Haiti's many natural attractions and the luxury accommodations in the new hotels. Estimé required peasants to wear shoes in the city. An income tax law was passed. A new look was taken at education and agriculture, and no foreigner was allowed to teach history.

The behaviour of the new black elite, now in privileged positions, caused problems. Their lack of discipline, and often mere greed, began to have repercussions. There was a political-business scandal in the banana industry. Also, some prominent black officials were charged with graft in the construction of the exposition. The rift between black and mulatto widened. The old elite found an ally in the army, particularly in the black strong man Colonel Paul Magloire. Estimé, in an attempt to placate the United States, which already viewed him with suspicion but upon whom he depended for financial assistance, opposed radical student and worker movements. Thus, opposition formed on both the right and left. His followers in the lower class were disorganized.

Once again Duvalier had a front-row seat at a power struggle, but this time he displayed deep emotional involvement. From his cabinet post he watched how agitation by students and workers played into the hands of the mulatto elite. When Estimé tried to push through a constitutional amendment which would allow him to run a second term, the end was in sight. Congressional elections had weakened Estimé. The new assembly refused to pass the amendment which would have given him another term in office. In retaliation, a pro-Estimé crowd wrecked the Chamber of Deputies. The crowd ran through the streets of the city waving pieces of broken furniture from the Chamber, crying *Vive Estimé*. On this occasion a fiercer side of Duvalier emerged, but always in private. Cabinet members recall he went to Estimé and asked permission to 'take care of Magloire and his clique'. Estimé demurred.

Rumours of an army *coup* were sweeping the city. Duvalier himself may have finally triggered it. He wrote a memorandum and circulated it, criticizing Magloire and accusing him of being disloyal to the administration. As a result, Estimé called each staff officer to his office and asked him to declare himself either for Estimé or Magloire. All opted for Estimé, but supported Magloire. Crowds that two days before had run through the streets shouting *Vive Estimé* now were yelling *A bas Estimé*. On 10 May 1950 Magloire, whose support had helped put Estimé into office, deposed him in a bloodless *coup*. It was the first time since 1915 that the army had moved alone and directly to change the government. There was no popular outcry.

During the nights following Estimé's overthrow Duvalier threatened to put the city to the torch, but did not. Neither did he accept the *coup*. He refused to follow other Estimé officials into the Magloire government. On 20 May 1950 Estimé took his wife and four children aboard a ship that sailed for Hoboken, New Jersey. From there he went into exile in New York, where he died three years later. A bitter, violently angry Duvalier went back to the US sanitary mission. He had seen the military at work again, and promised he would not forget it.

7
Magloire

The Magloire years generally were good ones for Haiti. The arts, encouraged under Estimé, flourished under Magloire. Tourists swarmed into Port-au-Prince. Abuses of power seemed minor when compared to Haitian afflictions of the past.

The black colonel began from an excellent position. The elite, the army, the Church, and the United States supported him, he had no quarrel with Trujillo, and he had a measure of genuine popularity. Even some of Estimé's followers liked him. He was at least black, and they discovered with some relief that, although they might not fare so well as under Estimé, they would not be stripped of everything. Magloire had something for almost everybody. Louise Déjoie was returned to his seat in the Assembly, and the ever-popular Daniel Fignolé became deputy from Port-au-Prince.

In the elections of 8 October 1950, all adults were eligible to vote except women. The inauguration was a gala affair, and Haiti soon became accustomed to gaudy celebrations under Magloire. It started on 5 December and lasted for three days. Magloire assumed constitutional power to a twenty-one-gun salute, flag-raising, and church services. He dressed in a black suit and surrounded himself with military wearing dress whites.

'I am a soldier. I am at the orders of the nation, and I shall not disobey,' Magloire said. He spoke of helping peasants, rejecting oppression and corruption, the dignity of man, the war against communism, and freedom of the press.

One of Magloire's first moves as President was to accept an invitation from Trujillo. In February 1951 the Presidents of the two countries met for the first time in fourteen years, spending equal time at the border towns of Belladère, Haiti, and Elías Piña, Dominican Republic. They signed a 375-word document calling for closer relations, co-operation against Communism, and regulation of migratory movements between the two countries. When the two friends embraced, Magloire's hand hit the butt of a .38 snugged on Trujillo's hip. Trujillo said later he knew Magloire's cane was a gun.

Duvalier continued working with the Americans, under the Point IV programme, as consultant at the American Sanitary Mission. His bitterness and determination to fight Magloire seemed to increase with time. He saw a former assistant, Clément Jumelle, one of his own favourites in Estimé's Department of Public Health and Labour, rise to become Magloire's Finance Minister and also a Magloire favourite. Jumelle, an ambitious man, argued that he did not leave the government when Estimé fell because he believed that the country needed a civil service system rather than a spoils system under which government employees changed with each administration. The Jumelles, a highly regarded black family from the little town of St Marc, lived just five doors away from Duvalier in Ruelle Roy. Under Estimé, Duvalier used to visit them often for meals, particularly on Sunday mornings. He would switch plates in order to eat the meal set before Clément. He always feared poisoning.

As the Magloire administration began, Duvalier met Clément Barbot, a dapper black with finely chiselled features who was to become a major influence in his life. Barbot lost a minor political job in the Department of Agriculture when Estimé fell. Barbot also came from St Marc, where he had been an elementary teacher and married the mayor's daughter. Duvalier helped Barbot get an administrative job with Point IV, and Barbot became part of a small group which even then regarded Duvalier as a political leader of Presidential timbre. The quiet, efficient Barbot paired well with Duvalier, supplying a badly needed knack for organization.

Oddly, under Magloire, the military man, the yaws campaign reached its peak and the disease was brought under control. This was partly because penicillin became more easily available. In 1945 it had cost four dollars per million units but in 1950 was down to fifty-five cents for the same amount. Because yaws struck so heavily at children, the United Nations Children's Emergency Fund (UNICEF) offered to buy the penicillin. With Point IV help, the Haitian government set up injection centres in 1951, put seventy-two medical aides on horseback and sent them out into the country to make the job complete. With a medicine kit and a hypodermic in the saddlebags, the medico would study a detailed map of his assigned area, then search out every resident and stab him in the buttocks with a needleful of penicillin. By 1953 this project was completed at a cost of $500,000 to Haiti and $650,000 to UNICEF. The American Sanitary Mission had been rechristened the Inter-American Cooperative Health Service (SCISP is its French acronym). Once the massive horseback attack throttled yaws, SCISP had the job of keeping it under control with sixteen clinics placed around the country. Duvalier worked in these.

Magloire in what could be called his golden years established a surface balance of colour and classes, though in fact he favoured the old elite. Police and the army rigidly maintained order, and the country enjoyed relative prosperity. Magloire did nothing to annoy the influential Trujillo, and relations with the United States were never better. Magloire improved on the base laid down by the pioneering Estimé. He introduced a five-year plan for basic development and industrialization, tourism reached its peak, foreign investors were given special incentives, progress continued in health and education, and he dealt for an improved position in the international coffee market.

If Haiti enjoyed it, Magloire literally basked in good will. The general became renowned as a playboy who liked whisky, women, pomp and circumstance. World figures came to Haiti to be decorated, or to attend celebrations. Magloire greeted them in fine suits wearing a diamond stickpin, or resplendent in uniform. *Time* magazine put him on the cover, and he probably became the first President of Haiti to achieve popularity in the outside world. Magloire installed blue lights around the

National Palace to give it a festive air at night. Haiti became 'in' with artists, writers, and theatre people. Noel Coward, Paulette Goddard, Truman Capote, Irving Berlin, and many others visited. Entertainment was lavish. In April 1952 the government appropriated $20,000 to entertain General Hector B. Trujillo, vice-president of the Dominican Republic, who came for a four-day official visit. In May the world premier of a movie based on the Kenneth Roberts novel about Haiti, *Lydia Bailey*, was held in a new air-conditioned theatre Magloire installed at the Casernes Dessalines army barracks near the palace. On his birthday in July Magloire dedicated a $120,000 soccer stadium. In August Dictator Anastasio Somoza of Nicaragua and his wife made a state visit, and at the palace balls the two generals contested to see who could be the more elegant and bemedalled. Magloire once appeared in a dark blue cutaway coat with epaulets and braid down the front wearing a plumed cocked hat.

There were unsettling events, too. Magloire's brother, Arsène, an engineer, was Minister of Public Works. While things were accomplished, there was an unusual amount of money spent. One crime against a public works employee named Désinor, though never solved, cast a shadow. Désinor was wounded and the rest of his family killed in a swift, unexplained attack by unidentified men. Magloire and his brother fell under suspicion because charges of graft were being made against the department. Désinor recovered and eventually went to New York in a diplomatic post. Years later in exile Magloire said he felt there was a possibility that the crime had been carried out by a Duvalierist group trying to embarrass the government.

When former President Estimé died in exile in New York in July 1953, Magloire brought his body home for a state funeral. The body lay in state and was accorded full military honours.

This was the year Magloire ordered special outfits of blue and gold for his palace guard at a cost of $50,000. He spent $7 million in a renewal programme for Cap-Haïtien, retaining the old port's flavour, while adding new harbour facilities and a sea wall. At additional cost he provided a new highway between it and Port-au-Prince. In the capital, the Champ-de-Mars was rebuilt and a square for Independence Heroes established in front of the palace, with statues of each freedom fighter, including a four-ton Dessalines.

That November anti-Magloire pamphlets were distributed around the city. One night policemen killed two men as they tried to flee after putting up subversive posters. Magloire visited the policemen involved and told them, 'You know that I have a horror of abuses, but whenever there are circumstances requiring action such as you took, do your duty. I will assume the responsibility.'

With the one hundred and fiftieth anniversary of independence approaching, Magloire prepared the historic city of Gonaïves for the celebrations. He erected a modernistic cathedral, refurbished two public squares, and produced a ceremony that was truly grandiose. There was a re-enactment of the last battle for independence. When the triumphant 'Dessalines' made his speech to the army, the wife of the French Ambassador was so moved that she cried. The British Ambassador was not so helpful as he intended when he consoled her by saying not to worry, the days of French imperialism were dead.

A scene depicting the last decisive battle was so complete that it even included the shooting of a horse in an episode during which one particularly valiant revolutionary general had lost his mount and an opposing French general was so impressed by his courage that he offered him another.

While diplomats and officials watched, General Magloire, also absorbed in the play, opened his tunic and thrust his hand inside while assuming a Napoleonic stance. Hundreds of peasants reacted emotionally when it appeared that the French were winning. In an impromptu display they swarmed up the hill en masse, hauled down the French tri-colour from the old fort, and routed the soldiers. Ceremonies even included the reading, by Brigadier General Antoine Levelt, of the Haitian Declaration of Independence and the grisly prelude by Dessalines's secretary, Boisrond Tonnère: 'To write this Act of Independence we must have a white man's skin for parchment etc. etc.' The day of festivity ended by moving to a dinner on the lawn before the ruins of the Sans-Souci Palace near Cap-Haïtien, at which US star Marian Anderson sang.

In January 1954 Magloire took official notice of a movement against him and assembled thousands of workers and government employees on the lawn of the National Palace to hear one of his most famous speeches: 'In 1946 I was but a major and I could repress them. In 1950 I put on my *cançon fer* [iron pants] and now I am obliged once more to wear my iron pants to repress some vagabonds.' Deputies Daniel Fignolé and Rossini Pierre-Louis were the major political figures arrested. They were accused of plotting against the state by inciting workers and students to strike and of circulating subversive literature among the armed forces calling for revolt against a 'backward regime'. Police also sought Senator Marcel Hérard but he escaped. Fignolé's newspaper, *Haiti-Démocratique*, was closed. He remained in jail until April, when the government declared complete amnesty for all involved.

By December Magloire began to show an interest in Duvalier's activities. He sent word to the Inter-American Cooperative Health Service (SCISP) officials to fire Duvalier for using the US job as a front for political activities. When Duvalier heard this, he went into hiding, and stayed under loose cover until August 1956. He hid first in a next-door neighbour's house and stayed in touch with his family, who were never bothered. Magloire later contended that he made no real effort to arrest Duvalier but just wanted to keep him on the defensive.

In September 1955 Duvalier changed hiding places. He went across the street to stay with a priest, Father Jean-Baptiste Georges, who was later to become one of the staunchest foes of the little black Caligula. The move was carried out as a major item of strategy. Duvalier dressed as a woman, and a friend picked him up in a car. They drove into the city along Harry Truman Boulevard and then circled back to the priest's home. Duvalier in his skirts got out of the car on an adjoining street and entered the house from the rear. It had all the drama of children acting out an adventure while a parent secretly watched.

Duvalier slept on a cot on the second floor of the priest's home. There also was a chapel on that floor, and when Father Georges said mass there, Duvalier would fold up his bed and lock himself and it inside the shower. Evenings he stretched his bed out in the office and read from the library. Barbot liked to say that Duvalier's favourite book, which he kept with him during most of his underground period, was Machiavelli's *The Prince*. Duvalier took his 'exile' all very seriously, even ducking low each time he passed the window at night. When not reading he wrote in schoolboy notebooks. From these literary efforts later came his first law on illiteracy and the groundwork for the School for International Studies.

He was not a troublesome boarder, however. Because of diabetes, he could not eat sweets, and he neither drank alcoholic beverages nor smoked. He especially liked imported apples and Seven-Up.

The priest, Father Georges, had studied in Canada for a doctorate in Canon Law. When he returned to Haiti in 1949 under Estimé, he became chaplain at the university. Next to his home there was a student centre. Its student treasurer had been a young man named Luckner Cambronne, whom Duvalier had previously met and whose talent for collecting money Duvalier found highly useful when he became President.

The Jumelles were good friends to Duvalier while he was in hiding, though he showed little gratitude for it later, killing off, in fact, as many of them as he could seize. As a cabinet minister, the only known business venture he had attempted was the purchase of a station wagon which he converted into the *tap tap* trade, Port-au-Prince's term for the public jitney (seven cents a ride). When Magloire's police arrested his driver, the Jumelles had him freed and the automobile returned. The car supplied Duvalier's family with money while he was in hiding. The Jumelles also used their influence to keep Duvalier's father, Duval, on the public pay-roll. The three Jumelle brothers also gave the family $150 a month.

Duvalier stayed with Father Georges six weeks, but it was

only one of many hiding places. As he moved about, plotting the overthrow of Magloire, Barbot became his constant companion and adviser. Duvalier also established a dubious friendship with Magloire's police chief, Marcaisse Prosper, who was apparently ensuring himself against the future by not pressing the search for him. Duvalier once hid at a house next door to a gasoline station. The house caught fire. Police rushed to the scene and one young officer opened a door to find Duvalier standing there. The policeman nodded and walked away. Many of Magloire's detectives became Tonton Macoutes under Duvalier. Some were expert marksmen. They had ample opportunity to practise, for they customarily shot criminals they apprehended rather than take the chance of seeing them later freed in court on a technicality.

President Dwight D. Eisenhower invited President Magloire and his wife to the United States for an official visit in January 1955, and they were given the full treatment. Vice President Richard Nixon greeted him, and there followed a parade down Constitution Avenue. The Magloires spent one night in the White House, and then stayed at the presidential guest home, Blair House. On 27 January Magloire addressed a joint session of Congress with a thoughtful, intelligent speech that contained more than the expected amenities. He reminded the Congress that the United States had looked with 'a certain reserve' on the rest of the hemisphere in the past, and spoke of 'suspicions' aroused by the Monroe Doctrine. He said that Abraham Lincoln first helped Haiti with recognition, but that not until Franklin D. Roosevelt arrived with his Good Neighbor policy (and, not incidentally, ordered the withdrawal of the Marines from Haiti in 1934) had an air of 'cordiality and fraternity' between the two republics existed. He complimented President Eisenhower, and observed 'No doubt, from time to time clouds darken this atmosphere of confidence. We often complain of insufficient aid while distant countries receive considerable benefits. But we believe that our destiny is closely linked to that of the great American democracy for better or worse.'

Magloire went from Washington to New York, for a ticker-tape parade up Broadway. At the press conference that followed he commented 'Since the decree against Communism nineteen years ago no red infiltration has been noted. Basically, the people of Haiti are immune to Communism because the goods are well distributed among everybody.' (There were peasants who would have disputed the last, and two small but persistent Communist parties already were beginning to organize and lay future plans in Haiti.) After visiting Chicago and Canada, the Magloires returned home via Jamaica. When he arrived in Port-au-Prince aboard the British aircraft carrier, *Triumph*, 50,000 Haitians gave him a hero's welcome.

Vice President Nixon and his wife came to Haiti in the spring on the way home from a trip to the Dominican Republic. Nixon, a royally welcomed visitor, was the first guest in Magloire's new luxury marble mountain villa in Turgeau. He almost made a campaign of it. At a garden party Nixon mixed a Haitian rum (Barbancourt) cocktail for Magloire and, during a press conference, said that governments always like to show their best projects, but in Haiti he had been able to see both the 'before' and 'after' of housing projects on the outskirts of the city. Nixon praised the change as fantastic.

He often stopped to question peasants. One such conversation was particularly memorable. He held up a young woman riding a donkey loaded with milk containers and talked with her through a government interpreter. Her first reply in Creole used a common Haitian slang expression, 'Tell this *cocoyé* to let me go on my way.' The interpreter translated this as 'She says she is happy to meet the Vice President of the United States.' Nixon then asked about her family, and the woman said she had no husband and three children, but the interpreter said 'She is engaged.' Nixon placed a hand on the donkey's rump and asked 'What is the donkey's name?' Her reply was 'He is crazy. It is called a donkey.' Then she loosed a stream of complaints. The interpreter told Nixon: 'She says it hasn't got a name, and asks to be excused because it is getting late.' The official group moved on, leaving the milkmaid sucking her teeth and muttering.

Despite all the fanfare, Magloire's troubles were mounting. Stories of corruption swept the city, and his enemies began to try to get the ear of the United States. In a congressional election the popular Fignolé lost his deputy's chair to an unknown Magloire man named André Jeanty, a Boy Scout leader. Since Fignolé was the most pcpular political figure ever known in Port-au-Prince, his loss – by 4,000 votes to 40 – was regarded as symptomatic of what was happening. No less significant was the Péligre Dam project to irrigate 80,000 acres of potentially rich farm land in the Artibonite Valley. The cost, originally estimated at $14 million, soared to $31 million. A hydroelectric plant at the dam was never built. There also were complaints about poor but expensive road construction. Despite the many good things accomplished, the 'golden' Magloire era was tarnishing. One project Magloire encouraged, which has lasted and has proved of great benefit to Haiti, was the Albert Schweitzer Hospital founded by Dr Larimer Mellon at Deschapelles in the Artibonite Valley. Magloire helped at the beginning with a generous grant of land and of some houses which had formerly belonged to the Standard Fruit Company. The cornerstone was laid in December 1954, and a modern hospital was erected in a primitive setting.

Early in 1956, while still in hiding, Duvalier's men contacted Carlos Prio Socarras, former President of Cuba who was then plotting against Batista. Duvalier made a deal with Prio (reportedly $20,000 and tactical advice) for help in the campaign against Magloire: after becoming President, Duvalier was to help Prio by providing bases for attacks to be launched against Batista. Prio sent a young Cuban, Temistocles Fuentes Rivera, to assist Duvalier. Fuentes Rivera described himself as president of the Federation of Cuban Students, and, apparently, was skilled in underground as well as political tactics. Duvalier succeeded, but Prio never received his end of the bargain. It all seemed forgotten in 1958 when Batista gave a $4-million loan to Duvalier's government.

Police blamed a series of May 1956 student disorders on Duvalier followers. A dozen students were injured as police broke up a series of demonstrations aimed at provoking a strike. Anti-Magloire pamphlets were distributed, and one boy was caught trying to burn down a school in Cap-Haïtien. Stories were told to frighten peasants and prevent them from bringing produce into the city. They were told that *loupgarous* (werewolves) were loose and that some of the *marchandes* had disappeared mysteriously while trying to enter the city. The growing opposition claimed that under the Estimé constitution Magloire's term as President ended 15 May 1956. The Magloire constitution in 1950, however, stipulated that 15 May 1957 was the end of the term.

The disorders prompted Congress on 21 May to declare a state of siege. On 25 May Police Chief Prosper made a statement to the newspaper *Le Matin* in which he described the movement against Magloire. Prosper named a half-dozen members of the Haitian Revolutionary Committee as responsible. The group included Duvalier followers. Two men arrested for spreading subversive literature among students were Paul Blanchet and Dato Daumec. Blanchet remained a close Duvalier aide during his Presidential years. Prosper noted:

> Certain of the plotters are known for their attachment to Dr François Duvalier, who happens to be still in hiding, under cover for more than a year, afraid to show himself, notwithstanding the Presidential clemency, but who is trying to make people believe that with the support of the American personnel of SCISP he is certain to accede to the Presidency, as if that were admissible. He [Duvalier] also maintains that he is the *successeur* of the political doctrine of the late President Estimé, and that in this capacity all the partisans and friends of the ex-chief are duty-bound to support his candidacy. ... The students of Lycée Toussaint seem to have been driven to white heat by the partisans of candidate Duvalier.

It was rather a remarkable statement from Prosper, because it served Magloire and at the same time clearly labelled Duvalier an underground activist, heir apparent to the popular reforms of Estimé, and possibly the United States favourite. The stuttering police chief with a love for money was a cautious man. When Duvalier came to power, he did not lose his quarter-million-dollar home in Gros Morne.

Through intermediaries Duvalier convinced Magloire that the plotting charges had been a lie and in August, with security guarantees, came out of hiding. He was ready to campaign in earnest. He visited the *Haiti Sun*, an English-language weekly, wearing his customary dark suit and keeping his hat on. Smiling, he asked the one question that was on his mind, 'What do the Americans think of me?'

Duvalier formally announced his candidacy on 7 September 1956, in a letter to the newspaper *Le Jour*, which was backing Clément Jumelle, the Magloire favourite and chosen successor. The letter gave a brief Duvalier biography, twelve-point programme and added the comment that his programme had been studied and 'planned during thirteen years of methodical political preparation.'

Duvalier was always quick to deny any involvement in the persistent public disorders, and few people could imagine the mild little man even setting off a firecracker. On 15 October he issued this declaration to the newspaper *Le Souverain*:

> I, the undersigned, Dr François Duvalier, candidate to the presidency, declare to the public and to all the organized institutions established in the country, that I decline any attempt . . . (or association with) . . . movements subversive of public order . . . desiring to face presidential elections in order, calm and peace. I declare besides that the order, in accordance with our programme already published, is given to all my friends all over the territory that the most absolute abstention must be observed. . . .

Magloire was off on another trip to the United States for a medical check-up. He returned on 22 October and was received by a tremendous crowd attracted by the excitement of the occasion as well as by the colourful chief of state who was received so well abroad. In his homecoming speech Magloire said that people in the United States had asked him about the coming elections and the candidates. Magloire said there was talk that Duvalier was the choice of the Americans working in Haiti, particularly those in Point IV, and was counting on their influence to win the elections.

'M. Duvalier, without doubt, has never collaborated with my government,' Magloire said. 'But he has no enmity against me. I believe him to be too great a patriot to connect him with playing on the American strings in order to ascend to the Presidential seat.' He also mentioned Louis Déjoie, Daniel Fignolé, and Clément Jumelle and noted: 'All good Haitians when they reach their forties have a more elevated objective than running for a seat in the Senate.'

Bombs continued exploding around Port-au-Prince during November. A favourite target was the old Iron Market, where a panic could easily be launched among the market women, sending them running wildly through the streets. Merchants would bang shut their heavy iron anti-revolution doors. Some people believed that the bombs were being placed by Magloire himself to create a climate that would be an excuse for postponing the January elections. Only years later did suspicion fall on Duvalier.

Magloire's own desire to stay in office and the subversive movements made him a suspicious man. He withdrew support from Jumelle, and even accused him of being a *mangeur de mulâtres* (literally a mulatto eater, but colloquially a racist). Déjoie and Duvalier, meanwhile, entered into a 'gentleman's agreement' to oust Magloire, a pact that lasted only as long as each thought he was benefiting. Déjoie emerged from this succession of events as the favoured candidate.

The afternoon of 29 October Batista police in Havana surrounded the Haitian Embassy, shot their way inside and killed ten Cubans who had sought asylum there. The following week in Port-au-Prince students demonstrated quietly against the attack by carrying a giant banner that read 'Reparations to the National Honour'. Carlos Prio Socarras's emissary to help Duvalier, Fuentes Rivera, made a fiery speech at the Cercle des Etudiants condemning the attack.

The campaign was truly heating up, and it became dangerous for candidates to go out into the provinces on tour. One November night Daniel Fignolé was almost ambushed on the road to Léogane. He escaped, but Police Chief Prosper decided it was time to call for order. Prosper spoke to all the major candidates, but he started with Duvalier. He accused Duvalier or his partisans of the attack on Fignolé, and called it an attempt to eliminate an opponent and throw suspicion on the government. But nothing changed. Bombings continued, and Duvalier issued another statement disapproving 'of all disorder or subversive action....'

Early in December Magloire called in US Ambassador Roy Tasco Davis and suggested that perhaps it would be better after all to postpone elections until peace was restored. A few days later, 5 December, Ambassador Davis and the Papal Nuncio advised Magloire that he had lost all support and should give up the Presidency on schedule. Magloire reacted as Estimé had six years before. He called in army staff officers and asked that they declare themselves. The only man to speak up was Colonel Léon Cantave, who told Magloire that the officers no longer supported him but were afraid to say so. Cantave was arrested. With a kitchen cabinet of three youthful, ambitious, and loyal officers, Magloire decided to hold on. He ordered the arrest of forty political opponents. Most escaped, but Déjoie was jailed. Typical of Haitian political contradictions, Magloire then released Déjoie long enough to complete a business deal with foreign businessmen for the raising of cherries.

The sixth of December was the crucial day. With a simplicity that was more insulting than deceptive, Magloire announced over the radio that he was conceding to the opposition and would step down as President. But he said the next in constitutional line to be President, Chief Justice Nemours Pierre-Louis, had refused the job. Therefore, the army would assume control of the country. He added that the army had asked him to remain Commander in Chief until order was restored.

This swift change in hats brought on a general strike of 'passive resistance'. Ninety per cent of Port-au-Prince closed down. Stores, shops shuttered their doors, lawyers refused to take cases, labourers would not work. In desperation, Magloire appeared personally at La Belle Créole, a large department store, accompanied by armed police, and ordered the proprietor to open. Then he summoned thirty-two leading merchants, some of them Americans, and asked them to sign a pledge that their stores would remain open. All signed the pledge; all their stores remained closed. A government communiqué blamed the strike on 'foreign companies and organs of the American government'. Magloire's ambassador in Washington protested American 'intervention'. The city, nevertheless, remained quiet as a morgue.

Magloire bowed to the popular will, and on 12 December again turned over the government to Chief Justice Pierre-Louis, who this time accepted. Magloire intended to return to the barracks even then (the year before Congress had named him 'general for life'), but Déjoie, out of jail and the leading political figure of the moment, demanded that Magloire leave the country before a coalition cabinet was formed. Captain Alix Pasquet and Lieutenant Philippe Dominique led a delegation to break the news to the general. Faced with opposition from two of his top supporters, Magloire accepted.

On a cool evening, 13 December, a Haitian army plane flew Magloire and his family to Jamaica, leaving behind his beautiful marble villa in Turgeau (which became the National Museum) and assorted other holdings. Out of the country, Magloire issued a statement explaining that he left to avoid bloodshed. And there was none, but in the uncertain political atmosphere that followed Police Chief Prosper disguised himself as a woman and fled to asylum in a foreign embassy.

Haitians, always responsive, rejoiced at the new political turnover and prematurely celebrated the beginning of a new era of democracy.

8

The Campaign

Since slavery Haiti has used songs to praise and chide its leaders. Magloire and his entourage, some of whom occasionally danced to the songs themselves, were portrayed as hard-drinking revellers. One went:

> Tous les jours M'sou
> Cé wikey M'bouè
> Tous les jours M'sou
> Nan sein maman – mouin, cé wikey M'bouè.

(Every day I'm drunk/It's whisky I drink/Every day I'm drunk/At my mother's breast it was whisky I swilled.)

In 1957 most of the Presidential candidates chose lively méringues for their followers to sing. Typically, Duvalier adapted 'The Happy Wanderer'.

Much of what Duvalier did in the campaign was unintentionally just as absurd, and his three opponents, Fignolé in particular, ridiculed him. With the drama of a Shakespearian actor and the earthiness of a street urchin, he heaped sarcasm upon ridicule. 'On my second soaping in the shower today,' was a typical Fignolé introduction, 'it occurred to me that Dr Duvalier is a profoundly stupid little man. . . .' Even Duvalier's workers and campaign managers often joked among themselves about him. They felt they were pulling the strings that would lead him to the palace.

There are conflicting opinions as to whether Duvalier deliberately created this role for himself as a campaign weapon. Some insisted that this was simply the real Duvalier; others were equally certain that Duvalier, having cunningly assessed the country, the campaign, and his opponents, had decided to play the deceptive role of a puppet. Later events proved that, if a Jekyll-Hyde character had not developed already, it was nevertheless in the process of emerging. The glimpses were startling.

Duvalier spoke in official French of honesty in government and promised a fair deal for the rural masses. He talked about his work in the US programme for the curbing of yaws. He described himself as a country doctor who had the support of the rural folks and the United States aid technicians. Duvalier's platform was simple: he promised to follow in the footsteps of President D. Estimé, whose stature had grown since death. Some of Estimé's former partisans formed what they liked to think of as a strategy board to guide Duvalier to victory.

Among the top aides was Roger Dorsainville, a shrewd politician, good writer, and speaker who had continued in government service, even holding several cabinet jobs under Magloire. He managed Duvalier expertly. Another was Lucien Daumec, former member of the Haitian Communist party who wrote most of Duvalier's speeches. Mme Estimé, too, campaigned for him. Duvalier seldom said anything to allay the fears aroused by his past as an anti-clerical writer and one who toyed with voudou and folklore. Confident Estimists would say: 'Duvalier is us.' One campaign manager laughed and said: 'Hell, Doc Duvalier can't even come up with a decent speech. He just showed me one he was going to make in Cap-Haïtien.' Expressing disgust, he added: 'I tore it up and wrote him a new one.'

The endorsement of Estimé's objectives won Duvalier the support of coffee speculators, the influential middlemen who loan peasants the money that keeps them going between harvests. The military also came to favour Duvalier – that harmless-looking little man who listened so intently to what was told him. He was a man who could be manipulated easily, they thought. Duvalier had directed his post-Magloire speech primarily to the army. 'The soldier renounces individual for collective destiny in order to safeguard human dignity and liberty,' he said. He called the army a 'symbol of vigilance' and urged it to 'remember its traditions in order that the electoral operations may be another beautiful page in the Haitian democracy.... I believe that its [the army's] will be an immaculate sword.' He added one last homage to the soldiers who broke up the Magloire 'slave system', and then thanked God, the clergy, youth, women, and all other Haitians.

Because of his studies of voudou, which had become fashionable, the quiet doctor also had some support among the intellectuals.

The next candidate was Louis Déjoie, born on 23 February 1896 in Port-au-Prince. His ancestry included the Marquis d'Ennery (died 1776), governor of Saint Domingue; Nicolas Geffrard, one of the four generals who fought for Haiti's independence; Fabre Nicolas Geffrard, son of the general who became President. As a boy Déjoie studied at the Petit Séminaire Collège St Martial in Port-au-Prince and later in Belgium at the Jesuit College St Michel in Brussels and the Institut Duprich.

In 1920 he received his diploma of 'engineer-agronomist' from the Institut Agronomique de Gembloux. The following year he returned to Haiti, where he held various government jobs. He was director of the Ecole Pratique d'Agriculture (1924).

From his early years Déjoie had style. He dressed well and even during a period when he was a government agricultural representative in the backwoods he dressed for dinner while his guests, usually other agricultural extension agents, wore their khaki uniforms.

Other positions held by Déjoie were: chemistry teacher at the Lycée Pétion; chemist for the Haitian-American sugar company; president of the Chamber of Commerce (1945), senator for the south in 1946, re-elected in 1950.

In Louis Déjoie the elite had a truly representative son. Wavy black hair and warm brown skin gave him the look of a matinee idol, and Déjoie often acted like one. He embodied most of the sentiments and theories of his class, but although ten years a senator, he distinguished himself as an industrialist and agronomist in the essential oil business which he entered during the Second World War with American financing.

A self-styled non-politician, Déjoie liked to see himself as the gentleman farmer going off in his wide-brimmed Stetson to look over his businesses in east and south-west Haiti. He took time out each week to have at least one black-tie dinner at his home at which American Embassy officials were often honoured guests. A dandy in every sense, Déjoie was a prisoner of his advisers and flatterers from the day he stepped out of jail after the ouster of Magloire until he followed him into exile. Those advisers were not always thinking about the good of the country or Déjoie. They thought and fought for their 'class'.

His followers called themselves *les forces du bien* (forces of good) and condemned the 'revolution of 1946' and the succeeding governments as a 'decade of social regression', proclaiming that Déjoie's ascendance to the Presidency would mean a new era of industrial and business prosperity. Their plan was to re-establish the old elite in power. Déjoie was supported by the clergy, the American Embassy, and high-ranking mulatto army officers, and he could count on the support of peasants who grew lemons or vetiver grass for the essential oils, or worked in his own oil plants.

Déjoie was fond of saying that the Haitian President had too much power; he proposed to establish a technocracy which would enhance the country's agricultural and industrial development. The 'Senator', as he was called, did not soft-pedal his claim that he had more US support than Duvalier, including the favour of US business interests and the American Embassy. In Haiti, support of the United States was almost tantamount to victory in the election. However, from the outset of the campaign Déjoie had antagonized the army, by criticism and the menace of thorough reform if he won the election.

Daniel Fignolé, born in 1913 of poor parents in Pestel, a village in the south-west, was from the other end of the social ladder. Fignolé's father cultivated his little land with his own hands and taught in a rural school. When the elder Fignolé died in 1927 the widow took Daniel and his brother to Port-au-Prince, where she worked to keep them in school. Fignolé did well in primary school, but because of illness and the pressures of helping his poor family, he had to repeat his final high-school year at Lycée Pétion. During this period he worked as a part-time teacher to help his mother. His bid to become a lawyer ended when he had to quit law school to feed himself and his mother. Returning to Lycée Pétion, he taught his favourite subject, mathematics. In 1942 his debating ability led him into a small political circle. That year he wrote an article criticizing the Lescot regime in the magazine *Chantiers*, which got him fired from his state job and formally launched into politics.

Fignolé liked to consider himself an activist in the revolution of 1946, but it was not until he founded the MOP that his name became notorious among the elite and the object of adoration in the crowded wooden shacks of La Saline, Lakou Bréa, Bolosse, and Bel Air (an olfactory misnomer if ever there was one).

Fignolé later claimed that Duvalier played no part at all in the 1946 upheaval, an accusation which may have a basis of truth to it. However, he avoids, to the point of outright refusal, discussing how and why he personally selected the little doctor as Secretary-General of his Worker-Farmer Movement (MOP), preferring to talk about his sixty-four days as Minister of Education under Estimé, during which time he received credit for two new secondary schools.

Once out of the government, Fignolé emerged as a labour leader of considerable influence when he began implementing the promises he had made as a politician. He organized the workers at the Haitian-American Sugar Company (HASCO), demanded and obtained a raise from the princely sum of 1.5 *gourdes* per day to five. In 1950, when he was elected to the Assembly from the constituency of Port-au-Prince, he received more cheers on inauguration day than Magloire. Until he lost his seat in the rigged elections of 1955 he was a champion of the urban working class. He served seventeen days in prison under Estimé, and three months under Magloire for 'oppositionist activities'. The elite called him Communist; those who knew him better plumped for Fascist. He liked to think of himself as a democrat in the Franklin D. Roosevelt mould. His 1946 radio broadcasts earned him the reputation of a rabble-rouser; these were so effective that some of his bolder supporters made open jokes about which gorgeous mulatto woman they were going to appropriate the day after his party took office: a tactical error.

It was a more mature Fignolé who emerged as a candidate in 1957. He was handicapped by a lack of trained followers in the all-important army (though the lower ranks in the Port-au-Prince garrison supported him to a man). Then, too, he lacked support outside the capital, where he had convinced the people of his sincerity by not moving into a fancy neighbourhood and assuming the airs and privileges of the successful Haitian politician.

Duvalier he regarded as his most powerful opponent and the little doctor became the prime target of his campaign speeches. A study in contrasts, Fignolé in private was vastly different from the crowd mesmerizer on the podium. A slim, handsome man – despite a heavily pockmarked face – he kept his own counsel and was almost reserved. Perhaps the knowledge that time was against him in his move to make himself known in the countryside added to his taciturnity.

The fourth candidate, Clément Jumelle, a big, intelligent black man with a disarming smile, was born in 1915. He graduated from the University of Haiti Law School in 1937, and a scholarship enabled him to study at Fiske University, from which he received a Masters Degree in Sociology, *magna cum laude*. His scholarship terminated, he worked as a taxi driver, door-to-door salesman, and labourer to pay for his studies in public finance at the University of Chicago. Upon his return to Haiti, he worked in the Ministry of Labour under Estimé, remained in his post under Magloire, and eventually rose to become the Minister of Finance, although he insisted that he ran a clean ministry, that he never was a Magloire man, and never had been party to any of the subsequent scandals. He called for a better understanding among Haitians and said that the country's most pressing problem – besides illiteracy – was the large gap between rich and poor. A dynamic leader, he wanted to add a 'technical dimension' to the revolution of 1946 and create a civil service.

The first provisional government, after the fall of Magloire, was headed by Joseph Nemours Pierre-Louis, who based his succession on Article Eighty-One of the Constitution, which provided that the Chief Justice of the Haitian Supreme Court assume the Presidency in an emergency. Justice Pierre-Louis's government lasted seven weeks.

His chief blunder was to form a coalition cabinet consisting of Duvalierists and Déjoists, thereby incurring the wrath of the excluded political sectors. He was further attacked for including in his cabinet two other Supreme Court justices (next in line and next), his personal physician, and an octogenarian friend.

A debate developed over whether Pierre-Louis's government was *constitutional* or *revolutionary*. Pierre-Louis refused to commit himself to either ideology (in reality, the debate hinged on whether the nation would continue to stagnate under the *status quo* or whether Haiti would continue the revolution of 1946). The most outspoken advocates of the revolutionary mode was the Parti du Peuple Haïtien, also known as *Le Souverain*. Outlawed under Magloire, it included many Duvalier followers. It was they who accused Pierre-Louis of sympathizing with Magloire and trying to put brakes on the December revolution.

Describing their mission as one of *justice populaire,* they organized commando units that struck swiftly at government agencies and forcibly ousted known Magloirists. (In Haiti it is normal that a new broom sweeps the public ministries clean, yet the harshness of the commando tactics was such that anarchy very nearly resulted.)

Two other major problems confronted by Justice Pierre-Louis were a staggering public debt and an empty treasury. A Déjoie man, Finance Minister Paul Cassagnol, devoted himself to a search for evidence that would pin the blame of the nation's bankruptcy on his predecessor, Clément Jumelle. The patched-up cabinet struggled against political anthropophagism, lack of ready money, and violence.

When four ministers, representing both the Déjoie and Duvalier camps, charged Pierre-Louis with purposely obstructing the investigation of Magloire's financial abuses, the end was in sight. By 1 February 1957 Pierre-Louis stood alone amid the shambles of his provisional government. He invited all the major candidates to a peace parley at the National Palace – a conciliatory move that ended abruptly when Déjoie and Fignolé demanded the President pro tem's immediate resignation. Two days later François Duvalier was also seeking Pierre-Louis's silvery-grey head; over the radio he and Déjoie joined forces long enough to call for a general strike. On 4 February Pierre-Louis resigned. The army, it was announced, would henceforth guarantee the nation's security.

The strike paralysed Port-au-Prince. Stores closed, private and public transportation ground to a halt for lack of gasoline. Radio broadcasts blamed Déjoie; over and over again, they said, it was he who was inconveniencing the people, keeping little children out of school, gradually starving the city.

On 5 February Daniel Fignolé pressed the button and his steam roller began to pick up speed. Shouting *À bas Déjoie*, mobs came out in force. On 1 February all the candidates – with the exception of Déjoie – submitted two names to the Assembly and asked it to choose the next President. The two compromise choices were lawyer Franck Sylvain, an insignificant Presidential candidate who agreed to give up the race if he be allowed to serve in a provisional capacity, and Dr Edouard Pétrus, who had been an instrumental figure in the eradication of yaws. He was considered by many as perhaps the sole apolitical man of any consequence in Haiti, although some said he leaned toward Clément Jumelle. Both he and Sylvain agreed to abide by the constitution if chosen.

The *Parti du Peuple Haïtien*, whose commandos had been largely responsible for the state of affairs, insisted that it also be represented. Sylvain and Pétrus agreed, and the name of a third candidate for the temporary Presidency was put before the Assembly, Colbert Bonhomme, a prominent lawyer in whose house the 'exiled' Duvalier had once hidden from Magloire.

As the Assembly convened to make its choice, the huge crowd that gathered was too restless for the army to handle. General Cantave first asked Duvalier to calm the crowd and make it step back. Duvalier made his appeal but to no avail. Then Fignolé climbed to a high spot, and silenced everyone by raising one arm. He added a few crisp words in Creole, and the crowd dispersed.

When the Assembly chose Sylvain, the people broke police lines shouting victory slogans and singing 'la Dessalinienne', the national anthem. The end of the strike and customary Haitian enthusiasm for a new leader literally had the people dancing in the streets. A stranger would have thought Sylvain an exceedingly popular man, but this was only the excitement of the moment. A week before many had never heard of the lawyer.

It soon became apparent that Sylvain favoured Duvalier. In 1955 he had been fired as a judge under the Magloire administration, and in April 1956 he was one of those who put in writing the opinion that Magloire's constitutional term should have ended in May 1956. As President, Sylvain continued the campaign to establish Clément Jumelle's guilt for the alleged misappropriation of public money during the Magloire administration. Both Duvalier and Déjoie wanted Jumelle out of the race.

Typically, it was a time to settle old scores. Sylvain appointed Colbert Bonhomme as Minister of Justice. At the public's request he took legal steps against those men who had been rumoured to be involved in the 1953 slaying of the wife and five children of Ludovic Désinor, a public works employee under Magloire.

Against this highly flammable background the Presidential campaign continued. Duvalier made a memorable trip to the old coffee port of Jacmel. He was met by people throwing rocks and he nimbly remarked that they were right – if the streets were paved, there wouldn't be any rocks to throw. He then promised to pave them when he became President. He never did. The little doctor also reinforced his bid for Church support with a visit to Our Lady of Fatima Chapel at Pernier, a few miles distant. After mass he spoke, emphasizing his Church education and Catholic faith and reminding those present that he had been a member of the Catholic Youth Organization.

Even then Duvalier was complaining about visiting journalists, few of whom wanted to interview him. They said that he was a dreary little man with doubtful chances who never did anything newsworthy. And rather than answer a question directly, Duvalier would reel off a long, 'mystic' statement which journalists would follow briefly; and then stop to wonder about the speaker. To a US newspaperman who kept pressing for a simple Yes or No answer to an equally simple question, Duvalier replied with fifteen minutes of broken-field rambling. Noting that his original question had still not been answered, the reporter respectfully reiterated his request for a direct statement. This irritated Duvalier. He instructed his interpreter to inform the reporter that 'I have had the benefit of an education, even if he has not. I answer the way I answer.'

To counter a persistent belief that American newsmen favoured Déjoie because he offered them highballs, Duvalier's men began entertaining the foreign press corps with warm beer.

While Duvalier claimed to embody the spirit of the Estimé days, Clément Jumelle had most of the technicians of that revolution on his side. They saw in him a man well prepared to run the country. But Jumelle's big liability, and one that he never could overcome, was his association with Magloire. Many of the black middle class reasoned that because of this drawback he could not win; despite Jumelle's qualifications and winning smile, they began drifting over toward the quiet, apparently agreeable, amiably eccentric (or slightly dotty) little doctor.

He had something for all. He promised social justice, education, and work, and asked collaboration from everyone, including capitalists, whom he said were necessary; he gave absolute guarantees that both local and foreign investments would be protected. He called on the elite to help educate the workers, and said that every man who wielded a machete had the right to qualify for university education. More and more Daniel Fignolé seemed the only man Duvalier had to beat.

As the campaign progressed, violence and wild charges became routine. Fignolists stoned a house where Déjoie stayed on a tour of the south, and Déjoie partisans came out shooting. Two persons were killed. After Déjoie had moved on to the next town, one of his workers, left behind, was beaten to death. As Duvalier entered Port-au-Prince returning from Jérémie, his entourage was stoned. When the dust cleared, one man was found dead with a bullet in his jaw.

Voter registration began on 25 March. Unhappy with the leanings of the pro tem Sylvain government, Fignolé called a meeting of candidates, political parties, and unions. President Sylvain called his own meeting, inviting candidates, police prefects, and newsmen. At the meeting in Fignolé's home, over an old mahogany table covered with a lace cloth, a letter was drafted to Sylvain. Neither Duvalier nor his representatives were present. The letter charged Sylvain with rigging the election for Duvalier, and reminded him that he had promised to remain impartial. It added: 'Indeed, Mr President, the unconstitutional electoral decree encourages frauds. State trucks driven by government drivers transport the electors of a candidate [Duvalier] at the exception of others. The Bureaus of Inscription function very irregularly, and the protests of the representatives are discarded by threats and police proceedings.' The letter further contended that state workers were hired with the condition that they hand over their voter registration cards to the local Duvalier political boss. It enumerated a variety of other abuses and called on Sylvain to fire his cabinet and to form another, 'representative of all political sectors'. The only candidate who attended Sylvain's rival meeting was Duvalier.

Louis Déjoie, as he had done with the government of Pierre-Louis, forced the issue with Sylvain. He sent Sylvain a telegram that read: 'Am sorry to inform you that money authorized by government for special public works – quite needlessly – is being shamelessly used ... to serve exclusively in recruiting of voters for Duvalier.' He warned Sylvain that unless such abuses were corrected, he would call a general strike.

To the Fignolé meeting and the Déjoie telegram Sylvain replied that he would accept the resignation of his cabinet with the condition that a representative political conference be called to recommend a new one. He made it plain, however, that he reserved the right to veto unacceptable names.

Fignolé, enjoying his role as king maker, called another meeting over his mahogany table and once more all candidates with the exception of Duvalier were represented. Another letter demanded that Sylvain dismiss his cabinet, suspend voter registration, and consult all candidates personally about a new cabinet.

Sylvain insisted that his cabinet should serve until the political conference was held. The opposition moved a step further and decided that the cabinet's resignation was not enough; they also wanted Sylvain to step down. Sylvain dissolved the Assembly that had chosen him and issued an order for the arrest of Clément Jumelle to seek accounting for 2 million *gourdes* ($400,000) which had been sent to New York under his signature when he was Magloire's Finance Minister.

On Monday, 1 April, a general strike began. The army secretly moved Sylvain to one of the mansions built by Magloire. That night the city throbbed to the racket of masses of people tapping on electric-light poles and anything else that would make a noise in a technique that was known as *ténèbres* (or shadow protest).

A bomb factory was discovered a few miles from Port-au-Prince, and a certain Daniel Francis was arrested. The army communiqué stated:

In the evening of 1 April 1957, the Army of Haiti was informed of the existence of a warehouse of arms and ammunition at Thor. Officers and soldiers dispatched to the scene found, at Mrs Esther

Poulard's, co-occupant of the house with Daniel Francis, a certain quantity of Molotov cocktails, hand grenades, and other explosives. While the Justice of the Peace was making his report an explosion took place in the house around 8.15 p.m....

Lieutenants Michel Conte and Frenel Andral Colon had the job of examining and dismantling the equipment. Acting Justice of the Peace Fournier Fortuné, filling in for Justice Duval Duvalier, sat at a table. Lieutenant Conte picked up what looked like a box of cigars. An explosion followed that threw the judge into a corner. Lieutenant Conte lost both arms and both eyes; Lieutenant Colon lost one arm and the sight of one eye. Hundreds of people streamed into the general ward of the hospital to catch a glimpse of the horribly mutilated men. They would pause at the foot of their beds, gape, and chatter among themselves excitedly, but, out of respect for their surroundings, in muted voices. It was all very innocent; the wounded officers' visitors were less after a thrill than an edifying experience, and since both men were under heavy sedation, the fact of their being on display made no significant difference to their general well-being. After a few days one died, and, a few days later, so did the other.

It was commented upon that candidate Duvalier's father managed to arrive at the bomb factory just as his subordinate, Acting Justice of the Peace Fortuné, was being led off profusely bleeding. Had someone warned Duval Duvalier in advance, Port-au-Prince wondered. Soon another rumour was winging around the city – someone had planned a 'red night' for Fignolé and Déjoie; their homes were going to be bombed.

Next the army entered the rumour fest. Chief of Staff General Léon Cantave charged that President Sylvain had received advance information about the bomb plot and had expressly failed to prevent it. It was significant, Cantave added, that the factory and warehouse were discovered just hours before the 'red night' was scheduled to take place. The same men responsible for the December 1956 and the January 1957 bombings were behind this latest piece of infamy. A communiqué, referring to the men as public enemies, was issued for the arrest of Fritz Cinéas, Charles Lahens, the Cuban Temistocles Fuentes, and a certain Clément Barbot whose name was soon to become very well known indeed. A thousand-dollar reward was placed on their heads.

These four fugitives from justice were generally believed to work for mild little Dr Duvalier – who denied that he had ever met any of them. He even went to Radio Port-au-Prince and broadcast his mystification that anyone in his right mind could actually believe that he, a man of medicine, of the people, a healer, might consort with, to say nothing of even knowing casually, brigands, terrorists, *public enemies* . . .

The remaining candidates called a meeting to decide what form the next provisional government would assume. In all, eight persons met. Clément Jumelle sent three personal representatives, who were judged unacceptable; Jumelle would have to take the chance of appearing in person before his rivals.

After much negotiating and bickering, Haiti found itself ruled by a kind of triumvirate. Each of the three major candidates was handed three cabinet posts; each of the minor candidates received one cabinet post.

Three of the minor candidates withdrew. The 'electoral college' emerged with eleven cabinet ministers and two additional subministers, one going to Fignolé and one to Déjoie. As soon as the new ministers began sweeping their ministries clean and passing out the spoils, trouble resumed.

On 22 April Duvalier publicly protested the new system. It was vitiating the country, he said. On 23 April his three ministers quit. On 24 April a minor candidate fired *his* minister for flirting with Déjoie's camp.

A communiqué from the remaining ministers informed Duvalier that his defaulted cabinet posts would be divided up between Déjoie and Fignolé. Impossible, said Duvalier, who added that in the spirit of patriotism he would try to persuade his ministers to return. General Cantave asked all the candidates to meet again and argue their positions.

Duvalier replied that collaboration was impossible when the fate of the nation was at stake and that this was his position.

He would not lower himself to argue it with men who sought personal gain and aggrandizement. Cantave adjourned the meeting until the next day, when he commented that the situation was serious and proposed that a military junta be established to rule until elections.

Duvalier quickly agreed, but Déjoie and Fignolé did not. Another meeting was adjourned. On the third day, when Cantave again urged army rule, Déjoie and Fignolé reacted by calling for a general strike directed personally against Cantave. He offered to resign, but the army supported his position and requested businessmen not to get involved. Still, the strike lasted eight days. During that time Cantave asked the opinion of the Supreme Court. The judges, noting they had no legal jurisdiction, said it was their opinion that the remaining members of the Council were the government. They added that the Council, appointed and recognized by the people, now was responsible only to the people. The candidates could not fire them. Cantave and the army abided by the opinion.

Once Jumelle and Duvalier were on the outside, they moved to sabotage the new government which, they felt, would throw the election to either Déjoie or Fignolé. Accordingly, they asked that the elections be boycotted. 'Without me the government is a farce and the elections a joke,' Duvalier said. A new US Ambassador, Gerald A. Drew, arrived and the United States recognized the Fignolé–Déjoie Council. Elections were scheduled for 16 June.

Voter registration began again. Each registrant was given a card that was to be turned in on election day at the ballot box. Because of the high illiteracy rate, it was a practice for most voters to entrust their cards to their favourite candidate until election day.

Duvalier, who had been abiding by the old Creole proverb *Throw the rock and hide your hand,* now began to move more openly. The second week of May, partisans of the two 'out' candidates set up road blocks with giant boulders on the road north, near St Marc. There was violent opposition to the elections in the south also, and tension mounted in the capital. The

Council countered by closing two radio stations which supported Duvalier and Jumelle. Police fired into the air to disperse stone-throwing mobs. On Flag Day, 18 May, the official crowd and diplomatic corps gathered at the Basilica of Notre-Dame and anti-government demonstrations broke out. Two persons were shot and killed, many others wounded. The army intervened while policemen were beating demonstrators in front of the church.

Haiti was once again in a state of crisis. The mutilated Council appointed the Chief of Police Colonel Pierre Armand to replace Cantave as army chief. Armand declined 'for the moment', and Cantave announced that he had dissolved the 'triumvirate' government to save the country from anarchy. Armand then changed his mind and accepted the appointment from the government which Cantave had just overthrown. On 25 May there was a confrontation. The army, in response to political pressures, split its support between General Cantave and Colonel Armand. Déjoie was Armand's main supporter.

But behind the internecine army war was a typical backroom power play. The army had not been paid for two months and an angel was found to provide Cantave with $46,000 cash for the soldiers. He was Clémard Joseph Charles and he made the contribution in Duvalier's name.

Cantave and his men bivouacked in the Dessalines barracks behind the palace and assumed defensive positions. He broadcast a call to troops in the provinces and to the people to rise and support him with Committees of National Salvation. In the meanwhile peasants armed with knives and rocks were fighting off soldiers who tried to remove the road blocks near St Marc. Armand gave Cantave and his men half an hour to surrender. He had planes drop leaflets on the barracks stating that most of the military supported Armand. When the half hour passed, a plane flew over and dropped a bomb. It bounced to a stop on the parade ground in front of the jail without exploding. Someone had forgotten to fuse it.

Masses of people gathered as close as possible to see the war. People rushed for ringside seats on the Champ-de-Mars grandstand in front of the barracks. Mobs roamed the streets. Newspapers, radio stations, and stores were sacked. Duvalier's guards drove off an armed attack on his Ruelle Roy home. One of Fignolé's steam rollers moved around a car on the streets and stripped it to the chassis in minutes, without tools.

Armand put artillery pieces along the Champ-de-Mars and had them open fire on the barracks. Cantave snipers picked off the artilleryman, and three of their guns were captured.

While the military factions mauled one another to a standstill, Fignolé was slipping off to the Casernes Dessalines to meet with Duvalier and Clément Jumelle. His defection from Déjoie shifted the balance of power and by the next morning the struggle was all over. Daniel Fignolé emerged as the new provisional President.

News of this triggered public rejoicing on a scale unprecedented in Haiti's history. An enormous throng gathered before the palace where, in a fit of *esprit de corps,* Colonel Armand embraced General Cantave. A prolonged battle was thus averted; the one-day civil war was over. Only seventeen people had been killed.

Both Armand and Cantave stepped aside for a new army chief of staff, handpicked by Haiti's new leader – General Antonio Th. Kébreau, soon to bite the hand that picked him. But, for the time being, all was splendid. Fignolé delivered a marvellously restrained inaugural address from the palace balcony: 'Under my administration [Haiti] will have a true democratic government. There will be no dictatorship. The United States of America doesn't like dictatorships, and neither do I.' Bells pealed; the crowd roared its approbation; the elite discreetly applauded; General Kébreau, perhaps even then thinking of cowboy movies, beamed. Fignolé received a twenty-one-gun salute, which proved to be two more than the number of days he held office.

So crafty was General Kébreau that the first inkling Daniel Fignolé received that all was not well in Haiti came when Kébreau kicked in the door to his office and arrested him in the middle of a cabinet meeting. Fignolé was whisked off into exile.

After the fact, Kébreau's sudden warm friendship with Rafael Trujillo was noticed and commented upon. Since the Dominican dictator hated Fignolé, some claimed to discern his long shadow behind the 16 June cowboy movie coup. This, however, has never been proved. For two days something resembling peace and quiet reigned in Port-au-Prince.

General Kébreau's junta declared a state of siege in effect and a stringent curfew was promulgated. Without its driver, Fignolé's steam roller seemed permanently stuck. Then, on the night of 18 June, the rumour that Fignolé was being held captive in Fort Dimanche began to circulate. The response was slow in developing, but when the protest did gather momentum it was truly awesome.

With a steady roar that could be heard miles away, Fignolists marked their progress through downtown Port-au-Prince by shattering every lamp in sight. Block by block, the capital darkened. The rioters attacked Fort Dimanche with sticks and stones. Using searchlights, the police methodically shot them down. After a pile of corpses had been created, the police counter-attacked, moving into the slums, seemingly bent on eradicating once for all Fignolé's power base from the face of the earth. Pitched battles of an indescribable ferocity resulted. The next morning the city was taut as a drumskin, but silent.

General Kébreau expressed regrets, but justified his measures by claiming that the city had been a 'jungle' the night before. Death estimates ran as high as one thousand persons – but this figure was never verified, since no one wished to be caught counting. After a while army units came in trucks and began hauling off the bodies. The fire department washed away all traces of blood. Things were back to normal.

On 2 August 1957 the Ministry of the Interior and National Defence announced that general elections would take place on 22 September. No registration was required. Ballots would be available at all polling places, but voters could bring their own. Election officials would be on hand to help the illiterate.

Violence, malfeasance of any sort (specifically, tampering with the ballot box) would draw heavy penalties. The decree added that the new President would be sworn in on the basis of the 1950 Constitution, but that the first task of the new National Assembly would be to draw up a new constitution to be ratified within a two-month period after all elective offices were assumed.

On 17 August 1957 Duvalier's old mentor, Lorimer Denis, died. Noting the little doctor's attachment to voudou, unfriendly voices whispered that he had 'given' his friend as a sacrifice to the *loas* (or spirits) in return for the Presidency. Like the death total on the morning of 19 June, however, this was never actually verified.

9
The Shaky Start

Left alone, François Duvalier might have been just another of the in-and-out Presidents Haiti has known through its history. But if early in his incumbency he revealed himself as a bungling, inexperienced administrator, the opposition, or what passed for it, showed even greater ineptitude. Instead of letting him weave his own noose, his enemies impatiently sought to bring him down with clumsy, ill-timed schemes that merely served to marshal around him the support of people who, under ordinary circumstances, would have been only too happy to do away with him.

The sense of transience that the Duvalier tyranny conveys even today was apparent from the start. The lack of bureaucratic organization stunned even those used to the hasty improvisations of past governments. Only in pruning enemies was there some efficiency, and the main organizer in this sector was Clément Barbot, whom Duvalier later polished off.

Even before he formally took office, Duvalier was to get a taste of the kind of plotting that overthrew many of his predecessors. There were bomb explosions, terrorism, and strikes; once he had assumed the Presidency, there were invasions and conspiracies which plumbed the depths of black magic.

The stage for Duvalier's early difficulties had been set by the elections, in which he had been spurned by Port-au-Prince, the financial and social heart of the country. The business community was cold toward the President-elect, and the urban masses were all for Daniel Fignolé. Understanding from the beginning that these circumstances would provide ammunition for his enemies, Duvalier set out to check his rivals. But he moved cautiously, so as not to alarm unduly either the

American Embassy or Trujillo, and in order to keep his opposition from uniting in one camp.

As expected, the election results quickly sparked disorders in the capital. A defeated Déjoie, claiming that the vote was rigged, announced that he would challenge the results before the Assembly and the official vote-canvassing tribunal. Asked about a strike to support his claims, Déjoie said: 'It's not my idea, but at the moment I'm no longer in control of my supporters.' When the strike did come, four days after the election, it turned out to be a poorly organized move launched in confusion. Less than 5 per cent of the capital's business firms closed their doors, and Duvalier's backers rolled up their sleeves in their first real show of force. The guns they had worn discreetly during the campaign now came out in the open and they lost little time in pressuring merchants into reopening for business. Anti-riot doors of steel mesh or corrugated iron were forced with acetylene torches; some stores were discreetly looted. The swift, efficient reaction of the Duvalierists, backed by the police, broke the strike and signalled its end as a significant political weapon in Haiti – at least for the duration of Duvalier's tenure.

Still, the opposition was not completely deterred. There soon followed terrorist attacks on isolated military outposts. One of these led to the new government's first international incident when terrorists disguised as ordinary citizens approached the sentry at an army post in the mountain resort town of Kenscoff, in the hills above Port-au-Prince one night. A prisoner in a back room of the outpost overheard a man ask the sentry for a curfew pass to take a woman in labour to a doctor. Soon thereafter gunfire broke out. The terrorists killed the sentry and three soldiers asleep in their bunks. A corporal, who slept in a back room, and the prisoner lived to report the massacre. The bodies were left all the next day in order to impress the curious who came to see what had happened.

Army officers were in an ugly mood. Martial law was declared by the junta that ruled until President-elect Duvalier formally assumed office on 22 October. Civilians as well as soldiers were empowered to 'apprehend or kill' on sight any person regarded as an outlaw. This is how a Haitian-born US citizen, Shibley J. Talamas, lost his life. Talamas, a three-hundred-pound six-footer, was a popular textile merchant of Syrian descent. He had once ruled as 'king' of the Port-au-Prince carnival. Three hours after the shooting of the soldiers in Kenscoff he was arrested in Pétionville where he had gone to fetch an obstetrician to deliver his wife's child. He got into an argument with the police and was held until mid-morning on charges of violating the 10 p.m. curfew. Upon his release he went to the Canapé Vert Hospital to see his new daughter, born at 11 a.m., and later to the residence of Ambassador Gerald Drew after being warned that the police had searched his home and were now seeking him. In the afternoon the US Consul and Vice-Consul, assured by a lower-rank police officer that Talamas would not be mistreated, convinced him that he should give himself up and escorted him to police headquarters. The police later said they had found in Talamas's home nine-millimetre ammunition similar to that used in the terrorist killing, along with a luger pistol, a hunting rifle, and a bayonet. They claimed Talamas, a known Déjoist, had been an activist during the 25 May fighting, when a high-powered Austrian rifle had been taken away from him. He was removed from the police station to Fort Dimanche, where he was beaten to death by his interrogators. Army officers attempted to deliver him, although he was dead, to the national penitentiary, but the duty officer there refused to admit a corpse. At first the army tried to hide the facts, suggesting that he died of heart failure and that the autopsy had revealed an old heart lesion. The official version stated that he had been struck when he tried to grab a machine gun during his interrogation. Getting no satisfaction, the United States halted three technical assistance programmes because, it said, Haiti was failing to keep up its share of the financial arrangements. Duvalier inherited this situation when he was inaugurated on 22 October, and after some three months of negotiations he made a formal expression of regret on behalf of Haiti and suspended for ten days without pay the two officers who killed Talamas, paid his American widow and child $100,000 in compensation, and renewed guarantees to US citizens' lives and property.

While the death of Shibley Talamas gave the opposition an opening to discredit the army and Duvalier internationally, Déjoie chose to challenge Duvalier's right to the Presidency on the grounds that his father was from the French Antilles and not Haitian-born as required by the Constitution. Duvalier was invited to publish his and his father's birth certificates to counter the attack. A government radio station accused the Déjoists of defamation of character. *Haiti Miroir*, the Déjoie organ, published a story which allegedly proved that Duvalier's father was not Haitian. But Duvalier did not produce the birth certificates as requested, nor did he offer any evidence that he was born of a Haitian father.

By and large, Duvalier was in good form during his first post-election press conference. When asked the reason for his victory, he replied with a smile: 'The peasants love their doc.' He sought to impress on all who would listen that he and Haiti were one. 'I am neither the red nor the blue but the indivisible bicolour of the Haitian people,' he said, referring to the flag that traditionally stands for the union of blacks and mulattoes. 'As President I have no enemies and can have none. There are only the enemies of the nation. And these the nation must judge.'

He promised constitutional rights, called for the other candidates to unite behind his administration, and commented that he hoped Haiti would become the 'spoiled child' of the United States 'like Puerto Rico.' Duvalier stressed the need for honesty in government and criticized the Magloire regime for making a 'private affair' out of government business. He said he would ask the United States for financial help to correct the nation's fiscal problems, promised to join private investors in the development of tourism and, startling even his own partisans, announced he would ask for a US military mission to collaborate with the armed forces. Throughout he emphasized the need for political unity and pointed out that an effort in this direction had recently been made by one of his ministers, who had played poker, socially, with Louis Déjoie, Jr, son of his chief opponent.

However, the road to unity was littered with the debris of the many attempts – even before he was sworn in – to keep him out of the land's highest office. The abortive general strike, the terrorist attacks, and the Talamas incident threw deep shadows over Duvalier's fanciful talk of political unity.

Before Duvalier's inauguration Trujillo had sent a delegation to Port-au-Prince to decorate General Kébreau. The Dominican dictator, still suspicious of Duvalier because of his links with his enemy Estimé, wanted to make sure he had an ally in Kébreau, whom he regarded as the potential military strong man.

On 22 October 1957, despite widespread maledictions, Duvalier entered the glistening white, three-domed National Palace and took the oath of office in the Salle des Bustes between the rows of bronze images of his long line of predecessors. Across the palace's green lawns he could see the rusty tin-roofed neighbourhood of his youth.

In the palace Duvalier occupied the ill-starred Presidential chair, said to be *rangé* – which is a voudou term for an evil spell that supposedly comes over any man who sits in it. The new President seemed as insecure as any of the provisional chiefs of state who had been ejected so easily from the chair during the past year. Conjecture was rife in Port-au-Prince about Duvalier's lasting qualities. Already at work were many conspiracies that were to blight his early years.

Beginning with Dessalines, Haitians have dispensed with titles and given their own pet names to their rulers. Pétion was known as *Papa Bon Coeur* (Papa Good Heart). The most recent Papa had been Daniel Fignolé who received complaints from 'his children' – the urban poor – in popular songs. In 1946 they sang out against the black-marketing of soap with 'Papa Fignolé, they hid the soap.' In 1957 they added new lyrics complaining about the shortage of water with 'Papa

Fignolé, they have turned off the tap.' But Duvalier's case was different: He christened himself 'Papa Doc'.

One of Papa Doc's first acts was to reward Kébreau. In a ceremony at the palace the President praised his loyalty and named him Army Chief of Staff for six years, an appointment usually lasting only three. Kébreau beamed with pleasure. In November Kébreau headed a fifteen-man delegation to the Dominican Republic to decorate Trujillo and his brother, Hector. The Haitians remained in Ciudad Trujillo celebrating for a week; in Port-au-Prince the word around the palace was that Papa Doc was not pleased with this performance. On his return Kébreau toured the provinces theatrically like a visiting potentate, basking in his power. He was acting as though he were still running the pre-Duvalier military junta rather than serving a duly elected President. He had taken seriously a comment attributed to Duvalier during the election campaign, when the mild little doctor-candidate told intimates that he had interest only in being President, adding that Kébreau could retain the real power. Trujillo's chief spy, Johnny Abbes Garcia, began to visit Haiti frequently and was given a warm welcome by Kébreau.

After a month in office Duvalier granted amnesty to all accused of political crimes during the campaign, except those involved on Déjoie's side in the 25 May upheaval. The move was clearly aimed at reinstating Clément Barbot and Fritz Cinéas who, during the campaign, had participated in the 'Red Night' April bomb plot. At the time Duvalier publicly denied knowing them. Officially reinstated, Barbot fast became the most feared man in Haiti. Sure of himself and his future, Barbot, even while a fugitive, had calling cards which identified him as 'chief of the secret police'. He did not need the cards, the mere sound of his German DKW jeep, announcing his visit, struck fear. Whenever an opponent to the regime was arrested, Barbot did the interrogating and he was savagely efficient. Prisoners talked or died, sometimes both. Word spread through the neighbourhoods about hooded Duvalierists who struck at night. Known as the *cagoulards*, they predated the Tonton Macoutes, and performed duties with which Duvalier did not wish to be officially associated. Their first action that drew public attention took place in January 1958. A half-dozen armed men broke into the home of Mme Yvonne Hakime-Rimpel, an opposition newswoman, swarmed upstairs where she and her two daughters lay sleeping, and severely mauled them. The daughters were left on the sidewalk while the men drove away with their mother. She was found the next day, semi-conscious, nearly naked, on a quiet back road near Pétionville, and rushed to the hospital in serious condition. The Ligue Féminine d'Action Sociale protested. The police did nothing. This was a blunt warning to the opposition.

Duvalier's relations with the American Embassy were strained, in part because of the Talamas affair, but mostly because he and his supporters resented US Ambassador Drew's thinly veiled support of Déjoie during the campaign. In making his bid for US aid, Duvalier tried to bypass the Embassy and deal directly with Washington. Nor did he like to seek Embassy advice on dealing with American firms.

Like Estimé before him, Duvalier found his collaborators more greedy than helpful. His top partisans fought for contracts providing them with kickbacks. In the scramble for personal profit, Haiti's poor resources were eroded and the new administration weakened. One businessman who knew Duvalier said that the President had decided very early in his career that all US businessmen and politicians had a price and dealt with them on that basis.

Trying to emulate the success of Trujillo, he hired a New York public relations firm headed by John Roosevelt, youngest son of the former President, and announced a $150,000 one-year campaign to promote the country. Trujillo had once hired Franklin D. Roosevelt, Jr, as public relations consultant.

Duvalier's duplicity showed itself early in the way he got money for his campaign from Cuba's former president Prio Socarras, on the understanding that the Cuban rebels fighting to overthrow Batista would have a base in Haiti. Once elected he obtained a multi-million-dollar 'loan' from Batista with the understanding that there would be no Cuban rebel base in Haiti.

A month after he moved into the palace he sent five top aides to Havana to work out the details of the loan. When the money was finally transferred from Havana to New York, Jules Blanchet, head of the 'watchdog' superior court of accounts, established by the military junta to control government spending, announced that the government had acquired a $4 million loan from the Banco de Colonos of Cuba at 5½ per cent for seven years. He said that the loan was guaranteed by $7 million in unclaimed deposits of Haitian sugar cane workers in Cuba, deposits whose ownership remained to be determined. (What Blanchet did not say was that the Batista men who helped negotiate the loan got a million-dollar kickback and Duvalier received $3 million, none of which was repaid.)

Those who worked for Duvalier during the campaign, and especially the men who carried out the difficult task of making bombs for him, were learning that gratitude was not one of Papa Doc's virtues. Temistocles Fuentes, the Cuban envoy of Prio Socarras who assisted Barbot and his underground team during their bomb-making days of 1956–7, returned twice to Port-au-Prince and was twice deported.

Batista later sent a delegation to Port-au-Prince to decorate Duvalier with the order of Carlos Manuel de Céspedes. The delegation expressed regret over an October 1956 incident in which Havana police had overrun the Haitian Embassy while looking for political enemies. They pledged Cuba's friendship and promised 'to maintain relations between the two governments in a climate of reciprocal respect and benevolence.' Duvalier had made his peace with Batista. A confirmation of this spirit of amity was the visit of Dr Rolando Masferrer, who assured Duvalier that Fidel Castro would soon be routed out of the Sierra Maestra in Oriente Province, the section of Cuba closest to Haiti. In the summer Duvalier decorated Batista with the Grand Cross of Toussaint Louverture. Duvalier instituted this decoration himself, and Batista was the first to receive it.

Clément Jumelle had dropped out of sight after Duvalier's election, and Déjoie went underground after the abortive strike attempt. On 16 February 1958 Duvalier announced that former Senator Déjoie was not being sought by police. A few days later Duvalier met with Déjoie in the National Palace. The Déjoie newspaper *Haiti Miroir* reported that the meeting was cordial and that Duvalier declared 'both M. Déjoie and himself were technicians in discipline, and as such both had the duty of meeting to discuss the problems of the country.' The *Miroir* said they talked about a variety of things, including freedom of the press and political parties.

On 12 March 1958 General Kébreau, while riding on the Pétionville road, heard a thirteen-gun salute. He quickly learned that it was to mark the installation of Colonel Maurice Flambert, a former Estimé aide, as the new Army Chief of Staff. Kébreau ordered his chauffeur to drive him to the sanctuary of the Dominican Embassy. His six-year appointment had not lasted six months. Kébreau remained under cover until one fine day when Duvalier suddenly appointed him Ambassador to Italy.

Within a week of the abrupt sacking of Kébreau, Trujillo's trouble shooter, Johnny Abbes Garcia, made a personal inspection of the Port-au-Prince scene. His trip was followed by critical block busters delivered against Duvalier in Creole on La Voz Dominicana, Trujillo's powerful radio station. The station sought to create an air of instability in Haiti, saying Communists were trying to take over the government. They specifically mentioned the name of Lucien Daumec, former member of the Communist party and now Duvalier's brother-in-law and personal aide, as one of the conspirators.

In April the Dominican radio announced that a clandestine station, calling itself Radio Freedom, was operating in Haiti, and Haitians began to tune in. Barbot took it upon himself to find the station but was unable to do so. Duvalier even asked a visiting US destroyer to help locate the radio with its technical equipment. The equipment placed the radio in the palace. It was close. The station was operated by a Cuban named Antonio Rodriguez, a Castro sympathizer and friend of Clément

Jumelle, who maintained a butcher shop across from the palace. Haitian authorities never learned of its location.

The new regime, in the meantime, was having problems on the financial front. Jules Blanchet, president of the Superior Court of Accounts, estimated that only one fourth of Haitians between fourteen and fifty-five were employed. Unskilled workers were receiving seventy US cents a day and skilled workers two to five dollars. The annual per capita income was estimated at about seventy-four dollars. Duvalier's first budget was trimmed, leaving him little room for development programmes. In a purely political manoeuvre, he contracted with a Miami firm to clean out the La Saline slums. La Saline was a nest of Fignolé supporters, whom Papa Doc feared. Blanchet estimated that the La Saline improvement plan to move out 5,000 residents, relocate them in new housing, and set up a shopping centre would cost $1 million. A project sign was put up, *Ici Bientôt,* 'here soon'. After a year or two the rotting sign fell down. Some of the people were moved to barracks outside of Port-au-Prince, called Simone Duvalier after the President's wife. La Saline, bigger and filthier than ever, is still there.

Plans were also made to build a hotel and a larger airport in Cap-Haïtien, and a jet airport in Port-au-Prince. Monopolies were handed out for the production and distribution of flour and cement. Clément Barbot figured in these deals, found them profitable, and soon branched out into fields other than Papa Doc's personal security. He made a lucrative arrangement with Trujillo, committing Haiti anew to provide sugar-cane workers on a dollar-contract basis for the Dominican Republic.

Haiti had a system of budgeted and unbudgeted accounts. Unbudgeted funds financed Duvalier's private needs, such as the *cagoulards* and the growing secret police, dual guardians of his power. These funds came from the profits of certain monopolistic concessions, including tobacco. The International Monetary Fund, which supervised Haiti's budgeted accounts and provided stand-by funds to keep the *gourde* stable, knew about but did not see the other accounts. Thus there was the puzzling spectacle of a financially troubled government, in default on international debts, making grandiose public works plans. Behind this dichotomy lay a considerable amount of administrative inexperience, but mostly greed and corruption. The *Haiti Miroir* exposed matters in a censorious editorial reporting that a French citizen had paid some 2 million *gourdes* ($400,000) to obtain a government contract. The newspaper's editor, Albert Occénad, was jailed for defamation.

Before April 1958 passed, Haiti exploded into turmoil again while government officials were busy fighting for fat contract fees. On 8 April a Presidential decree cancelled a thirty-year contract (after it had run nine years) which had given an Italian citizen the International Casino gambling concession. The Italian Ambassador protested what he called illegal 'nationalization' but the casino passed into the hands of Duvalierists. Barbot had become personally interested in it and, through a front man, the gambling concession changed hands three times, each change depositing more cash in Barbot's pocket. But Barbot claimed that all these deals were made in the name of Duvalier and that the money went directly to Papa Doc. The government also announced a twenty-five-year concession giving a Japanese firm rights to fish Haiti's territorial waters and to export the fish and by-products. But the tangle of Duvalier politics eventually prompted them to pull out.

On 14 April Duvalier celebrated his fiftieth birthday by releasing a number of political prisoners, including two high-ranking army officers arrested for their part in the one-day civil war the previous May. But other officers who also had participated in the fight on Déjoie's side were not released, for reasons unexplained.

On 30 April an explosion blew apart an old thatched-roof hut at Mahotières, some five miles south of Port-au-Prince, and Duvalier reacted harshly. It was the first bomb plot against him. The peasant hut had been the site of a little factory producing Molotov cocktails and other explosives which were to have been used against Duvalier in the May Day celebrations.

Armed with Duvalier's unconditional support, Interior Minister Frédéric Duvigneaud pulled no punches in the follow-up probe. Duvigneaud's appointment as Interior and National Defence Minister had drawn some private comment to the effect that he seemed an incongruous personality among the Duvalierists, because of his light colour and his background. A member of the elite, he belonged to the exclusive Bellevue Club and was married to an Italian; it was he who had played poker with Louis Déjoie, Jr, drawing Duvalier's favourable comments. Duvigneaud issued a communiqué:

> Louis Déjoie, principal instigator of the Mahotières bomb plot, is hereby declared an outlaw. Any person who gives asylum to the fugitive will be considered an accomplice of the crime against the security of the state and treated as such. A reward of 25,000 *gourdes* [$5,000] will be paid to anyone who furnishes information leading to the apprehension and arrest of the said Louis Déjoie.

Duvalier was also uneasy about Clément Jumelle, who was still in hiding. He issued a decree nationalizing the properties of two Jumelle brothers, Clément and Ducasse, ostensibly for involvement in the Mahotières bomb plot. The government claimed that, under questioning, two of those arrested had implicated them. Few Haitians believed this. The Jumelles were given forty-eight hours to surrender, after which they would be considered outlaws under the same terms as Déjoie. Shortly thereafter Déjoie requested asylum in the Mexican Embassy and was granted safe-conduct out of the country.

On 2 May the Assembly met to declare a state of siege; to give Duvalier emergency powers, and to suspend constitutional guarantees, including immunity from arrest for congressmen. The opposition had no wind of this move, which swiftly struck down a Déjoist deputy, Franck J. Séraphin. Unaware of the sword hanging over him, Séraphin courageously decided to orate on individual liberty. He invoked the constitution and asked justice for the jailed newsmen who had helped make the revolution against Magloire. At this the government-packed audience on cue shouted: 'Down with Séraphin', and tried to break into the section reserved for deputies. The police held them back. Séraphin sat down, and order was restored. Duvigneaud requested calm, saying that the session was of great concern to the government. Other deputies rose to support this view and commend the government. Deputy Josué Jean-Baptiste presented a palace-dictated resolution granting the extraordinary powers Duvalier sought. It was quickly approved. Duvigneaud thanked the deputies and followed with a charge 'that Séraphin's co-workers are preparing a conspiracy.' He said that, in spite of the government's charitable policies, the opposition had resorted to a malevolent propaganda campaign to sabotage Duvalier's programmes. 'You have been amusing yourself, Séraphin, by going into the garbage of the opposition to come back and call the government of 22 September *cagoulard* and *assassin*,' Duvigneaud said. The Assembly gave a thunderous applause.

Disorder erupted again in the audience and there were cries that Séraphin should be outlawed. Police drew guns to protect him, and Séraphin shouted, demanding to be heard, but was drowned out. The Assembly voted Duvigneaud's request for full powers for Duvalier and an increase in salary for the army. As the session ended, the screaming crowd tried to rush Séraphin, but soldiers put him in a car and carried him to prison. Séraphin later was sentenced, then pardoned. In 1960 he was rearrested and has since disappeared.

The offices of two newspapers, the *Miroir* and *L'Indépendance*, were wrecked one night and, despite Duvigneaud's denials, there was no doubt that Duvalier's *cagoulards* were responsible. Georges Petit, editor of *L'Indépendance*, was jailed for the seventeenth time in his life as a newsman. His first imprisonment took place during the US Marine occupation. Duvigneaud explained that both papers were involved in the campaign against the government and had been printing lies.

Duvalier, after only seven months in office, had driven the opposition either out of the country or underground. The Duvalierist mayor of Port-au-Prince, Laferrière, issued a threatening communiqué. Over the radio the mayor declared that the country was fully mobilized and threatened penalties which, he said, would make enemies shudder in memory fifty years later. The threat of a blood bath was quickly protested by the American Embassy, which was concerned for the lives and property of its citizens in Haiti. The Inter-American Association for Democracy and Freedom cabled from New York to army chief General Maurice Flambert: 'International conscience is shocked by continued abuses committed by President Duvalier's police.' The cable noted Laferrière's threats and said it would 'hold you responsible for lives of prisoners and for bloodshed or any massacres.' A few hours later Laferrière was dismissed from his post, but his message was clear to Haitians.

The homes of prominent opponents of Duvalier were fired on by Barbot and his agents. During the curfew under the state of siege, Duvalierists appeared on the streets, armed with submachine guns, checking all who travelled after dark. The Duvalierists were under the loose command of top government officials who operated around the city in almost autonomous units. The public now started calling them Tonton Macoutes, after the bogeyman of the folk tales. Instead of hiding behind hoods as they had done earlier, the Duvalierists were now proud of their role and hid only behind dark glasses and powerful weapons. During the curfew some twenty unexplained shots were fired at the residence of American Ambassador Drew as he, his wife, and two grandsons were sitting down to dinner. At this, Duvigneaud called a press conference to assure the government's good will toward the United States, and promised the Embassy full protection. He told reporters that it was not clear whether the Ambassador's residence was shot at deliberately or by mistake, and that in any case the assailants were unknown. He assured that the government was in firm control of the internal situation, and blamed Déjoie for the trouble. Duvigneaud added that Haiti was ready to provide the United States with 'every facility for guided missiles, tests, bases, or tracking stations.' The United States had tracking stations in the Dominican Republic.

On 18 May 1958, at Haiti's request, an eight-man Marine Corps survey team was dispatched from Washington. They were to precede the actual training team. Major General James P. Riseley, a tough leatherneck who had learned to speak Creole during his six years as commander of the Pétionville district at the time of the Marine occupation, headed the team. There already were US Air Force and Navy missions working with the Haitian Air Force and Coast Guard.

Seeing the Marines at Duvalier's side the opposition panicked. Following the occupation emotions had run so high that for many years Marine guards at the American Embassy were not allowed to wear their regular uniforms. Now the Marines were returning on Duvalier's invitation to train his army! The psychological impact was important. As usual, Duvalier smiled his half-smile and made no effort to justify his act. He often mumbled later that the army, torn by dissension because of the 1957 crisis, needed to be reorganized. In reality he wanted the Marines as a token of US support and to help ward off his enemies.

Duvalierists made a show of cleaning up the city. They founded the Police des Moeurs, which declared war on pimps, prostitutes, and street beggars, and asserted their authority forcefully over the Fignolists among the poorer classes. Traditional Creole songs, some risqué and some chiding the government, were banned.

Duvalier was so intent on snuggling up to the United States that he wrote President Eisenhower a letter regretting the treatment Vice President Nixon had received on a trip to Latin America (he was stoned in Venezuela). Dated 26 May, the letter said:

In the light of the greatest progress since President Lincoln in the field of personal liberty and individual freedom, I and my government regret the shameful treatment recently accorded your administration's representative, Vice President Nixon, on his trip. On behalf of the people and the government of Haiti we would welcome any visit of representatives of your administration and the US government. As leader of the free world, you and your people deserve the respect accorded to leaders of any great and good cause. The people of Haiti and I salute you, Vice President Nixon, and the American people, and reiterate that we are happy to be on your team. God bless you. Sincerely, Dr François Duvalier, President of Haiti.

Duvalier's letter commending the United States on progress toward individual liberty had been written the same month that a state of siege, censorship, and night curfew, and the removal of constitutional guarantees, had been imposed on Haiti; the same month that the American Ambassador's home had been fired on and that the mayor of Port-au-Prince had threatened a massacre.

Duvalier, in an interview with the *Miami Herald,* said that he had assurance of substantial US support. 'We have achieved political stability, and have the situation well in hand,' he said. On the same day the *Herald* carried an interview with former Haitian Army Captain Alix Pasquet, a Miami exile. Pasquet had sided with the Déjoie army faction during the May 1957 day of civil war, and then went into exile. He commented: 'Haiti can look forward to more killings, more imprisonments, and more poverty.'

In June Barbot and his band bombed out another newspaper, the triweekly *Le Patriote,* which had supported Jumelle's candidacy. About noon two bombs were hurled inside the entrance to the small editorial office and printing shop, injuring two printers. Police arrived and arrested the paper's owner, Antoine G. Petit, son of the old crusader Georges Petit, already behind bars.

On the evening of 29 June, in an explosion similar to the 30 April incident at Mahotières, another bomb factory located on the Frères road, a few feet from where Duvalier was to pass the next day to attend a festival, was discovered. The small *caille* used as a bomb factory was levelled and an iron-worker named Kelly Thompson was picked up at the scene with leg injuries and burns on his body. Thompson admitted complicity and was detained in the military hospital after disclosing names of others allegedly involved. Minister Duvigneaud claimed that Thompson confessed the plot had been financed by Jean Desquiron, a businessman and chicken farmer who had been a supporter of Clément Jumelle. Desquiron, his pregnant wife, and a dozen others were jailed. Because Duvalier attended the Saint Pierre's day festivities in Pétionville the next day, and then travelled to Frères, passing the gutted bomb factory, the government presumed he had escaped his second bombing.

Duvalier protested the sudden appearance of Louis Déjoie and his military aide Captain Maurepas Auguste, in Ciudad Trujillo from their exile in Mexico. Déjoie left the Dominican Republic after Trujillo took the hint that Duvalier could entertain his enemies just as easily.

Despite an occasional bomb and the fearsome visits of Barbot's bands, now well organized in the exercise of the night raid, Haiti was still a popular tourist spot. Tourists seldom if ever got a whiff of the political infighting. 'Cruise popularity moves Haiti to the top of the West Indies list', one headline boasted.

In mid-July, however, one little cruise ship, the *Mollie C.*, was already headed toward Haiti, bringing with it eight men from the Florida Keys who were anything but tourists. They had conceived an invasion so bold and bizarre that it almost toppled Duvalier. Three former Haitian army officers, two Florida deputy sheriffs, and three adventurers invaded Haiti with the fifty-five-foot launch.

The unlikely eight were former Haitian Captain Alix Pasquet, Lieutenant Philippe Dominique, Lieutenant Henri Perpignan, sheriffs Arthur Payne, thirty-four, and Dany Jones, thirty, of Dade County (Miami), Florida, and three other Americans, Levant Kersten, Robert F. Hickey, and Joe D. Walker, skipper of the *Mollie C.*

They chose the night of a full moon to leave the Florida Keys, loading up the *Mollie C.* with 1,173 gallons of gasoline for the 600-mile trip through the Florida straits, around the top of Cuba, and into Haiti's Gonave Bay.

The boat attracted little attention because the peasants were accustomed to seeing tourists at the popular bathing beaches. Tall, handsome Arthur Payne, dressed in swimming trunks, took the boat's dinghy and went ashore, posing as a tourist. Peasants offered him a variety of straw hats for sale. He had his picture taken with several hats atop his head.

Despite the stifling heat, the former army officers stayed aboard the *Mollie C.* and out of sight inside the cabin. Payne explained to the Haitians on the beach that he was having trouble with his boat and needed to arrange overland transportation to Port-au-Prince, where he could get a boat to tow the *Mollie C.* to port. Payne said he would try to get a station wagon to take him and his companion to the capital.

The *Mollie C.* remained at Délugé the night of 28 July 1958 until the moon came up. The boat then glided to a landing near a vacation cottage owned by a wealthy Haitian businessman some two hours before midnight. They quietly began to unload their carefully concealed arms.

Without the invaders' knowledge, however, one of the peasants reported their presence to the assistant *Chef de Section,* who gave the alarm. In response, the army post at nearby St Marc sent out a three-man patrol in a jeep.

The patrol drove up, caught Payne and the others unloading arms, and immediately opened fire. In the brief battle, all three in the patrol were shot and left for dead. Payne was wounded in the thigh.

The invaders took the jeep and headed for Port-au-Prince. They sped through the little town of Montrouis and past its army post without being detected. But near Arcahaie the jeep broke down near another army post. This was not far from the spot where a new home was being built for Duvalier.

With the Haitians doing the talking, they hired a *tap tap* (a pickup truck remodelled for use as a passenger bus) to take them to the capital. Painted across the *tap tap* was the legend: 'In Spite of All, God is the Only Master.' The invaders forced the owner to help transfer the weapons from the jeep to the truck.

All were dressed in khaki, like Haitian soldiers. As they entered Port-au-Prince Dominique drove past one of his old command posts, where he had once cared for an impressive string of Anglo-Arabian horses for President Magloire. He and Pasquet both had been staunch Magloirists, but later played key roles in presenting the military ultimatum which resulted in Magloire's ouster. The other officer, Perpignan, had been a close adviser of Magloire's and a member of his 'kitchen cabinet'. Perpignan had joined Magloire in exile.

Dominique raced the *tap tap* into Port-au-Prince, headed straight for the main entrance of the Casernes Dessalines behind the Palace. Pasquet barked an order to the sentry, saying the *tap tap* was bringing in prisoners. They drew a confused half-salute and roared through the gates.

Inside, Dominique made a swift U-turn and stopped. The men piled out, vaulted up four steps to the veranda leading to the army chief's administrative offices. By minutes they missed capturing General Maurice Flambert, who was taking a midnight stroll across the parade ground to the palace.

Pasquet, a former commander of the Dessalines barracks, and his team worked quickly. They burst into one office and caught the duty officer completely by surprise. When he reached for his gun, they shot him.

The sound of gunfire brought another officer running. He had been on a routine inspection tour. One burst from a machine gun killed his aide, and wounded him.

Within minutes the invaders had secured the barracks. They routed out sleeping soldiers and locked them in their quarters or made them sit on the floor in their underwear with their hands over their heads.

Pasquet took over the telephone and began trying to call the palace, the prison, the army headquarters, and private homes. He told the palace to surrender or be blasted out. He called Presidential aide Captain Claude Raymond and asked him to join the rebels, boasting that the alternative for Raymond would be death because the rebels controlled the barracks and most of the rest of the country. Pasquet ordered Prison Commander Major Gérard Constant to release Raymond Chassagne, a former lieutenant sentenced to a year in jail. Constant stalled and went to the palace to see what was happening.

But the invaders made two costly mistakes. First, they did

not know that the ever-suspicious Duvalier had moved most of the arms and ammunition out of the barracks and into the palace basement. Capturing these had been an important part of the plot, and Duvalier's literally sitting on the explosives crippled their chances.

The second mistake clearly tilted events in Duvalier's favour. For some unexplainable reason, Henri Perpignan, one of the invaders, developed an urge to taste his old brand of cigarettes, the Haitian-made Splendids. Just after dawn he sent one of the prisoners, a man named Marcel who drove for Mme Duvalier, out to buy two packs.

On the streets Duvalierists grabbed Marcel and took him to Under Minister of Interior Lucien Chauvet, who smoked the cigarettes while interrogating the driver. Chauvet learned that there were only eight invaders and relayed the information to Duvalier who, on learning of the invasion, had panicked, packed a bag, and prepared to flee with his family to the Colombian Embassy. Now reassured, he unpacked and sat down to deal with the annoyance. Even so, it took some time for Duvalierists to believe there were only eight men holed up in the barracks.

Until this point, the palace gates were open and the streets nearly deserted, and only sporadic bursts of gunfire issued from the palace. The invaders were awaiting word on their ultimatum; had they gone ahead and stormed the palace at this point, they probably would have succeeded. But they had lost their momentum and their early advantage. As day broke government forces began to rally. The official radio broadcast a call to arms and urged Duvalierists to hurry to the palace.

The broadcasts blamed Magloirists, and said they had joined forces with 'hated' Dominicans to take the barracks. They ordered: 'Go to the palace and aid your President. . . . Hated Magloirists have seized the Casernes! What is more, they have foreigners with them.'

Not sure what was happening, a few sailors appeared with rifles. Incongruously several market women with basketloads of vegetables on their heads strolled regally by, glancing curiously at soldiers who lay in the gutter opposite the palace cradling rifles in their arms.

Lieutenant Jean Tassy, later to become a secret police boss, approached the palace and asked what was happening. Told that more than two hundred rebels had taken over the barracks and were laying siege to the palace, Tassy turned and ran.

Duvalierists began to gather by one of the palace gates. The palace issued guns to anyone who would take them, including shoeshine boys. Periodically, a tightly bunched group of armed Duvalierists would get up their courage and make a run toward the barracks. But the mere sound of fire sent them scrambling toward cover.

Lucien Chauvet, Under Minister of the Interior, led a small group of Tonton Macoutes in directing fire toward an open third-storey window of the barracks. Some of the Tonton Macoutes carried only long sticks of wood. Each time shots sounded they would drop to the ground. Many of these Duvalierists later in the morning threw away their sticks when they were issued real arms.

The palace and barracks were back to back, separated by an area of about four hundred yards which became the battlefield. As the small size of the invading force became known, the knots of Duvalierists increased and their sorties became bolder. Captain Daniel Beauvoir moved troops from Pétionville to positions in the hospital behind the barracks. General Flambert, Clément Barbot, and Minister Marc Charles, who got out of a sickbed to join the fight, led a grenade charge. The palace opened up with .50-calibre machine guns.

At the peak of fighting, Colonel Louis Roumain, one of the invaders' prisoners, rocked his chair backward through an open barracks window and fell into the street. He was pulled clear of the fire unhurt and verified that only eight armed men were inside. Even so, some Duvalierists still remained sceptical.

Alix Pasquet died when a grenade was lobbed into the commanding officers' room. The back of his head was blown off and he fell face upward looking toward a photograph of a cynically smiling Duvalier hanging on the wall. The picture had a bullet hole in it.

When Duvalierists finally stormed into the barracks, they found Arthur Payne wrapped in a mattress, pleading for his life: 'I am a journalist, I am a journalist.' Bullets silenced his screams. Old blood-soaked bandages on his leg showed that he had lost a lot of blood from the wound received in the earlier skirmish at Délugé.

In the same room lay Dominique's bullet-riddled body. At one point he had hand-held a .30 calibre machine gun to drive off the Duvalierists gathering for the kill.

Near Dominique was an elderly man with a shock of blond hair, shot through the ear. An empty pack of Lucky Strikes was balanced on his neck, and his tattoed arms were outstretched. This was Walker, captain of the *Mollie C.*

Wedged behind a desk in the farthest corner was Dany Jones, half-sitting, a small hole in the centre of his forehead.

The 'invasion' was over. It was 9 a.m., 29 July. Maddened Duvalierists tore into the building to see the dead enemies, some soaking their handkerchiefs or pieces of their shirts in the blood. One Duvalierist, a furniture maker, dipped his handkerchief into the splatterings of Pasquet's brains, and ran into the street screaming: 'Look, look at the damn brains of that mad Pasquet.'

The other three invaders had managed to slip out of the barracks but they did not get far. Perpignan, slightly wounded, and Hickey crossed the street into the military hospital grounds, jumped a fence, and separated. Hickey, armed with a sub machine gun, was spotted by a soldier, who shot him dead with a Springfield rifle.

Perpignan ran into the yard of a house and ordered the houseboy to hide him in a chicken coop. The boy became frightened when he heard the mob moving down the street and tried to run. Perpignan fired a burst from his sub machine gun, wounding the boy. Hearing the shots, the mob closed in on Perpignan, shot, stabbed, and beat him savagely. His body was stripped and dragged through the streets to the palace. The mob carried the body up to Duvalier's apartment so that he could see the dead enemy.

Kersten had left the barracks alone. The mob caught him in the streets and sliced his body to ribbons with machetes. He also was stripped and the body paraded around the streets until officials ordered it taken to the morgue so an accounting could be made of the invaders.

When the barracks were captured by the invaders, Duvalierists had set up a .50-calibre machine gun in the palace yard in anticipation of an air attack. It never came. Federal agents in Miami seized a plane loaded with arms, ammunition, sixteen men, and some anti-Trujillo literature before it could take off, presumably for Haiti.

The fighting over, Duvalier, in a steel helmet and army uniform, wearing one .45 automatic on his belt and another in his pocket, posed for pictures with Minister Frédéric Duvigneaud, Captain Claude Raymond, and Lieutenant Gracia Jacques. He then drove around the city triumphantly, an entourage of gun-toting Tonton Macoutes at his side.

Later, the President issued a statement which said that the American Embassy had pressured for Payne's release in March; blamed Paul Magloire and Louis Déjoie for the invasion, and asked their extradition from the United States. He noted that the invaders came from US soil and included Americans, even deputy sheriffs, but said that 'in spite of the evidence, the international conspiracy will not affect relations with the United States.'

The American Embassy declined to reply to the statement directly 'to avoid further damage to Haitian-American relations.' Duvalier had the United States at a disadvantage and he tried to follow it up. In New York Jules Blanchet commented in an interview that the Haitian government wanted the United States to withdraw Ambassador Gerald Drew.

It was an incredible invasion, strange even among the weird twists and turns of Haitian history. In Miami a sheriff's investigation later revealed that the men were to receive $2,000 apiece but that as invasion time neared their funds dwindled and some even had to spend their own money to get the invasion off. It never has become clear who was funding the attack. There was evidence to indicate that both the United States and Haiti knew in advance of the invasion plans. Despite this, it still caught Duvalier by surprise and nearly toppled him.

For Duvalier the victory was significant: it taught him that he needed a personal army to stay in power. From this understanding came several new moves. Duvalier built the palace guard into an autonomous unit directly under his command and quartered them on the palace grounds away from the army barracks. As another balance against possible army disloyalty he built up the militia and accorded new status to the previously semi-secret Tonton Macoutes. Gates were built blocking off the barracks from the street and powerful floodlights were installed around the palace.

Duvalier's hold on the palace became tighter than ever. Thus Haiti began to feel the suffocating iron grip of its ruthless and implacable new master. The curtain had gone up on one of Haiti's bloodiest epochs, and occupying centre stage was Papa Doc, ironically the creation of his enemies, the product of mediocre and corrupt political leadership.

10
The New Dictator

In the aftermath of the 'Dade County Deputy Sheriffs' Invasion' Duvalier did his best to keep emotions stirred up and the United States on the defensive. He emerged from this, his first real test, physically altered, and Haitians soon took note of the change. There was nothing left of the quiet, humble country doctor in the photographs of him plastered around the city. He was shown snarling out at the world from under a large American army helmet. It and the khaki uniform he was wearing bore no insignia. They needed none. His cocky stance – gun at each hip – said it all. Duvalier's new look soon spread to his followers. They, too, wanted to appear tough.

While the Assembly met to vote him authority to continue his rule by decree with full powers for an additional six months on the grounds of national defence, government employees were rounded up for a march on the American Embassy. The fire brigade and police stood by while the crowd gathered around the Embassy fence. Some carried placards bearing freshly painted messages in English. 'USA, why do you protect dictators? Are you a democracy?' was perhaps the most striking and ironical. Other signs denounced Déjoie and Magloire and demanded their extradition from the United States: 'Send back Déjoie and Magloire. We want peace.' Keeping a careful eye on the clock, the demonstrators quit at exactly 2 p.m., the regular hour for government employees to go home.

Papa Doc followed this up with a state-of-the-nation address. Buried deep in its turgidity was a pleased comment that Batista had offered him men and arms. After commenting on Haiti's position, he revealed:

> Friends from abroad have understood all this and desired to express it in a tangible way. Far from the other side of the cordillera

comes to me here like a bugle blast the heroic accents of the message of descendants of José Marti and Maceo. Our Cuban brothers, rising to the level of common traditions, have spontaneously offered to expose their chests by coming to the aid of the immense, sacred band of Duvalierism to crush continuous assaults by the anti-patriots who have set out to reconquer their positions lost in 1946 and 1956. I wish to thank them from the bottom of my heart.

Duvalier knew more trouble was to come. He said:

It would be dangerously illusory, at any rate, to believe that the reaction is definitely wiped out, and that you can consequently enjoy the pleasures of victory tranquilly. With the sanguinary awakening of these forces of darkness, you will have to respond by a tenfold vigilance so that the government may, in a climate of peace and national unity, be able to work to transform into concrete reality your wishes and aspirations....

When on 22 September 1957 your votes put an end to the electoral campaign, fertile in emotions of an intensity and of an asperity unequalled so far, and brought me to the Supreme Magistrature of the State, that day, through the democratic means of the ballot, and the weight of your 700,000 votes, you have affirmed your definite and inflexible wish to see the government and the public administration of Haiti become a weapon of progress and of evolution of the people, and not an instrument of exploitation, pillage, personal riches, and corruption. For this election, by the character of the powerful interests involved, marks a decisive step in our national history. It concretizes the indignant protestation of all scorned and forgotten social classes upon the shoulders of which repose the riches of an egoistic and privileged minority.

The election was the victory of our miserable peasant masses for whom a just and equitable part of the national revenue is henceforth assured. This election signalled the victory of the working classes, too long tricked, who had decided to consolidate the conquests of 1946. This election signalled the victory of the middle classes delivered from a permanent fear of tomorrows. This election signalled the victory of our sclerotic provinces which profoundly aspire to break the chains which enslave their development. This election signalled a declaration of war against ignorance, utmost nepotism, and the prejudices *sans grandeur*. This election finally signalled the conquest of the nation by itself and by the people.

Delivered in stilted French, the speech passed over the heads of most of the Creole-speaking audience. Those Haitians who understood it were saddened that a man who knew the problems of the country so well would exploit them so cynically.

The same day Brigadier General Maurice Flambert, who had succeeded the grandiose General Kébreau as Army Chief of Staff, was promoted to Major General, the first time such rank had been awarded. The same decree unified all branches of the armed forces under his command.

Curfew continued for twenty-seven days after the invasion and censorship for months. The Penal Code was modified to provide the death penalty for plotters and imprisonment for those who spread malicious rumours about the government. Congress voted a National Defence Stamp to help a National Rehabilitation Fund which Duvalier planned to use for the purchase of arms. Duvalier announced that he had contributed one month of his salary to the fund and indicated that he expected other officials to do the same. Clément Barbot, now known as the head of the Tonton Macoutes, was decorated by Duvalier for mustering the attack which finally wiped out the July invaders. The state sold the Magloire properties and dissolved Déjoie's business; a military court sentenced the three opposition newsmen, Albert Occénad, Georges Petit, and Daniel Arty, to five years for 'incitement to revolt'.

The United States seemed intent on disavowing the guilt that had accrued as a result of the Florida invasion. A joint United States–Haiti communiqué issued on 22 August stated that relations had never been better and they would be 'further strengthened in the future'.

Before the month was over relations indeed were 'further strengthened'. Haiti was allocated some $400,000 in US funds for roads and irrigation systems.

The remains of three invaders, Payne, Hickey, and Jones, were shipped by plane to relatives in Miami. Walker and Kersten were buried at Port-au-Prince's Cimetière Extérieur. The three Haitian former army officers went into unmarked graves.

Barbot and his Tonton Macoutes located two of the Jumelle brothers and, with police Captain Jean Beauvoir, led a detachment of men to a little frame house in Bois Verna. Sleeping inside were Ducasse and Charles Jumelle, brothers of the former candidate Clément. They were shot to death. Both were almost fully clothed, and police arranged the scene for a little added drama. Flash camera pictures were taken of the two Jumelles lying on the road in front of the house with pistols near their hands. The photos also showed a trail through the gravel where the men had been dragged dead from the house.

Minister of the Interior Duvigneaud issued a communiqué within a few hours:

> Last night, in the interval of exactly one month from 29 July, the Forces of Order once again were faced with the old revolutionary demon and again triumphed. Charles and Ducasse Jumelle who, with their brother Clément Jumelle, were co-authors of the Mahotières and Pétionville bomb plots and the tragic events of 29 July, were killed last night . . .

The house where the two Jumelles had hidden belonged to Jean-Jacques Monfiston. He was taken to Fort Dimanche and slowly tortured to death in an attempt to force him to reveal the hiding place of Clément Jumelle. Members of the Monfiston family also were killed, but Jumelle's hideout was not revealed. It was Duvalier's policy to charge all his enemies with involvement in the bomb plots of Mahotières, Pétionville, and the 29 July invasion, even though these enemies had political differences and there were no facts to link them.

Ducasse Jumelle, sixty, had been a prominent member of the Masonic order in Haiti and was Minister of Interior under the Magloire administration. During Duvalier's underground period Ducasse had protected the family as well as Duvalier himself. Ducasse and Clément each had a $5,000 reward on their heads.

Clément had one other brother, Gaston, a doctor, who was in jail with two of their sisters. Friends of Clément said he never laughed again, and blamed himself for his brothers' death and the family's imprisonment. He had recognized Duvalier's post-election amnesty as fodder for foreign consumption. He and his wife used a variety of hiding places, often peasant *cailles*. He had been outlawed but refused to take asylum in a foreign embassy until he was forced by ill-health in 1959.

A variety of incidents, apparently the result of post-invasion jitters, followed the Jumelle murders. Arthur and Aggie Vincent, U S citizens who ran a restaurant on the Champ-de-Mars, were expelled without explanation. Two young Argentines on their way south from Miami landed their plane to refuel and were jailed for five days on suspicion. The Rev. Mauricé Balade, a Frenchman who had lived in Haiti twenty-nine years, was dismissed from his post as curé of Léogane and deported. A Columbia University graduate student, Alfred Mark Edelson, thirty, visited Port-au-Prince on a tour of the Caribbean and was arrested after a trip up the mountains around Kenscoff.

Two of Duvalier's pet projects, a U S Marine mission, ostensibly for the purpose of training his army but in actuality a symbol of U S support, and the building of a jet airport were revived. Airport planning fizzled again, and it was several years and many new plans before it was finally realized; but the Marine mission was within grasp.

William A. Wieland, chief of the Caribbean desk at the U S State Department, arrived in September with Marine Colonel Victor J. Croizart to talk about the training mission. An official communiqué said that the conversations were held 'in an atmosphere of cordial and frank friendship'.

When it appeared certain that the Marines would be coming, Duvalier began tidying up a bit. He brought the business community under tighter control. In a 13 October 1958 decree he stated that no business could close its doors or even go bankrupt without permission: 'There is a need to prevent all actions that could compromise the economic life of the country. In certain instances, the closing down of commercial, industrial, and agricultural establishments can constitute a means of provoking social and political agitations.' As the Haitian economy staggered, more and more firms went bankrupt, but they kept their doors wide open even though only creditors walked in.

Duvalier tried once more to cope with the growing financial problems. He agreed to a $338,000 contract with the Washington and New York firm of Klein, Saks, and Lehman Brothers to study the country's sagging economy and make recommendations for reform. But after the reforms were suggested, Papa Doc proved not to be very interested in following anyone's advice.

As a result of the Wieland conversations, a ten-man Marine temporary training mission under Major James T. Breckenridge arrived to carry out a ninety-day pilot project with Haitian army recruits. A Marine survey team the previous spring had said that such a mission was feasible, and this was a practical experiment with the idea. At a 138th-birthday party for the Marine Corps, US Chargé d'Affaires Philip Williams commented that the request for a mission reflected the high opinion the government had of the Marines.

Duvalier dispatched one of his top aides, Joseph Baguidy, to Italy with money collected from the National Rehabilitation Fund. He returned with 150 tons of war matériel, including arms, ammunition, and three American light tanks left over from the Second World War. Duvalier already had six similar tanks which had been given to Haiti during the war under a US military grant. They were armed with a .37mm. gun, one .50 calibre and one .30 calibre machine gun. However, they were in varying states of readiness because Haiti had no qualified tank mechanics, armourers, drivers, or gunners. Truck drivers and automobile mechanics were substituted and the tanks remained around the palace most of the time. Some of the machine guns were dismantled and set up at fixed emplacements. The new purchase swelled Duvalier's arsenal to about 600 M-1 rifles, some air-cooled machine guns, .60mm. mortars, and Browning automatic rifles. With these he had an air force of four Mustang P-51s, eight AT-6 trainers, and two DC-3s.

Duvalier changed the date of Army Day to 18 November in order to commemorate the decisive battle in the War for Independence against the French. A parade was held to exhibit his new military hardware to the Marines and the public. Word got around that the heavier weapons, such as anti-aircraft guns, would not be displayed – the message, which was not lost on Port-au-Prince – being that Duvalier had all kinds of matériel in reserve. The arms purchase was announced as totalling $60,000, but it was probably higher.

After a month of work by the Marines, Brigadier General Richard Mangrum arrived from the United States to inspect their progress. The Marines and Haitian officers, as well as a crowd attracted by the activities, watched the Haitian army go through the new drills they had been taught. Afterwards General Flambert personally decorated General Mangrum, Colonel Croizart, Major Breckenridge, and Captain Charles Williams with the Jean-Jacques Dessalines Order of Military Merit. Haitians did not miss the irony. Dessalines's legendary hatred of the white man is immortalized in a Haitian military march, *Dessalines pas vlé ouè blancs* . . ., or, literally, 'Dessalines can't stand the sight of white men', which was played at the parade.

A week later Duvalier finished his military housekeeping. He sacked the entire general staff, ridding the army of old-time officers and replacing them with younger men trained either by Haitians or by one of three small US military missions since the time of the Marine occupation. (There had been an Army mission from 1939 to 1945, a Navy mission since 1948, and an Air Force mission since 1950.) Retired were Major General Flambert, who, less than six months before, had attained the highest military position anyone short of a dictator had ever held, together with seventeen colonels. Flambert was a twenty-seven-year veteran; many of the colonels had served for twenty-five years.

These were the Haitian officers who dated back to the Marine occupation, and Duvalier, in a typical example of clear thinking, apparently believed they might either resist the Marines or perhaps become too close to them. He did not want too much foreign influence in the army, which he well knew meant trouble for past Haitian Presidents.

To replace Flambert, Duvalier chose the police chief, Colonel Pierre Merceron, and in a Sunday-morning ceremony at the palace he pinned the silver star of a brigadier general on each one of his epaulets. After slightly more than one year in office, Duvalier already had fired two army chiefs.

Other preparations for the Marines included a four-article decree issued on 15 December changing the name of a special unit at the palace to the Presidential Guard. The new guard was directly under Duvalier's command, slept on the palace grounds, and was groomed as Haiti's elite corps. It received the best of everything available: uniforms, weapons, food, and pay. Prime qualification for membership was loyalty to Papa Doc.

At the insistence of Barbot, and to prevent possible attacks from opponents across the Dominican border, Duvalier and Trujillo agreed on mutual assistance and co-operation. Barbot had replaced former General Kébreau in Trujillo's favour. He provided, at considerable profit to himself, Haitian sugar-cane cutters to Dominican plantations. Haitians bitterly called it 'slave trade'. Barbot reached this position through his friendship with Lieutenant Colonel Luis Trujillo.

The two dictators met on the humid salt flats on Haiti's side of the gateway fort to Jimaní, principal entrance to the Dominican Republic. Duvalier superstitiously set the meetings for 22 December 1958 (twenty-two is his favourite number). Two flag-decked stands had been set up, about one hundred yards apart. Precisely at the appointed time, 8 a.m., Trujillo stepped out of his dusty Cadillac in a light grey suit, and mounted the stand nearest the Dominican soil. His honour guard was dressed in ceremonial blue and gold with huge white helmets. Opposite them stood the Haitian guard in khaki. They waited for Duvalier, sweltering in the heat. After an hour Trujillo became irritable. His pancake make-up, which he sometimes wore at special occasions, was running in the heat. He ordered photographers away.

The Duvalier motorcade approached around the bend, with sirens wailing, at ten-thirty. Was it a deliberate slight? Duvalier was always late. Trujillo, however, had a reputation for being punctual. The idea of keeping Trujillo waiting thrilled Haitians. Many also chafed at a festive meeting with the man responsible for the 1937 massacre of 20,000 of their countrymen along this same border.

The pact they signed talked of fighting Communists, but the key phrase was one in which they 'further agreed not to tolerate subversive activities of political exiles whose actions prejudice good relations between the states.' Another agreement said: 'They shall consult each other to harmonize their respective positions at the United Nations and Organization of American States as much as possible and in conformity with the principle of inter-American solidarity.'

Johnny Abbes Garcia and Clément Barbot, responsible for this meeting, clinked champagne glasses in the background as the two dictators went through the formalities. Later Duvalier was pleased when he learned he had kept Trujillo waiting for so long and had gotten away with it.

Duvalier got his Christmas present from the United States at 5.20 p.m., Christmas Eve 1958. Foreign Minister Dr Louis Mars, American Ambassador Drew, and General Merceron attended a brief ceremony and formally declared that a permanent Marine training mission would be brought to Haiti. This was called a 'further demonstration of the close bond of friendship uniting the governments and people of the two countries.' The agreement was of indefinite duration: it stipulated that members of the mission would serve two years at a time and provided that either government had the right to end the agreement with three months' notice.

But before the Marines could land, a more important development in next-door Cuba shook the hemisphere and was to continue shaking it for years to come. Dictator Batista fled on New Year's Eve 1958, and a bearded guerrilla from the Sierra Maestra, Fidel Castro, inherited the country on 1 January 1959. The man who ran the Oso Blanco butcher shop across the street from the palace (which once housed a clandestine radio station), Antonio Rodriguez, the Cuban friend of Clément Jumelle, revealed himself to be the co-ordinator for

Castro's 26 July movement in Haiti. Rodriquez took over the Cuban Embassy, ran up the 26 July flag, liberated some duty-free scotch and champagne to toast the Cuban revolution, and then called on Duvalier, made nervous because of Castro's surprising triumph. Rodriguez demanded all Cuban rebels in Haitian jails be released, and a plane be furnished to fly them to Santiago, Cuba's nearest major city. Four Cubans were in jail awaiting trial on charges of having killed a Haitian boat captain in an attempt to seize his boat and head for Cuba. Duvalier, eager to accommodate his strange and apparently powerful new neighbour, quickly agreed.

Duvalier also offered to send medicine to Cuba. Aware of his public ties with Batista and his own reputation, he had the jitters. He was afraid that his opposition would find a new haven in Cuba, where they could get arms and aid. In an effort to improve his image, he recognized the Castro government on 8 January 1959, and softened his rule. Louis Déjoie, who had been tried *in absentia* and sentenced to death, was granted full pardon, as was Congressman Séraphin, who had served three days of a three-year sentence; also released were the imprisoned newsmen, Occénad, Petit, and Arty; Gaston Jumelle and the Jumelle sisters; Yves Bajeux, who had been harshly beaten and tortured, and his fellow plotters, all under death sentences. Haitians in asylum were granted safe-conduct out of the country.

Duvalier had still other reasons to worry. Trujillo also was on Castro's black list, and Duvalier was freshly tied to him. Dominican exiles had fought with the Castros and it was clear that Fidel now owed them support in their battle with Trujillo. He also had a personal score to settle with the Dominican dictator who had sold arms to Batista when no one else would, and then provided Batista with a place of refuge when he fled the country. Trujillo re-emphasized his ties to Duvalier by sending a navy corvette to Port-au-Prince as a show of helping Haiti guard against attack.

Peter Kihss of the *New York Times* interviewed Duvalier

later that month, on 15 January 1959, and asked a classic question: when was Duvalier going to stop being a dictator? 'I am not a dictator,' he was told. 'I consider myself a country doctor. I want to build up Haiti.' Duvalier said he would let his power to rule by decree expire, but added that the state of siege technically would continue until the Assembly lifted it. Duvalier admitted frankly Haiti was in 'a financial mess'. He spoke about the need for greater US aid, and added this interesting comment:

> I took everybody out of jail because I want to tell them that it is much better to think in terms of the nation, because the nation is the Haitian nation of all the Haitian people, not only for myself. I am only the chief. I did what I wanted to do as a Catholic.

While Haitian exiles flocked to Havana, some concern was being voiced in the United States over the new Marine mission. Senator Mike Mansfield, majority whip, urged the administration to 'go slow' on sending the mission.

The Marines, however, had landed. Colonel Robert Debs Heinl, Jr, a spit-and-polish Marine who looked the part of a crisp British officer in colonial India, arrived with four other Marine officers and four non-commissioned officers aboard the S.S. *Ancon*. Heinl, forty-two, a Yale graduate and son of a former *New York Times* correspondent, headed the mission, and he announced that it would arrive in echelons to train technical branches of the services and infantry. He spoke French, was enthusiastic about the mission, and despite Haitian hatred of Marines, expressed his intention of getting the job done. Heinl had been at Pearl Harbor during the 1941 Japanese bombing, served in the Pacific at Wake Island, the New Hebrides, Guam, Iwo Jima, and with the occupation troops in Japan. He was the author of several studies of Marine history. Heinl later said that his instructions, though never formalized in writing, were to ensure the pro-US orientation of the armed forces and to build up a broad base of professional, politically disinterested officers and non-commissioned officers. Heinl was told by William Wieland of the US State

Department (who also had been advising the United States on Cuban affairs) that US policy supported Duvalier and that he should do his best in that direction.

Ambassador Drew introduced Heinl to Duvalier at the palace the day after his arrival. Duvalier explained to Heinl how political tensions were being relaxed and added the opinion that the principal role of the Marine mission (officially called a Navy mission to avoid the emotional conflicts) was to assist in keeping the Haitian army out of politics. Duvalier also kept the Marines under close surveillance.

Colonel Heinl found a ready source of information in Clément Barbot, the powerful Tonton Macoute chief and now Duvalier's private secretary. A general staff member who failed to disguise his hostility toward the Marines was brought sharply into line by Barbot. Within six months the man was out of the army. Duvalier's opposition found in the Marines a handy target of criticism. They called them white Tonton Macoutes.

Barbot had become the man to see to cut through government red tape and he was very much in demand among the business community. Called 'the little muffler', he was rapidly growing in stature, dangerously crowding the shadow of the dictator.

Before January passed the former butcher, Antonio Rodriguez, came back as Cuban Ambassador. Rodriguez had lived in Haiti twenty years after beginning his days as a revolutionary under the Gerardo Machado dictatorship (1925–33). He had married a Haitian and lived in Port-au-Prince a long time. In a formal ceremony he presented his credentials to Duvalier, who accepted the new Ambassador as an additional problem. Duvalier knew him to be tough, and a staunch supporter of Clément Jumelle, who, along with the rest of the opposition, had no doubts about Duvalier's mercy or the value of his amnesty promises.

Haiti abounded with examples of Duvalier mercy. Police caught a man distributing what they called subversive literature early one January morning. Tonton Macoutes chased him through the deserted downtown streets with guns blazing.

When his car rammed across the sidewalk and into a building in front of the tourist shop La Belle Créole, the Tonton Macoutes riddled it with bullets and left him and the blood-stained car on the street all morning as a warning. The same week two other men were shot to death when they were caught trying to start a fire with a bottle of gasoline. The police report suggested that the men might have been responsible for 'subversive fires' started around the city.

In Havana the exiles, as Duvalier feared, were busy. They joined other exiles from all over the Caribbean flocking to the new hope, Castro, for help in overthrowing dictatorships astride their homelands. Castro had said that Cuba would help any revolutionary group.

At that time Louis Déjoie, the mulatto former champion of the Haitian elite, was the most active Haitian exile. He went to Havana three days after Castro took power to ask for help. Ernesto (Che) Guevara, who had landed with Castro from Mexico and came out of the revolution a leader, helped Déjoie set up a training camp on a farm about thirty kilometres from Havana. Déjoie also had a Havana office in the Refugio Building. 'They offered us 800 soldiers willing to disembark in Haiti with us and we had a landing barge which could carry 300 men put at our disposal. The training started, and all was going well,' Déjoie said when he reviewed the operation years later.

Déjoie, Daniel ('Steam Roller') Fignolé, and Jumelle supporters formed a loose association called the United Opposition, which broadcast in Creole three times a week to Haiti over Havana's Radio Progreso. Déjoie held a press conference in the Havana Hilton Hotel (later the Havana Libre) to denounce Duvalier. In a statement in Santiago de Cuba Déjoie predicted Duvalier's downfall, but denied plans for an armed invasion. He said that the United Opposition would continue its radio broadcasts. Fidel Castro had warned that since Haiti was a friendly country, the exiles could talk about but not predict invasions. Fignolé, in exile in New York, sent recordings which were used in the Radio Progreso broadcasts. In one he told the people in Haiti to be prepared to begin a general strike when he gave the word. Jumelle was still hiding in Haiti.

Duvalier tried to reach into Cuba and eliminate his foes but the plan backfired. Cuban police announced in late February that they had uncovered a plot to assassinate Déjoie and three other Haitians active in the Duvalier opposition. Police said they arrested three men as they arrived at Rancho Boyeros Airport. They quoted one as saying that the Haitian consul in Havana was supposed to supply arms and pay $10,000 for each killing. Besides Déjoie, Haitians threatened were his secretary, Robert Léger, and former army officers Pierre Armand and Maurepas Auguste.

Duvalier tried another tactic which proved to be more successful. In Déjoie's own words, this is what happened:

> Duvalier sent a mission to convince Castro that he would co-operate with Cuba if the Haitians in exile were discouraged. . . . Until then the training had been progressing. We had thirty Haitians who had joined the 800 Cubans. But Castro made the deal with Duvalier, and then we had nothing. Duvalier agreed to let the Communists infiltrate. Haiti then appeared to break relations with Cuba, but maintained consuls throughout Cuba and co-operated with Castro. The co-operation continues to this day [1962]. Later, some of my men tried an invasion from Cuba in the south of Haiti, but I was not really involved.

Déjoie said he left Cuba in May 1959.

At this point the United States moved openly to bolster the Duvalier government. State Department officials used the explanation that Duvalier had shortcomings but offered more stability than any of his predecessors. Even his immediate predecessor, however, Paul Magloire, had enjoyed greater rapprochement with the United States and given Haiti something to show for the money spent. The State Department was concerned because of poor economic conditions inside Haiti and the noise if not the reality of a threat from Cuba.

Between February and September 1959 the United States gave Haiti $7 million for its budget. This was a cash gift, not a loan, and was officially allotted as $3.5 million for the fiscal years 1959 and 1960 (ending 30 June), but it was spent within seven months in 1959. Haitian observers looked on with considerable amazement for Duvalier continued the free use of his 'unbudgeted' accounts estimated as from $4 to $7 million annually. This revenue was derived from government distribution of monopolies (not retail sales) in tobacco, soap, matches, sugar, lard, edible oils, and other articles. Duvalier did not hesitate to switch budgeted items around as it suited him. The official gazette once listed seventeen budget switches, all to the secret police. The US gift thus put Duvalier in the position of subsidizing not only legitimate debts, but freeing money for his own private purposes which were, in most cases, of a repressive nature.

Other Duvalier pals rallied around. Trujillo announced that he was forming a 'foreign legion' that would also defend Haiti. He said five retired Dominican generals were organizing a force of 25,000 men to be supplied with weapons by the government. US Congressman Victor Anfuso, a friend of Duvalier's American adviser Dr Elmer Loughlin, asked the United States to halt any invasion from Cuba if the Organization of American States did not act.

Meanwhile Papa Doc had his men hopping in Port-au-Prince. During the five days he expected the invasion, his friend Trujillo sent over a Dominican warship, *The President Peynado,* to help. The government cancelled all exit permits for Haitians and foreign residents, excepting only diplomats and tourists. One of the Presidential Guard lieutenants, Jean Tassy, personified Duvalier's mood. Tassy, driving a palace car up the Delmas highway, almost struck another driven by businessman Roger Denis (no relation to Lorimer). Tassy's arrogance affected his driving, and Denis, who never participated in politics, called out to him: 'So the road now belongs to you?' Tassy came back and arrested him, left Denis's wife, who could not drive, sitting in their car, took Denis to police headquarters, and charged him with subversive talk.

He ordered Denis, a man of fifty, tied with his hands under his knees. Policemen took turns beating him across the back and legs until he fainted. He awoke in a military hospital and was transferred to the private hospital Canapé Vert. There were no broken bones but his flesh had been beaten to a pulp. Reports of the incident were circulated, some with pictures, and some Haitians felt Tassy would be in trouble for this abuse of authority. He wasn't. Duvalier promoted him and Tassy became one of his most trusted aides. As soon as he could travel, Denis and his family left the country.

The home-front picture was further clouded by a drought in the north-west near Jean-Rabel. Thousands faced starvation and newspaper stories reporting it angered Duvalier, and, in what drew expressions of disbelief from the American Embassy, the Haitian government refused to transport food from the United States offered by charitable agencies. When pictures and additional reports documented the problem, CARE moved in to feed some 75,000 persons in the affected area. Such an example of callousness towards his own people did not deter the United States from loaning Duvalier another $4.3 million in April to complete an 80,000-acre irrigation system in the Artibonite Valley.

On the evening of 6 April 1959, Clément Jumelle found time running out on him. Just after dark Cuban Ambassador Rodriguez saw someone on his front patio. He looked out and saw two persons dressed as peasants: Clément Jumelle, lying on the ground, and his wife standing beside him. Jumelle, a fugitive since September 1957, was finally driven to ask asylum which he had stoutly refused until then. Servants carried him to an upstairs bedroom and the Ambassador called in six doctors, who pronounced Jumelle critically ill with uraemia, his condition further complicated by hypertension. They gave him oxygen, blood transfusions, worked around the clock trying to save him. Rodriguez brought two specialists over from Havana on a special Cubana Airlines flight, but it was too late. Five days later Jumelle died.

Rodriguez was tipped off that an attempt would be made to steal Jumelle's body when it was taken out of the Embassy. The reasons were not clear, but it was speculated that Duvalier either feared the emotions that might be aroused by a public funeral or that he wanted the body for voudou purposes.

The night of Jumelle's death Rodriguez drove down the steep driveway of his Embassy residence with a friend sitting beside him in the front seat. It was Jumelle. He had been dressed, taken out through the back door, and propped up in the car. As the Tonton Macoutes knocked at the front door, Rodriguez drove him to the house where Jumelle's eighty-five-year-old mother and his sisters lived. 'I did all I could,' he told them.

The following afternoon a hearse carrying the body moved slowly up the small street in front of his mother's home to the Church of the Sacred Heart for funeral services. Hundreds of mourners followed silently behind the slow-moving car. People flocked out of their homes to watch the procession, handkerchiefs held to their mouths in token sympathy. At the first intersection a police wagon roared up and braked to a stop in front of the black hearse. Police officers waving Tommy guns jumped into the hearse and, sirens wailing, sped away with the body. Wreaths were scattered on the street and the mourners, some with bloody heads, stood in the middle of the street astounded. Word quickly spread that Duvalier had ordered Jumelle's body brought to him at the palace so that Jumelle's heart could be removed to make a potent *ouanga*. The police continued through the city and then took the road to St Marc, where Jumelle was hastily buried. Feelings fanned by rumours of a voudou ritual ran high and the Catholic daily, *La Phalange,* reported that the police refused to let a priest bless the interment.

His February prediction of an invasion from Cuba never materialized, but Duvalier continued preparing for it. He began to bolster his civilian militia and announced that 25,000 men and women had volunteered to defend the country. The militia had no weapons, except when they were loaned them briefly for training, but Duvalier contended that they would be ready if trouble started. He said that the militia really had started during the 29 July 'Deputy Sheriffs'' invasion when citizens answered his radio appeal for help. Army Chief General Merceron ordered all the other civilians to turn in their firearms as a 'security measure', which struck some observers as odd preparation for an outside threat.

Duvalier took the further precaution of reshuffling his administration. He said it had become necessary to cope with growing economic problems, political unrest, and 'inefficiency in government'. Among those ousted were the tough Minister of Interior and Defence Duvigneaud, the Minister of Education Father Jean-Baptiste Georges (a Catholic priest), and Minister of Agriculture Marc Charles. All three had been considered loyal members of the government and in good standing. Father Georges had been popular with university students and was regarded as a hard-working man. Charles had been influential in Duvalier's election, and during the 29 July invasion had gotten out of a sick-bed to help.

When the Assembly reconvened in April some members made it plain that they took their elective offices seriously. Senator Jean Bélizaire chided his fellow legislators in an opening address that obliquely criticized Duvalier. 'Without respect for the principles of the Constitution there is no democracy,' he said. 'No respect either for the dignity or for the rights of citizens, there is no political stability and, consequently, there is no progress.'

Bélizaire, who was some six months away from a death sentence (he eventually was able to flee the country), was so vehement because he and his fellow senators were being pushed hard by the little doctor. One congressional delegation was almost bodily ejected from the National Palace where it had gone to present a petition. Tempers were not soothed when Captain Franck Romain of the Presidential Guard was promoted for his part in the skirmish. But Duvalier had many effective ways of cooling people off.

About the same time that Bélizaire was making his brave speech the Venezuelan Chargé d'Affaires Enrique José Miliani was declared *persona non grata*. His residence had become an island of asylum. In March alone seventeen persons were granted safe-conduct out of the country under Venezuelan protection. Others seeking asylum soon replaced them.

Police discovered 143 grenades in a small metal shop and announced that they had foiled another plot. A good propagandist, Papa Doc rose above it all with a grand new campaign against illiteracy. He plastered DDD signs all around the city – 'Dieu [God], the great worker of the universe; Dessalines, the supreme artisan of liberty; Duvalier, architect of the new Haiti.' Several roads and avenues were renamed for Duvalier, and one of the signs was planted before a workers' city built by Magloire.

The illiteracy campaign was a striking example of the 'Duvalierist revolution'. While the government admitted Haiti was ninety-per-cent illiterate, Port-au-Prince newspapers carried stories proudly announcing the departure of Haitian teachers for Africa, to help Africans learn to read and write. Duvalier was driving out the professionals and complaining because he did not have any. The same week he spoke of Haiti's great financial needs for education. Meanwhile the government had just spent $32,070 to open a Haitian Embassy in Tokyo.

Late in May 1959 the Information Ministry reported: 'President François Duvalier has been confined to bed by grippe and overwork.' But rumours said that Duvalier had taken a turn for the worse and an American specialist was being summoned for consultation. Haiti was in the middle of a grippe epidemic.

Duvalier had a heart attack that very nearly did what all the plots and invasions had not been able to. Sunday night, 24 May 1959, he almost died. His physician, Dr Jacques Fourcand, thought he was in a diabetic coma and administered insulin. Dr Fourcand was a brilliant, US-educated neuro-surgeon. He had been an early disciple of Duvalier, became more involved in politics than medicine, and was appointed head of the Haitian Red Cross.

In spite of the insulin shot, Clément Barbot noticed that there was no response. A young consultant, Dr Rosarion, told

Mme Duvalier that he thought Dr Fourcand had made a mistake. Acting on his advice, Barbot rushed out in the middle of the night, broke into the first pharmacy he reached, and brought back glucose. Dr Rosarion told Mme Duvalier it was peculiar that such a good doctor as Fourcand would make such a mistake and suggested it might have been deliberate. (Years later Rosarion quit the Tonton Macoutes in disgust and turned in his gun. He was arrested and beaten. Duvalier then brought him to the palace, apologized, saying he had not known of his imprisonment, and gave him an envelope containing $1,000 in what was, literally, blood money.)

Barbot took full command, called Ambassador Drew, who sent for a cardiology team from the US naval base at Guantánamo, Cuba. The Navy team worked with Duvalier for thirty days. Barbot clamped secrecy on the whole thing, but secrets are hard to keep in Haiti for any length of time. When word got out, Barbot had the Ministry of Information report Papa Doc had grippe and would need rest. Two specialists from New York, Drs D. Kispel and Lawrence Cone, were flown in for consultation. Barbot, and later the Navy doctors, saved Duvalier's life.

Barbot was now acting President. He began to function as chief of state as though he had been preparing for it all his life. He presided over cabinet meetings, issued press statements, made all the decisions. This was a grave mistake. If anybody knew Duvalier's penchant for chopping those closest to him, especially if they appeared to be developing a taste for power, it was Barbot – who wielded a polished if slightly blunter axe himself, as Rodriguez, Fidel Castro's former Ambassador to Haiti, can attest.

Early on the morning of 6 June 1959, after a tour of Port-au-Prince's night life with a fellow Cuban, Rodriguez was ambushed by unknown men sporting Tommy guns. Fairly used to this sort of Caribbean reception, Rodriguez and friend succeeded in driving off the attackers with only superficial flesh wounds and powder burns received. The Ambassador's car, however, showed 52 bullet holes in its side. A formal complaint was lodged, and Rodriguez was called home to give a personal account of the incident. Before leaving for Havana he complained that Mme Clément Jumelle's request for safe-conduct out of the country was being unnecessarily delayed. It arrived the following day, something that never would have happened if Rodriguez had not been in the habit of wearing a Colt .45 at all times.

Apparently Trujillo was behind Barbot in the plot. A month earlier as Rodriguez, his wife, and pregnant daughter sat in their car awaiting restaurant kerb service, a Dominican Embassy Land Rover drew up next to them. A man got out and walked over to the Rodriguez automobile. In Spanish he said, 'Good evening, Mr Ambassador', and dropped a grenade into the front seat. Rodriguez grabbed it and threw it out; it exploded in mid-air. The Land Rover disappeared.

When Ambassador Rodriguez returned from Cuba, he brought his own colourful little army with him. Four *barbudos* came along. They dressed in neat olive drab, wore black-holstered pistols with extra large ammunition chargers, carried knives in their belts and grenades in their suitcases. Two of the four were officers and had Tommy guns. Rodriguez meant business. Haiti now not only had Marines wearing colonial helmets and carrying swagger sticks, but gun-toting former Cuban revolutionaries. When Rodriguez went shopping, large crowds formed just to see his entourage.

With Duvalier ill and Cuban invasion rumours going strong, tension built in the city. The fourteenth of June was a significant day for the island as a whole. A fragmentation bomb exploded in the casino, killing four and injuring five persons. The same day Dominican exiles out of Cuba tried to invade the Dominican Republic by air and sea. A C-46 plane carrying fifty-six of them took off from Manzanilla and landed at the Dominican mountain village of Constanza. The invaders fought briefly with the Constanza military post and then retreated into the hills. Trujillo's efficient military machine followed, and those who were not killed at the landings at Maimon and Estero Hondo beaches were executed in Ciudad Trujillo. That date, 14 June, later was adopted as the name of a leftist Dominican political party with strong Castro sympathies.

Fire broke out in the Dessalines barracks that month and a new panic swept the government. Smoke billowed over the palace and the city. Soldiers ringed the palace, and Duvalier called for his tanks to circle the grounds and asked the US Marines to man them. Armed Tonton Macoutes combed the streets in automobiles, and gunfire was heard throughout the city. Firemen fought the blaze for two and one-half hours, but a wing of the barracks was destroyed. The actual threat to the government, if any, has never been made clear. An official announcement said that the fire had been started by a short circuit in the air-conditioning system.

A bomb exploded at a religious festival, injuring forty-two persons, and Minister of Interior Jean Magloire (no relation to the former president) was wounded in the back and legs when a grenade was thrown at him as he walked on the balcony of his two-storey home. Magloire was up the next day to attend a military review marking Duvalier's official return to duties.

At a forty-minute, full-dress parade by the Presidential Guard, Duvalier sat on the palace steps and watched. He wore a black suit and black hat, and his cabinet, Ambassador Drew, and Colonel Heinl sat with him. Tanks and armoured cars stood guard on the palace lawn, and only government officials and known Duvalier supporters were allowed inside the iron fence.

On 30 August 1959, while the Organization of American States was meeting in Santiago, Chile, a boat pulled up near the isolated village of Les Irois in south-western Haiti. Thirty men clambered ashore. All were Cuban, except their leader, Henry Fuertes – alias Henri d'Anton – an Algerian who had married Louis Déjoie's cousin when he had lived in Haiti and who later won a commandant's commission fighting Batista in Cuba's Escambray Mountains. Fuertes's men easily captured the mud huts that comprised the little Haitian fishing village, recruited local guides, and gave them Haitian liberation badges to wear. The recruits happily carried supplies, and the entire 'army' pushed off into the hills toward Les Cayes. Fuertes's band, wearing uniforms of the Cuban revolution, passed out Cuban cigars along the way. In the group only Fuertes spoke Creole. A soldier at Les Irois escaped to Anse d'Hainault and sounded the alarm.

When news finally reached Port-au-Prince, Colonel Heinl and Clément Barbot climbed into a Marine helicopter and flew down to survey the situation. Haiti protested to Cuba and to the OAS meeting in Chile. Castro claimed he knew nothing of the invasion, and it appeared he did not. News reports described him as angry.

Barbot kept things hopping. The first countermove was to airlift 150 Haitian soldiers trained by the Marines as a mobile unit from the Casernes Dessalines into the war zone. Marine advisers worked out of the army's field headquarters in Jérémie.

The invaders trudged along through the hills, almost as if they were on a training hike. Haitian units began to hunt them down. Duvalier's first victory was claimed when some of the invaders were caught by surprise as they were eating a noon meal of goat and cooling their feet in a mountain stream. The army opened up with automatic weapons and sent them scattering so fast that they left their boots behind. Another unit came upon a group in a peasant *caille* and literally pulverized it and the peasant family it harboured with gunfire. Fuertes himself was trapped in a cave. The guerrillas were handicapped for cover because most of the area's heavy vegetation had not grown back after the most recent hurricane.

With his customary efficiency, Barbot went to work in the litle villages through which the invaders had passed. His vengeance was so thorough that more peasants died than either invaders or soldiers. Those who collaborated, willingly or not, even by furnishing food or shelter, were exterminated. Peasants in the area were used to trading with yachtsmen who sometimes anchored in coves along the peninsula. After this invasion all visitors were treated as suspect.

With the Coast Guard working offshore, and surveillance

by planes overhead, the invaders lasted only until 4 September. All were killed or executed except four, who were brought back to Port-au-Prince as trophies. Many Haitians had doubted the dramatic news, which circulated only by gossip because initial reports were suppressed in local newspapers and all roads to the south had been closed to prevent any local Duvalier opponents from joining the invaders. Although it had complained repeatedly to the Marines that more modern weapons were vitally necessary, during the invasion the government boasted that its superior firepower had guaranteed victory.

When the four prisoners were flown to Port-au-Prince, a crowd of some 2,000 gathered at the airport to see them. Cabinet ministers, Barbot, and General Merceron congratulated themselves on their success. But instead of awesome *barbudos,* the astonished crowd saw four beardless terrified young men in handcuffs. 'Look, they are children,' someone shouted.

To Duvalier's great relief, Cuba recalled Ambassador Rodriguez. Haiti also recalled its ambassador from Cuba, but relations between the two countries were never formally broken. Duvalier kept Cuban consulates open, and as late as 1964 a consul in Santiago communicated by cable with Duvalier. Haiti's relations with the Vatican were also strained. The archbishop of Port-au-Prince, Monsignor François Poirier, was critical of Duvalier. As a result, Duvalier issued an arrest order for the archbishop. It was later suspended but not rescinded.

With solid Marine assistance on hand, the Cuban invasion defeated and Rodriguez out of the way, Duvalier turned his attention to those congressmen who continued to irk him with lofty statements about constitutionality, rights, and the dignity of man. When he asked for decree powers again on 19 September, six senators had been opposed, but the measure passed. The Chamber of Deputies took the practical approach by saying decree powers were not necessary. They did not add, or need to, that Duvalier exercised whatever power he felt necessary.

Papa Doc handily disposed of the dissident senators by a special decree he had published in a special edition of *Le Moniteur*. On the charge that the six men were plotting with the Communists, he declared them henceforth impeached; two immediately fled the country, and three, including Jean Bélizaire, sought refuge in the Mexican Embassy. They had all been close to Duvalier in the 1957 electoral campaign.

The sixth senator, Yvon Emmanuel Moreau, a thirty-nine-year-old Episcopalian minister, refused to run for cover. Instead, he issued a statement saying that the charges were 'pure invention' and that the Communist issue had been raised 'simply to make an action such as this acceptable to the US State Department.'

> They had to invent a story to dispense with me. I am a believer in democracy and I thought I was doing my job when I criticized what should be criticized to protect the welfare of the people and the country. . . . I have never been involved in any subversive activities and I don't intend to be used now by any group of politicians. Despite the action taken against me, I will continue a normal life.

In November 1960 Moreau was arrested. His mother went weeping to Alfred Voegeli, the American Bishop of Haiti, pleading with him to intercede on her son's behalf. Voegeli spoke to his old friend Duvalier, and that ended the friendship. Moreau was never heard from, or of, again.

11
Sneak Elections and US Aid

So fierce were anti-Duvalier appetites growing that his rivals decided to fight fire with fire and resort to voudou, suspecting as they did that their President had more than an anthropological interest in the subject.

One dark night oppositionists repaired to the cemetery where Duval Duvalier – Papa Doc's father, who had died some five weeks before his son took office – was buried. They removed Duvalier *Père*'s corpse from its grave and heart from its body, since they needed the latter to work a powerful *ouanga* or hex on Duvalier *Fils*' alleged Special *loa*-granted Powers. Human ordure was then smeared over both corpse and tomb.

But Papa Doc continued, publicly at least, to thrive now that he had recovered from his heart attack. Certainly his double-talk continued unabated. 'My habit is always to take out of jail,' he informed a press conference, 'to release people.' He went on to say that in all Haiti there were but two political prisoners, one of whom – an old friend – he would be only too happy to free, 'except the police department has asked me to wait.' He then began haranguing the newsmen about 'Communist infiltration' and his ceaseless fight against it, unemployment, and illiteracy. He denounced the latest series of bombings and finished on the cryptic note that 'some people get crazy. They are not responsible [for their actions], and I am a doctor.'

By 1960 US aid had become the paramount issue in Haiti. Duvalier sought massive assistance with no strings attached. Public opinion in the hemisphere counselled against granting him any financial assistance since Papa Doc was now a full-grown tyrant and money would only help tighten the stranglehold on his little fiefdom.

The United States was in a dilemma since not only had Duvalier shown himself for the ruthless dictator he was, but he had openly refused to comply with even the most elementary requisites in qualifying for assistance. Just across the Windward Passage, however, lay Cuba and Fidel Castro.

The projects that interested Washington were mostly designed to raise the standard of living in specific agricultural areas. Since the majority were long-term, Duvalier and his henchmen remained unimpressed; they wanted short-term schemes which, supervised by the corrupt Haitian bureaucracy, could be much more readily milked. Preliminary explorations yielded a paradox to Washington fact-finders: American technicians were moving into a land whose own professionals were leaving in droves for jobs abroad. There was thus a shortage of trained men who could be further taught, together with a 'base' illiteracy rate in excess of 90 per cent.

State jobs went to Duvalierists. Period. In mid-March 1960 Duvalier fired a competent Haitian engineer in charge of the Artibonite Valley development project. To replace him, Papa Doc, without bothering to consult the US aid agency which was supplying the funds, named a minister he had earlier jailed for misuse of public funds. In this manner he began to pressure Washington, which, he felt, had no alternative but to aid him.

The newly built US aid offices in Port-au-Prince became the scene of lengthy talks between Duvalier's representatives and the Americans. The United States sought an agreement that would give it supervision of job distribution. The little tyrant was miffed. He let it be known that he and only he had hiring and firing rights on any programme and that to say otherwise was not only an affront to national dignity but a discourtesy to Haiti's sovereignty. The few aid programmes under way were suspended while the talks went on. The diplomatic seesawing was to last for months.

Use of the threat of Communism as a handy blackmailing tool probably had its genesis on 17 May 1960, when the leftist

National Union of Haitian Students, who had been given a free hand by Papa Doc, began a national congress. The far-leftist slant taken at the meeting had never before been seen so blatantly open in Haiti. On 18 May the Education Minister, Rev. Hubert Papailler, a Roman Catholic priest, attended the congress and complimented the students. He noted that they were conducting their 'first congress under the double sign of anti-segregationism and anti-colonialism.' *Le Matin*, a government organ, revealed that Duvalier would honour the congress by issuing a 'stamp of solidarity' which the students' union could put in circulation. Haiti, ignoring its own staggering problems, announced that proceeds from the sale of the stamps would go to aid black students in South Africa.

Duvalier wanted the American Embassy to hear the anti-imperialist slogans chanted at the leftist student rallies. He travelled to the old coffee port of Jacmel to dedicate a new American-built wharf, and read on 25 June a memorable speech which subsequently became known as 'The Outcry of Jacmel', a cloudy but ominous major policy speech in which Haiti was presented as a friend rejected by its powerful and ungrateful neighbour. 'We are at the limit of the time of sacrifices. We are breaking,' he said. His government had depended on the United States; its loyalty had gone unrewarded.

> In hope of frank and loyal friendship between the Haitian government, the Haitian people, and the American government and the American people, in the hope of a test-proven collaboration, of an effective and wide co-operation in order to help the Haitian nation in being ready to participate in all destinies of the United States in particular and of the continent in general . . . in order to prevent the collapsing of the Haitian democracy in hate and wrath, I geared all the political and economic action on the moral support of this great neighbour and on its effective material help.
>
> I refused to offer to any other nation that which I offered the United States and its government. I have called on American capital to develop the economy of the country. I have called American technicians to organize and reorganize the institutions of my country; to their economy my underdeveloped country still is a sure market.
>
> But for thirty-three months my government and its people have

been living on promises, smiles, encouragements, recommendations, hesitations, delays, and misunderstandings.

We need a massive injection of money [300 million was the sum sought] to reset the country on its feet, and this injection can come only from our great, capable friend and neighbour the United States. It can come in different ways: generous help for American security; loans, easy credit terms....

He blamed Magloire's regime for 'criminal squandering of dollar reserves' and the 1954 hurricane for staggering the Haitian economy. He said that his government had received from the United States 'only an insufficient loan of $4.3 million for two development projects.' He neglected to mention the $7 million grant to his budget in 1959, and another $6 million already promised for the fiscal year ending 30 June 1961.

Duvalier then issued what was interpreted by all as a warning.

Two great poles of attraction lure groups of people and associations of countries to a pilgrimage during which they always lose some pieces of their flesh and suffer lacerations of the soul. All postures are converging on them and they seem to be the only sovereigns having to talk and make decisions in the name of humanity and its way of life. Observing and living in such an international context, in the area of international interdependence, where the scale of the new order of size of the problems of relations between people is immeasurably complex, we need solid ground to make a choice.... Communism has established centres of infection.... No area in the world is as vital to American security as the Caribbean.

The American Embassy got the message clearly, and it stung. Duvalier had described Haiti as a nation 'rotting in misery, hunger, nudity, sickness, and illiteracy', and had said Haiti had to choose between 'two great poles of attraction in the world today to concretize its needs.' Translated from diplomat language, it was a threat to turn to Communism if the United States didn't live up to expectations.

In reply, on 5 July the American Embassy reviewed its aid programme to Haiti, in particular to the Duvalier government. It said the United States had given (not loaned) Haiti $40.6 million since 1950, and that $21.4 million of this had gone to the Duvalier government.

Duvalier unleashed his press on the United States. Paul Blanchet, anti-American Minister of Information, used his newspaper *Panorama* to ridicule the Embassy report. Other newspapers dug up every conceivable complaint against the United States and churned out headlines of, to say the least, an inflammatory nature.

The same month, the United States cut Cuba's quota of subsidized sugar sales to the United States and raised Haiti's quota by 25 per cent. The United States also announced a new large-scale economic-aid programme to all Latin-American countries except Cuba. The purpose was to fight the spread of Communism in the Western Hemisphere. The *New York Times* observed that 'growing political tensions in Haiti, a slowly deteriorating economy, and a resentful president' made Haiti a prime candidate for President Eisenhower's preventive programme.

Another contribution came from Fort Lauderdale, Florida, where the county school board decided that two US Navy surplus seventy-five-foot patrol boats were too expensive to maintain. They had been gifts from the Navy, and now the school board, with United States approval, gave them to Haiti, thereby increasing the nation's Coast Guard by 20 per cent.

Taking a page from Castro, Duvalier outfitted his militia in denim shirts, blue jeans, red arm bands, and red foulards around the neck. Significantly, this uniform was borrowed from the garb worn by the old *caco* fighters who battled the US Marines during the occupation. Duvalier liked this historic appeal to anti-US sentiment and lost no opportunity exploiting it. The ragtag militia was viewed as a force to counter-balance the Marine-trained army. It was not a fashionable period for pro-US sympathies, as some Duvalier cronies discovered.

The dapper Clément Barbot, whose Sten gun and bullet-proof vest were as much part of his habitual dress as his dark suits, returned quietly home with his wife and an escort of Tonton Macoutes the night of 14 July 1960, after attending the Bastille Day party at the French Embassy. A well-armed company of Presidential Guard troops caught him by surprise and quickly disarmed him and his escort as they entered the house.

During the next six hours he was kept prisoner in his home, but after he tried to escape hiding in a bag of dirty laundry, Duvalier ordered his imprisonment in Fort Dimanche. In the days that followed Barbot underwent interrogation in the same manner to which he had subjected so many when chief of the Tonton Macoutes. One of the questions put to Barbot was the source of a large amount of cash found in his house. Another question was where the 'rest' of the money was? Barbot's last business deal had been yet another resale of the franchise of the International Casino and he had told the men involved that Duvalier had urgent need of the 'fee' to build a hospital. In true underworld style Barbot had not cut his boss in on the take.

Two Americans had purchased the casino monopoly. They bought it in the hope of giving it the Las Vegas–Havana glamour treatment and siphoning off the lush Cuban flow of tourists that quickly faded under Castro.

With Barbot in jail, the arrangement did not last long. One day in September, after the new owners had announced the beginning of $150,000 in renovation work on the casino, they were expelled from the country. At the same time, though apparently in a separate case, the American manager of a flour mill, Joseph Cichowski, was also expelled. There was no explanation, except that the men had dealt with Barbot.

Barbot had been a good husband and father. When his son, studying medicine in Germany, suffered a nervous breakdown in November 1959, he had quickly flown to Germany to be with the boy. His absence from the palace gave rivals jealous of his power the chance they'd been waiting for. They fed Duvalier's suspicion of his 'good friend', and by the time Barbot returned the undermining was almost complete.

Their job was easy, Duvalier had been suspicious of Barbot's ambitions since his heart attack of 1958, when Barbot had saved his life by turning to the Americans and then had run the country efficiently during the period of his recovery. Barbot was close to Colonel Heinl, head of the Marine mission, and his frequent dinner guest. Ambition and friendliness with the Americans spelled treason to Duvalier.

Even those who hated Barbot said that though he operated savagely, he showed more fairness and efficiency than anyone else in the Duvalier inner circle. He and Papa Doc had shared much together. Without Barbot, Duvalier quite likely would not have reached the Presidency. When the palace had been under attack or threat of attack, the Barbots and the Duvaliers had lived together as one family. Mme Barbot and her children were the closest friends of Mme Duvalier and her children.

Two months after Barbot's return from Germany the struggle for influence around Duvalier had moved into an ugly and desperate phase. During the last day of Mardi Gras, 1 March 1960, explosions suddenly were no longer firecrackers but gun shots, and the internecine Tonton Macoute struggle became rough. Duvalier and his family were watching the carnival parade from a downtown vantage point when the disturbances began. The only victim was one of Barbot's top bodyguards, and the assassination attempt was directed not against Duvalier but against Barbot by other Duvalierists who sought to supplant him. Wednesday night, 2 March, after the funeral of Barbot's bodyguard, big, hefty Dr Roger Rousseau had just locked his car in the street and was about to join his wife and eight children in their house when a friend approached. His last words were 'What have I done to you?' before he was riddled from head to toe by machine-gun bullets. The erstwhile friend was Barbot. The victim had been a top Duvalierist with his own group of Tonton Macoute followers.

Now, with Barbot and his gang either in prison, dead, or exiled, a tough trio took over his duties and power as secret police chief and Tonton Macoute boss. The men Duvalier chose were Elois Maître and Luc Désir; the third man was Major Jean Tassy, known for his loyalty to Duvalier.

Strangely, although Duvalier would not permit a doctor to enter the Barbot home and treat his sick son, Barbot's daughter was allowed to continue at her job in the Finance Ministry as if nothing had happened. One of Barbot's last jobs for Duvalier (and some say that he executed Rousseau on Duvalier's orders) was the seizing of a letter that purportedly revealed a plot against Duvalier and involved exiled Louis Déjoie.

The Haitian Student Union continued to promote anti-US feelings. As a youth congress in Havana opened on 26 July to celebrate the anniversary of the Fidel Castro political movement, the Haitian student union sent greetings:

> We take this opportunity to reaffirm the anti-imperialistic position that we adopted during our May congress beside the youth of Cuba and all the progressive youth of the world. Haitian students are watching attentively the evolution of the situation in Cuba. They see with great satisfaction the efforts of the revolutionary government to carry the country out of the claws of the American eagle.... It is that situation that leads us, the Haitian students united under the banner of the UNEH (Union Nationale des Etudiants Haitiens), to look with sympathy toward the Cuban people raising their chins in front of the American colossus.... The Cuban people take their destiny in their hands and the Haitian students applaud.

The Haitian press gave the student message wide and thorough coverage, a sure sign that Duvalier wanted to keep the pressure on the American Embassy. With his encouragement, Haiti's Communists were acting up.

The President was shaken a little later in the month when the OAS met in San José, Costa Rica, and condemned Trujillo. The OAS passed a resolution recommending that member nations sever ties with the Dominican Republic. The action was based on an assassination attempt made by Trujillo against President Romulo Betancourt of Venezuela, traditional foe of all dictators. Duvalier complied within a month. The December 1958 pledges to Trujillo were no longer convenient.

On 1 August a parade was organized by Duvalier to commemorate the second anniversary of the forming of the militia. Eight hundred militia men and women in blue shirts and dark blue denim pants marched to the palace, went through tactical exercises, and listened to speeches.

Léostène Nicoleau, a militia commander, said: 'Excellency,

the gun that Sonthonax gave us to defend our liberty and that the American occupation had taken away from us is the gun that, without fear, you have given back to us – be assured that this gun will not be used against you.' Sonthonax was a member of a civil commission sent to Saint Domingue, the French colony that is today Haiti, in 1796. He gave guns tc the slaves, saying: 'Here is your liberty: he who takes this away from you will try to make you slaves again.'

Le Matin joined the anti-US chorus by declaring that the United States either was confused or prejudiced. But it noted: 'History has shown that a rain of dollars can heal many a wound . . .'

The duel with the United States broke in Duvalier's favour when the Embassy announced that it had agreed to supply the equipment necessary to modernize the army.

Meanwhile, American Ambassador Gerald Drew, an old Duvalier adversary, was withdrawn (16 July) at the end of his regular tour. Duvalier greeted this as a new sign of victory. Upon Ambassador Drew had fallen the brunt of the anti-American newspaper campaign, and Duvalier had blamed him personally – as was to become his habit with American ambassadors – for obstructing relations between him and his great and good friend, the United States.

Duvalier showed his good faith by cracking down on the left. In September twenty students were arrested secretly, among them Joseph Roney, treasurer of the student union. Word of the arrests spread quickly, however, and students began to agitate in an effort to build pressure for their fellows' release.

With the students now providing the appropriate scare, Papa Doc began badgering the United States anew for money. Mayor Jean Deeb of Port-au-Prince rephrased Duvalier's famous 'Outcry of Jacmel'.

'We can't take it any longer. We must go one way or another,' Deeb said. Communists were causing trouble; Haiti was a poor, starving nation caught up in a world struggle for power. 'We don't even have a public works programme.' He warned that unless the United States helped its friends, 'it will be left alone in this hemisphere.'

Duvalierist officials said that Haiti needed $150 million from the United States. Typically, while awaiting a new ambassador, Duvalier left the harsh statements to others and presented himself as a reasonable and misunderstood man. Said Duvalier: 'I've written several times to President Eisenhower about the needs of this country, but we are going down and down every day.... Haiti will never turn to the Communists.... I merely said at Jacmel what I have been saying to the United States, but they didn't understand it.'

The Embassy exchanged notes with the Haitian government in October about the new arms agreement. Philip Williams was Chargé d'Affaires. Article two of the agreement specified: 'Equipment and material provided the government of Haiti ... will be used solely in Haiti's self-defense, in maintaining its internal security, or to participate in the defense of the area of which it is a part, or in the United Nations' collective security arrangements and measures.' Whatever the wording, Duvalier's army had new weapons, and the old ones passed on to the Tonton Macoutes and militia.

An item in *Le Moniteur,* the government gazette, indicated things to come. It published a Presidential decree announcing a special credit of 200,000 *gourdes* for 'special expenses of the secret police', because 'Certain unforeseeable expenses must be met.' That same month of October a half-dozen well known Haitians were jailed, including a lawyer, former diplomat, and two planters from Léogane. One of the planters was named Riobé, a name that became significant in 1963.

On the third anniversary of his election (22 September 1960) Duvalier inaugurated two kilometres of main street repaved in concrete and financed by means of bonds purchased by O. J. Brandt, a Jamaican and Port-au-Prince businessman. After the dedication ceremony Duvalier (as Haitian Presidents had before him) scattered handfuls of coins along the streets. Men, women, and children scrambled in the dirt for them. The Presidential motorcade always brought people running.

Student agitation for release or at least trial of the twenty arrested students reached a peak in November, just after Robert Newbegin arrived as the new American Ambassador. Duvalier received him warmly, and commented that now US–Haitian relations would improve because the United States had an ambassador who, he was sure, would understand Haiti's problems. It was an act he went through with American ambassadors until they inevitably displeased him. During the honeymoon period both made friendly gestures. The Marines helped build a pontoon bridge when waters of Lake Miragoane rose and covered part of the road to the south. Without it, the southern tip of the peninsula would have been isolated. The bridge and six miles of road approaches on either side were completed in one month by Seabees brought from the US naval base at Guantánamo. Duvalier reshuffled his cabinet, replacing Raymond Moyse as Foreign Minister with Joseph Baguidy. Moyse was regarded as lukewarm towards the United States.

In response to pressure from the agitating students, and perhaps as a gesture to Ambassador Newbegin, Haiti finally acknowledged that it had indeed arrested twenty students 1 September. It added that one was a militant Communist and that the others had been helping him distribute propaganda.

Baguidy, the new Foreign Minister, who also served as education minister, said the government had 'palpable and irrefutable proof of the Communist origin of the movement.' When he presented his 'proof' to the press, it consisted of a piece of white cloth bearing a Soviet hammer and sickle and the inscription: *Vive la Liberté, Vive le 26 Juillet, Vive l'URSS*. Unofficially, the government spread word that Jacques Alexis, Haiti's most famous living novelist and poet and also a Communist, was behind the student agitation. It said he had been preaching Communism at clandestine meetings held in vacant garages round the city.

The effect was to inflame the students further, and on 21

November they called a strike, closing the university and high schools as a 'last effort' to have the twenty who had been jailed turned loose. Duvalier responded swiftly. He gave a twelve-hour ultimatum to return to classes, declared martial law, and described the strike as 'Communist-inspired'. (Haiti had been under a state of siege ever since Duvalier had assumed power.) Next he ordered all youth associations, including the Boy Scouts, dissolved. As the army surrounded the university, bombs began to explode around town.

The police and Tonton Macoutes were out in force searching for anti-Duvalierists. One night a little group of armed Tonton Macoutes penetrated deep into one of the long, dusty winding 'corridors' of Bel Air, a section of thousands of small tin-roofed shacks of the lower class. Word of their arrival had spread. One man, who detested the Tonton Macoutes and Duvalier, waited until he spied them through the crack in the side of his little single-room home and then with a quick movement emptied a bucket of the night's toilet waste upon them. The Tonton Macoutes cried out angrily and the man yelled a quick apology, saying 'Sorry, neighbour, I didn't see you out there.' The neighbour who had witnessed the episode replied 'I am in my home. It must be thieves out there.' He was convincingly fearful, and the Macoutes left quietly, muttering to one another what a pigsty Bel Air was. But Bel Air laughed for months.

Other anti-Duvalierists, or those suspected of being, were not so fortunate. A British storekeeper, sixty-one-year-old Cromwell James, had been arrested on 1 November, held without bail, and severely beaten. On 22 November his lawyers obtained a hearing and found that James was charged with, of all things, highway robbery. James was freed the next day and, on 27 November, died of gangrene poisoning due to untreated wounds.

The second day of the strike Duvalier advanced Christmas holidays a month, giving students no reason to gather at the university or in the schools. He then ordered all businesses closed, thus keeping people off the streets. Government radio programmes made the surprise announcement that the Catholic archbishop of Port-au-Prince, Monsignor François Poirier, had been expelled from the country. He was charged with giving Communist students $7,000 to help overthrow the government. Tape-recorded broadcasts in Creole were repeated over and over denouncing the prelate. During the morning the Archbishop had suddenly been arrested, escorted to the airport, and put aboard a plane to Miami in his white cassock and purple sash, carrying one dollar and a book. Only after the plane was airborne did the government reveal what it had done.

Duvalier did not mention Archbishop Poirier when he spoke to some 6,000 partisans who had marched through the streets to gather on the palace lawn. They carried signs saying 'Down with Communism' and 'Duvalier is the last resort', 'Protector of the weak', and 'Duvalier or Death'. With members of the cabinet and his staff nearby, Papa Doc thanked them.

> You have lifted the morale of the man who directs the destiny of the nation so as to signify to him that his mission, his sacrosanct mission, has just begun. . . .
>
> Dear friends, they have tried to use youth, the fine flower of youth, for shameful purposes. The power I have from you, the power I have from you alone, no power of this world can take away from me, can stop me from fulfilling my mission. . . . Lizards who provoked the American occupation, who engineered the troubles of 10 May 1946, whom Estimé has ousted, now want the youth as a screen to overthrow the government. Dear friends, those lizards I know where they are, who they are, where they hide. . . . There are some people, some backward people, who can think only of destruction. . . . They have become mad.

And as Duvalier had said before, when people 'get crazy', Papa Doc had to take care of them.

The Vatican appointed Bishop Rémy Augustin as apostolic administrator of the archdiocese of Port-au-Prince to succeed

Poirier. In 1953 Augustin had become the first Haitian to be consecrated a bishop.

A debate ensued as to whether Duvalier had been excommunicated by the Vatican for his action against Poirier. The government pointed out that Poirier had been under an arrest order since August 1959; the order, later suspended, but not rescinded, was issued after the Archbishop had been highly critical of Duvalier when two French priests were expelled for 'reasons of national security'. At that time the government stated it had no quarrel with the Church but with 'certain French priests who have involved themselves in internal politics, contrary to the Concordat between Haiti and the Vatican.'

Army troops closed off one water-front district and made a house-to-house search for student and labour-union strike leaders. The Catholic newspaper *La Phalange* was ordered not to publish any information about the political situation except what was released in official bulletins.

One government radio broadcast, Voice of the Republic, increased to four shows daily, all prepared by the Ministry of Information and expounding at length the virtues of Duvalier, 'the spiritual leader of the Haitian people'. Under government prodding, all newspapers reminded their readers that the Communist party was outlawed and that any subversive activities against the government were punishable by death.

Three months after their arrests Joseph Roney and the other nineteen students were freed. But first, Roney's father and brothers had to sign a paper prepared by Port-au-Prince Prefect Lucien Chauvet which declared that politicians had manipulated the students into activities beyond their intention. This move to re-establish peace set up the first major break in Duvalier's favour. A week later (8 December) the United States announced an $11.8 million grant for special economic and technical assistance to Haiti, including direct budget support. Duvalier didn't get the $150 million (much less the $300 originally demanded), but he was moving in the right direction.

New US aid came as a shattering blow to the opposition. With a new Ambassador and a new young President about to assume office in the US, John F. Kennedy, there was some hope that the United States would not be blackmailed. But Duvalier now had US money, US arms, and US Marines in his corner. The combination appeared invincible.

This was a busy period in Duvalier's reign. He shook up the board of directors of the Banque Nationale; arrested Georges Rigaud, the dentist and one-time PSP Presidential candidate, and a number of other men including the heroic former Senator Yvon E. Moreau; and, smelling out what he believed to be an army plot, Duvalier purged the officer corps again.

He began to apply a more 'legalized' form of pressure to the striking students. He issued a decree changing the name of the university (to the State University of Haiti) and its status, placing new restrictions on both students and parents in preparation for the reopening of classes.

The decree ruled that each student would need a police certificate 'attesting that he does not belong to any Communist group or association suspected by the state' and a certificate of good conduct issued by the civil court; any student violating school rules would be expelled; unauthorized demonstrations were banned; students could not abandon classes without permission; if a minor were absent three days without a doctor's excuse his parents would be liable to heavy fines or imprisonment ranging from one month to one year.

Duvalier justified the decree on the grounds of 'international Communism, the mentality of Haitian politics, the permanent state of insecurity of Latin America.' High Schools were scheduled to reopen on 9 January 1961, and the university on 16 January. School directors were ordered to hand in daily lists of absentees.

Before schools could reopen the United States broke diplomatic relations with Cuba, and Haiti immediately lined up alongside its 'good friend' the United States. Foreign Minister Baguidy proudly declared that 'Haiti ended relations with Cuba more than a year ago', following the thirty-one-man invasion. In fact, however, relations had not been formally broken and, as already mentioned, at least one Haitian consulate in Cuba continued to communicate with Duvalier.

When some students continued their strike after classes resumed, Duvalier proclaimed a new state of emergency and a curfew which authorized police to shoot anyone seen on the street after 10 p.m. Total censorship was clamped on messages inside Haiti or to foreign countries.

Bishop Augustin, Poirier's successor and the first Haitian to attain this office, was routed out of his quarters and placed on a flight to San Juan. The move came so swiftly that the bishop didn't even have time to put in his false teeth. *La Phalange*, the Catholic newspaper, was seized. The edition that day was to have carried a pastoral letter from Bishop Augustin, voicing a plea that the new university decrees be rescinded. The closing of *La Phalange* ended any pretence of a free press.

That evening Duvalier ordered the expulsion of four other priests. All were accused of supporting the Communist student strike.

The expulsion of Poirier, Augustin, and the administrators of the diocese left the Church temporarily headless. The Vatican responded by excommunicating the Haitian authorities involved in what was the first major excommunication in Latin America since 1955, when it had acted similarly against the Juan Perón dictatorship in Argentina. Despite censorship inside the country, Haitians heard the news over the Santo Domingo Radio.

Two days before the university reopened (14 January 1961), martial law and the curfew were lifted. This was part of a move to blunt the emotions of the strike and was coupled with a Duvalier drive to split the strikers by making appeals to those students who had Duvalierist ties or inclinations. Some were offered special concessions. One Roger Lafontant, a medical student, was given an all-expenses-paid honeymoon at a tourist hotel to celebrate his recent marriage. He also received a car and in time became a prominent Macoute and chief of the anatomy department at the medical school while still a resident. The university reopened on schedule but a majority of its students refused to attend, and a large number of high-school students remained out.

Foreign Minister Baguidy announced that the government

considered the crisis over and blamed 'French priests' for causing it all. He ignored the Vatican excommunication and complained that foreign priests for years had been dabbling in Haitian politics in what he said amounted to spiritual colonization.

A week later striking students exploded bombs on the streets and Duvalier moved again in anticipation of serious trouble. He called the militia in from the provinces and stationed them in the streets of Port-au-Prince. They lounged around the Bord-de-Mer (downtown section) in their ill-fitting blue denim uniforms and aroused fears by the inexpert albeit sincerely devoted manner in which they fondled their weapons. As noise bombs popped around the iron market and market women stampeded through the streets, the militia panicked, too, and fired their weapons indiscriminately. Car-loads of Tonton Macoutes circled the city, gun barrels bristling from rolled-down windows.

Jean Tassy, now sitting in Clément Barbot's old office, had Tonton Macoutes killing on suspicion alone.

In Gonaïves, where Bishop Jean-Marie Paul Robert was in his twenty-fifth year of service, a mob formed outside the two-story bishopric shouting for Robert to leave the country. It broke into an adjoining Catholic storehouse used to keep charity food for distribution to the poor and building materials for schools. The mob looted the storehouse and moved a short distance down the road to military headquarters.

The army made no attempt to interfere with the looting, and a military delegation called on Bishop Robert, one of the tough old Breton priests, to tell him he must go immediately to Port-au-Prince. The officers said they could not guarantee his safety because his presence incited crowds to riot. That evening an army car drove him without incident to Port-au-Prince, where he sought refuge in the home of Papal Nuncio Monsignor Giovanni Ferrofino. Told he could not return to Gonaïves, Bishop Robert took up residence in a retreat house, where he remained until November 1962, when Duvalier had him expelled on trumped-up charges.

Robert's eventual expulsion caused something of a sensation in Haiti. The government said he had instructed his Gonaïves priests to omit the prayer for the President at the end of mass which was prescribed by the Concordat. The Presidential order to go on including the prayer had infuriated most priests, who knew of Duvalier's excommunication, and many either slurred over the prayer or omitted it altogether. But only in Gonaïves, at the modernistic new cathedral, was an issue made of it by the government.

A bizarre note was added when Zacharie Delva, Duvalier's fearsome roving militia chief, held a voudou ceremony on the steps of the cathedral itself. Delva, a *houngan*, officiated and the public was invited. He had considered holding the ceremony inside the church but decided instead to have it on the steps so that more people could attend. The rites included the sacrifice of pigs as blood offerings to the voudou gods.

In a new peacemaking effort, Duvalier called a group of students to the palace, spoke warmly of Haitian youth and its responsibilities, and called on all students to return to classes. At the same time he ordered the publication of a copy of a letter written by Dr Joseph Verna and Fritz Hyppolite of the Communist and clandestine Party of Popular Accord. Dr Verna was in jail at the time and the palace handed out copies of the letter to the press.

It was a curious manoeuvre. The government was circulating a letter from the Communist party, which participated in the strike. The letter accepted Duvalier's version of events, calling on the students to call off the strike. In effect, the Communist party said that the strike had been subverted by the clergy and Déjoie supporters. It also noted that Jacques Alexis, the writer and Communist, had left the country three months before the strike began, refuting an earlier unofficial government claim that Alexis organized it all.

Using a fake passport with the name Bernard Celestin, Alexis had slipped out of Haiti early in August on a passing ship. During November he attended a World Conference of Communist Workers Parties in Moscow and signed what was known as the

'Declaration of Eighty-one' for the Party of Popular Accord. Later he went to Peking and then to Cuba. He did not return to Haiti until April 1961.

Officially the strike lasted until 16 March, but the heart of the opposition was gone. Duvalier had scattered enemies in two influential areas among youth, the Association of Secondary School Teachers (where he removed leaders, replacing them with Duvalierists) and the university (where the surprising support from a variety of sectors for the leftist National Union of Haitian Students was combated by pruning the faculty and its rights, clamping new regulations on students, and controlling other supporters through the army). The cry of *Communism* had restrained the business community from providing greater help and barred any sympathy or tacit aid from the American Embassy.

Thereafter the sons of Tonton Macoutes or others in government favour received priority for admission and scholarships. Despite their odd call to quit the fight and preserve their future, the Communists appeared the losers.

Duvalier cleverly and ruthlessly baited the United States. During the crisis he had moved to eliminate known and suspected enemies. He gauged the Cuban scare and the United States change of administration, and methodically plotted his course to take advantage of it all. Whether rumours of an impending Cuban exile invasion of Cuba had penetrated Haiti or not, Duvalier rode the crest of the confusion. He threatened, cried wolf, and triumphantly saw the United States again return to his side with an open pocketbook.

During March, although Duvalier often boasted of having broken relations with Cuba, Haitian Consul Lamy Camille continued to travel back and forth to Santiago de Cuba.

As the long months of student agitation settled, Duvalier received US Congressman Victor Anfuso, New York Democrat. He gave a reception at the palace for Anfuso and told the Congressman he would give the United States the north-western port of Môle Saint Nicolas (which the United States had sought and even pressured for in the nineteenth century) as a naval base and missile tracking station, replacing the base at Guantánamo, Cuba. Duvalier, supposedly a fierce nationalist and defender of Haitian soil, took the peculiar position of initiating an offer to bring the foreign military to Haiti on a permanent basis in contradiction to the stand of men in history whom he had hailed as patriots. US military men confessed privately that the bay was not suitable for a modern naval base. In a few days the United States announced that it had given Duvalier a half million dollars to improve his streets, which were branded a 'traffic hazard'.

The same day (6 April 1961) he offered the naval base, Duvalier announced that he was dissolving the bicameral Assembly. Ignoring legislative terms as prescribed in the 1957 Constitution, Duvalier ordered an election to be held on 30 April for a unicameral assembly. The 1957 Constitution had recommended such action but not until the regular terms ended in April 1963.

Events over which he had no control or influence once again intervened to benefit Duvalier. The Cuban exile Bay of Pigs invasion (17 April) captured US attention and, when it failed, put the United States on the defensive throughout the hemisphere. In the wave of anti-American feeling it aroused Duvalier found further room to manoeuvre.

Because the Cuban invasion came so soon after the offer of Môle Saint Nicolas as a military base and tracking station, some thought that the United States might have staged the operation from there. Soon, it was confirmed that the invaders were trained in and launched from Central America.

There was, however, some action in north-west Haiti.

Haitian author Jacques Alexis, who had stopped in Cuba on the way home from his trip to Russia and Peking, tried to slip into Haiti with four other men on his thirty-ninth birthday, 22 April. He moved across the Windward Passage from Baracoa, Cuba, to land at Môle Saint Nicolas. Alexis, who in his books championed the cause of the peasants, was betrayed by them. Fearful of reprisals, they reported his landing to local officials.

A small military detachment which guarded the approaches to the Môle with an ancient field artillery piece took the five men prisoners. They also seized a bundle of Communist literature and $20,000 in US currency. Some of Alexis's friends later said that the money consisted of royalties from his four books, but others were equally insistent that it was a contribution from the coffers of world Communism. It was learned that Alexis had led Communist leaders to believe he had 50,000 followers in Haiti.

The invaders, bound with sisal cords and thrown into a cell at the Môle, drew a select contingent of Tonton Macoutes and military officers from Port-au-Prince to handle the situation. The Alexis band was dragged to a grassy field in front of the old British fort, Saint George. There peasants and urchins, under the effective urging of the Tonton Macoutes, stoned them in true Middle Ages style. Alexis's right eye was torn out of its socket, and the stoning left all five dead or very close to it.

Duvalier decreed $100,000 for the 30 April 1961 congressional election expenses. All candidates were Duvalierists, varying only in degree of loyalty. Cockfights were suspended for election day, and all government employees were ordered to be on their jobs, even though it was Sunday. The weekly newspaper, *Oedipe*, run by Duvalierist Jean Magloire, commented: 'The people, it must be recognized, will vote as much to elect their representatives as to approve the policies of President Duvalier.'

Election eve there were indications that the election would be an unusual one. As Paul Kennedy, *New York Times* correspondent, ate dinner at the Oloffson Hotel, Police Major Jean Beauvoir informed him he must not leave the hotel during the night and that he would be expelled from the country on the morning plane. Kennedy had previously been expelled from Haiti by President Magloire, but two days later had had the satisfaction of being on hand in Jamaica when the banished Magloire himself arrived. At first Kennedy was given no reason for his expulsion. Then he was told that the government thought he might write 'something funny' about the election, which indeed turned out to be a travesty.

In Cap-Haïtien government officials even insisted that US citizens attached to a local aid programme actually vote. Under duress, some did. Few voters considered it unusual that the name Dr François Duvalier was printed at the bottom of each and every ballot.

Late that evening rumour spread that Duvalier – with two years to go on his current term – had declared himself re-elected for an additional six years because his name had appeared on each ballot. On 4 May Attorney General Max Duplessis declared to the Electoral Board – called the Census Committee – that Duvalier indeed had been voted another term in office. Crowds were organized to collect before the palace and applaud this view. The Attorney General said in his ruling:

> It is essential that immediately, even before counting the votes obtained by the candidates, we insist upon the principle which, far from being new, constitutes the very essence of national sovereignty. This principle can be defined: the members of the electorate, when presented with an electoral decree or law which looks to them incomplete, have the right to fully manifest their will to complete the law or decree and to designate a civil servant or a group of civil servants whose election was not foreseen. The intangibility of the principle once established, it will be easy for us to understand that the electorate of Port-au-Prince Arrondissement (used to establish legal precedent) has acted within its full sovereign power by designating François Duvalier for a new term under the title of President of the Republic

In three days the Census Committee convened, agreed, declared President Duvalier re-elected, and announced that he received more than 1.3 million votes. His party, the National Unity party (PUN is its rather apt French acronym), was declared the only legal one in Haiti. All fifty-eight congressional seats, of course, went to Duvalierists.

The new legislature ratified the election (14 May 1961), and Duvalier responded: 'I accept the people's will because being a revolutionary I do not have the right to hear the people's voice.' An editorial in the *New York Times* commented 'Latin America has witnessed many fraudulent elections throughout its history but none has been more outrageous than the one which has just taken place in Haiti.'

A committee was set up to raise $100,000 for a 'colossal' celebration at the swearing-in ceremonies scheduled for 22 May. It delivered a cheque for $77,340, which proved to be barely enough. The government used every truck and boat it could get its hands on, commandeering them from foreign companies, charity agencies, and private citizens to flood the city with peasants.

As the trucks deposited the rurals in Port-au-Prince they swarmed everywhere, despite lack of sanitation facilities; slept where they could; cooked communal meals in little tin pots over open fires. Some were seeing the city for the first time and gaped at its wonders. Some stayed on one side of the street rather than cross the blinking traffic lights, which made them uneasy. They danced and sang songs like 'Papa Duvalier, dig your feet in deep'. Even when it rained, it was another Mardi Gras.

The government announced that 300,000 persons had gathered at the inauguration; there was certainly a mammoth crowd, a sea of straw hats and flags and placards, but a more reliable estimate placed the number at 100,000.

Duvalier took off his helmet, put on top hat, tails, and a red-and-blue sash. He entered the Congress by a side door, though an honour guard awaited him in front, and took the oath of office with his hand raised in an Olympic salute. Noticeably absent was US Ambassador Newbegin, who had gone to Washington for 'consultation' in order to miss the affair. But Colonel Heinl in a Marine dress uniform and American Embassy Second Secretary David Thomson represented the United States.

Military Junta President Gen. Antonio Th. Kebreau (right) and Capt. Andre Fareau, Minister of Justice and Labor, prior to the September 1957 elections. (Photo: Bernard Diederich)

Professor Daniel Fignole at his school, prior to becoming provisional president in 1957.

Meeting of presidential candidates at the home of ex-Senator Marceau Desinor on April 5, 1957. Seated candidates Louis Dejoie, Dr. Francois Duvalier, and Daniel Fignole. Standing: two aides to Duvalier, Roger Dorsainville and Jean David. (Photo: Bernard Diederich)

Duvalier, his wife Simone, and three of their children, including five-year-old Jean-Claude, at their Ruelle Roy home prior to elections. (Photo: Bernard Diederich)

Duvalier on election day, September 22, 1957, standing before a painting of Emperor Jean-Jacques Dessalines. (Photo: Bernard Diederich)

Duvalier on election day angrily orders partisans to go to downtown Port-au-Prince to stop vote buying by Dejoie advocates. His coat flew open to reveal a pistol in his belt. (Photo: Bernard Diederich)

Soldiers deployed during election day, 1957. (Photo: Bernard Diederich)

Ex-Senator Louis Lajoie leaving for exile, being escorted to the plane by the secretary of the Mexican embassy, where he had taken political asylum. (Photo: Bernard Diederich)

Major Claude Raymond, head of a new presidential guard, hands his sword to President Duvalier during a ceremony creating the new elite force on December 15, 1958. American Ambassador Gerald Drew and Col. Robert Heinl (USMC) in white dress uniform observe. (Photo: Bernard Diederich)

Aboard the Mollie C en route from the Florida keys to Haiti. Former Haitian army Lieut. Henri Perpignan and Dade County (Miami) Sheriff Dany Jones prepare ammunition for their July 1958 invasion of Haiti. (Diederich collection)

Anti-Duvalier guerrilla leader Baptiste (left) with an aide discussing his campaign against Papa Doc in the field in 1964. (Diederich collection)

The National Security Volunteers (VSN), also known as uniformed Tontons

Left to right: Capt. Claude Raymond, Interior and National Defense Minister Frederic Duvigneaud, President Duvalier, and Lieut. Gracia Jacques pose after defeating the Pasquet invasion in July 1958.

Left to right: Jean-Claude Duvalier in 1960 watches his father on the rifle range along with Ltd. Gracia Jacques, Claude Capt. Claude Raymond, and Capt. Jean Tassy, one of the heads of Duvalier's secret police.

A woman member of Duvalier's militia.

Duvalier meets with neighboring Dominican Republic dictator Gen. Rafael Trujillo Molina on December 22, 1958, at the border. Clement Barbot, chief of Haiti's secret police, wearing dark glasses, stands behind Duvalier. (Photo: Bernard Diederich)

American Ambassador Raymond Thurston presents his credentials to President Duvalier. (Diederich collection)

President Duvalier in 1960, fully recovered from a heart attack.

President Duvalier shortly before he died, poses with his hand on the shoulder of his chosen successor, his 19-year-old son Jean-Claude. (Collection Bernard Diederich)

12

The Dictator Unmasked to the World

On 28 May 1961 the *New York Times* wrote that Haitian officials 'are threatening to withdraw political support for the United States in international organizations if they are molested ...' (i.e., if the officials are directed towards even the most rudimentary goals of social rehabilitation in return for financial aid).

The article went on to say that the price of Haitian support in the hemisphere would be continued assistance (to the tune of some $12.5 million annually) and the maintenance of the US military missions. Duvalier, apparently, was winning every trick.

But on the evening of 30 May Generalissimo Rafael Trujillo's thirty-one-year reign over the Dominican Republic ended abruptly. His unmarked but unescorted chauffeur-driven car was riddled with bullets, one of which killed the Dictator, who had been en route to an assignation with a new mistress. The fact that the assassins had been close to Trujillo, *seemingly loyal supporters*, was what fascinated and appalled his Haitian counterpart.

For weeks after the event Duvalier ordered every scrap of information coming across the border brought to him instantly. He spent hours going over, and brooding on, Trujillo's last days. The only comfort he derived from the event, an aide later revealed, was that it threw the hectic Caribbean into even greater turmoil which, it was reasonable to expect, could only mean greater US 'co-operation'.

Perhaps Trujillo's positive evidence of mortality was what prodded Papa Doc into his next series of excesses; perhaps, however, these are inherent in dictatorships. In any event, Duvalier succumbed to the urge to perpetuate his administration, and after less than four years in power began a truly monumental undertaking – Duvalierville.

For its site he chose the pleasant little village of Cabaret, twenty miles north of Port-au-Prince. Here he would build a showplace to Duvalierism, one that would unite all that was typically Haitian with all that is progressive, modern, dynamic. Tourists would come in droves to see *la vraie vie haïtienne* – its beaches, its cement plant, its alcohol and sugar-cane refineries. More pilot projects like Duvalierville, such as irrigation ditches, were promised.

On 21 July 1961 Luckner Cambronne, the rising young Duvalierist and deputy from Cabaret, dedicated the village to its new purpose. In his acknowledging speech Papa Doc told the peasants, among a great many other things, to 'make it [Duvalierville] a flower city, whose principal industry will be touristic good will.' The President even promised to establish a residence there himself which he would visit often 'to renew at the warm sources of your fervour my strength of an untamable and untamed fighter, and my faith as believer in all the possibilities of my race.' Cambronne began a concerted fund-raising campaign almost immediately.

Government employees, businessmen, and members of the armed forces were asked for generous monthly contributions. A toll booth was put on the Duvalierville Road. Congressmen voted to contribute ten dollars each from their monthly salaries. Under this system, either you paid or the Tonton Macoutes paid you a visit. The donations made to the National Renovation Movement were neither accounted for nor declared in the budget.

As the drive grew, the NRM began asking for lump sums. One large company's contribution was assessed at half a million dollars. But the business community was not the only one that paid up. Even school children, whose parents sacrificed necessities just to get them to classes, had to 'volunteer' a dime apiece.

These were the beginnings of the golden days for Duvalier's secret police. Haitians, who once ridiculed Dominicans for submitting to the Trujillo dictatorship and talking in whispers while looking over their shoulders, were now doing exactly the same thing. Taxi drivers and others who mingled with the public were looked upon as possible spies, and some were. Tonton Macoutes in the capital took on an affluent look, wearing dark glasses even at night, a fedora, and their trademark, a bulge at the hip. In the countryside militiamen and little Duvalierists tried to emulate their brothers in the city, but because Duvalier wanted arms only in the hands of the most trusted, they carried toy pistols and guns to symbolize their new-found authority.

Tonton Macoute status was loosely defined. Nearly all government employees belonged, and were subject to off-duty call. Some received a monthly stipend, thirty dollars to fifty dollars, but others operated for the prestige of it or the unwritten licence it gave them to swagger and steal and, sometimes, literally get away with murder.

In Gonaïves in early 1961 the militia made a house-to-house search to rout out all merchants and tell them what their NRM donations would be. One businessman, told to send fifty dollars, returned a cheque for ten dollars. The cheque was sent back, this time with a request for $1,000. A reluctant merchant sometimes found himself tapped on the shoulder as he walked down the street and taken to Cambronne's NRM office. If he started to protest he was met with a reproach: 'Ah, ah,' the official would say, 'just pay.'

There was corruption however, even within the NRM. Some Tonton Macoutes, using Cambronne's name, made their own collections. Haitians with friends in high places did not pay. One victimized businessman was angered when his cancelled cheque came back endorsed by a mistress of one of Duvalier's top officials.

An insistent report of a torture chamber in the basement of the palace circulated. It became a persuasive factor for many who preferred not to see it personally in the to-pay or not-to-pay dilemma. Of those reportedly taken there, few left whole men. Some former Duvalierists claimed that the room was painted brown from floor to shoulder height so that blood spatterings would not mar its neatness.

Luckner Cambronne became the symbol of Duvalierism. He once declared in the legislature his golden rule on how a Haitian should support the President: 'A good Duvalierist stands ready to kill his children, or children to kill their parents.'

One of his classic moves was to send out telephone bills dating back several years, even though the phone system did not work. Some bills for the non-existent service ran as high as $500. Cambronne explained that when all the money came in, the system would be put in working order.

When he consented to see newsmen, he greeted them in his air-conditioned office, behind a desk with three telephones, wearing a gold ring, a gold watch, and an expensive black suit. Often bobbing solicitously nearby was Colonel Jacques Laroche, who described Cambronne unblushingly as one of the 'dynamic new generation'. Cambronne usually wore a grim, businesslike air, but this could change magically when cash was produced.

Before making a statement to newsmen, he would grab the palace phone – Cambronne's intragovernment telephone service worked – and talk with Duvalier. At those times, too, his serious mien became all big smiles. His end of the conversation consisted of rapid '*Oui, mon Excellence; oui, oui, mon Excellence*' replies. Then he would put the telephone down and make statements like the following:

The Duvalierville project is the answer of the Haitian people to the call of their President. All Haitians have decided to help each other to help the government release them from misery and hunger. Everybody will come with what he has, one cent or one dollar, everything he has, to improve the general economy.

Duvalierville is a pilot project to test our possibilities. It will be completed in six months. This is where the Haitian peasant is making more effort by himself than anywhere else. This is a voluntary effort. People give. They know the government has no economy. This is not part of the Haitian budget. This is the people giving because of their great feeling for their President.

The amount donated cannot be listed. People give effort, stones, concrete blocks, and things that cannot be listed. We have plans in

Duvalierville for living quarters and all kinds of facilities to attract tourists and permit them to see Haitian life as it really is . . .

Six months later Duvalierville was a village in slow-moving construction with few accomplishments to view. There was an empty, modest, but modern farmers' market set in the midst of rubble, the beginning of modern dwellings constructed in single-file motel fashion. Workers lugged boulders about. There was activity but no showplace. The most impressive item was a large billboard, which displayed plans for what Duvalierville would, one day, hopefully become.

Ernst Biamby, former army colonel purged during the student strike, became the central figure during late August in a plot to assassinate Duvalier. After his ouster from the army Biamby had been approached by friends, including in-laws who had influence in Duvalier's top circles, with the plan. From his Venezuelan exile, Louis Déjoie sent two Frenchmen to contact Biamby and help organize the assassination. One was André Rivière, a former lieutenant in the French army who fought in Indo-China, the other Claude Martin, a former corporal in the Foreign Legion.

Rivière and Martin brought with them three machine guns and explosives. The plan was simple: to catch Duvalier outside the palace and shoot him. But some of the plotters were too anxious. Rivière and Martin later complained that every time they handed out a gun the man would make a premature move.

Roland Rigaud, son of the dentist who disappeared during the student strike, heard that Duvalier often attended incognito a drive-in movie on Delmas Road with his two daughters. Rigaud armed himself and went there nightly for nearly a month, taking a position so that he commanded a view of each car as it entered, prepared to shoot.

One night Eric Brièrre, a youthful Olivetti technician, heard that Duvalier was driving along Harry Truman Boulevard. He found Rigaud, and they went gunning for him. Along the bay they asked where Duvalier was, and discovered he had never left the palace. The Tonton Macoutes reported the questions to Duvalier and an investigation started.

Justin Napoléon, active as an explosive expert in the underground, was arrested first. From him police got the name of Eric Brièrre. Police arrested Brièrre's father, a tax-office employee, and posted a guard at the house. When Eric came to investigate his father's disappearance, he, too, was arrested and taken to Fort Dimanche. Rigaud found asylum in a Latin-American embassy, later left the country, and went to New York.

Eric Brièrre was tortured so badly that a report at the time said that an officer became sick when he saw him being dragged past his father's cell. The elder Brièrre had to listen while his son was being beaten to death in an upstairs room.

A sympathetic police officer tipped off other plotters that they had been discovered. Rivière and Martin left the country, later breaking with Déjoie in Venezuela and joining the exiles in the Dominican Republic.

The Tonton Macoutes rounded up the plotters, arresting Biamby and his brother Roger, former Captain Daniel Bouchereau, Captain Chenon Michel, pharmacist Frédérick Bouchereau and Gérard Lafontant. Several others sought asylum. Ernst Biamby was tried in February 1962 by a military court, convicted, and sentenced to death. A month later, through the intervention of influential friends, Biamby was granted a presidential pardon. Out of prison, he and his family went into asylum at the Dominican Embassy and were given safe-conduct out of the country.

Other significant changes in the army followed the arrests of the Biamby group. General Merceron was named Ambassador to France, reportedly because Duvalier was unhappy with what he considered soft-heartedness in the Brièrre case. Named to replace him as chief of staff was Colonel Jean-René Boucicaut. Duvalier commented that Merceron had served with 'fidelity and zeal', but added that the General 'needs a rest in a temperate country'.

Major Gracia Jacques replaced Major Claude Raymond as head of the Palace Guard. Major Frédéric M. Arty took over from Daniel Beauvoir as police chief, and five colonels, one major, and one captain were retired.

Luckner Cambronne's Renovation Movement, acting as a spur to Tonton Macoute lawlessness, caused incident after incident and contributed to a growing conflict with the United States.

A sailor off an American Merchant Marine ship became drunk in Port-au-Prince and was thrown in jail for twelve days before the American Embassy received a smuggled message and had him released. What had been a night watchman of an international aid agency was found garrotted, riddled with bullets, and strung up on barbed wire.

An American tourist declined three times to hire a persistent taxi driver and walked away. The driver insisted on knowing where he was going and the tourist angrily asked him to stop meddling. The American spent five hours in jail before he was released through the intervention of the American Embassy.

One incident stirred antagonism between Marine Colonel Heinl and Duvalier on a personal level. The Colonel's twelve-year-old son Michael, riding from his home to classes in Port-au-Prince in a bus, made a remark that the driver, a Tonton Macoute, considered derogatory to the government. The driver left his route and drove directly to the National Palace, where he handed the boy over to the special guards whose job it was to receive oppositionists picked up by the Tonton Macoutes. As Michael was being led in, protesting he was the son of Colonel Heinl, Jean-Claude Duvalier, whom he knew, saw him. The President's son confirmed that the boy was indeed Heinl's son and he was released. But Heinl had already heard of his son's arrest and was livid. He was quoted as saying if the boy wasn't released immediately, his Marines would storm the palace. American Embassy officials also pounded on the palace gate with protests, but Michael already had been freed. Washington sent two formal notes demanding an official apology, but received no reply. From that day forward relations became strained between the Marine Corps and Papa Doc.

A crisis had finally developed in the issues over the handling of U S aid as well. Since the end of the U S fiscal year (30 June) no new allocations had been made. Aid projects, the funds for which had been voted previously, continued running, however.

The United States was stalling, hoping to impress Duvalier that safeguards must be established. The United States wanted administrative checks to 'stop waste, misuse, and corruption.'

There were other complaints, too. The United States considered the April 1961 sneak election illegal. It disapproved of being in the position of shovelling money into a country which was using the unbudgeted accounts of the Régie du Tabac and the National Renovation Movement for a variety of political purposes while letting basic development needs be shouldered by foreign aid. It disliked the abuse of American businessmen or other American citizens who ran afoul of the peculiarities of Duvalierism.

The Haitian position was that the United States should donate the money and Haiti should spend it. Duvalier viewed any other arrangement as a violation of Haitian sovereignty. Earlier conflicts along these lines had been worked out. Many in Washington took the position that Duvalier's government was incompatible with the goals of the Alliance for Progress. Part of the US ability to make policy decisions was resolved (September) when Congress passed a measure (the Dirksen Amendment) which specified that foreign aid would be cut off to any country that did not meet its obligations to US firms or US private citizens.

One example of what was happening involved the American Development Services, a California firm. Contracting engineers, they had been operating in Haiti since December 1960, on a variety of assignments from the US-financed Organization for the Development of the Artibonite Valley (ODVA). The total of contracts came to some $200,000 and included the building of a rice-drying plant, food mill, canning plant, wharf, and other items.

The company had complained that the Haitians had not provided living quarters for the engineers as promised, had delayed needed machinery at customs, and had held back salaries from local labourers as long as two months, creating discontent. A showdown developed during the building of a wharf at Saint Marc. One of the engineers, Albert Van Zyverden, was sent word that the new police prefect, Félix Douyon, wanted to see him. Van Zyverden and his foreman went to his office.

Douyon told them that there was a problem, but he would help them solve it. He said a group of Haitian engineers and contractors objected to the US firm getting so much work and had petitioned President Duvalier to stop it and deport Van Zyverden. Douyon said that the President had placed the entire matter in his hands. The decision was whether to start deportation proceedings. Van Zyverden related it this way:

> But Douyon explained that even though he was a new prefect, he had heard of the many excellent projects we had completed in the Artibonite Valley. And he said he had no intention of deporting me. In fact, he was willing to see that the company got a good write-up in his own newspaper, *La Masse,* that would ward off any future protests. He said he already had gone to Duvalier and discussed the matter and the President approved.
>
> However, there was one other matter which the President had mentioned. He instructed the prefect to obtain a contribution from me for Duvalierville.

Van Zyverden said he later asked his Haitian foreman what he should do. The foreman said that the prefect, a powerful man, could cause a lot of trouble, and that it would be better to pay. Van Zyverden wrote a cheque for $200 and gave it to Douyon, who looked at it and walked away without a word.

Next day the foreman came to Van Zyverden, very worried. He said that the prefect was not happy with the $200 payment and had expected at least $300. He advised Van Zyverden to give another $100 so that the prefect would be a friend, and that he then would solve any labour trouble or other difficulty that arose. It was the sale of 'protection' in US gangster style.

'Since I did not have my cheque-book with me, but had two fifty-dollar bills in my pocket, I gave them to my foreman and he immediately used my car to take the money to the prefect,' Van Zyverden said.

This time Douyon was satisfied and an article appeared (9 November 1961) in *La Masse*. 'It was so flattering I considered the $300 well spent,' Van Zyverden said.

A month later, as Van Zyverden and another engineer, Ed

Reed, were working at the wharf site, a chauffeur-driven car pulled up. It was the prefect.

'He did not get out but called me over. I shook his hand and we talked for a minute or two. Then he told me that President Duvalier had instructed him to get another $400 from me. I told him I couldn't pay it, that we couldn't give any more. I figured then it would be a continuing thing, a sort of blackmail. Before he drove off he said, "I'll see you at your house tonight."'

Van Zyverden at that point lost his 'protection'. Reed and Van Zyverden had lunch and when they returned to the wharf an officer and two soldiers put them under arrest.

'They charged me with hitting a native with my automobile,' Van Zyverden said. 'They took me to the hospital and a native in bed there pointed his finger at me and said, "That's the man who hit me." I was not the driver and we definitely had not hit anyone. It was a frame-up.'

That was a Saturday, and Van Zyverden was told to appear before a judge on Monday. Sunday the head of the ODVA, Roger Cantave, told Van Zyverden not to worry. 'He told me he was sure it was a frame-up and that he would send his lawyer with us Monday to have the case cleared up.'

To Van Zyverden's shock, when he went before the judge on Monday, the accident case was never mentioned. 'Instead, we were told that we had to be deported because we had no work permits. When I asked them about the hit-run charge, they told me it had been dropped.

'The matter of the work permits had been brought to M. Cantave's attention time and time again and he had always assured me not to worry about that. I had asked him about them nearly a year previously and he said we did not need them because we were working for the government.'

Police put Van Zyverden and Reed in a car, drove them to Port-au-Prince, where Van Zyverden was put in a detention room and Reed in a cell with three men facing criminal charges. Police stripped Reed of all his belongings, including his belt. In about four hours they were released and went to the American Embassy. They left the country.

Another US citizen, Richard J. Arbour, had a similar experience. Arbour had been hired by an American firm (Freeman H. Horton Associates of Palm Beach, Florida) to collect overdue debts from the Haitian government. He arrived in Port-au-Prince, spent some four weeks discussing the situation and trying to verify his claims with Duvalierists in the Finance Ministry. He met with Duvalier (16 December) and reported to the American Embassy later: 'The president was quite cordial and friendly and agreed to pay me $75,000. The meeting lasted two hours....' Arbour said afterward that Finance Minister Hervé Boyer told him to return on 18 December and pick up the cheque. 'He also added that he wanted to take a sum of money off the top of that $75,000 and I would not know the amount until 18 December.' That evening Arbour visited two tourist hotels and left one, El Rancho, just after midnight. He caught a taxi which had several other people in it, and it took him directly to a police station. From there he was taken to another police station and then jailed. The American Embassy secured his release the next day and he was ordered out of the country.

Haitian officials charged that Arbour had made statements detrimental to the government. Arbour denied it. His ouster was delayed as he made additional attempts to collect payment and payment was promised. By 22 December he decided that Haiti had no intention of paying and left the country.

During November the United States announced that Ambassador Newbegin was being reassigned to Washington after a little more than a year in Port-au-Prince.

That fall the Assembly again voted Duvalier full economic powers; General Boucicaut was awarded the military medal of Dessalines. A new income tax law was decreed that looked good on paper, but in practice was used as a weapon against those who balked at Duvalierism. But, like an earlier law arbitrarily reducing rents by 25 per cent, it made good grist for the propaganda mills.

Duvalier opened 1962 with an Independence Day speech in which he made another half-threatening, half-cajoling pitch for US aid on his own terms. He spoke of 'widening of the gap between the small Negro people of Haiti, an underdeveloped country, and the great developed nations.' He added that 'anxiety and doubt of being misunderstood have found their way' into the Haitian people. He wanted massive injections of aid that would solve the country's problems in one spectacular swoop. He was impatient with the long-range health, education, and welfare programmes that called for any kind of co-ordinated effort. He questioned both the sincerity and the efficacy of John F. Kennedy's Alliance for Progress programme.

In all, it was a restatement of his basic position of aid without strings. Privately, US officials estimated that 80 per cent of the money received was being wasted through mismanagement and corruption.

On the same day of this 'peace and bread to survive' speech, Duvalier received Aleksander Bekier, the Polish Chargé d'Affaires. During their talk, he praised the Polish people's courage and patriotism and said how Haiti had never forgotten the way her ally, Poland, had sided with her time and again during her wars of independence. The two allies then discussed how mutual commerce might best be encouraged. The meeting did not go unnoticed by the American Embassy and its new Ambassador, career diplomat Raymond L. Thurston. Nor was it intended to.

While Duvalier complained of his country's needs Haitians discreetly referred to the fortune his family had amassed in jewels, real estate holdings, and foreign bank deposits – sufficient in themselves to underwrite an aid programme. The *Christian Science Monitor* pointed out that Duvalier's government had received more than $116 million in grants, loans, and other types of foreign assistance, most of it stemming from the United States, whose yearly grants averaged over one-half the nation's annual budget.

On 8 January 1962, after formally resuming ties with the Dominican Republic, Papa Doc delivered another speech on the theme of how he would lead the Haitian people to economic liberation. This was the signal for yet another fund-raising drive under the efficient stewardship of Luckner Cambronne and it added to the already fearsome mechanism of his National Renovation Movement.

An organization called the Permanent Council for Economic Liberation was authorized to sell $6 million worth of government bonds. Purchase was mandatory. Duvalier set the example by contributing 15 per cent of his monthly $2,000 salary. The Port-au-Prince jet port was designated as the Council's first project.

Ambassador Thurston, once settled, began a series of trips designed to acquaint him with Haiti and US aid projects. He visited the Poté Colé (or Operation All-Pull-Together) Project in the north and was favourably impressed by the increased food production it was making possible. At the same time he remarked that $3 million had gone into it since 1959.

On his way north Thurston made an unscheduled stop at Duvalierville. All the activity and half-finished construction he saw hardly justified the amount of money officially spent on this 'flower city'. There is no record of whether the Ambassador attempted to ascertain the unofficial amount of money spent.

More or less concurrently in Punta del Este, Uruguay, where the Organization of American States was meeting, the United States was busy trying to persuade the various foreign ministers to condemn Cuba. Haiti joined a group of six nations who were abstaining from the vote – a stand that made the censure fall one short of the necessary two-thirds majority.

Duvalier tergiversated until the eleventh hour, then instructed the Haitian delegation to vote along with its big brother to the north. When a newsman asked a member of the US delegation what had changed Haiti's mind, he was told 'diplomacy'.

The annual Mardi Gras began with the theme Joy in Austerity. One citizen built himself a papier-mâché castle which he carried out into the streets and, in a parody of the National

Renovation Movement, began demanding pennies from the crowd for 'maintenance'. He received many laughs until the arrival of the Tonton Macoutes.

Another group, with homemade shovels, pretended to be repairing the pavement. Each time they pantomimed asking for their wages the boss would produce a pistol and point it at them. They, too, vanished into the maw of Fort Dimanche.

Foreigners never ceased to marvel at the Haitians' seemingly endless ability to tighten their belts and survive. At carnival time NRM Director Luckner Cambronne announced a new lottery to benefit economic liberation. Besides an official state lottery, the Haitian people's every move was taxed and 'donations' were for ever being demanded. Cambronne ruthlessly enforced Duvalier's decree that the new lottery was 'compulsory for employees of the public administration ... pensioners, autonomous services, commercial and industrial societies, shopkeepers and their staff.' Payment for coupons was deducted from salary cheques on a sliding scale.

By the end of March Cambronne announced that the work at Duvalierville was half-finished, but he did not mention costs. Under the guise of a slum-removal project, yet one more fund-raising gimmick was instituted, a twenty-cent surcharge for the compulsory auto inspection every three months. Foreign diplomats, bombarded with complaints about the NRM, met and decided to protest to the Foreign Ministry. The British Ambassador, Gerald Corley-Smith, was chosen as their spokesman.

'This Corley-Smith is a man whose like you don't see much any more,' one ambassador said. 'He tells the truth.' Another commented: 'He does what all of us would like to see someone else do – to satisfy our own sense of righteousness.'

The British Ambassador complained to Foreign Minister René Chalmers about treatment of foreigners by the NRM. He said it had created a climate of fear. Chalmers demanded to know what they feared. When Corley-Smith replied that they feared the Tonton Macoutes, Chalmers said this was an insult. (The government had not yet officially recognized the existence of the Tonton Macoutes, as it did later, and considered the term a dirty word.)

A diplomat described the meeting this way: 'Corley-Smith was less than diplomatic, but he said what needed to be said. He said quite frankly that the people weren't contributing to Duvalierville voluntarily, but because they were afraid of the Tonton Macoutes.'

Corley-Smith was ordered out of the country, and Haiti withdrew its ambassador to London, Colbert Bonhomme, by request. The British Foreign Office announced that this change was taking place because of 'the unsatisfactory state of Anglo-Haitian relations.' But the British left a chargé d'affaires in Port-au-Prince. The London *Economist* commented: 'How much longer this extraordinary rule of blackmail and harshness will last depends largely upon the Americans. So far, with more at stake than the British, they have been vastly more susceptible to blackmail.'

One law had already appeared (mid-February) indicating Duvalier would accept aid on Washington's terms. Duvalier decreed a Special Control Committee to liquidate all Haiti's debts with US firms and with US private citizens. This action was taken in response to the Dirksen Amendment. The decree also indicated that 'essential' economic programmes for aid would be coming out of Washington as soon as debts were satisfied. It gave Americans three months to submit their claims.

Within weeks (8 April) Ambassador Thurston announced a $7.25 million aid allotment 'to assist the Haitian people in their efforts to raise their social and economic standards.' The funds were directed to specific projects and it was emphasized that they would be subject to control from the US Agency for International Development (AID). Plans included Poté Colé, the Artibonite Valley, the Péligre watershed, and a $3.4 million loan for the 44-mile highway south, regarded as part of the Punta del Este payoff.

It was apparent that the United States was renewing aid – on condition that the corruption and mismanagement of the past not reoccur. It was reported that the United States at the same time sought a release of political prisoners, end of rule by decree, and a public accounting of the Régie du Tabac funds.

The United Nations announced that it had hired seven Haitian judges to serve as judges in the Congo government, bringing the total of Haitian specialists working for the UN there to some one hundred and fifty.

At the Pan American Press Seminar held at the International House in New Orleans, Haitian publisher Frank Magloire of *Le Matin* defended the press in Port-au-Prince. He denied a resolution by the Inter-American Press Association stating there was no freedom of the press in Haiti. 'I don't say that the Haiti press is as free as any in the world but as for myself and one other well-established newspaper in Haiti, we aren't having any trouble. We are an information paper and are not partisan.' Magloire said that his paper did not refrain from covering political corruption or government brutality – which must have surprised his readers back home. He said that his statement referred to papers in existence at least five years and did not apply to government newspapers or political journals.

At about the same time Watson Sims of the Associated Press visited Haiti and commented upon the restrictive measures in force. He pointed out that citizens could not hold a meeting of any kind – cultural, social, or otherwise – without written government permission. At sanctioned meetings, he said, the entrances had to be well lighted so that all those attending could easily be identified.

Late in the month (27 April) the United States sent a secret note to Duvalier stiffly protesting a speech he made to the Haitian Assembly (16 April) in which he suggested that the new US aid constituted an endorsement of his government.

In Washington the United States made it clear that it did not consider the April 1961 election legal and that it felt Duvalier's constitutional term would end on 15 May 1963.

As the 1962 Day of National Sovereignty approached (22 May), the US State Department called Ambassador Thurston to Washington for 'consultation', continuing the practice begun under Newbegin of snubbing the Duvalier celebrations. Five other ambassadors also left the country.

With thousands of peasants trucked into the city to provide a receptive audience, Duvalier again spent the greater part of his speech on jabs at the United States. He took the line that the United States was discriminating against Haiti (not enough money, too many strings) because it was a Negro nation and suggested that the United States wanted him to surrender both pride and dignity in the name of democracy. 'Would this be democracy or masqueraded colonialism?' he asked.

> The Haitian democracy is not the German or French democracy. It is neither the Latin-American or US-type democracy. It is defined in full, according to the ethnic background of the people, its history, its traditions, its sociology, all overflowing with humanism ... in view of all these goals Haitian democracy is defined and redefined as a national discipline within the revolution....

The same month, a twelve-man team representing the Alliance for Progress left for Washington after having spent six months surveying Haiti's needs. They planned to put together a two-year development plan and make recommendations for fiscal and land reforms which would bring Haiti maximum benefit. The committee had been created by agreement between the Haitian government and the Alliance for Progress, and their work included contributions by both Haitian and Latin specialists. The problem, of course, was that just such scientific planning was regarded by Duvalier as usurpation of Haiti's sovereign rights to waste or steal foreign aid if it so chose.

The conflict over handling of aid continued to boil, then spilled over into an open challenge on all fronts late in July with a dramatic letter from Marine Colonel Heinl to Haitian Army Chief of Staff General Boucicaut. Since Heinl and Boucicaut were friends, it was assumed that the letter came as no surprise to Boucicaut, although it did to most others. It later became apparent that this was the first in a series of US steps to force a showdown and hopefully to force Duvalier out.

The letter was a military appraisal of the effect of Duvalier's militia on the Haitian army. It called the militia useless, expensive, and dangerous, and recommended that it be abolished. Heinl in effect was conceding that the Marines were being used to keep Duvalier in power by indirectly training and equipping the militia.

Two days later General Andrew O'Meara, chief of the Southern Forces Command based in the Panama Canal Zone, came to town. The General, Ambassador Thurston, and Colonel Heinl talked with Duvalier, apparently about the letter. The General then talked with General Boucicaut, Haitian chief of staff.

The situation began to burst at the seams. Mimeographed copies of the letter began to circulate around the city in both English and French. Ambassador Thurston said that the United States had no part in circulating them.

There were rumours of an army plot, but it did not clearly take shape. There seemed to be no question, however, that the US actions constituted a message that the United States now opposed Duvalier.

Within a week Washington announced that it was suspending most aid to Haiti (interestingly, the controversial jet airport loan remained in effect), but it kept a bargaining hook. Of the last $7.25 million allocated to Haiti only $1.6 million had been put to work. The remainder could be offered again if the situation improved. The United States revealed that Haiti had balked at the programme of specific projects and strictly accounted long-range planning. Duvalier rejected aid altogether, a policy that seemingly preferred to let Haitians starve rather than deprive Duvalierists of the privilege of stealing.

Boucicaut, who first had given a terse denial to the Heinl letter, sounded out several fellow officers for support in opposing Duvalier and failed. The President called Boucicaut to the palace and ordered him to go on television that night and repudiate Heinl and his letter. Instead of going downtown to the television studio, Boucicaut collected his wife and four children and drove up the hill to asylum in the Venezuelan Embassy.

Colonel Gérard Constant became Duvalier's fifth army chief in five years. In a ceremony at the palace Duvalier said: 'My old dear friend Boucicaut, having reached the age of limit, is retired, according to the regulations of the armed forces of Haiti. I wish to give you the investiture, my dear Constant, as the chief of the army staff ... believe sincerely that in your function you will preserve the military honour and that your sword never will be "prostituted."' The official announcement simply said that Boucicaut, forty-four, had retired and was being replaced by Constant, forty-eight.

The Assembly met in September and granted Duvalier powers 'to take all necessary economic measures'. As the new fiscal year began (1 October) Duvalier observed it was his first budget in four years which would not have foreign (US) support. He promised that Haiti's development would continue through the National Renovation Movement.

Duvalier did get a measure of foreign help when the International Monetary Fund entered into a stand-by agreement under which Haïti could draw up to $6 million to keep its currency stable.

The OAS Human Rights Commission requested permission to investigate human rights in Haiti and received no reply. Manuel Bianchi, head of the commission, repeated (9 October) the request and received a cable from Foreign Minister Chalmers declining on the grounds that it would represent a violation of Haitian sovereignty.

Bianchi sent another cable pointing out that Haiti had approved the OAS provision which gave the commission the right to investigate. This time he received no reply.

William L. Ryan, Associated Press special correspondent, wrote (12 September) a story in which he said 'responsible people' had heard Duvalier, indignant that Kennedy would not let him spend US money without restraint, say that he intended to 'bring President Kennedy to his knees'.

But another Cuban crisis was building, and the problem of Duvalier took a back seat. President Kennedy announced (22 October 1962) that the Soviet Union had established long-range missiles in Cuba and the United States began its quarantine on military shipments to Cuba.

Ambassador Thurston had the unpleasant job of delivering to Duvalier a letter President Kennedy wrote to the chiefs of state of the Latin-American nations, soliciting their support in the missiles crisis. On 26 October 1962 Duvalier came out in support of the United States and, publishing Kennedy's letter, issued a communiqué stating that the Haitian armed forces and the 'Volunteers of National Security' (militia) had been placed on alert throughout the Haitian territory, and the country's ports and airfields were at the disposal of the United States. Duvalier took advantage of this bid for co-operation from the United States to christen the militia officially the VSN (Volontaires de la Securité Nationale). Four months after Heinl's criticism of the militia as unnecessary and burdensome, Papa Doc was saying that this militia was an official entity and on the side of the US Marines in the fight against Cuba. The alert of these Lilliputian forces, however humorous, gave the Duvalierists a certain pleasure in seeing that the big neighbour had called on them.

Heinl reacted to Duvalier's psychological needle with one of his own. With US forces saturating the Caribbean, two ships operating in the Cuban blockade took advantage of the offer to use Haitian ports and docked in mid-November. Six hundred steel-helmeted, battle-ready Marines came ashore. They paraded five miles along the water front in what Heinl called 'Operation Stretchlegs'.

Meanwhile, Father Paul Robert, the Catholic Bishop of Gonaïves removed from his diocese in 1961, was expelled from the country. He was accused of ordering priests to omit Presidential prayers, and old charges were revived that he had pillaged 'archaeological and folkloric riches of his diocese' when he tried to stamp out voudou, and that he had defamed Duvalier during the 1957 election campaign. Three other priests were deported at the same time and, within a month, several more were sent out. The Vatican responded by recalling the Papal Nuncio, Monsignor Giovanni Ferrofino, and announcing that all Catholics responsible for the Robert expulsion automatically were excommunicated.

Minister of Finance Hervé Boyer spoke at the dedication

of a new bridge built across the Croix des Missions River six miles north of Port-au-Prince:

> We are now in the last phase of our revolution, the most difficult of them all. It calls for great courage, sacrifice, political sense, and consistency ... the task is made more difficult because at this stage he [Duvalier] must expect desertions, deviations and surprising turnabouts from the insincere leaders, former companions of the road who had in their mind nothing more than the hidden motive of catching the revolution for their own personal profit. In order to overcome their criminal purposes he had to and he must force himself to continue to, in spite of his will, sacrifice some personal friendships to preserve the interests of the national community.

Boyer, the former Communist with a sumptuous villa and impressive bank account acquired under Duvalier, did not seem an ideal example of revolutionary sacrifice. Nor did Duvalier. His name was on everything, from stamps, schools, bridges, police headquarters, streets, and avenues, to flashing neon signs. Hard-pressed Haitians would not have minded the pyramiding taxes so much had community benefits grown from them. But their only notable results were the entrenchment of Duvalier and the fattening of Duvalierists.

It was no secret around Port-au-Prince that the United States was looking for a respectable opposition group which it could support. Professional men, merchants and military elements were being appraised with this end in mind.

Late in the year Ambassador Thurston put the US position on record in a frank interview with Richard Boyce of the Scripps-Howard News Agency:

> I do not believe President Duvalier himself is a Communist but he finds it useful to throw them in our face, and so far he seems to have them under control. We also know that the Communists here maintain links with Castro's Communists in Cuba and with the international Communist base in Mexico. Although we do not feel all this represents an immediate threat, the longer it goes on the better is the chance the Commies will get control. And when President Duvalier finally goes – by whatever means – there could be a Castro-type takeover from the top.

13

U S Challenges Papa Doc

The year 1963 was heralded in Haiti with an editorial, 'The Psychosis of Fear', by a well-known Duvalierist, former cabinet minister and ethnologist Lamartinière Honorat. It was a veiled criticism of the terror perpetrated by the regime and of Haitians as well for allowing themselves to become paralysed by fear. Both fear and terror reached their height that year.

The world soon became aware of a new internal situation in Haiti. The Kennedy administration made it clear that it wanted no part of Papa Doc and openly condemned him. Nations in Latin America going along with this censure were Venezuela, Costa Rica, and the neighbouring Dominican Republic under its first freely elected President in more than thirty-one years, Juan Bosch. Duvalier seemed to have not a friend in the world, nor for that matter did he appear to want any.

Constitutionally, Duvalier's six-year term ended on 15 May 1963. Early in the year U S Ambassador Thurston told visiting newsmen that the United States felt that after 15 May Duvalier would have no legal claim to the Presidency. It became an open confrontation between Duvalier and the Kennedy administration. Duvalier continued to claim that his April 1961 'election' gave him another six-year term that would run through 1967. When he ignored the constitutional date for elections, 10 February 1963, a variety of forces, encouraged by open U S opposition, gathered against him.

Three young leftist students marked the day on which the new elections should have been held by going into the streets at night and painting anti-Duvalier slogans on the city walls. One sign read 'Caca Doc'. For this act of subversion one was tortured to death and the others released only months later, after being interrogated and personally tortured by Duvalier.

At no time in the past six years of Duvalier's reign had there been so much speculation concerning his assassination or overthrow. Few Haitians, even the Duvalierists, could imagine how Papa Doc could survive with such formidable forces in and outside the country against him. In the old days it had been sufficient for the American Embassy simply to spread the word that it would welcome the President's overthrow. Duvalier was changing the pattern. He seemed the only person in Haiti unconcerned about the situation.

On his rare public appearances he was always surrounded by a sea of denim-clad militiamen and Tonton Macoutes, their guns drawn, fingers at the trigger. It was a marvel that Duvalier was not killed accidentally amid the ocean of cocked pistols waving around him.

The periodic electricity blackout in the capital – ordered to preserve power – added to the climate of nervousness. The only areas spared from the nightly blackout were the National Palace and the neighbouring Champ-de-Mars.

One night in January the explosion of a transformer plunged the palace into darkness. Trigger-happy Tonton Macoutes instantly began firing in all directions, converting the surrounding park into a no-man's land. The incident generated further apprehension.

One of the early measures by which Duvalier probed the new US position was to call for the removal of Colonel Heinl, whom he now considered hostile to his government. Heinl had only a few days of his second two-year assignment left when Duvalier made this decision. Heinl left on 1 March, and was replaced by Colonel Roy Batterton.

Taking additional precautions to ward off any possible *coup,* Duvalier ordered Father Jean-Baptiste Georges exiled to the southern town of Grand Goave and placed under twenty-four-hour surveillance by twenty-six militiamen. Father Georges had been constantly plotting Duvalier's overthrow since he was fired from his post as Minister of Education in 1958. Georges, who had given haven to Duvalier during his days in hiding from Magloire, was one of those to whom disillusion with Duvalier came early. Two weeks after being detained, the priest obtained permission to visit Port-au-Prince for 'spiritual exercises' and slipped into asylum in the Dominican Embassy.

Duvalier systematically went about the job of neutralizing any threats at home. A new danger for him was an exile group in the Dominican Republic.

Following the collapse of the Trujillo dynasty in 1962, Haitian exile leaders abroad began soliciting resident visas from Santo Domingo. One of the early arrivals was Roger Rigaud, a former army officer and politician, who was close to US labour organizations in Latin America. He managed to get the Dominican National Civic Union to sponsor his visa. Rigaud was soon followed by his brother Pierre, a former diplomat, and by Paul Verna, who had been a secretary in the Haitian Embassy during Trujillo's time and had important military contacts. The junior officers he befriended during his assignment in the Dominican Republic were now in command of the army. The two former diplomats launched an organization they called the National Democratic Union (UDN) and invited all to join.

Louis Déjoie was also attracted by the possibilities in the neighbouring Dominican Republic. Déjoie had done the Caribbean circuit, having set up a military camp in Havana during the early days of Fidel Castro and later organized an anti-Duvalier radio programme from Caracas.

But new faces now appeared among the exiles. They were the young men who, unable to pay for a plane or boat ticket to exile, had hidden in the rugged Haitian hills until the Dominican Republic was no longer unfriendly. They also sought to marshal their forces for the fight against Duvalier.

Pierre Rigaud began recruiting daring youths to slip back into Haiti to distribute UDN leaflets and raise money. Port-au-Prince contacts would deliver cheques drawn on foreign banks to these couriers. Rigaud would cash them.

Rigaud soon ran into a problem that was to become commonplace in later years – the exile-opportunist. One promised Rigaud he could get a supply of revolvers from the Dominican town of Barahona. Rigaud gave him money and transportation and awaited the arms. The next day, as he walked through Independence Park, Rigaud spotted his 'agent' sitting in a restaurant with friends, eating and drinking in a style which only the weapon money could have paid for.

Treatment of Dominicans in Haiti did not endear Duvalier to Juan Bosch. The Dominican Consul in Aux Cayes, Gerardo Blanco, was found dead in his garden one January morning, his throat so thoroughly slashed that he was nearly decapitated. The Dominicans demanded a 'satisfactory' investigation. Tension between the two countries mounted.

Haiti had no friends in the Organization of American States, and Haitian Ambassador Fern D. Baguidy had boycotted a meeting on 27 February 1963 because he took offence at a remark made by Costa Rican Ambassador Gonzalo Facio on a national television programme stating that Duvalier appeared to be violating the principles of the OAS.

Months before the 15 May deadline official apprehension mounted over the confrontation with the United States. This was the date, according to Washington, that marked the constitutional end of Papa Doc's term. As early as January 1963, official apprehension started to mount over the 15 May confrontation. Some Haitians, sensing the axe about to fall, took refuge in Latin-American embassies in Port-au-Prince or made the more dangerous journey overland to the Dominican Republic. Major Louis Moïse, his wife, and three children moved into the Venezuelan Embassy to join former General Boucicaut, whom Duvalier had denied safe-conduct out of the country.

Haiti accused yet another Venezuelan, Chargé d'Affaires Francisco Millan Delpretti, of housing anti-government activists and declared him *persona non grata*. Haiti said he had helped Colonel Biamby's wife and eight children reach asylum in the Dominican Embassy.

Duvalier brought in new Communist influence to badger the United States. On 12 March he welcomed a three-man

Czechoslovakian commercial mission which had come to study the potential for trade exchanges between the two countries. A Polish diplomatic and trade mission had been in Port-au-Prince since 1959.

Duvalierists quarrelled among themselves. In Gonaïves in early March three Duvalierists from Port-au-Prince found their authority disputed by the local militia. A fight developed and the Port-au-Prince agents were killed. In the following days the Port-au-Prince Tonton Macoutes had to be restrained from taking revenge on the Gonaïve militia.

Even the countryside was restive. A new tax on the production and marketing of rice ran into resistance from peasants in the Artibonite Valley. People bartered their rice rather than pay the tax. To halt the bartering the authorities had Tonton Macoutes set up road blocks and began confiscating rice on which taxes had not been paid. There were riots, and peasants were jailed. Discontent spread.

Duvalier declared in a speech that there was a kind of undeclared war being waged against him. But the foxy little President promised to be around long after the deadlines they were setting for him: 'We received constitutional power from the people legitimately. I will accomplish with all the force of my patriotism the mission confided in me even if we have to disappear in flames ... no power in the world can come and give us a lesson in democracy.... Haitian democracy is not German democracy, or French, or American.'

Despite the frequent purges and loyalty checks, a group of army officers, who had benefited as pro-Duvalierists in 1957 and had risen rapidly in the ranks, had been plotting his overthrow since January 1963. With US encouragement, they sounded out most of their key fellow officers, found little opposition, some fence sitters, and considerable support.

In determining their own strength, they also unwittingly tipped off Duvalier that something was afoot. A loose watch was kept on some of the key conspirators. The leader was Colonel Lionel Honorat, assistant chief of staff. Although the Honorat family was close to Duvalier, the Colonel had been studying accounting during his free time in case he needed a civilian career.

The plotters decided to strike at 6 p.m., 10 April, but were persuaded by Armed Forces Chief of Staff General Gérard Constant that four the next morning would be a more propitious hour.

The officers expected the American Embassy to supply them with weapons, and when the arms did not materialize they took a fatal step. They decided to seize what arms were left in the armoury of the Casernes Dessalines. They made a grave mistake in approaching Lieutenant Valmé to ask that he secure the keys to the armoury. Valmé mentioned their request to his brother, a rabid Duvalierist; Lieutenant Valmé found himself hauled before Duvalier to explain.

Duvalier responded quickly to what he heard. The same night, 10 April, all colonels were ordered to report to the palace immediately. Many were attending a soccer match. Four officers, including Honorat and Lieutenant Colonel Kern Delince, fled to the Brazilian Embassy. Honorat carried in his pocket a written declaration for the Haitian people of the formation of a new military junta that was to be announced once the radio stations were captured.

Charles Turnier, a popular black colonel with a good army record and a reputation for staying out of politics, refused to flee. He believed his personal status would protect him and that he would be in a position to revive the plot once things settled. As so many before and after him, he was in error. Turnier was additionally handicapped by being known to be pro-American.

Four days later he was arrested at his home by a group of Duvalierist officers. They took him to the Casernes Dessalines, where he was murdered. What really happened was obscured by the government propaganda. There are former Duvalierists who say that Turnier was beaten nearly to death in a futile attempt to get from him the names of other plotters. The end came, according to these sources, when an army officer put a pistol behind Turnier's ear and pulled the trigger.

The government version was that Turnier was killed in an attempt to escape. The palace announced that Turnier had used a concealed weapon to kill an army sergeant who brought him breakfast, and then forced his way out for a single-handed attack on the palace. His beaten, bullet-riddled body was left in a bloody heap on the parade grounds as an 'exhibit' and a warning to others.

In the two weeks following Turnier's death, seventy-two officers were discharged from the armed forces. Colonel Yves Cham of the general staff signed the orders discharging sixty officers, then fled to asylum in the Brazilian Embassy. Duvalier announced that 'certain foreigners resident in Haiti' were implicated in the army plot but did not reveal their names.

Former army officers were becoming more numerous than officers on active duty, and Duvalier decided to neutralize another potential threat. He personally prepared the list of officers to be arrested and taken to Fort Dimanche. He began by arresting men known for their sympathies for the opposition since 1957. Tonton Macoutes raided their homes and arrested relatives who had not taken asylum in Latin-American embassies.

Meantime, exiles in the Dominican Republic were having difficulties in organizing. A unification meeting was called the night of 17 April in Santo Domingo, but two of the best-known exiles, Pierre Rigaud and Louis Déjoie, had plans of their own and refused to attend. Other leaders met and tried to carry on.

First to speak was Raymond Cassagnol, one-time owner of a sawmill at La Miel in Central Haiti. He was from a well-known Haitian family and had fled after the Tonton Macoutes pressured him for active co-operation and frequent 'donations'.

The second speaker was an old Duvalier foe, Antonio Rodriguez, the former Cuban butcher friend of Clément Jumelle, who had been Castro's first Ambassador to Haiti. Since leaving Haiti he had served Castro as Ambassador to Guatemala and finally to Pakistan, where he defected.

Cassagnol proposed formation of a Haitian revolutionary

movement (MRH is its French acronym); Rodriguez, wearing a white Cuban *guayabera,* or leisure shirt, urged exiles to sacrifice their self-interests in a united effort to overthrow Duvalier.

Rodriguez and Cassagnol made frequent trips to the United States, and the Cuban returned one day with funds for a projected invasion of Haiti. The first exile training camp was set up beside the rifle range of the Dajabon army garrison in the north-western part of the Dominican Republic. The Dominican area commander, Colonel Ney Garrido, a burly, tough, Creole-speaking officer, co-operated. The first troops arrived in style aboard the Cuban's newly acquired white Chevrolet pick-up truck. Three dozen exiles were in training, although in Santo Domingo the camp's many 'commanders' put the figure at around 200. The small invasion force worked diligently with Tommy guns and rifles, but the nightly tropical downpours made the new military life difficult if not altogether unbearable. Despite quarrels over leadership, the exiles were encouraged by the active support of the Dominican military establishment as D-day neared. Two Dominican officers gave twice-a-week instructions in guerrilla tactics and urban warfare, although the training mostly emphasized shooting.

But it was not the exiles or even the army that Duvalier had begun to worry about. It was his once great friend, Clément Barbot. Long regarded as broken, Barbot returned to the little arena like a ghost to haunt his former boss.

Duvalier had ordered the release of Barbot after eighteen months in the hot, fetid Fort Dimanche without explanation, and the day after his liberation, sent him a new Vauxhall as a gift. It was generally believed that Barbot, Papa Doc's former hatchet man, had undergone a change in prison that had made him repentant and devoutly religious. From his well-guarded home, in the foothills overlooking Port-au-Prince, he ventured out only to attend retreats in the Jesuit house of Villa Manrèse or mass at the Sacré-Coeur Church of Turgeau. It was presumed that Barbot was atoning for his crimes.

The morning that Colonel Turnier's battered body was displayed on the barracks parade-ground shots were heard in

Barbot's neighbourhood. He reacted as did most Duvalier foes. He thought the move to oust Papa Doc was on. That morning, as his daughter drove the Vauxhall from the house, she waved a greeting to the guards at the gates. Barbot was curled up on the car floor. In town he kissed his daughter good-bye and went quietly underground to seek vengeance against Duvalier. He had sworn to kill Duvalier for the harsh treatment his family had received, particularly for his denying medical care to Barbot's mentally ill son.

Shortly before dawn on Sunday morning, 21 April, a small plane took off from a Dominican airfield and headed for Haiti. Over Port-au-Prince it dumped out bundles of neatly printed leaflets bearing a message in French from the exiles in Santo Domingo.

The plane was gone before the palace knew what had taken place. The wind carried the leaflets up the city's hills. Back yards and rooftops were littered. When the palace finally learned of the drop, Tonton Macoutes were sent out to destroy the leaflets.

The leaflets announced 'operation dry cleaning' against 'all noxious insects who accompany the gorilla Duvalier.' They called on the armed forces to join the revolution and warned that foreign residents and diplomats 'accredited to the tyrant-voudouist' should evacuate the city before 15 May. All Haitians living in the vicinity of the National Palace were told to evacuate the area before that deadline.

The little plane, later to be christened 'that butterfly' by Duvalier, gave the opposition in Port-au-Prince a lift. They speculated that the next move would be a real bombing of the palace.

The day after the leaflet raid Duvalier decreed an official Month of Gratitude to himself, to continue until 22 May, the second anniversary of his inauguration for a second term. During that month all public figures were called on to make speeches praising him and expressing the country's thanks for him. This was a way of putting his servants in a for-me-or-else position. There was no middle ground. In some cases Duvalier supplied the speeches to be read. Thus in a time of stress and vengeance officials had to place themselves on record as Duvalierists, which meant that they would have to fight for their own lives and Duvalier's if revolution came.

The Month of Gratitude theme was expressed best by Dr Jacques Fourcand, the pistol-packing president of the Haitian Red Cross and Duvalier's personal physician. He spoke at the Rond Point of Liberty on Harry Truman Boulevard in the heart of the city, and his words were among the most blood-chilling ever heard – even by Haitians. He warned that if Duvalier were attacked it would cause the greatest slaughter in history, producing a 'Himalaya of corpses'. He added:

> Blood will flow in Haiti as never before. The land will burn from north to south, from east to west. There will be no sunrise or sunset – just one big flame licking the sky. The dead will be buried under a mountain of ashes because of serving the foreigner.

Dr Fourcand clearly established the 'foreigner' as the United States; he criticized the United States for racial intolerance, attacking those who 'under a protocol of foolishness' loosen ferocious dogs in the streets to prevent Negroes from attending universities. He accused American racists of refusing restaurant service to Negro women and of raping Negro girls. Dr Fourcand even dredged up the Marine occupation; cited what he called military repression and asked: 'What right have they to advise us and give us a lesson in constitutional law?' In a final insult he called the United States a 'democracy of sluts'.

When he finished, Duvalier congratulated him. Other similar speeches of gratitude followed throughout the month. Minister of Public Works Luckner Cambronne suggested that the people 'keep machetes and guns ready' in case trouble started.

Some of the speeches hinted that Duvalier might declare himself emperor and touched on the creation of a dynasty. In one broadcast a group of Duvalierists from Trou Sable, a poor neighbourhood in Port-au-Prince, swore to defend Duvalier to the death and declared that if anything happened to the president they would put his son, eleven-year-old Jean-Claude, in the palace.

Clément Barbot finally struck. But it was several days before Duvalier realized that his old lieutenant was back in business. At 7.25 a.m., Friday morning 26 April 1963, a Presidential limousine pulled up to the Methodist College as was its custom every school day and delivered the Duvalier children, plump Jean-Claude, eleven, and his sister Simone, fourteen, to the front door. As the children were entering the school door and the limousine was moving out of the gate into the tree-lined street, three blocks from the palace, a series of shots rang out. The Duvalier children's chauffeur and two bodyguards were shot dead. Witnesses later told how one car had been awaiting the arrival of the palace limousine and another had been following it. There was no attempt to kidnap or harm Duvalier's children, but this was not apparent at first because of the panic the incident created. Most Haitians speculated that it was an attempt to kidnap the children for a handsome ransom: Duvalier's resignation.

Like all previous anti-Duvalier moves, they considered it bungled. The government radio declared that there had been an attempt on the lives of the 'two tiny little children'. The Duvalierists' response was typically blood-chilling.

The school was cordoned off. The army went into the streets. Grim-faced, they crouched behind trees and bushes around the palace facing in every direction. Road blocks were set up and all cars searched. Duvalierists put on their militia or Tonton Macoute battle gear. They moved, guns in hand, about the city arresting anyone they regarded as an opponent of the regime. The word from the palace was that all former army officers must be arrested. As the radio blared out a call to arms, families rushed to schools to take their children home, fearing the worst.

Duvalier's anger was fearsome to behold, according to those who saw him that day. He was convinced that only an experienced sharpshooter could have shot his children's escort with such precision and rapidity. The marksman, he decided, was a handsome black army lieutenant, François Benoit, one of those to fall in the army purge after the Honorat plot was uncovered. Benoit, an honour student at the US anti-guerrilla school in the Panama Canal Zone, had for several years led Haiti's rifle team to victory in the Panama contest with other Latin-American nations. Two days earlier police had gone to Benoit's home to ask him to return his M-1 rifle. When they knocked on the front door of his parents' old two-storey wooden house in Bois Verna, Benoit decided to resist arrest. He awaited them upstairs, a grenade in each hand. But when he saw the maid downstairs talking to them with his infant son in her arms, he took flight. He escaped through a rear second-floor window, raced through neighbouring back yards, and finally reached asylum in the Dominican Embassy residence.

Convinced that Benoit was involved in the attack, Duvalier ordered his Presidential Guard to instigate reprisals. They streamed out of the palace in two trucks and headed for Bois Verna. Benoit's parents had just returned from morning mass at the nearby Sacré-Coeur Church. The former judge tried to calm his wife, who was worried because François had been away two days and had no clean clothing. Another son, Jean, a lawyer, came by to take a shower (Port-au-Prince's uncertain water system was furnishing none at his own house). Jean promised his mother that he would take François some fresh clothes, kissed his parents good-bye, and left for the American Embassy, where he worked. Shortly after his departure palace guards and Tonton Macoutes began their rampage. En route to the Benoit residence, the truck-loads of troops and hired killers raced up one-way Ruelle Saint Cyr in the wrong direction. As they passed the home of the mistress of Presidential Guard Commander Gracia Jacques, a guard near the doorway was stirred to action. He ordered all parked cars away from the lady's home. Lionel Fouchard, son of Duvalier's dean of the civil court, was too slow in moving and was shot dead at point-blank range. Fouchard's companion, a pregnant co-worker, was speechless for days and a week later lost her baby.

The heavily-armed troops assaulted the Benoit house as if they were attacking an enemy pillbox. When they arrived, the elderly couple was standing on the steps talking with a visitor. A servant hovered nearby. The troops opened up with rifle bursts that almost cut the old people and the visitor in half. They kept shooting until the wooden house looked like a sieve. One servant got as far as the street before being machine-gunned. The officers then ordered what remained of the house set afire.

Benoit's infant son Gérald was normally in his crib on the second floor. There was a report that he was taken out before the fire, but one Latin-American diplomat who devoted almost two years to the search for the child was finally convinced that he died in the flames that quickly consumed the house and one next door. The fire brigade watched the flames without stirring; they were interested only in protecting nearby property owned by a Duvalier Minister.

The hunt for Benoit was on. Fifteen Tonton Macoutes rushed into his brother Jean's house. When they left, his frightened wife gathered up their valuables and fled. Friends hid the couple until they received asylum in the Argentine Embassy. Mme Jacqueline Benoit, eight months pregnant, had been warned that the Tonton Macoutes were coming for her, and she got away in the nick of time, just before they stormed the small primary school where she was teaching. Tonton Macoutes told the teachers to be thankful 'that she is not here, because what you would have seen would have been more dreadful than you could ever imagine.' Mme Benoit reached asylum in the Ecuadorean Embassy. Her whole family was taken to jail.

An elderly lawyer, Benoit Armand, was shot to death in his home by the Tonton Macoutes. The fact that his first name was Benoit was reason enough.

The Presidential Guard proceeded from Benoit's house to the chancellery of the Dominican Embassy, which had moved the year before into a modern house on the Delmas Road, between Port-au-Prince and Pétionville. They blocked the road and went into the Embassy, searching it from top to bottom.

They treated the Dominican woman secretary present curtly, and only then did they realize their mistake. Asylum as a rule is granted not at the offices of the embassy, but in the residence of the ambassador.

The guard and Tonton Macoutes surrounded the Dominican Embassy residence in Pétionville and moved into the yard prior to storming the residence with its twenty-two refugees, including Benoit. The Dominican Chargé d'Affaires demanded they leave the grounds, pointing out that it was sovereign territory of the Dominican Republic. The soldiers responded by climbing into the flamboyant[1] trees along the driveway and setting up machine-gun positions around the grounds adjoining the El Rancho Hotel.

While this was going on, terror ran rampant through the city streets. André Poitevien, a former Coast Guard commander, was caught in front of his home by a group of Duvalierist militia women and shot to death. They were responding to a standing order that all former military officers be shot or arrested.

A block away from the burning Benoit house, two bodies lay on the sidewalk all day, flies covering their wounds, a soldier standing guard. One of the 'bodies' was a neighbour of the Benoits. He had been hurrying home to his wife and five children when he was shot for going too close to the Benoit massacre scene. Despite the pain and the flies, he played dead all day and only when night fell, and the guard left, did he let the startled neighbourhood know he was alive.

Another of Haiti's top marksmen, Major Monod Philippe, considered a steadfast Duvalierist, fared better than Benoit. He was arrested at the national prison, of which he was commander, and taken before Duvalier, who slapped him across the mouth repeatedly. He was released and later returned to duty. But the national prison was doing little business. The hundreds arrested that day were taken directly to the palace or Fort Dimanche. It is not clear what happened to them. They just disappeared. It has never been confirmed whether

1. *Delonix regia* or the Royal Poinciana. In bloom, its flare-coloured flowers are spectacular.

they were quickly executed and dumped into common graves at Fort Dimanche or kept in prison and liquidated whenever Duvalier was seized with the urge to kill someone. For years relatives of the missing men have held out hope that in some far-off isolated jail they might still be alive. But Duvalier later crushed these hopes by saying again 'I have no political prisoners.'

Tonton Macoutes patrolled the streets, sirens wailing. Road blocks were everywhere. It took hours to cross town or travel up the hill to Pétionville, where the road checks were both tedious and rough. Some former army officers, having no idea of the danger they were in, drove to pick up their children at school and on their return home were arrested at road blocks and never seen again. Their cars were pushed to the side and, in some cases, confiscated by the Tonton Macoutes. Detentions went on throughout the night. In the morning it became a delicate matter to comply with a decree ordering all civilians (without Tonton Macoute status) to turn in all weapons to police. The difficulty was transporting guns to police headquarters through the road blocks – for anyone caught with a weapon was arrested.

One of the first men Tonton Macoute Chieftain Elois Maître went looking for, after the Duvalier children's bodyguards were killed, was Eric Tippenhauer, a well-known Haitian entrepreneur who had been close to both Estimé and Magloire in business deals. Tippenhauer was considered one of the shrewdest businessmen in Haiti. Alerted by a top official that they were after him, he left his office and went to his mountain home in Laboule. His young sons, one married to an American, were totally removed from politics. Three of them were arrested and disappeared. Tippenhauer was caught in his house in the mountains. To make his trip to jail more agonizing, he was shot in the leg.

Jean Chenet and his American wife had a popular jewellery business. They lived on the beach at Arcachon, several miles south of the capital. Some Tonton Macoutes remembered that Chenet, an artist, had been friendly with the late Charles Turnier. They went to Chenet's home, shot him, and then dumped his body in his front garden.

One of hundreds arrested was André Riobé, a mulatto sugarcane planter near Léogane, who distilled 'clairin' and who had only recently been let out of jail. Two Tonton Macoutes grabbed him as he drove toward his home at Martissant, a suburb. His son Hector escaped. Riobé disappeared and his car was confiscated. Weeks later the Tonton Macoutes took everything the family owned, including their savings, as payment to assure Riobé's safety. While his mother was paying this ransom, Hector discovered that his father had never reached jail. They had murdered him on the street. Hector's bitterness led him to become an activist – and a martyr – in the anti-Duvalier fight two months later.

Merchants feared to open their stores yet dreaded not to, since this might be interpreted as the sign of a general strike.

In less than a week the United States issued five official protests to the Haitian government over six separate incidents involving US citizens or Embassy personnel. The Brazilians, Dominicans, Ecuadoreans, and Venezuelans also protested similar incidents.

The American Embassy sent notices to the 1,031 Americans in Haiti advising precautionary measures 'to meet the present situation and prepare for any further disturbances.' A number of Americans were appointed wardens to serve the American community. All Americans were asked to keep in their homes several days' supply of drinking water, cooking gas, and other essentials; to stay away from downtown areas as much as possible, especially at night; to avoid all disturbed areas; to cooperate with local authorities; to await advice from the warden on new developments.

Trying to force Dominican President Bosch into ousting Haitian exiles from their new sanctuary in the Dominican Republic or perhaps merely to frighten him, Duvalier welcomed three nephews and a niece of the late Dominican dictator, Rafael Trujillo, from Spain, where they had been in exile. Luis Reynoso Mateo, José Rafael Trujillo Lara, Francisco José Reynoso Mateo, and Teresa Oviedo Reynoso apparently came to see whether the Trujillo interests might find new Dominican political opportunity in the current turmoil. They checked into second-floor rooms at the Excelsior Hotel on the Champ-de-Mars, two listed their occupations as businessmen, the others as a farmer and a housewife. Luis Reynoso, former Trujillo military attaché in Port-au-Prince, was in familiar territory.

As the world became aware of the bloody turmoil inside Haiti, repercussions began. The Dominican Republic's new President, Juan Bosch, reacted first. On 28 April 1963, two days after the Benoit murders, he went on the air to tell Dominicans: 'We have been suffering with Christian patience all manner of attacks by the present government of Haiti.' He listed some of the Dominican citizens who had been jailed or maltreated, and continued:

> In January of this year, when I was only President-elect, the Haitian government began a plot to kill me and designated a former member of the SIM [Trujillo's secret police], Michel Brady, a Haitian, to commit the crime. In March the Haitian government named this Monsieur Brady Haitian Chargé d'Affaires here in Santo Domingo, but we rejected the proposal, informing the Haitian government in diplomatic language that we knew why this gentleman was coming.

Bosch censured the presence of the Trujillos in Haiti. He said they were behind the radio and press campaign in the United States accusing the Bosch government of being Communist. Bosch then told of the Benoit incident and gave details on the invasion of the Dominican Embassy.

> Two Haitian guards bearing police badges numbers 491 and 533, and armed with rifles, entered the chancellery of the embassy and consulate general of our nation in Port-au-Prince, searched the ground floor, climbed to the second floor, threatened the secretary Katia Mena, who was alone because the only two diplomats we have at this moment in Haiti were not there, and began to question her at rifle point. Only a government of savages, of criminals, is

capable of violating the sanctity of a foreign embassy and threatening with rifles a woman who is also an employee of the embassy. This action is a slap in the face of the Dominican Republic, an affront which we do not intend to ignore.

Since Thursday armed guards have surrounded the Dominican Embassy residence in which are twenty-two asylees, including women and children, who are living through indescribable hours of terror, because every minute of the day and night they expect the attack which will cost them their lives. This also is unpardonable . . .

The situation is grave. . . . We have suffered with great patience the outrages . . . but these outrages must end – now. If they do not end within twenty-four hours we will end them.

El Caribe, the Dominican Republic's leading newspaper, responded in a front-page editorial: 'The entire Dominican citizenry will back whatever action the chief of state considers appropriate to repair the grave offences against our free and sovereign people.' And the country did respond. There was a rush of volunteers for the army, telegrams of support, offers from business for donations to the war effort.

Sunday, 28 April, at 1 p.m. the Dominican Radio began broadcasting an ultimatum to Haiti in Creole. The Dominicans announced that they were friends of the Haitians and the quarrel was solely with Duvalier.

The broadcasts announced that they would bomb the palace if Duvalier did not heed the ultimatum, and instructed the people to evacuate the surrounding area. Monday Duvalier's Voice of the Republic began answering the Dominicans with broadcasts in Spanish.

The day before Bosch's speech Foreign Minister Andres Freites had sent a long cable to Haitian Foreign Minister René Chalmers delivering the twenty-four-hour ultimatum. Chalmers replied with a long cable in French denying the charges and announcing the end of diplomatic relations between the two countries.

Freites cabled back, repeating the charges and demanding safe-conduct for the twenty-two persons, including François Benoit, in asylum in the Dominican residence. Chalmers replied with the charge that Dominicans had violated the rights of asylum by allowing the Haitians to keep their weapons, allowing Benoit to leave the Embassy to make the attack on Duvalier's children, and asserting that Bosch was using the 'whole affair to divert the attention of the noble and unhappy Dominican people from the internal situation.' He repeated that Haiti was breaking relations.

The same afternoon (28 April) the OAS Council headed by Costa Rica's Gonzalo Facio met in Washington and called for an emergency session at 10 p.m.

The Dominican Ambassador to the OAS, Arturo Calventi, listed twelve charges against Haiti during the meeting, repeated the twenty-four-hour ultimatum, and warned that gunboats would sail on Port-au-Prince the next day unless Haiti pulled its troops back from the Dominican Embassy residence in Pétionville.

Calventi charged that Haiti, unable to get help elsewhere, had gone to the Communist bloc for aid. He said that Haiti had established secret relations with Czechoslovakia and Poland and cited missions of the two countries in Port-au-Prince as proof. The Polish mission had been there since 1959, and the Czechs had arrived in March. Calventi said that Haiti was receiving 'all forms of political counsel from Poland' and had signed 'a secret economic treaty' with Czechoslovakia under which Haiti would aid 'Communist infiltration in the Caribbean'.

Haiti replied that it would defend itself by 'all means available' if the Dominicans attacked.

The OAS voted (sixteen 'ayes'; two abstentions) to invoke the 1947 Inter-American Treaty of Mutual Assistance to make sure that Haiti would observe its international obligations and to form an investigating committee to go to Haiti and make a report.

It urged Haiti and the Dominican Republic to keep the peace until the committee finished its work. Ambassadors from Colombia, El Salvador, the United States, Ecuador, and Chile were named. The United States declined and was replaced by Bolivia.

The *New York Times*, in a story by Max Frankel, commented:

> The United States has wished for some time for the downfall of the Duvalier dictatorship in Haiti, and it may have found encouragement in this weekend's Caribbean crisis....
>
> By a variety of diplomatic affronts it has demonstrated its revulsion against what it regards as a corrupt, brutal, and inept regime. There are indications that Washington, in secret, may have done even more.... Thus, though Haiti is small and insignificant in the swirl of world and hemisphere diplomacy, the problems she has raised for Washington have been great and fundamental. How the United States could tolerate Duvalier's government while trying to promote freedom, justice, and economic development in Latin America is a question that has haunted the Kennedy administration since the start of the Alliance for Progress program two years ago.

In anticipation of new trouble, American citizens began leaving Haiti upon the advice of the Embassy. One evacuée said: 'The Tonton Macoutes searched everyone. Everywhere you see people with their arms in the air, being patted under the shoulders as police frisk them for guns. But Friday was the worst. We live in Pétionville, about five miles from downtown Port-au-Prince, but because of all the check points I had to go through, it took me ten and a half hours to get home.'

In this setting, Duvalier, owlishly manipulating terror from the palace, decreed an out-of-season Mardi Gras. With blood and bodies still on the streets, a band, costumed dancers, and colourful government-sponsored floats added another macabre touch by marching through the streets to lively musical accompaniment.

Ambassador Facio, Costa Rica's delegate and president of the council, announced for the OAS that Haiti had agreed to restore diplomatic guarantees to the Dominican Embassy and residence, and would pull its troops back from the residence grounds. The Dominicans responded by extending the war deadline, while the OAS investigated. Colombia agreed to assume responsibility for the Dominican residence and the twenty-two persons in asylum there when the Dominican Chargé d'Affaires left.

However, President Bosch moved troops and mechanized units up to the Haitian border and ordered warships to position themselves for attack. Romulo Betancourt of Venezuela, in a personal telephone call to Bosch, offered full military support. In Washington Admiral George W. Anderson, chief of Naval operations, said that the United States was ready to move 'in hours if not minutes' to evacuate Americans from Haiti and to carry out the directions of the OAS. The State Department announced that thirty more Marines and ten members of the Air Force mission were being withdrawn from Haiti at the request of the Haitian government, leaving fifty-five US military personnel in Haiti.

In Santo Domingo Bosch stated: 'It is a very ugly situation there. One smart and capable Communist could convert Haiti because social and economic conditions are so bad. It is ripe for revolution.'

Bosch said that there could be no peace on Hispaniola as long as Duvalier was President of Haiti. 'Duvalier is not only a dictator, he is a madman. There is no control over him. I hope the Haitians get the job done as the Dominicans did,' he said, referring to the 1961 assassination of Trujillo.

Hundreds of students gathered and stoned the Haitian Embassy in Santo Domingo. Riot policemen arrested ten, drove off others with tear gas. Inside the Embassy Haitian Consul Jean Louis Charles decided it was time to quit: 'It appears to me that my place must be among the forces fighting to regain the prestige my country deserves.' He asked for political asylum.

The OAS investigation committee arrived in Port-au-Prince at 8.30 a.m., 30 April, and perhaps never in history has a group of nations been so thoroughly insulted in one day. Duvalier did tidy up some, however. He had the rotting bodies, still lying at the charred Benoit house around the corner from the Sans-Souci Hotel, buried.

There was a classic confrontation at the palace between Duvalier and the committee. When they were seated, Duvalier sat silently for an embarrassingly long time while the OAS ambassadors waited. Then he nodded his head to each as though giving a personal greeting. Actually, he was quietly cursing them in the foulest Creole possible. The ambassadors nodded and smiled, gratefully unaware that their parental origins were being questioned. That was all they got before leaving to hear Duvalier's speech, which added another rebuff.

Throughout the day trucks had hauled thousands of peasants into the city and dumped them into the downtown streets. Duvalier wanted a carnival atmosphere for the OAS and he knew how to mix the necessary ingredients. Free rum passed liberally through the crowds, drums beat, bands played, and placards appeared saluting Duvalier. The city donned a mask of revelry.

Late in the afternoon the crowds were directed to the palace, where they pressed around the iron fence until the gates opened, then they poured across the lawn and fanned out from the steps. Duvalier appeared at a balcony, raised his hands victoriously, and smiled his slow, cool smile to a throng intoxicated with rum and excitement. It was an effective contrast. Drums pounded, dancers twisted like corkscrews, and partisans chanted appropriately 'Duvalier or death'. About five thirty the official party stepped out to a small platform erected on the palace steps. The crowd had swelled to some twenty thousand, chanting, dancing, yelling. The OAS committee watched and listened.

Antoine Rodolphe Hérard, former Consul in Chicago, spoke first. He called the Dominicans liars and blackmailers and struck at the United States for cutting off aid. 'We prefer liberty to a crust of bread,' he said. 'If the foreigner wants to take our liberty in return for a crust of bread, we have no need for it.'

Duvalier stood before the microphones, a small, bespectacled man in formal black, swathed in a calm so complete that it seemed narcotic. Tonton Macoutes and officials stood close by. Foreign newsmen crouched directly in front of him, taking notes. He smiled condescendingly, slowly, showing one gold tooth, patiently shushing the crowd with hand pats. When he started speaking without notes his hands hung limply at his sides, never twitching, never clasping, never moving. The unnatural sheen of his face gave him an other-worldly look, which was perhaps intended.

Some of his words, half in French, half in Creole, were vulgar and shocked even his audience. Sometimes he became incoherent.

> Listen carefully, people of Haiti, it is only once every forty years a man is found capable of becoming the symbol of an idea. Every forty years. I am the personification of the Haitian fatherland. Those who wish to destroy Duvalier wish to destroy the fatherland. I am and I symbolize a historic moment in your history as a free and independent people. God and the people are the source of all power. I have twice been given the power. I have taken it, and, damn it, I will keep it for ever.

His face never changed expression, but when he spoke of power, the words ricocheted angrily over the crowd. The reference to 'forty years' was interpreted as a reminder that forty-eight years earlier President Vilbrun Guillaume Sam on 27 July 1915, ordered the slaughter of 167 political prisoners when he was threatened, an act that had brought on the Marine occupation. It also had brought Sam's death. A mob tore him to pieces.

> Those who shot at my children, shot at me. They know that bullets and machine guns capable of frightening Duvalier do not exist. They know that they cannot touch me because Duvalier is firm and unshakeable. I ask you, Haitian people, to raise your souls to the height of the spirit of your ancestors, and to prove that you are men ... put a little marrow in your bones, and allow the blood of Dessalines to flow in your veins....
>
> I don't take orders or dictates from anybody, no matter where they come from. When I had just received my medical diploma, I didn't accept or receive orders from anybody, not even from my own father. As President of Haiti today I am here to continue the

tradition of Dessalines and of Toussaint Louverture ... *I am already an immaterial being....*

No foreigner is going to tell me what to do.

Duvalier declared himself to be a 'predestined' leader with 'a historic mission to fulfil'. He praised the three men who died during the 26 April attack, and joked about the plane that dropped leaflets warning of Operation Dry Cleaning. 'You all know that airplanes have flown over Port-au-Prince, but these little planes are nothing but butterflies.' When he spoke about the men killed, he forgot to mention one by name, and the radio audience clearly heard someone tell him in Creole: 'President, you forgot one.' Anger returned as he spoke of his enemies at home. 'I want to speak about those who entered a foreign embassy in order to give the impression that a man of the people is not capable of directing the affairs of his country. They are filth.'

That was the end of the twenty-minute speech, a remarkable performance despite an explosive anger so uncontrolled that he stumbled over words, started sentences in French and ended them in Creole. But this terrible rage seemed to vanish, like a summer storm, as he walked back into the palace, a cynical smile of victory lighting his face.

The crowd was hoarse with excitement. Their patriarch, their absolute master, had spoken. In small knots they broke off and walked away, some with eyes aglow, heads nodding appreciatively, as if they'd been privileged to witness a true miracle.

Papa Doc had once more made it abundantly clear – this time before a large foreign audience – that he regarded himself above natural law, a Solomon of unquestioned wisdom, a black messiah responsible only to himself, with absolute powers of life and death over every citizen, over every human who dared shadow his path.

14

The Deadline Passes

The person least concerned in Haiti about the confrontation with the United States was Duvalier. He had unshakeable faith in his own words that whatever happened 'we will be here.' And while harried aides and cabinet ministers made anxious suggestions, Papa Doc sat confidently in the gleaming white palace.

But to the world outside Haiti the curtain appeared very certainly descending on the Duvalier regime. The end of the bloodiest tyranny in a hemisphere whose history is rich in dictators appeared to be only a matter of days off. If there was indifference to the situation in the little republic's highest office, there was genuine anxiety throughout the lower echelons, and hasty defence preparations began to take shape. Machine-gun emplacements sealed off the entrances to police and military headquarters and barracks. The price of approaching the palace without authority was one's life. Road blocks were everywhere and mass arrests continued.

Duvalier imposed martial law and announced an 8 p.m. to 5 a.m. curfew in an effort to curb night-prowling terrorists. The United States told American citizens to observe it, and warned them to be ready for evacuation.

Haiti agreed to issue passports for fifteen refugees in the Dominican Embassy residence but insisted that the other seven – including Benoit – must remain, since they were conspirators against the government. It also pulled the troops back from the residence grounds. Among the fifteen who left were Father Georges and former Army Colonel Paul Corvington, once head of the Haitian Military Academy. One of the lucky ones who left said that the seven men left behind 'feel completely insecure. It is a thing of terror. Duvalier lost his mind a long time ago.' Father Georges agreed: 'All the people are terrorized. Duvalier is not sane. To remain in power, that's all he wants.'

Dominican President Juan Bosch talked with newsmen at his home in Santo Domingo and sent them rushing to the cable office with explosive new statements. 'I am going to ask for a break in relations of all American states with the Haitian tyrant,' he said. 'On the next aggression by Haiti we will announce our actions to the OAS, but not from the Dominican capital – from a neighbouring capital.' Bosch was saying that he would invade Haiti and explain to the OAS afterward.

'Duvalier is a menace to the peace of the hemisphere, as he demonstrated when he said that only God could remove him from power.' Bosch denied helping Haitian exiles.

> We are not a nation of conspirators. We are a legal government acting in the full light of the sun.
>
> The situation between Haiti and the Dominican Republic is not similar to tensions which might arise between two other Latin-American nations with the same language, heritage, and customs. ... We share a common frontier. We have not forgotten that we once were occupied by Haiti. An abnormal situation in Haiti is equivalent to an abnormal situation in our internal affairs from the political point of view.
>
> In January in Madrid enemies of the Venezuelan government and the Trujillos met to organize a conspiracy against Venezuela and Santo Domingo with the support of Duvalier. The plot is now under way....

Bosch, with his troops massed on the Haitian border, proposed that Venezuela and Costa Rica join the Dominicans in establishing a 'democratic Latin-American force' to oust Duvalier. He said that the OAS should not allow its tradition of non-intervention to prevent it from exercising 'its responsibility for observance of democracy and human rights which cannot be subordinated to any other principle.'

A few days later, on Sunday, 6 May, war seemed probable. Bosch leaked word that he planned to invade at dawn. The US Ambassador to the Dominican Republic, John Bartlow Martin, talked with Bosch on the telephone, and one Embassy officer called on Foreign Minister Freites. Another warned newsmen at the El Embajador Hotel to be ready for anything. But the attack did not occur.

Martin, Bosch claimed later, argued he should call off the attack because Duvalier would abandon the country before 15 May. Bosch was also told that the United States planned to evacuate some of its citizens and that the OAS would assure diplomatic guarantees in Port-au-Prince.

A rumour soon started that Duvalier would indeed leave before the deadline. It began with an Associated Press report out of Curaçao in the Netherlands Antilles that the Haitian government had asked landing permission for a four-engine plane with six unidentified 'military' men. The Dutch government conferred with the American Embassy in the Hague. The Dutch agreed to let the plane land if the United States would accept Duvalier as a political exile, but then Haiti cancelled the request. This development has remained a mystery to this date.

But other arrangements were made. Hosner Apollon, director of the Régie du Tabac (the 'tobacco' monopoly which funnelled funds into Duvalier's unbudgeted accounts), bought some $6,000 worth of Pan American tickets for the Duvalier family with reservations for 15 May. The destination was Paris, and in addition to the Duvaliers there was one other name, Luckner Cambronne.

A US Naval task force headed by the *USS Boxer* steamed into the Bay of Gonave. The *Boxer* followed a triangular course which brought it within six miles of the Haitian coast. 'We're just standing by,' said Commander M. B. Jackson.

With the *Boxer* were the carrier *Shangri-La* and the *Taconic,* flagship of the Atlantic Fleet Amphibious Force. The task force also included an attack cargo ship, high-speed transport, a dock landing ship, and a tank landing ship. Some two thousand Marines stood ready to land by helicopter (the *Boxer* had twenty) and surface landing craft. The *Shangri-La* offered tactical air support. The force had been on routine mission in the area, but cancelled an exercise which would have taken it away from Haiti.

The British sent a Royal Navy frigate, the *Cavalier,* to the area to be used for the evacuation of British nationals if necessary.

In Washington, 7 May, a State Department official said that the Duvalier government appeared to be 'falling apart', ordered evacuation of dependents of U S government personnel, and urged all other U S citizens to leave because of the 'continued deterioration of the situation in Haiti and the difficulty of ensuring the lives and safety of U S citizens.' Pan American put on special flights to accommodate those who wished to leave.

Bosch commented that if the United States considered the situation grave enough to evacuate Americans, 'we shall continue to think that the problem is even more serious for us. The situation is not easy. We don't know what will happen but we know that Duvalier has killed and terrorized many people and has caused several blood baths. We have to be careful and vigilant.'

Evacuees arriving in Miami told tales of terror.

Internal pressures on Duvalier increased. The Argentine Embassy halfway up the mountains to Pétionville accepted five new asylees. Mme Clément Barbot walked to the Embassy with her three daughters and her sick son, twenty-three. His family safe, Barbot began to manoeuvre more openly.

On the outskirts of Port-au-Prince a band of Barbot men ambushed militiamen in trucks with automatic weapons and grenades; a report said that forty-five were killed. The legends that sprung up around Barbot became magnified out of all proportion.

A group of Tonton Macoute chiefs and militia sped to Martissant to relieve another unit being attacked by Barbot, and stumbled upon the Barbot stronghold. They believed they had him trapped in the house and they showered the house with gunfire until it seemed nothing inside could live. When they kicked down the front door, only a black dog ran out. No one was inside; but Barbot had left behind his stock of weapons and grenades. Some Haitians decided that the shadowy Barbot had the power to change himself into a black dog. They said Duvalier ordered all black dogs shot on sight.

Barbot carried his campaign to Duvalie himself. In Haiti,

where few telephones worked (government telephones to the palace were an exception), Barbot found one that did and got through to Duvalier, promising he would kill him. Duvalier is said to have replied: 'Clément, you will bring me your head.'

One morning Duvalier's secretary found a note on his desk repeating Barbot's threat.

Duvalier put a $10,000 price on Barbot, and during the curfew hours launched house-to-house searches. It became a deadly game of hide-and-seek between two ragtag commando bands dealing death to one another in the alleys and dark streets. In a city already braced for possible revolution and the landing of the Marines, the personal duel between Barbot and Duvalier added an awesome touch.

Barbot deliberately spread word one afternoon that he would be in Pétionville. Major Jean Tassy, one of the Tonton Macoute chiefs, had the area surrounded, and waited. Meanwhile, Barbot slipped into the grounds at Fort Dimanche, disarmed sentries, and stole their weapons for his men.

On board the *Boxer* a 1,200-man Marine force staged a landing drill within sight of Haiti's coast line. Troops charged down the flight deck in full combat gear, boarded waiting helicopters, and flew toward the beach – stopping just short of Haiti's sovereign waters. The force had enough supplies for fifteen days of independent action ashore. Marine officers said that the drill was routine and not related to any specific mission.

In Santo Domingo President Bosch maintained his military on the alert. The OAS committee, which had spent five days, 30 April to 5 May, on the island, went back to Washington to make its report, leaving two members in Santo Domingo in the hope that their presence would be a deterrent to war. The OAS authorized Gonzalo Facio, president of the Council, to enlarge the committee to six members and voted (18 to 0) to give the committee authority to recommend solutions rather than just investigate.

With Facio four members of the committee flew to New York to confer with Haitian Foreign Minister Chalmers, who had taken his country's charges against the Dominican Republic before the UN Security Council.

Chalmers emphasized to the Security Council that Haiti was a small nation, and suggested that it was the victim of racial prejudice.

> The very honour and pride of a small black people have been attacked. Accomplices have been given the task of leading the destruction and bringing about the death of the only Negro republic of the American continent.... In the name of the black world, Haiti, with glory and honour, has carried high [the torch of liberty] and that today, together with the brother peoples of Africa and coloured peoples in general, it will continue to hold high.

The Dominican Ambassador, Dr Guaroa Velazquez, rebutted by citing documents sent to the OAS and reviewing the problems: 'A chaotic situation exists in Haiti. It is a focus and danger spot in the Caribbean. But the reasons for its existence lie in the very nature of the political situation in Haiti, and it does not depend on pressures exercised from the territory of the Dominican Republic.' He suggested that the Council let the OAS handle the dispute.

After a talk with Facio and the OAS group, in which they 'demanded' his support, Chalmers buckled and agreed to let the OAS handle it. Until now the Soviet Union and its chief delegate, Nikolai T. Fedorenko, had been reluctant to enter the dispute for fear they would appear to be on the side of Duvalier. But Fedorenko did get mileage out of the situation. He said that the threat to peace was not in the attitude of the Dominican Republic, but in that of the United States. 'A well-known Japanese proverb says the crab has fun without emerging from the water.' He said that the United States openly was interfering and cited US press reports stating that 1,000 US citizens and a US investment of $50 million in Haiti were a reason. The OAS decided to send three members of its expanded committee to Haiti and keep three in the Dominican Republic.

In another address to the nation Bosch said: 'Haiti is a powder keg and we are a lake of gasoline. We do not know what can happen at any moment ... let the OAS carry out its duty as we have to carry out ours.'

Duvalier changed his stance not at all. 'I am a revolutionary in every sense – not a sentimental type but one of the hard kind. . . . I have for my companion my rifle.'

'If the OAS wants to help,' Bosch said, 'I suggest they send a psychiatrist down to examine Duvalier.'

Jean Richardot, head of the United Nations mission in Port-au-Prince, found Haiti slow in issuing exit permits to UN employees. He cabled a long protest to UN Secretary General U Thant and twenty came through quickly. When Richardot had members of a food and agriculture team evacuated, Duvalier expelled him. US Ambassador Raymond Thurston, faced with the same problem, told Duvalier bluntly that the United States would use force if necessary to get its citizens out of Haiti. The US exit visas also began flowing.

Ambassador Thurston's performance during the month of May set a memorable standard for US diplomats in Haiti, even though over all the United States came off poorly. If he spoke bluntly in May, it was only after frustrating months of trying to reason with Papa Doc. When this failed, Thurston got tough. In his first week as Ambassador, he had spoken enthusiastically about developing a working relationship with Haiti. He found, as had most other ambassadors, that he could not both represent the best interests of the United States and please Duvalier. Now, to protect US citizens, he spoke a language Duvalier did not like but understood. But it was all talk and Duvalier also knew how to interpret it.

As the month progressed, the initiative seemed to slip away from the United States, and to pass to Duvalier. As it was the annual custom of US ambassadors to be out of the country on Duvalier's favourite date, 22 May, Thurston scheduled a trip to Washington on 13 May. This was then changed to the tenth, then cancelled, and finally it was decided that he should sit out the crisis in Port-au-Prince.

The heavy May rains added a touch of soggy gloom to the city. It rained hard most nights and during the day cars and carts sloshed through a sea of sticky grey-brown mud. Many poorer Haitians wrapped up a few belongings, piled into buses or *tap taps*, and headed to what they hoped was a quiet countryside until the storm blew over.

Along the border Haitian and Dominican army patrols maintained normally friendly relations and both avoided anything that might develop into an incident.

Dominican war fervour also had cooled off. Their military leaders were having second thoughts about the invasion. A military appraisal made by US officers in Port-au-Prince stressed the vulnerability of any enemy force penetrating Haitian territory through 'Malpasse' – literally, the bad pass. This was a narrow gorge through which the thin, rough dirt road passed from the Dominican border twenty-three miles to Port-au-Prince. This report somehow got into the hands of Dominican officers and suddenly President Bosch was confronted with a reluctant army with which to back up his tough war talk of the previous days.

Bosch was also having political troubles at home, most of them involving a *coup*-prone military long suspicious of his 'democratic Leftist' ideology. Far-rightist officers began to suspect that Bosch's ploy was to get rid of them while they were out in the field making war preparations. The Dominican President also was having a serious problem on the labour front, and together these problems served to cool off the war-like ardour. In his book, *Unfinished Experiment*, written after his overthrow later the same year, Bosch revealed his war plan for Haiti: he did not intend to go all the way into the neighbouring country; he would scare Duvalier out of office with a minimal penetration backed up by leaflet raids over the palace.

Those suspicious of Bosch also thought he might want a military exercise, perhaps victory in an easy war, to enhance his military popularity and divert attention from the home front. This may have been an unjust view, but there was evidence that the sweep of public feeling – so overwhelmingly for him when he first revealed the Haitian insults – had now turned against him. Since Duvalier had backed down on the points of embassy protection and had allowed some refugees out, the crisis began to look like a war of words and Dominicans seemed willing to let the OAS handle it.

While the Trujillo military machine was far superior to Haiti's in number and equipment, it was a repressive force that no longer had the brutal dictator to guide it. The forces lined up against Haiti were: a 10,000-man army; a Navy 6,000 strong; 4,000 Air Force and 10,000 national police. The Air Force was the best organized and equipped. It had paratroops and an armoured force created by Ramfis Trujillo as an elite corps.

Haiti's leader-lorn army numbered 5,000. Except for the Port-au-Prince units, the militia was composed mostly of untrained youths who carried battered rifles, clubs, or machetes. The Presidential guard of 500 existed only in order to protect the palace. The mobile Marine-trained tactical Dessalines battalion, the sole unit groomed for war, would probably be kept on Duvalier's orders as further palace defence.

Most of the army's modern equipment came from the United States. The tactical battalion was equipped with M-1 rifles, mortars, and machine guns. These were the weapons Duvalier obtained after the Marine training mission was set up in 1959. This equipment, worth approximately two million dollars, technically still belonged to the United States but Duvalier had control of it. In the original agreement, the United States retained a right of inventory as a safeguard that the weapons were used by the army only, and not by the Tonton Macoutes. In practice, US knowledge of how the arms were used was sketchy. About half the weapons were distributed to the army and the other half stockpiled in the palace basement.

The Month of Gratitude speeches continued, but some days they did not follow schedule. Gérard Latortue, head of a highly regarded school of business administration, rejected a pro-Duvalier speech he was told to deliver at La Saline, and instead sought asylum at the Guatemalan Embassy. Emmanuel Mompoint, professor of law at the university, refused to make a speech outlining the legal argument for Duvalier's claim on the Presidency. He entered the Chilean Embassy.

Duvalier, who had not left the palace in three weeks, moved out 300 yards, 12 May, to inaugurate a new five-storey tax building. A public show of confidence was an important part of the psychology of his rule. But even on this abbreviated trip he was accompanied by a heavy guard.

Plaster busts of Duvalier were being sold on the streets, sometimes with something more than just salesmanship. The starting price was ten dollars and they were offered to those who wished to express sympathy for the government.

Haitians, meantime, with a resiliency born of years of want and repression, had adapted their lives to the ways of the tyranny in order to ease their own difficult existence. It was a form of 'accommodation' in which they either suffered indignities quietly or obtained protection at a price, or through the sometimes available sources of influence.

The Duvalier governmental machine was peopled with innumerable opportunists at all levels. There were others who, looking for their own future protection, were open to pleas for help. Thus, Haitians finding themselves in difficult straits with some government agency or official were able to neutralize the threat to themselves by obtaining the help of higher-ups with whom they had a social, monetary, or blood relationship.

This, together with the easygoing Haitian character, may explain the absence of an internal upheaval that would have ended Papa Doc's rule at this opportune moment. Unlike his hot-blooded and usually impulsively violent Latin-American brother, the Haitian lets off steam verbally, and his small wars usually involve a lot of arm waving and angry epithets. He abhors physical violence. He could not believe such ruthlessness, such contempt of human life, as demonstrated by Duvalier, were possible in another Haitian. This is perhaps why it took so long to evaluate their leader in his true light – by which time it was too late.

Diplomats in Port-au-Prince grumbled because the OAS Committee did not investigate violations of human rights while it was in Haiti, but Duvalier would not let it. 'The Haitian government certainly cannot permit any meddling by any state or superstate in its internal affairs,' Duvalier said. In 1962 an OAS commission which wanted to make such an investigation was not allowed in the country.

Among the exiles, Louis Déjoie and Daniel Fignolé went to San Juan, Puerto Rico, and announced the formation of a Haitian government in exile. They listed a sixteen-member Assembly.

The United States ignored the Déjoie–Fignolé move and Bosch angered Déjoie both by declining to recognize the 'government' and by commenting: 'The criterion of the Dominican administration is that a government is not an ethereal juridical entity. A government must have domination of a territory, although this may be small.' Déjoie complained obscurely and mistakenly that Bosch might be in league with Duvalier.

When existence of the Haitian exile training camp at Dajabon in the Dominican Republic became generally known, Bosch was accused of lying when he denied helping the exiles. Events of the next few days indicated that the support was being given without his knowledge. There was also every indication that the corrupt Dominican military was 'milking' the Haitian exile movement, extracting what money they could and promises of greater rewards later for permission to use Dominican territory for training purposes.

New recruits from across the border swelled the exile trainees to sixty-seven and a plan of attack began to take shape. The exile band would cross the Massacre River on 15 May. They expected to be joined by internal resistance forces, secure the city of Cap-Haïtien, reasonably easy to defend because of its geography, announce a provisional government, and call on OAS nations to help them. This became an almost basic goal in all the invasions that followed later.

Dominican Colonel Garrido added panache to the training programme. A gun belt wrapped around his sizeable middle gave him the air of a Hollywood-type Mexican bandido. Garrido, who had attended Catholic school in Cap-Haïtien as a boy, had been a one-time Trujillo military attaché in Port-au-Prince. Some of his Haitian relatives had suffered under Duvalier and he consistently claimed that he helped Haitians 'out of love for Haiti'.

One midnight another prestigious figure visited the camp. When the Dominican Armed Forces Minister appeared, the Haitians scrambled to the rifle range and formed in columns to salute him. He shook hands with each, told them he was satisfied with their behaviour, and promised his support.

The Haitians were elated, their morale lifted, and they talked of the coming invasion with enthusiasm.

The next day a plane flew over the camp and the Haitians hid, thinking it was Haitian. It proved to be Dominican but equally troublesome, apparently scouting for Bosch.

The next day, 13 May, a Haitian hurried into camp to warn that the group was going to be disarmed and should strike across the border immediately. As the confused exiles discussed the situation, Rodriguez and Jacques Cassagnol arrived and called off the invasion. A variety of excuses were given, but it seemed that Bosch had learned of the camp and ordered its dissolution. It was one of Bosch's many clashes with the military.

Jacques Cassagnol told newsmen that he 'disbanded' his '200-man United Revolutionary Forces because of the threat of foreign occupation of Haiti.' He suggested that the United States was supporting another exile group, which he didn't name, and said that the plan was to provoke a Marine occupation of Haiti. He implied that he disbanded his forces rather than contribute to that plan.

A story by Tad Szulc in the *New York Times* said that 'a well-armed anti-Duvalier guerrilla force' belonging to the *Jeune Haiti* Movement was ready to move. He said that the group was headquartered in Santo Domingo, had the support of Dominican student associations, and was directed by the Rev. Gérard Bissainthe, a Roman Catholic priest.

But this attack did not materialize either. For the moment, Duvalier's enemies had eliminated themselves. News stories out of Santo Domingo said that the exiles 'bogged down in bickering'.

US Senator J. William Fulbright, Arkansas Democrat,

chairman of the Senate Foreign Relations Committee, left a Haiti briefing at the State Department fuming because the OAS would not act. He said that the OAS had not shown 'much determination or concern' over a 'chaotic situation'. He added: 'Personally, I regard it as a situation in which the OAS should assume responsibility for what action seems appropriate.' He said that the United States should take unilateral military action if necessary to prevent Communists from taking the country.

Costa Rica's Gonzalo Facio answered: 'The organization has no power to take any action when there is not an international conflict. At present the possibility of armed conflict between Haiti and the Dominican Republic has practically disappeared.' He concluded, with some discouragement: 'I'd like to overthrow him [Duvalier], but we don't have any international justification right now.'

A. A. Berle, former Assistant Secretary of State, listed known Communists in the Haitian government as Minister of Finance Hervé Boyer, Minister of Commerce Clovis Désinor, and Economic Adviser Jules Blanchet. A State Department official commented that Communists in Haiti came from two sources – 'the people's misery and Duvalier's extraordinary tolerance of them.' He said Communists suffered far less repression than any other opposition group, that Duvalier 'thinks they're tame', and that the conspiratorial nature of Haitian society favoured them.

The fifteenth of May was a clear, hot day, and the dazzling white National Palace was set off nicely by grass and shrubs turned deep green by the rains, and by the olive-drab tanks and khaki-clad guard. Duvalier called a press conference.

When Haitians turned on their radio, early in the morning, even the most sceptical began to believe that he was really leaving. For the first time since 26 April radio threats had stopped. Gone were the Duvalier *méringues,* the fiery speeches, and the haunting trouble theme song: *Du feu nan caille-la* (fire in the house). The government station which for twenty days had been calling Duvalierists to arms, threatening government enemies, blasting foreigners, and lauding Duvalier, alternated soft Haitian tunes with classical music. The road blocks had disappeared. Haitians sat home and huddled around their radios. Not a word was uttered – besides station identification – until five in the afternoon, when the press conference was rebroadcast.

Inside the palace two guards stood at the foot of two red-carpeted staircases. Between the staircases were a bare desk and more guards, with their pistols hanging loosely in their pockets or stuck in their belts, rifles in their hands. A big sign pasted on the desk warned: 'No armed member of the military is authorized to enter the President's office.'

The press conference was scheduled for 1.30 p.m. and newsmen sweated in the hot, humid air as they waited. Just before 2 p.m. their names were checked against a list, a guard asked if they had any weapons, and they were ushered into the Salon Jaune next to the President's office in the east wing of the palace.

A large portrait of Toussaint Louverture looked down from the south wall and toward the open window and balcony overlooking the palace yard. Beautiful pink roses decorated a centre table, their fresh touch contrasting with the cobwebs laced across the wooden chandelier and the dusty yellow drapes.

Sirens sounded and a parade of thirty-eight vehicles, mostly trucks loaded with peasants and militiamen, drove inside the grounds and began circling in front of the palace. It was a performance to impress the newsmen. About 2.15 p.m. Colonel Gracia Jacques followed his pot belly out a small door, paused, and announced dramatically: '*Le président de la République*.'

Duvalier came out the door with his head bowed. He walked slowly to his desk, sat for a moment, then peered up through his thick glasses and smiled faintly. It was an entrance both humble and masterfully timed.

An aide quietly read a short statement in English. He stressed points by punching the air with an index finger. Copies of the statement were passed out and one newsman asked if the total censorship would be lifted so that they could telephone or cable stories.

'Yes,' Duvalier said, 'because this is a democracy.'

Duvalier formally assumed the title Chief of the Revolution and accused the United States of trying to create panic in Haiti by evacuating its dependants, but said he believed relations now would improve. He denied reports that he had requested landing clearance for a plane to carry his family to Curaçao. He did not answer direct questions, but covered subjects raised by questions which had been submitted to him in advance on paper.

He denied repression and said that there had only been necessary acts against armed subversion and invasions. 'Unfortunately, this situation has been brought about by the shortcomings of certain men of the United States who should have directed their efforts toward understanding Haiti and its people by studying, comparing, and consequently judging.' The reference was to Ambassador Thurston.

> There is no doubt that the Naval and Air Force missions of the United States have provided valuable technical knowledge to the armed forces of Haiti, as well as to other small countries. However, when some irresponsible officers misuse their knowledge and training, in effect betraying their assigned mission, by meddling in the internal affairs of the host nation, there can be no alternative but to ask for their withdrawal.

He referred to US Colonel Heinl, the former chief of the Marine mission.

Duvalier said that he would never proclaim Haiti a socialist state, as had been rumoured, and that he knew of no provision which allowed the OAS to curb a country's internal violence. 'If it does exist, why has it not been used in Birmingham where there are not only possible threats of violence but actual acts of violence? I sincerely sympathize with the President of the United States in what must be an extremely difficult situation.'

At the conclusion he smiled and said: 'I would like to stay more with you but I'm very busy today.' He rose slowly and shuffled back out the small door into his adjoining apartment.

In New York, at 5.30 p.m., the Haitian Consulate called Pan American World Airways and cancelled the Duvalier reservations on an 8.30 p.m. flight to Paris.

A few minutes later in Port-au-Prince 1,200 members of the militia staged a parade, goose-stepping through the city. About two hundred were armed. One platoon leader crossed the rifle resting on his right shoulder with a machete in his left hand. They wore a crazy-quilt attire of khaki, blue denim, and assorted civilian garb.

Just before 7 p.m. explosions were heard and there was a rush to see if the revolution had come, after all, but it was only exuberant Duvalierists setting off fireworks.

By accident or design, Duvalier outmanoeuvred his enemies. He led the United States to believe that he intended to abandon the country but apparently had considered that possibility only as an option, and perhaps then only for his family. Reports circulated that he had been offered a large amount of money to leave, that he had rejected it angrily. One story said that through US business interests in Haiti a Haitian lawyer persuaded the United States that Duvalier planned to leave and won US co-operation in allowing the situation to remain quiet until he did. Even the Voice of America announced that Duvalier was leaving.

Ambassador Thurston had invited US newsmen on 15 May to his hilltop home, with a splendid view of the city and bay. Some thought it was to watch the fleet sail in and perhaps land the Marines. The fleet did sail around the bay but then headed out to the open sea once more. The *New York Times* commented editorially:

> President François Duvalier of Haiti has weathered heavy storms and is now embarked on his second six-year term of office. He is sailing a pirate ship that is a danger to the Caribbean, the United States, and the whole of Latin America. The longer Dr Duvalier stays at the helm, the greater the danger. Strong, personalist, cruel dictatorships of his type build up violent forces that threaten chaos and anarchy when they are released . . .

One Latin-American diplomat in Port-au-Prince described the situation as like a stalemate in chess – the game ends because Duvalier won't move. 'This time they won't dare have any attitude at all. Some time ago they would have sent Mr Thurston away ...'

The United States did not seem sure what to do next. In Washington, State Department press officer Joseph W. Reap issued a statement to define the U S position:

> We are reviewing the whole Haitian situation, including the constitutional position of the present regime. The question of our relations with the Duvalier government is a matter under urgent study and is being discussed with other governments. We are in a position to protect the interests of the United States and its citizens. As in other similar cases involving recognition problems we are in consultation with other governments in addition to those of all the American republics.

The statement was designed to give the United States time and flexibility to manoeuvre. In Port-au-Prince Ambassador Thurston cut off all contact with the Haitian government, said the United States had 'suspended' relations with Haiti. It was not to be regarded as a 'break' and no official word of the suspension was communicated to the Haitian government. The Dominican Republic, Costa Rica, and Venezuela had broken relations, and Ecuador followed the United States in suspending ties.

Haitian Foreign Minister Chalmers, who learned of the suspension in the newspapers, commented: 'This is a state of affairs that does not exist. It has no basis or precedent in international law.' He added that Haiti did not consider it a provocation. One OAS diplomat, frustrated at being unable to move against Duvalier, said of Chalmers: 'I tried to get a response out of him to give us an excuse to move ... but he just agreed to everything. He couldn't be insulted.'

As 22 May approached Duvalier made many public appearances designed to help regain an air of normalcy. He appeared publicly seven times in three days (19 to 21 May).

Security precautions the first day included a sixteen-vehicle escort with wailing sirens and a staggering assortment of armed guards who milled through the crowd before he arrived, an hour late, for two separate university ceremonies – one at the Medical School and the other at the School of Economics. Two economics professors lectured on the inconveniences necessary for progress. Duvalier appeared at the Rond-Point in the afternoon and stood in the rain as a band played the national anthem in an effort to crank up another parade. Dressed in his usual black, he carried a carbine during the limousine ride back and forth.

The next day he cut a ribbon to inaugurate the new Carrefour Road, made appearances at a special session of the Chamber of Deputies, and at a meeting of the Chauffeurs' Union.

The third day some fifteen thousand more peasants were trucked into the city to prepare for the next day's ceremony. In the afternoon 5,000 of the rural militia paraded through the city led by a detachment mounted on small horses, donkeys, and even oxen. Duvalier went to the Haitian-French Institute to hear himself praised by Haitian judges.

Revived terrorism by Barbot brought back tight censorship. Ten persons were killed as bombs popped around the city in an effort to discourage participation in the ceremony. Sounds of beating drums, police whistles, singing, screams, gunfire, and sirens mingled in the damp air.

A bomb exploded in the back yard of the home of Major John W. Warren, US military attaché, but caused no damage. The Embassy lodged another formal protest when 500 Haitians, some armed, marched noisily across its grounds to a bivouac area.

At the United Nations Secretary General U Thant announced that Haiti had lost its right to vote in the General Assembly because it was two years behind on paying its assessments. Four days later Haiti paid up $22,500 to retain its vote.

As promised, on 22 May Duvalier celebrated the second anniversary of his second term before a screaming crowd of 50,000, mostly peasants brought in to provide the cheers. Standing on the palace steps under a blazing sun, he told Haitians that they faced 'a difficult and even frightening' future. He said Haiti's problems were economic, not political, and announced that a 'new order' was beginning.

He said that an emergency economic plan would be

launched, asked tight discipline 'of all orders and institutions', and said that the nation must pool its resources in a 'national *coumbite*'.[1]

Clément Barbot chose the same day to reveal himself. While Duvalier had his Tonton Macoutes and militia scouring the city for him, Barbot talked with Jerry O'Leary of the *Washington Star* and allowed an Associated Press photographer to take pictures.

Barbot said he had plenty of men, weapons, and confidence. 'I have many friends who say they are with Duvalier now, but inside they are with Barbot.' He said that if he succeeded in overthrowing Duvalier he would abolish the militia, reorganize the army, restore law and order, and hold free elections within six months in which he would be a candidate. 'Duvalier is a madman,' Barbot said. He told O'Leary of repeated conversations with Duvalier in which the President stressed that he wanted to kill 300 persons a year – not 150 or 200, but 300. He said he and his brother Harry, a paediatrician, had almost been caught a few days before. While they were watching television in a hideout, sixty militiamen surrounded the house. In the fight that followed Barbot said he missed having a rifle butt slammed against his head only because he tripped. Flat on his back, he shot the militiaman with a pistol.

The United States still lacked a happy solution to the Haitian dilemma, and it was obvious that a new policy toward Port-au-Prince had to be forged. Duvalier, however, wanted Ambassador Thurston removed and made this point clear to Washington. Seeking to head off this crisis, Washington announced on 3 June the resumption of normal relations with Haiti and the withdrawal of a US Navy task force from the Bay of Gonave. US officials underlined that Duvalier still controlled Haiti and it was in the best American interests to maintain relations.

Papa Doc, sensing weakness in Washington, then moved against the US military mission, ordering its removal. Washington complied and followed up by revealing Thurston's re-

1. A voluntary rural co-operative work team.

call at Duvalier's request. Haiti recalled its Ambassador from Washington.

Thurston's departure provided comic relief to a tense, difficult situation. The day he was scheduled to go, the entire diplomatic corps turned up at the tiny, cramped airport, a sign of rebuke to Duvalier and sympathy toward Washington. The day was typically white hot, the sky cloudless. Minutes before the arrival of the Pan American commercial aircraft that was to take Thurston from Port-au-Prince to Santo Domingo, then Washington, the skies suddenly clouded over and a drenching rain began to fall. Moments later Pan American announced with regrets that because of the storm the plane inbound from Kingston, Jamaica, had overflown Port-au-Prince. The announcement was barely over when the storm stopped, the skies cleared, and a scorching sun returned. As the diplomats filed out of the airport, one turned to another and, pointing skyward, remarked: 'Do you think Thurston believes in voudou?'

The next day Duvalier demonstrated his total repudiation of diplomatic norms and contempt for Thurston or Washington, or both. Instead of waiting two days for another commercial flight to take him out of Haiti, Ambassador Thurston summoned a US military craft, a DC-3, to fly him to Santo Domingo. Only Embassy staff members turned out this time to see the Ambassador off early the following morning. Solemn good-byes were said and Thurston boarded the uncomfortable cargo plane. He stood at the open door and waved. But at that moment, a Haitian officer emerged from the nearby Air Force headquarters and dashed toward the phone. He talked to Thurston briefly and then to Embassy staff members gathered at the door. The Ambassador got off. The officer had told him that the plane had not been cleared to leave Haiti. The officer was exceedingly pleasant as he explained that permission was being requested. There was a long wait. The hot tropical sun leaped up over trees and the temperature mounted. Angrily, Embassy staffers suggested all kinds of alternatives, including an emergency call to US Navy units at nearby Guantánamo, Cuba. Finally it was decided not to wait for permission any longer. Thurston reboarded the plane, again waved good-bye, and the DC-3's engines roared. Just then, however, ancient Haitian Air Force P-51 Mustangs also went into action. Three of them rumbled out of a nearby ramp and in deft ground manoeuvres boxed in the DC-3 so that it couldn't move in any direction. Hopelessly hemmed in, the DC-3 cut off its engines. A visibly angry Thurston emerged once more from the plane and conferred with his aides. The pleasant Haitian Air Force officer, acting almost as if thoroughly sympathizing with the Americans, joined them, then went back to his quarters, apparently to press for permission to let the US aircraft leave. Finally, after some thirty minutes of waiting, the Haitian officer re-emerged from his office, stood on the porch, and clapped his hands to get the attention of the Americans. Then he signalled them, with a wave of his hand, that it was all right to leave. As if by signal, the three P-51s once more lumbered into action, slowly circled out of the way of the DC-3 which Thurston once more boarded and which took off.

This was Duvalier's triumphant *fini* to a confrontation many believed would be his end.

Later an official Haitian note was translated as saying that Thurston no longer was welcome and could return 'only' to pick up his personal effects. This turned out to be a bad translation. When the State Department advised Haiti that Thurston was returning to get the furniture the Haitians fired off an angry cable to Washington saying that Thurston positively could not return. The original note was reviewed, translated again, and discovered to read that Thurston could not return 'even' to pick up his belongings.

15
Invasions Fail

The concentration of Haitian exiles next door in the Dominican Republic deeply concerned Duvalier. Although they were far from a serious threat, he recognized their potential for trouble. Papa Doc moved in typically brutal fashion to halt any further exodus.

One Sunday morning early in June 1963, Dominican border guards on the five medieval-looking towers spaced along the International Road, the middle link of the 129-mile-long boundary, looked out on a curtain of fire and smoke. At 3 a.m. Duvalier's militia and Tonton Macoutes had set fire to hundreds of thatched-roof *cailles* on the Haitian side and begun to burn a swath three to five miles deep, '*a cordon sanitaire*', to be regarded as a war zone. Anyone moving through it without a special permit was to be shot.

Peasants and their livestock were herded back into Central Haiti to grub for a living as best they could. Their crops were burned or abandoned. Haitians could still slip across the border, but the risk was far greater since the refuge previously offered by the friendly peasant was gone. With the peasants removed, Tonton Macoutes and militiamen privileged to travel in the war zone inherited the small but lucrative contraband business between the two countries.

To ensure the war zone's inviolability, Papa Doc named as supervisor a voudou priest and renowned smuggler, Dodo Nassar. Backing up the new appointee was another voudou official, the sinister Zacharie Delva, chief of Duvalier's militia.

Since the latest (April) military purge, former army officers had been filtering across the well-guarded border in twos and threes, hoping to join an exile force rumoured to be forming in the Dominican Republic.

One of these fleeing officers had witnessed, by accident, the massacre touched off by the escape of sharpshooter François Benoit and, having been seen at the spot, had to run for his life. Another trudged for hours, with his pregnant wife at his side, along the rough border terrain without realizing he had crossed into Dominican sanctuary until a peasant brought them water with ice in it. One officer was overcome by heat exhaustion near the border, became dazed, and unknowingly turned back towards Haiti. His dejection was such that, seeing a truckload of militiamen approaching, he offered to surrender. The militia miraculously overlooked him, in full uniform, in the crowd of peasants by the roadside.

Into this ambience of despair, confusion, and desperate hope came the tall, dignified figure of General Léon Cantave, a professional military man who had distinguished himself in the 1956–7 crisis. He arrived in Santo Domingo from exile in New York to help organize the men he once commanded. The year 1963, so full of promise in the beginning, had reached its midpoint. Searing summer heat, that so erodes effort in the tropics, had settled over Hispaniola.

The officers grouped around Cantave faced enormous problems. Many of the rank-and-file recruits were illiterate peasants; they needed weapons and a site for training. Twice Cantave got training under way and twice President Bosch intervened to frustrate the Haitians. Bosch told Cantave that his feelings were sympathetic to the exiled Haitians, but international agreements tied his hands and internal problems demanded all his attention. He said that the Dominican Republic could not be used as a base to attack Duvalier. Cantave gave up trying to win over Bosch and began to work with Pierre Rigaud and Paul Verna, whose Dominican army contacts had been useful before.

The life of an exile is hard anywhere. Differences that at home might have seemed unimportant, or at least subdued, become exaggerated. The politicians brought their prejudices with them, and the little people their distrust of politicians. Some young civilians resented the former army officers for having served Duvalier so long. The exile groups also lived in squalor. Some self-styled leaders used fictitious exile patriotic organizations to raise funds abroad. Few of the exiles in the streets of Santo Domingo could afford the fifty centavos a night for the cramped dormitories such as the 'Dormitorio Hilton', and slept where they could. They spent much of their time looking for money and arms. They quarrelled often over petty matters. Suspicion was rife among them. They accused one another of being informers either for the CIA or one of the many Dominican secret services.

Jeune Haiti had the advantage of some CIA financing, but Father Bissainthe in Santo Domingo still faced an inflexible Bosch. The young Haitian priest, unskilled in the subtleties of Caribbean intrigues, openly told Bosch's aides that he wanted a military camp. They ignored him. He finally returned, disappointed, to New York.

Hemispheric concern over Haiti had not subsided completely. *La Prensa* of Lima, Peru, commented:

> Duvalier had hardly taken over the power when it became obvious that he was incapable of solving the urgent economic, financial, and social problems that beset his country.... His whole personality changed completely, and seemingly overnight.... The cruelty he now exercises to hold his power is almost inconceivable – such a concept could only emanate from a mind affected by the use and abuse of power.... The presence of Duvalier in Haiti is a reproach to the conscience of the civilized world.

In France *Paris-Match* carried a photograph of Duvalier sitting with a carbine between his knees and captioned it: 'President's best friend'. The magazine stirred official anger in Port-au-Prince and the picture was scissored out of copies on the news-stands.

The United States announced that it was suspending the $2.8 million jet airport loan agreement because Haiti had stopped payments on its other loans.

Secret military trials had begun for the officers who took refuge in foreign embassies during the April purge. Duvalier charged them with corruption, desertion, and plotting against the security of the state. Sixteen, including Lieutenant Benoit, were condemned to death *in absentia*.

When asked about Haiti, Juan Bosch said: 'The OAS must find a solution to the situation, but I know they have neither the strength nor the authority to handle it.'

Duvalier, still surrounded by floodlights, tanks, and guns, installed steel doors to replace wooden ones at the palace. He had not gone out since 22 May. Foreign Minister Chalmers and his staff attended the American Embassy 4 July reception, hosted by Edward G. Curtis, the US Chargé d'Affaires.

Inside Haiti two startling events shook and inspired the exiles in the Dominican Republic, particularly Cantave's group, into action.

Clément Barbot and his brother Harry had big things planned for 14 July. They were hiding in a little house near the police post at Cazeau, three miles out of Port-au-Prince on the road north. The house was a few hundred yards from Radio Commerce, visited frequently in the afternoons by Information Minister Georges Figaro and other high officials. All had easy access to the palace. Barbot's plan was to seize Figaro and use him to slip two cars loaded with ten men dressed as militia into the palace that night at eight. Once inside, Barbot expected to be joined by at least twenty Tonton Macoutes whose loyalty he still commanded. The objective was to kill Papa Doc and take over the country.

Barbot was in contact with two other groups, one headed by a former Duvalier congressman and the other by embittered young Hector Riobé, whose father had been slain in the streets by Tonton Macoutes who had then stripped the family of its wealth.

But a hitch developed on the morning of the attack. A peasant told authorities that a man he believed to be Barbot shot at him. Duvalier quickly sent a strong force to the area designated by the peasant. Barbot and his men managed to escape from their hideout into a sugar-cane field. The Duvalierists found the field of tall sugar cane, set fire to it, and shot the men down like rabbits as the flames and smoke flushed them out. Among those slain were Clément and Harry Barbot. Two captured Barbot men were employees of the Régie du Tabac and

Tonton Macoutes. Barbot died three years to the day after Duvalier ordered his arrest and imprisonment at Fort Dimanche.

It was the end of one of Haiti's most unusual figures, a man both hated and respected for his capabilities. More than any other single individual he was regarded as responsible for Duvalier's consolidation in power in the early years. Many who knew him could not believe that the duel unto death had ended in Duvalier's favour. His family, who remained in political asylum for the next year, refused to accept his death as fact, even when the government released pictures of the body. Madame Barbot was certain that her husband would miraculously reappear as he had before.

Despite Barbot's fate, however, Riobé proceeded with his attack. He and his group of young men had assembled a crude armoured car and home-made flame thrower. Just after dusk the same 14 July they drove the heavily laden vehicle up the Delmas Road to Pétionville, scattering tyre-puncturing devices along the road behind them. The heavy armour plating caused the engine to overheat and as they turned to climb the road to Kenscoff the car stalled just in front of the Pétionville police station that also serves as army barracks for the area. The soldiers offered their help to the young uniformed men whom they mistook for militiamen on patrol. The young men refused gracefully the offer of help and when one soldier became too curious and peered inside at the assortment of weapons and the flame thrower, a member of the group panicked and shot him. Exposed, the Riobé band raked the barracks with gunfire, then fled to the mountains on foot.

En route the boys made the mistake of stopping for help at the home of a relative of a member of their group. After they left, the nervous relative informed the police and orders soon went out to arrest members of the youths' families.

In a daring move the boys captured the Kenscoff army post and deliberately set off an alarm. Tonton Macoutes who came running in answer to the call were mowed down. At this point the band could have escaped to the safety of the Dominican

Republic. But Riobé wanted to fight, and what followed earned him a place high on Haiti's growing list of anti-Duvalier martyrs. A planned retreat led them to a cave previously stocked with food, water, and ammunition for a long siege.

The cliff-side cave had only one conventional approach, up a slope devoid of any obstructions suitable for protection. Attempts by the militia and Tonton Macoutes to move in frontally proved suicidal. Dynamite charges lowered by rope from the top of the cliff were ineffective. The battle raged for three days. Although every official effort was made to cover it up, the sounds of the fight could easily be heard over the city.

As a last resort Duvalier sent in his US Marine-trained Dessalines tactical battalion, armed with modern field weapons, including mortars. They, too, were stalemated. Papa Doc's final card was to send Riobé's mother, riding a donkey bareback, up to the cave's mouth to plead with her son to surrender. The reply was a single gunshot. Then silence. The boy, the last survivor in the cave, had given Duvalier his answer.

Even after hours of silence from the cave fortress, Papa Doc's nervous troops refused to budge. When they did, it was behind a barrage of field-weapon fire fit for a major war effort.

How many of Papa Doc's troops paid the final price in the Riobé clean-up may never be known. Eye-witnesses, however, later reported that the stream of ambulances screaming up and down the hill from the city to the cave indicated sizeable casualties on the government side. Unofficial estimates ran to forty Duvalier troops killed; uncounted wounded.

Only two rebel youths were caught. One, Jean-Pierre Hudicourt, wounded in the shoulder in the Kenscoff attack, sought help from a peasant woman who mistook him for a thief and when he fell asleep beat him severely on the head with a pestle. Another youth was killed by Tonton Macoutes as he climbed out of the mountains south of Port-au-Prince. Hudicourt was subjected to the worst tortures the Tonton Macoutes could devise to force him to reveal the names of Riobé's companions. When he lapsed into a coma, Dr Jacques Fourcand, the President's aide, performed a brain operation in an attempt to revive him. His family sought diplomatic refuge. The father,

Pierre Hudicourt, a former diplomat, got into an angry discussion with Mexican Ambassador Bernardo Reyes about whether he qualified for asylum. Hudicourt told him to look up the Latin-American treaty on political asylum and he would find that the Haitian signatory was Pierre Hudicourt. He was accepted. His wife went into the Chilean Embassy.

The heroism of young Riobé fired up the exiles in the Dominican Republic. During the battle they frantically sought weapons so they could open a second front. Léon Cantave proved to be the man of the moment.

Early in July the Dominican army opened its training centre at Sierra Prieta, eight miles north-west of Santo Domingo, to Cantave's recruits. A combination of former military, young civilians and illiterate peasants, called *congos*, and recruited from the cane fields, made up the seventy trainees. They wore Dominican uniforms, steel helmets, and spent most of their time learning to shoot.

But they soon had a problem. The civilians did not like taking orders from Haitian officers whom they had hated in the recent past. Second in command was Colonel René Léon, who had been the commander of the force that crushed an anti-Duvalier Cuban invasion in 1959.

Bosch discovered the camp, summoned General Renato Hungria Morel, Army Chief of Staff, and demanded to know what Haitians were doing training in Dominican army installations. This was one of the two times the camp was broken up. Cantave huddled with his Haitians, then with the Dominican officers and, within a week, training was resumed at Sierra Prieta – this time without the disgruntled civilians. New men were recruited to raise the total again to seventy.

In Washington, meantime, the OAS investigating committee released its findings. It recommended that Haiti observe 'the principle of respect for human rights' and noted that there was an undeniable relationship between violations of human rights and the tension on Hispaniola. The United States expressed concern that Haiti would not let the committee investigate reports of these violations.

On 3 August 1963 the United States officially announced the closing of its AID mission, which it had been phasing out since June the previous year. The United States moved out of a new modern building it had constructed to house its multi-aid offices, and handed the building over to the Haitian government. The only US help in Haiti was for malaria eradication and the food-for-peace programme.

Cantave's exile forces began their long-awaited mission on the steamy night of 2 August. It was 11 p.m. when they crammed into big army trucks and headed north to Dajabon, the border town 350 miles away. The men wore khaki uniforms and new boots. The boots had been a problem for the broad-footed Haitian peasants and they spent the weekend getting their feet adjusted. The truck dropped them at a point near where the Massacre River spills into Manzanillo Bay in north-west Dominican Republic.

Only when they plunged into the river up to their necks and started across were they given the weapons for their mission. The weapons were US-made, the same ones Fidel Castro was said to have given Dominican exiles invading the Dominican Republic from Cuba on 14 June 1959, trying to topple Trujillo.

At daybreak on 5 August the invaders marched into the little rope-making town of Dérac across the bay from Fort Liberté. Dérac could have fallen without a shot being fired, but some of the invaders – with 150 rounds of ammunition apiece – felt they were at war and necessarily had to do some shooting. Against orders they shot two militiamen and one soldier in an outpost. Another invader killed six Tonton Macoutes before he could be stopped. The other Tonton Macoutes were rounded up and jailed. Dérac and all of North Haiti had been warned that the exile invaders were coming but had waited passively.

This corner of Haiti is one vast sea of sisal, a cactus-like plant used, among other things, for the making of rope. The area is the domain of the American-owned Plantation Dauphin, the largest sisal farm in the world. Colonel Léon of the invading army, most recently an employee of Plantation Dauphin, commandeered several jeeps and trucks for the assault on the next town, Fort Liberté. With Fort Liberté in front and Ouanaminthe army barracks to their rear, Cantave decided to hit Ouanaminthe first. From Dérac he called the commander to demand his surrender. A stuttering Captain Paul Edouard refused, surprising Cantave, who had contacted Edouard previously and received assurances of co-operation.

It turned out that Duvalier, aware of the invasion plans, had Edouard under Tonton Macoute guard during his telephone conversation. As a penalty, the commander, many of his soldiers, and hundreds of townspeople were trucked to Port-au-Prince and thrown into Fort Dimanche. Edouard was eventually brought back to Ouanaminthe and publicly executed.

With Ouanaminthe unexpectedly hostile, Cantave proceeded against Fort Liberté, a military sub-district of twenty men under the command of a lieutenant. Cantave sent a captured soldier to the fort with a demand to surrender, and in turn received a reply challenging Cantave to take the fort if he could.

Unknown to Cantave, the commanding officer had quietly evacuated his men from the fort to good positions in nearby colonial ruins to wait out the attack.

It was not much of a battle. A bazooka brought up by the exile force to fire on the fort jammed. Cantave's next heaviest weapon, a .30-calibre machine gun, fired one round and also jammed. One eager invader threw a grenade that exploded near Colonel Léon, wounding him on the left buttock.

With the noise of war the invading army of peasants seemingly crumbled. Cantave, worried about the condition of the arms his men had been handed in the dark, and by a possible attack by Duvalier troops from Ouanaminthe, ordered a general retreat to the Dominican Republic.

Two invaders were left behind, toasting their success prematurely with girl friends and clairin. When they awoke, Cantave was gone. Both were executed on the spot.

The exiles split into two groups for the retreat. Colonel

Léon and his men bored through the sisal in the Dauphin vehicles and scrambled across the Massacre River not far from the compound of the US Grenada Fruit Plantation at Manzanillo. Unluckily, it was a deep spot in the river and they lost most of their arms and ammunition.

Cantave's group moved directly towards the border, and almost ran into a company of soldiers out of Ouanaminthe. There was a debate whether to attack or ask the soldiers to join their force. They compromised and let them go by without a challenge.

Back in Santo Domingo Paul Verna was handling the 'war' news with enthusiasm. Verna, former newsman, diplomat, and Rigaud's friend, worked from the Jaragua Hotel. He gave a skilled performance. When the battle first broke on 5 August Verna announced that a 250-man force had invaded Haiti from an 'island in the Caribbean'. He asked one newsman if he would like to accompany the invaders to Cap-Haïtien that morning or wait until the next day. Fortunately for him, the cautious newsman waited.

Pierre Rigaud, the suave former diplomat who had also gone in with the invaders, suffered a loss. His porter left a briefcase full of documents behind on the battlefield. While Rigaud came home from the 'war' and, unnoticed, sneaked back into his hotel room just down the hall, Verna kept the battle going on paper. He reported that the striking force had grown to more than five hundred as defecting members of the Haitian military joined their ranks. It made good copy, especially one imaginative story he released about two columns advancing across Haiti in a pincer movement.

A few days later, with the help of the Dominican military at the border, a show was put on for the OAS investigation commission and newsmen at Dajabon. Reports had reached Santo Domingo that some Haitian exiles had crossed the border fleeing into the Dominican Republic. The fact that the entire Cantave force had returned was kept secret. When newsmen and the OAS arrived to inquire as to what had taken place they were shown by the Dominican military to a palm-thatched lean-to where eighteen Haitians lazed in the shade. One of these, a young Haitian who convincingly introduced himself to the visitors as Marc Sylvain, was actually a Cantave trooper named Timothé. He gave a colourful, first-hand account of how he defected from the Haitian army to join Cantave's forces. He spoke just enough English to make himself look legitimate, even for the television cameras of the major US TV networks.

When asked where Cantave and the rest of his army were, Timothé answered by tossing his head in the direction of the blue Haitian mountains. Actually, the leaders of Cantave's army were within shouting distance behind the grey walls of the nearby Dominican army fort, and the rest of the rebel force was in a camp on the safe Dominican soil.

The OAS Council in Washington had called an emergency meeting on 6 August to hear Haiti's charge of the 'new aggression' by the Dominican Republic. Haiti accused Bosch of allowing an invasion to be launched from Dominican territory. The Dominican Ambassador denied the charges, and once more an OAS investigating commission headed for Hispaniola. Haiti had declared the north-east of its territory a war zone and quickly announced that the invasion had been routed. The first official news published in Port-au-Prince came on 7 August in a communiqué stating:

Armed bands from the Dominican Republic attacked the outpost of Meyac the night of 4 to 5 August. They proceeded to Dérac where, at 5.30 a.m., they attacked the post, seriously wounding a corporal and two militiamen. At seven thirty 100 men under the command of former General Léon Cantave, seconded by Colonel Pierre Paret, Lieutenant-Colonel René Léon, Captain René Jacques, Lieutenant B. Philogènes, Lieutenant Louis Villemenay, and Lieutenant Louis Elie attacked the Casernes of Fort Liberté with automatic arms and grenades. The battle lasted two hours and the rebels were defeated. They fled, leaving behind dead and wounded as well as arms and ammunition. They were clad in khaki uniforms worn by the Dominican army and had shoes of Dominican make. The rebels fled, some of them throwing themselves into the sea. Others, the former officers, returned to the Dominican Republic in two cars obtained from the Dérac cordage factory.

Except for the usual mass round-up of anti-government suspects by the Tonton Macoutes, Port-au-Prince remained calm through the brief invasion. There was a flurry of excitement when a US businessman from Dérac said that the invaders had executed twelve Tonton Macoutes, and when the government airlifted reinforcements to the threatened area. The government later allowed newsmen to fly to Cap-Haïtien, which one erroneous report claimed was under attack, to show that all was calm. Major Joseph Lemoine, security chief in Cap-Haïtien, refused to let foreign newsmen go by car to Fort Liberté. 'We just don't want you to go there, that's all,' Lemoine said. Instead, they were flown over the area.

Before the invasion quickly collapsed the United States rejected a plea from the Cantave–Rigaud group for aid to the invaders and to recognize a provisional government. President Bosch was angry with the military, who were in turn unhappy with Cantave who had promised to take Cap-Haïtien the first day. Cantave was miffed at the military for giving him what he described as defective weapons. He claimed in numerous cases that the ammunition his men were handed did not match the guns they were carrying.

Following the fiasco the *New York Times* published an editorial commenting: 'Haiti remains Haiti'. Duvalier interpreted this as an insult and called in his new press adviser, Gérard de Catalogne, who had just returned from Europe on a mission to decorate every West European newsman who would accept the distinction. The white-skinned De Catalogne cranked out a reply that raked the United States. In part it said: 'The United States thinks they can treat the Negroes of Haiti as they treat the people of colour in America. We are Africans by race, French by language, and American only by geography.' The editorial was broadcast repeatedly for three days.

Cantave pleaded and won Dominican military support for another chance. The Haitians moved to a border camp at Don Miguel, almost within a stone's throw of their homeland. Cantave lived in a little tobacco shed and his army slept on the ground under palm fronds. Their second chance came on 18

August. This time they numbered seventy-two, and Colonel Léon led the column.

The day was specially chosen. It came as the Dominicans were celebrating their day of 'Restauración', liberation from Spanish rule. The celebrations offered an excellent cover.

President Juan Bosch visited the border town of Capotillo, where insurrection against the Spanish began on 16 August 1863. He received a twenty-one-gun salute and the Dominican Air Force flew past in review. From there Bosch went to the city of Santiago for a full military parade. In preparing for these festivities the Dominican army had broadcast over the national radio in both French and Creole advising Haitians near the border that the celebrations included gunfire and they should not be alarmed. But not all the firing that day came from celebrating.

At 6 p.m. the preceding night, 15 August, the exiles under Colonel Léon left their camp, moved across the Massacre River, and followed a peasant guide up the rugged hills that led to the pleasant little coffee-growing centre of Mont-Organisé. Unknown to the invaders (Cantave preferred they be called liberators) Duvalier was in the process of replacing the garrison. The day before he had ordered eighteen men at the mountain post trucked down to Ouanaminthe to be taken to Port-au-Prince, leaving on temporary duty only one medical corps corporal and two soldiers.

Colonel Léon took the town easily. The two soldiers fled in their underwear and the corporal surrendered and joined the raiders. The medic told them that a replacement garrison was on the way.

Colonel Léon had twelve men set an ambush a mile and a half down the road at Croix Rouge, where a steep curve slowed traffic. The men sat under a hot sun and watched a new detachment chug its way up the mountain road in two trucks and a Volkswagen. The waiting made them anxious, and Timothé, who had done an imaginative job of playing the part of Marc Sylvain for US newsmen at Dajabon, fired before the convoy entered the trap. Their cover broken, the other exiles threw grenades. One scored against the first truck, destroying it and most of its occupants. But the other backed down the road out of danger and the little Volkswagen peeled off in a swift turn and raced away at full speed. Soon thereafter a Haitian Air Force AT-6 came over on reconnaissance. As it flew low over the hill town, the raiders tilted up their old .30-calibre machine gun (the same one that failed against Fort Liberté) and riddled the plane's tail assembly. It limped back to Cap-Haïtien for repairs.

While part of the raiders patrolled, the others set up camp at the little army post. They told the townspeople that Duvalier had fallen in order to quiet their fears about later retaliation from the Tonton Macoutes.

At dusk an advance guard sent back word that he heard shooting and believed government troops had arrived and were trying to surround them. Colonel Léon, keenly aware of his disadvantages in weapons, ordered his forces to retreat to the border.

Again not all the raiders heard the withdrawal order. Some who were drinking with townspeople stayed, as did the twelve-man ambush group at Croix Rouge. With their commander gone, the stay-behinds had an uproarious time in town. Two Tonton Macoutes were killed and five had their homes burned.

Colonel Léon and his main group crossed the Dominican border at Trinitaria, and the rest of the band dragged in several days later bringing with them fifty villagers who were afraid to stay behind and face the new Duvalier troops. When all arrived at Dajabon, they found reinforcements of their own preparing to cross the border. Twenty-six exiles had missed joining the invasion by hours.

Colonel Garrido, the Dominican military commander at Dajabon, told newsmen: 'If the Americans want to see Duvalier fall, they should get some machine guns to these poor bastards.'

Foreign Minister Chalmers again protested to the OAS in Washington and threatened to take his case to the United Nations. He told an emergency meeting of the OAS Council that the Dominican Republic had been guilty of direct aggression in the invasions of 5 August and 15 August and indirect aggression by allowing Haitian exile broadcasts over Dominican Radio asking Haitians to rise up against Duvalier. Chalmers asked the OAS to appoint a committee to supervise the border area and prevent new incursions. The Council adjourned without taking action, suggesting that the investigating committee appointed look into the incidents.

The Dominican representative, Dr Arturo Calventi, again denied the charges, and said they were made 'by a dictatorship that has violated every basic Inter-American principle and which is hardly in a position to accuse others.'

In Haiti, on 23 August, a special session of the legislature suspended constitutional guarantees over individual rights and gave Duvalier extraordinary powers for six months. Since there had been no guarantees or individual rights anyway, and Duvalier already had complete power, these measures did not draw as much attention as a decree stripping fifty-four Duvalier foes of their citizenship and their property. Among those named were Cantave and his officers and Paul Magloire, as well as the heads of the known exile organizations.

The legislative session was regarded as part of a show staged to impress the OAS Committee, which had returned to investigate. A crowd of government employees cheered as speakers in the legislature called for action against the exiles.

The OAS Committee met with the diplomatic corps and heard warnings from the ambassadors that unless the committee did something about the forty-four people in asylum, the OAS was going to fall into disrepute. They wanted the committee to press the issue of safe-conduct out of the country for the asylees. One ambassador said that the situation 'has turned our embassies into jails for President Duvalier's political opponents.' The ambassadors also complained that the government did not guarantee the sanctity of the embassies or even of the persons of the ambassadors.

A story began to circulate in Port-au-Prince about a new game called 'Haitian roulette'. You played it by driving past the heavily guarded palace at night on four bad tyres. 'If you have a blowout you lose.'

The International Commission of Jurists, with headquarters

in Geneva, Switzerland, issued on 15 August a press statement on Haiti:

> For over a year the International Commission of Jurists has been collecting testimony and first-hand documentation on the political and social situation.... What emerged showed that human rights and fundamental liberties are totally disregarded by the government of François Duvalier. But before reaching a conclusion with respect to this regime, the Commission wanted to check the documentation it had gathered by making direct investigation within the country. With this in mind, the President of the Commission sent a personal letter to President Duvalier on 11 April 1963, asking him kindly to authorize the dispatch to Haiti of a group of observers who could gather information about the state of affairs on the spot. As no reply was received, a cable was sent on 30 May 1963, and, later, a second letter on 11 July. These were also ignored. ... The International Commission of Jurists [thus] considers that it is free to make public such information as has come to its notice....

What followed was as devastating an indictment as has ever been handed down against any regime. Coolly and implacably, the Commission revealed the political, social, and economic conditions of Duvalier's Haiti; the Tonton Macoutes were directly referred to, some of their multitudinous victims named; their extortion and blackmail practices were investigated, their methods of 'interrogation' revealed. The total cost (approximately fifteen million dollars per year) of maintaining the Tonton Macoutes, the 8,000-man militia, and the palace guard, 500 strong – in short, for keeping the police of a police state – was documented. (Their maintenance amounted to more than one half the country's yearly budget – approximately twenty-eight million dollars.) No stone was left unturned, or unthrown. Freedom of the press was investigated – and found totally lacking, 'despite the fact that there are no legislative provisions for any sort of restriction or censorship. In the absence of legal means ... the government uses physical force.' Individual liberties – to worship, to leave and re-enter the country, to organize trade unions, to be tried by one's peers ... to be tried at all – were delved into and found simply not to exist.

The Commission ended its report by examining Luckner Cambronne's highly lucrative National Renovation Movement whose

> programmes of work are pure fiction; it is not hard to guess where the funds of the NRM go....
>
> This aspect of the dictatorship of François Duvalier gives it a unique character. In today's world there are many authoritarian regimes. Generally speaking, they are the reflection of some ideology. The tyranny that oppresses Haiti does not even have that excuse; its only object is to place the country under tribute in order to ensure the future affluence of those now in power.

In New York Cantave persuaded the *Jeune Haiti* exile faction to join him and won some CIA financial support. United States officials were convinced that forces outside Haiti could overthrow Duvalier. The CIA aid given Haitian exiles, their leaders complained at the time, was limited and a manner of keeping their 'fingers on the exiles' pulse'. To show the CIA the exiles could muster an offensive and keep it going, and also to create an impression there were still rebels in Haiti, Cantave sent still another group across the Massacre River. Theirs was the minuscule unit of eighteen inexperienced men who had missed the Mont-Organisé expedition. This tiny group made a one-day move against the little Haitian town of Ferrier, killed the mayor, and raced back to Dominican soil.

After this incident, Duvalier moved more Tonton Macoutes to the north, but was careful not to weaken the defences of Port-au-Prince, where he maintained his greatest concentration of strength. He regarded the border attacks as possible diversions for a major thrust on the capital.

The Ferrier action, limited though it was, showed good faith and the CIA continued supporting Cantave. His force grew to 210 men, and one night he received a new arms supply from the United States, for which he had long waited.

Dominican Colonel Garrido and two Haitian rebel officers went to a clearing some two miles from Dajabon, near the military airfield, lit flares, and waited. At midnight on 26 August a heavy plane flew in low from the coast, and made two passes over the flares, parachuting crates of arms and ammunition. A truck carried them to Dajabon, where they were stored in a spare room at Garrido's house.

An argument developed between Garrido and Cantave over the arms. Cantave wanted the men to train with them, and the Colonel felt that they should be distributed only when the men crossed into Haiti. Cantave said that the men had gone into Haiti three times with arms handed them at the last minute. He demanded that they be allowed to train with the attack weapons. Garrido finally agreed, and the rebels were handed the kind of weapons they had dreamed about – mortars, bazookas, M-1 rifles, .30-calibre machine guns, and M-3 sub machine guns. At this point Cantave was paying $400 weekly to Garrido for camp expenses.

Early in September Foreign Minister Chalmers submitted a letter to the United Nations Security Council requesting it to consider Haitian charges against the Dominican Republic. He said that the dispute might 'threaten hemispheric security and international peace.'

Shortly the OAS Committee submitted its investigative report on the happenings in Hispaniola. It offered a peace plan that called on Haiti to be more careful in observing the rights of diplomatic asylum and to hurry in granting safe-conduct out of the country for the refugees. This number had been reduced on 1 September when Duvalier released twelve from the Brazilian, Chilean, Ecuadorean, and Guatemalan embassies. The committee also urged the Dominican Republic to prevent subversive activities by Haitian exiles in its territory and to take special measures to prevent exile border raids.

Haiti was not impressed and rejected the plan, apparently because it did not condemn the Dominicans. It called for a UN investigation leading to such condemnation. 'The regional system OAS having failed, it is now appropriate for Haiti to bring her case to the United Nations,' the Haitian UN representative said.

Cantave worried constantly about Bosch dismantling his new camp. The Dominican army meanwhile insisted that Cantave next attack Ouanaminthe. They even set the time and date, 22 September. As had happened before, word of the attack spread across the Massacre River and through North Haiti.

Duvalier reinforced the garrison at Ouanaminthe. The commander, a Major Lherrison, was reported to have prepared his men by holding a voudou ceremony, letting the blood of a bull in sacrifice. The defenders smeared it on themselves in the hope that it would make them immune to bullets.

Cantave delayed agreement on the 22 September date, but gave in when told that it was either the attack or the disbanding of the camp. Some of Cantave's officers had wanted him to move into the south of Haiti close to Port-au-Prince or stage a guerrilla-type action in the hills. They did not want a make-or-break frontal attack on Ouanaminthe. Cantave, at fifty-three, was not equipped physically to lead a guerrilla campaign even if he had been free to do so.

Garrido had powerful arguments of persuasion, including a promise of air and artillery support if needed. A Dominican plane was to be painted with exile markings.

At 4 p.m. on 22 September the rebels assembled and were issued khaki uniforms. Except for fifteen porters all 210 men were armed. Officers carried M-3s and wore .45 automatics. There were thirteen .30-calibre machine guns, mortar squads, bazooka teams, and all the ammunition they could carry.

Four trucks moved them down river, and at 10 p.m. on a moonlit night they began crossing. A Dominican sergeant assigned as guide led the first platoon across and on the Haitian side raised his rifle and fired a shot. The rebels hit the ground, thinking they were under attack. Cantave, this time equipped with walkie-talkies, called the advance platoon to ask what had happened. A lieutenant explained and the angry voice of Cantave crackled back: '*En avant*, even if we have been betrayed.' Whether the shot was accidental or a signal to indicate the platoon had reached the other side of the river safely, or even a betrayal to Haitian forces, could never be established. The raiders themselves, however, later felt that the shot tipped their hand. Considering the effectiveness of the Haitian grapevine it might have been an unnecessary warning in any event.

Once inside Haiti they faced a long march across a savannah to Ouanaminthe. It was rough marching in the moonlight, and even rougher when clouds obscured the moon. Colonel Léon, second-in-command, collapsed from what was believed to be a heart attack and was left behind with a former Haitian medical student.

An all-night march, lengthened by a mix-up in directions, had exhausted the raiders by the time they reached the outskirts of Ouanaminthe the next day. (Some felt that the wandering had not been accidental.) They met peasants moving out into the field to work and were told that Ouanaminthe was expecting them.

At 6 a.m. fifty raiders had their target in view: the two-storey yellow barracks. Their first shot, a bazooka round which fell short, started the battle. Government troops answered with a barrage of .50-calibre machine guns. As had happened at Fort Liberté, the defenders had moved out of the barracks and assumed advantageous positions. This time they dug in at a cemetery, took positions inside a school, and even placed one light machine gun in a tree dominating the field. As bullets flew, no co-ordinated battle plan presented itself.

Cantave himself made a suicidal run at the fort, firing a carbine, but a self-appointed bodyguard knocked him to the ground.

The Haitian defenders remained in their positions and laid down heavy fire across the field, which had been stripped bare of cover. One rebel platoon made it to within a few yards of the fort, and was met by a group of militia who yelled and beckoned them to enter the fort. The squad leader did not accept the invitation, which turned out to be a trick to get them to break cover.

Cantave received word that the platoon assigned to take the airfield had failed. Its mortar fire had sailed over the defenders and into the town of Ouanaminthe. At 10 a.m. a Dominican P-51 made two passes over the battlefield. It was not the exile plane, however. Haitian defenders fired at it on both passes. It banked hard and flew back toward the Dominican border.

Cantave again ordered retreat. The platoon assaulting the fort, led by young Fred Baptiste, had skirted the cemetery and did not hear the orders. It continued fighting. Some pockets of defenders were eliminated, but most were so well dug in that it would have been a costly task even for a professional army to dig them out.

Baptiste, and practically every member of his squad, suffered wounds early in the fight, but carried the battle on into the late afternoon, when they realized they were alone at the attack. At 2 p.m. a Haitian Air Force plane flew over the battlefield and landed at the Ouanaminthe landing strip, which was clear indication that the Cantave forces had not taken it, one of their early objectives. Baptiste and his men fought a rearguard action to evacuate the wounded who had been left on the battlefield. But the defenders of Ouanaminthe stayed in their dug-in positions all night and through part of the following morning, firing all the while as if the enemy were still before them.

When the battle opened in the early morning – and already some of Cantave's lost invaders had decided to return to Dominican soil – a .50-calibre machine gun on top of the Haitian border customs-house opened fire on them, and the bullets splattered against the Dominican customs-house at the opposite side of the Massacre River. Bullets from the Haitian machine gun also struck a Dominican schoolhouse. The sound of battle gave many Dominicans the mistaken impression that their town was under attack from Haitian forces across the river. Reports of the town of Dajabon under Haitian bombardment spread quickly to Santo Domingo and the military command in the area did nothing to clarify the situation.

Bosch was informed that Dajabon was under Haitian bombardment and Foreign Minister Hector Garcia Godoy called in foreign diplomats to acquaint them with what was supposedly taking place, describing the situation between Haiti and the Dominican Republic as 'very grave'. He said that Dajabon had been attacked and its 8,000 inhabitants had fled in panic. A noon report on the official Dominican radio confirmed the attack, stating that Bosch was once more giving an ultimatum to Duvalier. This time Haiti had three hours to cease the aggression, punish the guilty parties beginning with Duvalier, and offer immediate satisfaction and reparation. The broadcast ultimatum was repeated in Creole with the added warning that Haitians living near the palace should clear the area because it might be bombed. The Dominican Air Force reported its readiness to make a leaflet-drop over Port-au-Prince with the same warning.

While the misinformed Bosch government treated the matter of Haitian aggression with urgency, the remnants of Cantave's army were straggling back across the Massacre River to the safety of the Dominican Republic. Dominican soldiers, aware of the resale value of firearms, stripped the Cantave raiders as they clambered up the riverbank. Weapons too large to conceal, such as bazookas and .30-calibre machine guns, were stacked in neat rows in the archway of the customs-house on the Dominican side of the international bridge in full view of the Haitian border.

Back in Dajabon, Cantave peeled off his blood-soaked uniform, showered away signs of battle, and put on a light business suit. When the plane of army investigators arrived from Santo Domingo along with newsmen to investigate the 'aggression' they met a cool, nattily dressed Cantave carrying an overnight bag stuffed with Kent cigarettes.

Fifteen of Cantave's men did not return. Thirteen were killed in battle and two of the wounded were taken prisoner. Despite the gravity of their wounds they were made to load the dead on trucks. The two wounded men were then tied atop a pile of corpses for the long, bumpy ride to Cap-Haïtien. In Haiti's second city, after digging their own grave they were executed. Three rebels were back at their jobs in Puerto Rico after a weekend of war as if nothing out of the ordinary had taken place.

One of the first raiders to die was a brash, tough army veteran, Captain Blucher Philogènes, who had bragged that he was immune to bullets. On the battlefield he acted that way and was cut in two by machine-gun fire.

On the orders of the President, Lieutenant Abel Jérome cut Philogènes's head off and placed it in a pail of ice. Duvalier dispatched a special Air Force fighter to fetch the head. Why did Duvalier want the head delivered to him at the palace? Weird stories circulated around Port-au-Prince which told of Duvalier sitting alone with the head for hours, trying to communicate with it. In superstition-prone Haiti, where the dispensing of gossip is one of the few free pleasures of life, only Duvalier knows the truth.

The army investigating commission of high-ranking officers were greeted in Dajabon by the now jovial Colonel Garrido, a picture of innocence, who explained that the shooting was really nothing but Haitians firing at rebels fleeing into the Dominican Republic. But Bosch, in the Dominican capital, had made a request to the OAS to investigate the Haitian attack. His move threatened to reveal the history of the four Cantave attacks and the Dominican army's involvement before the legal hemispheric body. But the Dominican army leaders were not perturbed, knowing that the OAS investigators seldom get past diplomatic protocol.

Although Ouanaminthe had been a complete failure for Cantave and another victory for Papa Doc, the Dominican army leaders felt it was useful in setting the stage for a *coup d'état* against President Bosch that came two days later.

The ouster of Bosch quickly obscured the Ouanaminthe episode and there was little public realization of the role played by the Dominican military in Cantave's failure.

The Dominican military, at 7 a.m. on 25 September 1963, announced that Bosch had been deposed, and later in the day proclaimed the installation of a civilian junta to replace him. The military in their communiqué, endeavouring to justify their *coup,* stated that there was 'a chaotic situation', that the country was saddled with 'incapacity', and complained of 'dangerous improvisation of international incidents which in addition to endangering the prestige of the Republic could have led to a serious and unnecessary international conflict.' Although this was one of the army's official excuses for the overthrow, the reasons were well known to most Dominican and foreign observers: the army feared Bosch and the democratic leftists, and, above all, sought to retain its privileges.

Antagonism had built up towards Bosch among segments of the Church, business, and labour as well as the military. Loud accusations of Communist infiltration in his government and the embarrassing Haitian intrigues, of which he was innocent, made him an easy target. In exile a year later, Bosch wrote of his seven months as the Dominican Republic's first freely elected president in thirty-two years. In his book, *Unfinished Experiment,* he attempts to analyse Papa Doc:

> Psychologically, Duvalier is a type of man found in primitive societies. The more power he acquires, the more he is filled with a haughtiness that day by day transforms him physically, numbing him. So that he resembles nothing so much as a puppet that keeps swelling and swelling until it must either flop over on its back or explode.... In such creatures the effects of power are more than physical; there are also corresponding changes in the soul, which gradually desensitize them to all human feeling, until they become only receptacles of uncontrolled passions. These men are dangerous. They create an aura of sorcery. They deny being simple human beings, mortal and fallible, and consider themselves living representatives of the dark forces that govern the world.

Following his defeat, Léon Cantave was kept in detention at the 27 February Army headquarters camp across the Ozama River from Santo Domingo. Then on 18 October he was permitted to leave the country for New York.

Duvalier, delighted that his arch-enemy Bosch had been overthrown, decided against pressing his protests. He preferred not to stir anger among the new Dominican leaders.

The remainder of the Cantave army, except for the wounded left behind in the Dajabon infirmary, was loaded into two big trucks from the Esperanza Sugar Mill and dropped at the unused former Nigua Lunatic Asylum, about twelve miles from Santo Domingo.

Another frustrated exile episode developed after Ouanaminthe. Three exiles assigned the task of infiltrating Haiti, armed with sub machine guns, .45 automatics, and grenades, waited nine months at their appointed places for Cantave's invasion. They survived by buying the loyalty of local Tonton Macoutes (standard rate, twenty dollars). Finally giving up, they picked their way back. One caught a ride on a fishing boat and ran into a new bunch of exiles – this time anti-Castro Cubans – operating out of Punta Presidente, the Dominicans' closest point to Cuba. The Cubans turned him over to Dominican authorities.

Cantave's camp was finished. The raiders were left to scratch for a living as best they could, for he no longer could help them. Some borrowed money to rent a house, ate corn meal donated by the Catholic Welfare Services (CARITAS), and tried to make the best of a miserable situation.

Some of the *Jeune Haiti* group, which had found CIA support before, went back to New York and found it again. A chosen group was picked up quietly, taken to upstate New York for processing, then driven in covered trucks to a Special Forces training camp in North Carolina.

The Haitians were trained in guerrilla warfare, from 1 October until 1 November, and coached in the objective of dropping five-man teams into Haiti to form and train local guerrillas in clandestine operations. But suddenly the organizers of the scheme had a change of heart. The little group was taken back to New York. It was the beginning of the 'don't rock the boat' policy toward Haiti that was continued by the Johnson administration after the 22 November assassination of President Kennedy.

The old soldiers having failed with their orthodox invasion attempts, it was now the turn of youth to attempt the overthrow of Papa Doc.

16
President for Life

When Georgia-born Benson E. L. Timmons III arrived in Port-au-Prince in January 1964, Duvalier finally had a US Ambassador to his taste. Like his predecessors, Timmons assumed his post eager to exercise diplomatic skills within the US policy described as 'cool and correct'. But unlike Drew, Newbegin, and Thurston, Timmons's favour lasted beyond the usual honeymoon period.

He did have an uncertain start, however. Duvalier made Timmons wait five weeks for an audience and, when it was granted, treated him to a lecture (described in Washington as 'unpleasant') on how a diplomat should behave.

While Timmons went out of his way to maintain a working relationship with Duvalier, many others were not so successful. Nestor Chavannes, Duvalier's inspector of Caribbean embassies, returned from a trip to Nassau and at the airport heard that he was wanted at the palace. He fished a return-trip ticket to Nassau out of his pocket, used his diplomatic passport to get back on the plane, and left minutes before the arrival of the Tonton Macoutes.

Duvalier on 3 February 1964 ordered his legislature into special session to brand five deputies as traitors and strip them of immunity and office. The purge took a surprising twist when it included his brother-in-law Lucien Daumec and Cap-Haïtien Tonton Macoute chief Jean-Baptiste Sam, his wife, and son. Daumec, the short, lean former Marxist intellectual who affected the Papa Guédé garb so favoured by Duvalier, had a long history in the Haitian left. He had been part of the *La Ruche* student group which touched off the ouster of President Lescot. He was a devoted follower of Estimé and a member of the Haitian Communist party, when it dissolved itself to avoid embarrassing Estimé. Daumec had married the sister of Duvalier's wife, and worked in the palace as a high-level adviser and speech writer. He had survived the difficult years as Duvalier solidified his power, two cabinet shake-ups and then, like most others who stayed too close for too long, was struck down. After his arrest Duvalier saw to it that his wife got an immediate divorce. More purges were in store.

When two Canadian Jesuit priests returned after a visit home, a delegation of priests met them at the airport. Tonton Macoutes searched the luggage of the arrivals, Father Paul Laramée and Brother François-Xavier Ross. They found a picture of a man whom they identified as former President Paul Magloire, a letter, and some magazine articles which they viewed as subversive. Laramée, Ross and one of the greeting delegation, Father Paul Hamel, were arrested and taken to Fort Dimanche.

The 'evidence' was never shown to the Papal Nuncio or to Canadian Embassy representatives who protested the arrests. It turned out that the picture, which did bear a resemblance to Magloire, was of a construction boss named Félix. It had been taken at the Jesuit retreat house Villa Manrèse in 1959. Magloire had been out of the country since 1956. The letter was a copy of a request to the German church organization, Misereor, outlining conditions in Haiti and asking for a $50,000 donation. The articles included one from the *Reader's Digest* about Haiti and the 1963 International Jurists' report on Haiti. Ironically, the charity request had been approved, but was cancelled after the priests' arrest.

The 'evidence' was unimportant. Duvalier wanted to get rid of the Jesuits. Before the month was over, eighteen Jesuit priests and brothers were expelled for an 'attempt against the security of the state'.

Father Gérard Goulet, superior of the Jesuits in Haiti, commented that 'the Jesuits in Haiti received, for the second time in two centuries, the order of expulsion. In 1763 they had been found to be too devoted to the religious interests of the black slaves; in 1963 they were found too influential and dangerous for the security of the state. Deep down it was under new pretences the same traditional calumnies ...

'One throws stones only at trees loaded with fruit, says a Haitian proverb. Our mission has not ripened all of its fruit yet, but the numerous buds await the favourable hour.'

The three priests were interrogated by ten officers and three cabinet ministers, including Foreign Minister Chalmers. The questions dealt mostly with the retreat villa's radio station: how it operated, how it received its news, what they knew of the activities of the late Clément Barbot, who had frequented the villa following his release from prison, whether any had heard Barbot's confessions, what knowledge they had of the Tonton Macoutes.

After five days Father Hamel was released from Fort Dimanche and put under house arrest. The next day Police Chief Fred M. Arty led a delegation of police and Tonton Macoutes to close the Villa Manrèse. He demanded a list of all the people who used the retreat, searched every corner, and began sealing the villa. Priests were told to take 'what they need'. The domestic staff, three girls, were imprisoned. The nuns were sent to their motherhouse and the brothers to the archbishopric.

On 8 February the government held a meeting with the remaining Catholic bishops in Haiti, and two days later closed the seminary, also run by the Jesuits, placed the priests under house arrest, obtained addresses of the fifty-two seminary students, sent them back to their homes, and ordered them to report daily to police posts. The priests asked that they be allowed to complete the school year and were told in apparent seriousness: 'We cannot take the risk, the danger is too great. The Jesuits can overthrow the government in four months.'

On the thirteenth day after their arrest Father Laramée and Brother Ross were taken out of prison and with the other priests – eighteen in all, including those from the Jesuit parish Quartier-Morin – escorted to the airport and expelled from the country.

From Ottawa, Canada, Foreign Minister Paul Martin sent a strong protest, but Haiti simply ignored it and repeated that the Jesuits were expelled 'to preserve internal peace and the territorial integrity of the country'. The reply added that

Haiti had terminated the agreement of 1953 under which the Jesuit mission had assumed directorship of the seminary.

The closing of the seminary, along with the expulsions, was perhaps the greatest single Duvalier blow against the Catholic Church. Already leaderless, the Church now had its avenue of growth stunted.

With what he regarded as a tame US ambassador on hand, Duvalier renewed his periodic pitch to bring back American tourists and American aid. On 28 February Foreign Minister Chalmers issued the following communiqué:

In a cordial atmosphere, conversations took place recently at the palace between their excellencies M. René Chalmers, Secretary of State of Foreign Affairs and Cults; Clovis Désinor, Minister of Finance and Economic Affairs; Dr Hervé Boyer, Minister of Commerce and Industry; Luckner Cambronne, Minister of Public Works, Transportation, and Communications; Dr Adrien Raymond, Assistant Minister of Foreign Affairs, and his excellency Mr Benson E. L. Timmons III, American Ambassador, assisted by his counsellors. They brought to light the desire of the Haitian government and people, in their well-known tradition of generous hospitality, of giving a new impulse to the tourist trade in Haiti, favouring: 1, renewal of the visit of war units of the American fleet; 2, those of the tourist cruises organized by the different shipping lines; and 3, in general the arrival of American tourists in Port-au-Prince. Ambassador Timmons welcomed this policy and declared that the US government would take it into account when furnishing information to interested sectors of the American tourist industry as well as to private sectors, and in the scheduling of visits to different countries by the Naval units of the American war fleet. The Haitian government hopes that in a while the efforts made will have a favourable effect on the development of tourism in Haiti.

Yet tourism sank to a new low that season. During the winter only two of eighty cruise ships to the Caribbean touched Port-au-Prince. Passengers arriving by air were subjected to close checks, for Duvalier was afraid of imported assassins.

To give the new communiqué a boost, Duvalier ordered the

multitude of beggars around the waterfront and shopping districts cleared out. They were rounded up and deported to the country.

The newspaper *Le Nouvelliste* published a palace-inspired editorial stating: 'Will not this communiqué mean the opening of a true dialogue between two partners and two countries bound for over a century by a friendship and solidarity which were born on the battlefields of Savannah and which manifested themselves throughout history?'

These were mere words, for at the practical level the Haitian government did nothing to improve working relations with the United States. An excellent example of Haitian neglect is its abuse of the American-owned electric company.

The government rarely paid its electrical bill and ran up debts into the millions. It added to the company's losses by increasing taxes, and complained that electricity rates, twelve US cents per kilowatt hour, were among the highest in the world. Yet the government always stopped short of putting the company out of business. Neither could the company collect from many of its private clients. Approximately half of its power was siphoned off illegally by a variety of ingenious wire gadgets known as the Cumberland. Through the Cumberland, enterprising Haitians bypass the company's meters. Since the company can neither abandon its investment nor collect its dues, it rations electricity through regular blackouts.

The company has found it not only can do little about the Cumberland, but faces liability for any accident which results from its use. After one man installing a Cumberland was electrocuted, his family sued and won a $15,000 settlement. Company trucks comb neighbourhoods pulling down the current taps, but they quickly reappear.

The current taps draw their name from an American named Dr W. W. Cumberland who was general receiver and financial adviser to the Haitian government during the US Marine occupation. Cumberland ran a tight ship and gained near-legendary stature among Haitians for his ability to cut corners and get things done neatly and efficiently. Haitians memorialized him with their own corner cutting.

A new campaign of adulation for Duvalier began in the newspapers and it soon became clear that Haiti was in for another ritual of reverence. He was preparing the public for an 'election' whose purpose it was to name him President for Life. Paul Blanchet organized the campaign, bringing a variety of delegations to the palace to pay homage to Duvalier.

The *Haiti Journal* on 4 March declared without the hint of a smile:

Duvalier is the professor of energy. Like Napoleon Bonaparte, Duvalier is an electrifier of souls, a powerful multiplier of energy. ... Duvalier is one of the greatest leaders of contemporary times ... because the Renovator of the Haitian Fatherland synthesizes all there is of courage, bravery, genius, diplomacy, patriotism, and tact in the titans of ancient and modern times.

Blanchet's propaganda campaign reached full proportions as the annual Mardi Gras drew to a close. Street bands included among their carnival songs and dancing some new numbers based on the theme *Papa Doc pour la vie*. The National Security Volunteers, a label Duvalier put on the militia for the sake of respectability, paraded to the palace. Blanchet issued special gasoline rations to the Tourist Guides Association (taxis) so they could provide horn-honking accompaniment as the militia marched through the rutted streets.

The next day, 1 April, the army played its role. A delegation of officers visited the palace and General Constant read a declaration in which the army swore allegiance to Duvalier for life

with all the ardour of our patriotic convictions ... thanks to you, Excellency, and under your prestigious command, the armed forces of Haiti have many times fulfilled with honour and competence the sacrosanct mission of maintaining territorial integrity, victoriously holding battle against occult forces which had organized with the aim of compromising national sovereignty and independence.

Blanchet announced that the day's ceremonies were in response to nationwide public demonstrations urging that Duvalier rule for life. He said the army's statement was made after officers had signed appeals urging they be allowed to approve Duvalier as President for Life.

Duvalier responded with a major speech:

'I am happy that you understand it is necessary to join the revolutionary crowd and come here this morning to render homage to the constitutional chief of the armed forces in a new oath of allegiance.' He told the crowd that he understood their feelings and then spoke directly to his army chief of staff:

General Constant, Duvalier, the President of the Republic, who is prouder of his title of revolutionary chief than of that of chief of state, accepts and appreciates your gesture. I understand you, for I remember you were a lieutenant in 1957 when you risked your position in greeting me in Jacmel ... and now you are a general.

Not to make anyone jealous, I would also like to credit the present chief of the Presidential Guard, Colonel Gracia Jacques, for welcoming me in Verrettes, home town of the immortal Dumarsais Estimé, like a chief of state when I was only a candidate. He was second lieutenant and now he is a colonel ...

You know I cannot abandon my civilian children who had faith in me, my military children whom you represent here. I cannot abandon them to adventure.

Should I disappear in flames I must maintain the power which the people entrusted to the man in whom it has full confidence. My dear friends, it is not easy to find a man having full confidence in himself, in his country, such as I have.

It is not possible to find easily a revolutionist. You will find him every fifty years or every seventy-five years, but I who am speaking to you now ... I have full confidence and I synthesize the aspirations and I concretize, at this moment when I am speaking to you, the aspirations of the motherland and of the nation that we all love. I know where I can go because I am a revolutionist. I am less a chief of state than a revolutionist. When you will see that the man has the necessary power, you will equally know what is reserved to you.

It is because I want to avoid catastrophes. It is because I want to protect you, both military and civilian Duvalierists, who were with me in 1956 and 1961, that I want to go always higher to meet the thought of Toussaint Louverture who in article three of the Constitution of 1801 said that in the present state in which the colony of Saint Domingue was he could not hand over constitutional power. He had to keep it . . .

It appeared to the world that Duvalier formally had accepted the Presidency for Life in a prepared ceremony of acclamation, but it was only window dressing. He kept stirring the waves of adulation until 14 June, when an 'election' was held in the best Duvalier tradition to make it official.

While the rest of the world may have been startled to hear of Duvalier's declared intentions there was precedent for it inside Haiti. Since 1804 seven Haitians, three as monarchs, had decided to rule for life. In fact, few Haitian presidents ever left office voluntarily. Dessalines, Christophe, and Soulouque had proclaimed themselves respectively emperors and king. Sylvain Salnave, Pétion, Jean-Pierre Boyer, and Fabre N. Geffrard had assumed life terms. Salnave, elected in 1867 for four years, two years later decided to hold the office for life, which he did until shot by a firing squad.

Between the April declaration to the army and the election of 14 June Blanchet continued forming delegations to go to the palace and praise Duvalier.

A march was organized by Minister of Public Works Cambronne from Duvalierville (Cabaret) to the palace. The populations of Pétionville and Port-au-Prince were told to join it. Prefect Windsor Day ordered all cockfight pits closed, and all peasants within sight were rounded up to participate.

There was a brief pause in Duvalier worship, on 24 April, when Bishop Alfred Voegeli, American head of the Episcopal Church in Haiti since December 1943, and the man who had personally interceded for the life of Yvon Moreau, was expelled from the country.

Two days before Bishop Voegeli had been scheduled to lead a church delegation to the palace as part of the Praise Papa Doc Movement, immigration officials forced their way into his home at gunpoint and gave him two hours to leave. By noon he was on a plane to Puerto Rico. Duvalier ignored American Embassy protests.

Bishop Voegeli left behind eighty-two churches and their clergy, all Haitian but three, some 40,000 persons, and 14,000 communicants devoted to the Episcopal Church. He had been a firm supporter of Haiti and had established needed institutions of learning in the country. These included the Saint Pierre College, the Saint Vincent's School for Handicapped Children, the coeducational school of the Holy Trinity, and an old ladies' home.

Despite protests by conservative elements in the church, fifteen years earlier Bishop Voegeli had commissioned Haiti's newly discovered primitive artists to paint murals on the ceiling and walls of the Saint Trinity Church. The objectors one night painted the murals over in black but the work continued and, when completed, constituted one of the most rewarding views of Haitian art in Port-au-Prince.

The same week the Assembly met, voted Duvalier full powers for an unlimited period, suspended constitutional guarantees, carried out a Duvalier order abolishing the 1957 Constitution, and appointed a fifteen-man committee to draft a new custom-made constitution for a President for life.

One voice was raised in the Organization of American States against the actions to assume lifetime power. Doctor Gonzalo Facio, Costa Rica's delegate, called it a 'preposterous action'. He said that Duvalier had taken Haiti outside the OAS and the organization should move for its ouster.

Duvalier reacted angrily, branding Facio 'a valet'. He said he noted the Facio statements with 'irony and even contempt. Facio came here when some wanted to soil our national territory at the border last year, but he was only a valet. He was playing a part. I will never permit an international institution or a valet within an international institution to infringe upon our national dignity.'

Jean Julmé, president of the one-house assembly, echoed Duvalier's charges against Facio and suggested that Haiti withdraw its OAS representative from Washington. He warned the OAS that Facio should be sanctioned for his declarations. 'We hope OAS members will not fail to make Mr Facio understand how and why he must act to avoid Haiti withdrawing its representative.' Julmé struck the point that Haiti's OAS vote had been important to the United States. There were no more comments from the OAS.

Blanchet's delegations continued trooping to the palace and Duvalier regularly responded with words of self-deification. He denied rumours that he planned to declare himself emperor. To a delegation from Carrefour he commented: 'You have in front of you a revolutionary who could not accept the title of emperor with any kind of name be it François I or others. He will remain what he has always been, a man from the people who took power and took it forever. Never will he leave this palace which is so loved.'

A Bel Air group heard him say: 'I will not hesitate, as I have always said, to make a red night for the triumph of my cause.' The comments were so militant and so threatening that they sometimes seemed less a statement of Duvalier's intentions than an attempt at self-persuasion.

All palace worshippers were frisked for weapons as they entered the Duvalier presence, and watched carefully during their performances. They came to praise Duvalier, and the Tonton Macoutes and Presidential Guard were on hand to insure that no Brutus slipped in to bury him.

Depending upon his mood, Duvalier sometimes would lapse into vulgarity. To a militia delegation from North Haiti on 10 May, he said:

If someone thinks he can turn his ass left or right, I will crush it into flour and pass it through a sieve.... I am an intellectual, a doctor who has known only books, but I remind you that it is one of the greatest intellectuals of the great Russia who organized the Russian army at the side of Lenin.

What's the matter? Yes, what's the matter if a Negro in the Caribbean organizes his combat forces to make respected the sacred soil of his Fatherland? I will do it until you of the north come to join the militia of Port-au-Prince to put me to rest in the tomb.

But that is not the way I would will it. I do not need a funeral. You will simply go lay me in my tomb to the roar of bullets and machine-gun fire. A revolution is not made with literature. Revolutions equal gunfire. If a man thinks, whoever he may be, he is going to take this power the people have given me, besides I have taken the power for ever.

Duvalier sometimes got carried away by his words, leaving sentences unfinished and obscure.

I will not let any foreigner teach a lesson to Dr Duvalier. When you hear that things are 'this way, that way', you don't need an order. Come and occupy Port-au-Prince.... Duvalier will govern even under cannon fire. It is a formal order I give you. It is the chief of the revolution speaking to you. He will soon be President for Life. You don't need an order when you hear something is going on in Port-au-Prince. Come and join me. I will be with you.

To raise money for a May Day gift to Duvalier, Cambronne and his National Renovation Movement extorted twenty-five-dollar 'contributions' from businessmen and used them to buy a gold emperor-sized medal for Duvalier and a diploma which hailed him as 'chief of the revolution and grand-protector of commerce and industry'.

Deputy Ulrick Saint-Louis, head of the constitutional revision committee, drafted a nineteen-page report explaining why the Constitution had to be changed and presenting the new one. He said the new constitution, Haiti's twenty-first, provided a 'revolution through law', which he called the ultimate aim of a democracy. It had 201 articles, the most significant of which gave Duvalier the Presidency for Life and absolute powers. Throughout the constitution Duvalier was referred to as 'Le Souverain', a title so liked by Emperor Faustin Soulouque. The rubber-stamp assembly on 25 May approved it with what was called 'respectable' speed. And Duvalier announced that a Presidential referendum for approval would be held on 14 June.

To justify the Constitution, Deputy Saint-Louis quoted Robespierre: 'The greater one's power, the freer and more rapid his action.' Saint-Louis was rewarded by being named president of the Assembly.

With a new Constitution and a new term about to be established, Duvalier wanted to change the flag and did so, the red and blue colours becoming red and black. The original Haitian flag was created by tearing the white out of the French tricolour, leaving red and blue, but Duvalier contended that Dessalines had established a red-and-black emblem and that Alexandre Pétion changed it to red and blue. Duvalier issued a statement: 'At a time when the Haitian people give total adhesion to a mystique which joins that of the country's forefathers, we must again consecrate this emblem. No standard can better express the joy of the nation of finding again in the strong mystique, the faith of its ancestors, than the black-and-red flag of Dessalines.' On his personal flag Duvalier added a guinea hen on a conch shell.

At the annual 22 May celebrations another US position on Duvalier was broken: Ambassador Timmons participated by attending a high mass commemorating Duvalier's rule. Ambassador Newbegin had begun the practice of leaving the country each 22 May as an expression of US disapproval of Duvalier tactics. Timmons, instead, was conspicuously present and the effect was noted in and out of Haiti. A picture was taken of Timmons and Duvalier shaking hands and smiling, Timmons taking a plunging bow, and distributed by the news services. *Le Nouvelliste* commented on it. Next door in the Dominican Republic newspaper *El Caribe* viewed it as a 'step backward'. *El Caribe* said it noted with sadness that the US policy of a 'cordial *abrazo* for democratic governments and cold handshake for dictators' had been put aside. It expressed 'concern that US Ambassador Timmons conspicuously participated in actions celebrated by the tyrant to glorify himself.' It added that from the Trujillo experience it knew that such participation 'is exploited by dictators to bring to the souls of the people despair and pessimism, and thus anchor more firmly their despotic system.'

Another newsman in Haiti for 22 May saw it differently. Henry Raymont of the *New York Times* interpreted Timmons's actions to mean that the United States was seeking quietly closer ties with Haiti because it was apparent Duvalier had a firm hold on power. He noted a 'quiet but sustained effort' by Washington to encourage private investment in Haiti; that Ambassador Timmons had recommended shore leave in Haiti for US Naval personnel in the Caribbean; that the Alliance for Progress had extended an investment loan guarantee of $4 million for an oil refinery to be built; he cited the Inter-American Development Bank loan to improve the water system. In an interview Duvalier told Raymont that 'misunderstandings' and 'bad faith' by previous American ambassadors had caused poor relations with the United States. Duvalier expressed satisfaction with Timmons and said that 'there is a better understanding of our problems' because of him.

Following high mass on 22 May 1964, Duvalier sat in an overstuffed chair on a reviewing stand before the palace for four hours and watched a demonstration and drill by 6,000 members of the militia, about 20 per cent of whom were armed. The crowd assembled around the palace and cheered on schedule. After each drill, militia leaders read a proclamation swearing allegiance to Duvalier and demanding that he stay in office.

Duvalier's speech in reply was a new adventure in self-dialogue:

> As for myself I am a realist, I can listen to very beautiful speeches, but I remain a doctrinaire and a realist which means I never permit myself to be intoxicated. I remain equal to myself. While I listen to the speeches, I talk to myself ... I am at a new phase in my political life. ...
>
> President for Life means something. ... I know what I am doing. ... There is no revolution without gunfire. The nation must be under arms. The supreme chief must always be ready beside his soldiers to make respected what must be respected which means you, which means me.

Following additional festivities that night by militiamen, Duvalier added: 'I am not saying anything more. A chief, a supreme commander of the armed forces and commander of the civilian militia, a commander of the police does not speak to his soldiers or at least does not answer the speeches of soldiers.'

Amazing even to Haitians, the Blanchet propaganda campaign leading to the 14 June referendum continued. Delegations poured into the palace, repeating their sycophantic phrases and listening to Duvalier's fierce, pompous responses.

To a group from South Haiti he described himself as 'this giant capable of eclipsing the sun because the people already have consecrated me for life'. He declared himself a 'Bible-lover' but proceeded to say that his true god was the 'Africa mater' and that the African gods had made it possible for him to 'ascend and assault'.

Another group heard this comment:

> Nobody is capable of stopping me from fulfilling my sacrosanct mission.... The leader of the Haitian revolution has the right to do with Haiti what he wants to do for the welfare of the country, like the great Indonesian leader [Sukarno], the leader of the great China [Mao Tse-tung], and the leader of the eternal France [De Gaulle].

Duvalier displayed anger before a group of judges from Jacmel:

> This is the only judicial group which up until now has presented itself to pay homage to the chief of the revolution and the man who already is the President of the Republic. One cannot prevent some men from nourishing certain ambitions, but to feed those ambitions and covet the Presidency of the Republic, one must have courage like the little doctor of 1957 [Duvalier] who was not afraid when he had to declare his candidacy.

The 'ambitious' judge to whom he referred was chief of the supreme court Adrien Douyon, a Duvalier appointee who had strayed from favour. Rather than being ambitious, Douyon and other judges apparently had been slow in responding to pressures for public expression of adulation for Duvalier.

Douyon's successor, schoolteacher and Civil Court Judge Luc Boivert, led sixteen supreme court judges before Duvalier on 4 June to pay their respects, and heard Duvalier read a speech.

Duvalier said that he felt a 'secret bitterness' while listening to their homage. What he meant by 'secret' remains, for the large part, exactly that. For, as his appetite for power grew, his rhetoric became even more turgid.

Duvalier said he had judged the assembled judges 'not guilty' for slowness in expressing homage but reminded them that all power rested with Le Souverain. 'As a highly responsible chief I will remain deaf to pity for any political fault against the revolution.'

A Kenscoff delegation heard Duvalier declare:

> After this political act [referendum] there will never again be an election to elect a chief of state on the soil of Haiti.... I shall be lord and master.... I have always talked with the wild energy that characterizes me; with all the savagery which characterizes me ...
>
> The revolution is the revolution. If you must be a deputy at the chamber, you will be because the revolution is like a river. If one puts himself across the river he will be carried away.
>
> Everyone is turning his ass the way he can.... Why can't the Haitian people turn their ass the way they want? Why not? They are starting to recognize that Duvalier is not the Lucifer of the Caribbean....
>
> Well, each one turns his ass the way he wants. We have what is called a democracy. It is one of the most beautiful ones. De Gaulle has a democracy; it is one of the most beautiful ones. Mao Tse-tung has a democracy; it is one of the most beautiful ones. Well, let every country develop its functions, customs, and traditions, because it is an ethnologist talking to you....
>
> You know that Dr François Duvalier even under cannon fire will not back down. I have already said it. If my militia is afraid, it just has to look at my face. If the Duvalierist cohorts feel a tinge of fear, they will have to look at my face. My face stays just like you have known it in 1956. The man will remain equal to himself.

This speech, later run in a newspaper under the title *Un Dialogue Passionnant*, seemed an effort by Duvalier to match up his personalities. The little doctor was striding hard to keep pace with the 'sun-eclipsing giant' of his other self.

Voting, if it could be called that, began at 6 a.m. Sunday, 14 June. Blue, pink, red, and yellow ballots were handed out by the fistful. Kids made gliders of them, even pasted some together for kites. To vote was embarrassingly easy, for all the ballots said the same thing.

Oui was the only answer, and if anyone had the temerity to try a write-in *non,* he faced charges of defacing a ballot. Government employees hurried to the polls early so that they could be seen. The radio blared out 'Duvalier for Life' *méringues*. Little red-and-black flags flew. Peasants, trucked into the city, danced to rara bands and drank clairin. Everyone, including foreigners, was invited to step right up and vote. Militiamen thoroughly enjoyed themselves. By 11.15 a.m. Duvalier appeared on a palace balcony with his acceptance speech:

> Today the people have already manifested their desire. I mean that at this time that I am speaking to you I already am President for Life of the Republic....
>
> What the government wants is that you must fight, look, and watch so as the traitors of always, those who betrayed Jean-Jacques Dessalines the great, those who betrayed General Salomon, those who betrayed General Soulouque, so as these same traitors may know that now things have changed and that Dr Duvalier is neither Dessalines, nor Soulouque, nor General Salomon, of whom he is, however, the pupil. But he is a very distrustful man. He wants to lead as a master. He wants to lead as a true autocrat. That is to say, I repeat, he does not accept anybody else before him but his own person.
>
> A great man on the other side of the Atlantic knows what he is doing. He is called General De Gaulle. He is a great Frenchman. Another one who may be compared to Duvalier is President Sukarno of Indonesia. He is a great man. He knows what he is doing. Other great citizens who lead their countries with firmness and with all the necessary savagery know what they are doing. Duvalier also, ever since he was practising the profession of doctor, knew what he was doing.

Following this remarkable speech, Duvalier went to the polls and cast a *oui* ballot for himself. Newspapers reported 2,800,000 *ouis* as against 3,234 *nons,* although it was never clear how even this handful managed to vote against Le Souverain.

That night some 3,000 supporters sang and danced before a

twenty-four-foot-high monument 'to perpetuate the memory of the Duvalierist revolution'. The 'flame' was a flashing sign of revolving red, blue, green, yellow, and violet neon tubes. On 22 June 1964, Inauguration Day, the flame officially was lighted. One observer remarked: 'It is a true monstrosity; a fitting end to the day.'

The three days of celebrations for the inauguration were marred, in Duvalier's eyes, because a priest at the Te Deum in the cathedral inserted a clemency plea for political prisoners in his sermon. Duvalier made the priest, Monsignor Claudius Angénor, resign and placed him under house arrest.

The new Constitution gave the new *Président à Vie* a host of new titles: Supreme Chief of the Haitian Nation; Uncontestable Leader of the Revolution; Apostle of National Unity; Renovator of the Fatherland; Chief of the National Community; Worthy Heir of the Founders of the Haitian nation . . .

Article 106 credits Duvalier with provoking a national *prise de conscience* (decision) for the first time since 1804 'through radical political, social, economic, cultural, and religious changes in Haiti. . . . [Thus] he is elected President for Life so as to ensure the conquests and permanence of the Duvalierist revolution . . .'

Article 197 credits Duvalier with, among other things: making possible the reconciliation of the political factions strongly opposed at the downfall of the 1950 regime; 'realizing economic and financial stability of the state in spite of the pernicious action of the conjugated forces of the inside and outside'; and of 'undertaking and completing the alphabetization of the masses and thus fulfilling the aspirations of the small and humble for more light and welfare.'

The Constitution also praises him for ensuring peace and order through a reorganization of the armed forces, laying the bases of national prosperity through 'works of infrastructure' for the promotion of agriculture and industrialization; organizing the protection of the working masses and giving justice to the peasant; creating organizations for the protection of mother, children, women, and family – creating a strong nation, the pride of its sons!

But the most staggering bit of self-flattery of them all was a government-printed booklet, *Le Catéchisme de la révolution*. It contained litanies, hymns, prayers, doctrine. It substituted the Roman Catholic explanation of the Holy Trinity with a Papa Doc version.

(Q) Who are Dessalines, Toussaint, Christophe, Pétion and Estimé?

(A) *Dessalines, Toussaint, Christophe, Pétion and Estimé are five founders of the nation who are found within François Duvalier.*

(Q) Is Dessalines for life?

(A) *Yes, Dessalines is for life in François Duvalier.*

(This same question and answer were listed for the other four historical figures.)

(Q) Do we conclude then that there are six presidents for life?

(A) *No, Dessalines, Toussaint, Christophe, Pétion, and Estimé are five distinct chiefs of state but who form only one and the same President in François Duvalier.*

There were pictures of the flag, of the President, and his First Lady, and then the 'Lord's Prayer' followed:

Our Doc who art in the National Palace for life, hallowed be Thy name by present and future generations. Thy will be done at Port-au-Prince and in the provinces. Give us this day our new Haiti and never forgive the trespasses of the anti-patriots who spit every day on our country; let them succumb to temptation, and under the weight of their venom, deliver them not from any evil . . .

17

The Guerrilla Challenge

Duvalier's decision to become President for Life and do away, as he said, once and for all with the electoral system was a challenge that few Haitians found they were prepared to meet.

In Santo Domingo a handful of exiles managed to overcome their bickering and launch a shoestring guerrilla operation which kept Duvalier busy for the second half of 1964 personally directing an anti-guerrilla war from his office in the National Palace. And in New York thirteen young Haitians took up the gauntlet. For nearly three months the 'thirteen', as they have become known in Haiti, fought over much of the rugged southern peninsula against Duvalier's total might.

Only the 'soldiers' of Cantave's army were left in the Dominican Republic, the officers having followed Cantave to the United States, and these men joined other political exiles on the benches of Santo Domingo's tree-shaded parks planning the perfect anti-Duvalier revolution and cadging cigarettes. Sugar-cane workers, who numbered around thirty thousand, blamed the political exiles for the road home to Haiti being closed. Most Haitian labourers preferred, at that time, to return to Haiti where their earnings went further than in the high-priced Dominican Republic. As the months passed exile seemed to spawn only would-be-leaders. Ambition nibbled even the most unlikely exile as respect for the traditional Haitian leaders appeared to have vanished for ever.

Duvalier made no distinction between returning labourer and exile when it came to executing Haitians found in his border 'war zone'. His voudou curtain was still drawn along the border, but some daring Haitians were able to sneak across. Some didn't make it. There were recurring reports of Haitians being intercepted on one side of the border or the other, killed, and dumped into shallow, unmarked graves. Duvalier didn't want them to escape, and many Dominicans preferred that they did not come at all.

Early in 1964 a Catholic priest, Jean-Baptiste Georges, left Santo Domingo and went on a tour through South America to raise funds for a liberation army. In Colombia he confidently told newsmen that a new invasion force was preparing and would be inside Haiti before the end of the year. Fred Baptiste, a key figure in Cantave's battle for Ouanaminthe, had scraped together forty dollars to rent an earth-floored, thatch-roofed house some twelve miles from Santo Domingo to give a home to the remnants of the Cantave invasion force, who were literally living in the bushes, having vacated the unused Nigua Insane Asylum and left it to the animals, its regular tenants. Many of the men still had fresh wounds that needed caring for.

Henry Clermont, who left his studies at Fordham University to join *Jeune Haiti*, inherited a refugee house. To add to what aid was available for his group, Clermont worked in Wimpy's Supermarket in Santo Domingo. Louis Déjoie, the former Presidential candidate, worked as a commission agent for a Miami construction firm and sold the Dominican navy a kitchen. He also subsidized a group of exiles from his apartment. Raymond Cassagnol, who with his half-brother Jacques had made a 1963 attempt to organize an invasion, opened a French pastry shop.

The refugee centres, as they were called, were not military camps but places where Haitians could find some food and shelter. Father Jean-Claude Bajeux, exiled in February 1964, following the Jesuits' ouster from Port-au-Prince, heard of the plight of his countrymen in the Dominican Republic and moved down from New York to help. With the aid of some prominent Dominicans he formed the 'Friendship of Peoples Foundation'. His help often meant putting on his flowing robe and striding into the police headquarters or army centres to plea for hapless Haitians in trouble. He often had to assume duties that Haitian diplomatic representatives would normally fulfil.

In a survey, Bajeux's foundation reported that there were 30,000 to 50,000 Haitians in the Dominican Republic.

> Most of these Haitians live in the most pitiful conditions of filth and hunger around the sugar-cane *bateys* ... incredibly crowded, the wooden shacks are totally without sanitation or running water. The mud floors are vermin infested. The 'lucky' Haitian has a piece of corrugated cardboard to serve as a 'mattress' between himself and the damp mud.

Bajeux built a staff among exiles from the Christian Trade Unions Movement. Father Bissainthe and the International Rescue Committee in New York accepted donations on behalf of the Foundation and the Dominican government officially recognized it.

Bajeux, thirty-three, had studied theology and philosophy for nine years in France, and while there collaborated on several books dealing with the problems of the national clergy. He later spent five years in Africa, teaching philosophy and editing a newspaper. He returned to Haiti in 1962 to teach philosophy, edit the Catholic cultural youth magazine *Rond-Point,* direct the Catholic Youth Centre, and help launch another religious magazine called *Church on the March*. He spent twenty-one days under house arrest in July 1963, for having tried to establish a residence for youth chaplains in Port-au-Prince.

Andrew McClellan, Inter-American representative of the AFL-CIO, made a series of statements on Duvalier and Haitian cane cutters in the Dominican Republic that help spotlight Bajeux's cause. McClellan said that since 1957 Haiti had supplied 30,000 cane cutters a year to work in the Dominican fields. He said that Duvalierists were paid fifteen dollars a head for each cutter delivered and received half of the cutter's wages. He said Duvalierists received some six million to eight million dollars a year from this practice.

The Dominican man in the street, with the terror of dictatorship still fresh in his mind, was in principle sympathetic to the Haitian exile, and in the early days gave generously to a Haitian movement. But the Dominican became mystified by the fervour of the interexile animosity and could not understand the frequent denunciation by one Haitian exile of another when Duvalier was supposed to be the enemy. In reality, for many exiles, some of the other leaders in exile were as much the enemy as the man sitting in the palace in Port-au-Prince. No coalition was possible. Dominican citizens soon began to regard all Haitians with some scepticism.

From a morass of discontent, a group of young exiles finally launched a movement. They cloaked their moves from other exiles, as if they were all Duvalier agents; indeed, in many cases, other exiles unwittingly did aid Papa Doc. Fred Baptiste, a former Déjoist, shunned the banners of all the old-time politicians once he gained exile. He and other young Haitians who had moved into a little shack in a Santo Domingo slum where they had to take turns sleeping on the limited floor space at nights, spent their days doing the rounds in search not of food, but of arms with which to attack Duvalier. Most of these youths had opposed Cantave's attack on Ouanaminthe even though they had taken part in it. They had pleaded, instead, to be permitted to fight a guerrilla war.

With the new and modern arms Cantave had received, they dreamed of pursuing this war in the hills. But those weapons were in a Dominican arsenal, and no amount of pleading with the Dominican military could obtain their release. In the frequent park-bench conferences they held, the youths decided that guerrilla was a dirty word, denoting Communist militants. They hit upon the idea of calling their movement *Camoquin*, the name of an anti-malarial pill in Haiti. Baptiste liked to explain that the peasants called the rebels this because they were the answer to the disease that was killing Haiti – Duvalierism. Father Georges became the godfather of the *Camoquins*. The Haitian priest said he wanted nothing more than the overthrow of Duvalier. After weeks of searching, Baptiste and the priest found a suitable camp, a little unused chicken farm on the Villa Mella Road, some six miles from the capital. It was set in quiet, rolling farm land far enough away from

Santo Domingo (formerly, Ciudad Trujillo) to be out of range of the prying eyes of other exiles.

Recruits, carefully selected from the legion of exiles, quietly slipped out of town to the training camp. Nights they trained in the dark and slept in the chicken coops. Days they studied warfare from the blackboard and went through manoeuvres in the little back yard out of sight of the road and the neighbours. Most of the *Camoquins* had become proficient with rifles, sub machine guns, and even bazookas during training in the various camps that preceded Cantave's attack on Ouanaminthe. Some were former soldiers. Those who did not have any training with firearms got it by way of a rifle carved out of wood and from designs drawn on the blackboard. To have a firearm in the camp would have been too dangerous. New recruits were called 'aspirins' and put through rigorous initiations, so tough that one country boy fled in the belief that the fierce young exiles were true *loupgarous*.

Most of the exiles who had any interest in training visited the camp and found it a serious effort, tightly disciplined by Baptiste, then thirty, assisted by his younger brother. The *Camoquins* learned Morse Code as part of their training, mostly as a matter of exercising discipline, for they had no radio or communication apparatus. Daily they raised and lowered the Haitian flag from a flagstaff with a ceremony worthy of any military establishment.

But the *Camoquins* suffered serious setbacks in March 1964, that nearly ended the effort like dozens of attempts before it. Fred Baptiste worked himself into a case of ulcers trying to feed and equip his men, and went to the hospital. Other exiles had finally spied out the location of the camp and, with the backing of one of the 'leaders', set about to destroy it. Many 'leaders' felt if an invasion was not made in their name against Duvalier then they did not want to see it succeed. These exiles considered the efforts of the youths a dangerous adventure that should be stopped at all costs. They called on Dominican General Elias Wessin y Wessin and told him that the Villa Mella camp was a Communist movement. An anti-Communist zealot, Wessin y Wessin wasted no time in destroying the camp.

Sunday morning, 15 March, Wessin's personal secret service, which had kept the camp under observation for three days, moved in force. Swinging gun butts, they ploughed through the group of exiles who were doing Sunday-morning chores. One soldier broke the butt of his San Cristóbal rifle on the head of an exile. At gun point they were told by Wessin's secret service chief to admit that they were Communists. Their clothes, books, and small supply of charity food and cooking utensils were gathered up and taken, along with the men, to Wessin's headquarters. The outlandish accusation was that Baptiste and his companions were in league with both Castro and Duvalier and that they intended to invade Haiti with Dominican arms. Instead of fighting Duvalier they would hand over the arms to the Dictator in an attempt to embarrass the Dominican civilian junta during an Inter-American Press Association congress to be held the following week in Santo Domingo. Baptiste pleaded their innocence, but Wessin y Wessin handed them over to the national police. Henry Clermont and Frenchmen André Rivière and Claude Martin were picked up in their rooms in the city. Wessin reported that his men had found Communist literature and a Castro guerrilla training film at the camp. This evidence was taken before the president of the ruling triumvirate, Donald Reid Cabral, who found that most of the literature had come from the US Information Agency except for a guerrilla warfare handbook written by Che Guevara. President Reid then went with Wessin's intelligence chief to view the Castro training film at Radio Santo Domingo's studios. What they saw surprised them further. The film showed Dominican army officers training Haitians in the art of firing a bazooka near Dajabon the year before. The *Camoquins* were released, but without their boots, clothing, and food. They also had to contend with a suspicious General Wessin who already had at least one Haitian in his spy network.

Realizing that without the patronage of a politician all the effort they made might be in vain, the *Camoquins* named Pierre Rigaud and Father Georges co-ordinators of the movement which translates in English as 'The Haitian Revolutionary

Armed Forces' (FARH is its French acronym). With this high-sounding name and the protection a well-known politician can offer, their enemies could no longer point them out as Communist.

In New York another Haitian priest, thirty-four-year-old Father Gérard Bissainthe, continued his organizational work on behalf of *Jeune Haiti*. Bissainthe, the son of a lawyer, had studied in France and served as a teacher and chaplain of youth groups in Port-au-Prince schools. He called the movement non-Communist, and said it favoured a system of socialist-oriented co-operatives in the style of Israel's *kibboutzim*. He said that *Jeune Haiti* planned armed action against Duvalier.

Duvalier was aware of what was happening. During the ceremonies leading to the President-for-Life referendum he had Foreign Minister Chalmers send a message, on 7 June, to the United Nations Security Council warning that an invasion was being prepared by exiles in the Dominican Republic. The warning went largely unheeded until late in June when Baptiste and his *Camoquins* finally struck.

With at least three known secret services and the police keeping independent watches on them, the *Camoquins* managed to slip out of Santo Domingo undetected on 27 June 1964. That afternoon a little van picked up the twenty-nine revolutionaries and drove them to a party at an apartment in residential Santo Domingo. From the party, the guerrillas were shuttled through the streets of Santo Domingo out on the big four-lane main highway to a shoreside spot near the international airport, some twelve miles from the city. Except for their leaders the *Camoquins* did not know they were Haiti-bound until the last minute. Their biggest concern of the moment was possible arrest by traffic police because their van had no rear lights.

At about 11 p.m., as the last international flight took off from the airport, a *Camoquin* leader sent a message from the shore on a cheap walkie-talkie. An answer came back from the sea, and shortly thereafter a boat arrived. The rebels scrambled aboard, and the little vessel moved out to the open sea and turned west toward Haiti. The boat was from Miami and not accustomed to carrying invaders. Her normal cargo was contraband, but this time she carried in her hold secreted weapons and ammunition acquired from the flourishing Miami-Cuban exile arms business.

Passing Beata Island, a Dominican coastal patrol boat challenged them. They refused to heave to, and the patrol boat fired a warning shot across in the darkness. The captain of the clandestine ship battened a seasick bunch of *Camoquins* in the hold, goosed his motor, and soon outdistanced the Dominicans.

At dawn the boat anchored off Saltrou on Haiti's western shore. A heavy sea was running but the captain wanted to deliver the men and weapons and get out. The *Camoquins* began to unload the weapons into a dinghy to be ferried ashore. They had trouble immediately.

Guy Lucchesi, twenty-four, a student from Cap-Haïtien anxious to do battle despite a crippled arm, did not hear an order to stop loading the dinghy. He and another *Camoquin* called 'Chien Méchant' piled in, and the dinghy capsized. Both drowned. Their explosive detonators also were lost.

Some of the people at Saltrou, including Tonton Macoutes, spotted them offshore and came to help. The *Camoquins* were dressed in olive-green fatigues and looked like members of the Haitian army.

One big fisherman brought a battered old sailboat alongside, helped unload the arms and medical supplies and carry them ashore. The *Camoquins* stepped on Haitian soil on 29 June. Two other *Camoquins,* exemplary during training, were so terrified by the hectic landing without a gun in their hands that they deserted and made their way back to the Dominican Republic. When the fisherman learned that the men were anti-Duvalier rebels, he shouldered a case of ammunition and joined them as a volunteer.

Another witness to the landing was Duvalierist Army Lieutenant Célestin, unnoticed because he was dressed in civilian clothes. The *Camoquins* were told who he was and that he had left for Thiotte, a garrison town on a fair-weather road that led across the mountains to Port-au-Prince, shortly after spotting them. They pursued the Lieutenant and caught him and two Tonton Macoutes. Célestin died from a machete blow.

The *Camoquins,* their original number reduced to twenty-five by the two drownings and two desertions, moved towards the La Selle Mountains through one of Haiti's most rugged areas. Duvalier learned of their presence on 30 June, a day later, and, enraged, sent an army detachment under the command of Major Sonny Borges to combat them. Borges's men had mortars and automatic weapons. The *Camoquins* had old, battered M-1 rifles and three First World War British Enfields equipped with telescopic sights. They had also fashioned home-made grenades from explosives they carried, but they had lost most of their detonators in the landing.

The Duvalierists rarely saw them, though they often fired at what they believed were rebels. Once Borges thought he had the *Camoquins* encircled, and his men shelled the area thoroughly. For about three weeks Baptiste's band effectively harassed Duvalier as a hit-run force and stirred rural imaginations even though they did not carry out a military campaign of strategic significance.

Duvalier reacted by donning his khaki uniform. He went to Fort Dimanche and ordered Mme Max Adolphe, the warden, to choose twenty-one prisoners. His cold manner did not reveal his rage, and reports later said that Mme Adolphe thought Duvalier – as the new President for Life – planned to free some of the prisoners. Among those she picked were several she regarded as friends. Duvalier had the twenty-one executed.

The next day Duvalier chose an official whose word the American Embassy could be expected to believe, and had him reveal the executions to them. The President thought the United States in some way was involved and wanted to show that he could act as well as talk tough.

On 3 July Foreign Minister Chalmers cabled a long complaint to the United Nations accusing the Dominican Republic of aggression. Chalmers said that the invaders planned to dynamite bridges and gasoline tanks as part of a general campaign of arson and sabotage, and 'assassinate the closest collaborators of Haiti's head of state' (Duvalier carefully refrained from mentioning that he, too, was on the death list).

In naming the exiles behind the invasion, Chalmers showed no real knowledge of the Dominican situation. The cable ironically lumped every known exile together, listing Louis Déjoie, Henry Clermont, Father Georges, Léon Cantave, and Paul E. Magloire. At the time, both Magloire and Cantave were living in New York, Cantave not far from the United Nations. Most were bitterly opposed to each other.

The United Nations' complaint was censored out of all publications appearing in Port-au-Prince, but, as always, word still seeped in of the invasion in the south-west, partly because of the military activity. Duvalier's small Air Force began making regular sorties, and he prepared for a possible attack on Port-au-Prince by sending truckloads of militia into the mountains above the city, throwing up road blocks both on the road to Kenscoff and the road south to Jacmel.

Systematic arrests began. A group of students in Jacmel were jailed and beaten, some fatally. All suspected anti Duvalierists who had relatives in exile were picked up, including women and children.

One of the most striking cases of gratuitous brutality involved the arrest and disappearance of Maurice Duchatelier, his wife, baby, and part of his wife's family. Duchatelier had been an assistant manager for Pan American Airways for many years, then transferred to a job as sales manager of Texaco Oil Company. His wife worked as a secretary at Air France. Her brother, former Army Lieutenant Claude Edline, was in exile in New York. Former Army Lieutenant Francois Benoit, the sharpshooter, still in political asylum, was her brother-in-law.

Just before the Saltrou invasion Edline left New York to go to Baltimore and inquire about a teacher's job. Duvalier spies in New York reported Edline out of town. In Port-au-Prince the government assumed that this meant that he was with the rebels.

As Duchatelier and his wife drove home from work in a company car, the Tonton Macoutes picked them up. The maid tried to save the baby by giving it to neighbours, but the Tonton Macoutes found it. The Duchateliers were never heard from again.

Edline went to the Haitian Consulate in New York to show that he was not with the invasion force and save his family. It was too late.

In Port-au-Prince the people found it encouraging that the invasion appeared a sustained effort and that no boastful propaganda had been issued out of Santo Domingo in the early days of the landing. Not until 8 July did Duvalier allow an official mention of the *Camoquins'* invasion in Port-au-Prince newspapers. The first official *révélation* came in the following highly coloured report:

They [the invaders] were armed with M-1 rifles, .45-calibre revolvers, and grenades. Harassed as soon as they landed by the peasants of Belle-Anse[1] wildly devoted to the person of his excellency Dr François Duvalier, President for Life of the Republic, they left five dead and had to flee to peak La Selle, where, harassed day and night by the population, surrounded by the detachment of the armed forces of Haiti and of the corps of the National Security Volunteers, without water or food, they have no other alternative but an unconditional surrender or pure and simple annihilation without delay.

From the interrogation of prisoners fallen in the hands of the loyal forces, it was found out: 1) that the rebels left from Boca Chica about thirty kilometres from Santo Domingo; 2) that they were grouped before in a military training camp organized with the assistance of the Dominican authorities and placed under the direction of Rev. Father Jean-Baptiste Georges and Pierre L. Rigaud, both traitors to the Haitian motherland and under pay by a foreign power; 3) they are backed by the Dominican parties of the left and the 14th of June movement of Castro sympathies.

The government of His Excellency the Hon. Dr François Duvalier, highly conscious of its responsibilities before the nation, has already ordered all the measures tending to put an end to this daring enterprise of the *apatrides* [men without a country]: 1) strict patrols organized on the south-west coast by the Units of the Coast Guard Service of Haiti and the Air Force block effectively the ar-

1. Belle-Anse had formerly been named Saltrou, or 'Filthy Hole'.

rival of eventual reinforcements; 2) constant shelling of peak La Selle by heavy artillery and mortars has already started.

The government of the Republic regrets to have to state the backing given by the government of the Dominican Republic to the enterprise of the rebels, in contempt of international custom, of the most formal dispositions of the charter of the United Nations, of that of the OAS, and of the treaties signed in 1874 and 1884 between the two countries sharing the sovereignty of the island.

A week later Foreign Minister Chalmers said that his report was still correct as issued and he had nothing to add. 'Did Castro issue a statement at Playa Giron [Bay of Pigs] until victory was achieved?' he asked.

Duvalier's militia and army were not anxious to go into the mountains after a guerrilla force of uncertain number and weaponry. For the most part, they contented themselves with occupying the markets in the lowlands, wreaking vengeance on any whom they suspected of trying to assist the rebels. It was sound strategy, for the barren hills yielded little in the way of supplies to the *Camoquins*. If a peasant was found with as much as two or three dollars on his person, it was considered an inordinately high amount and he was shot on the premise that the money must have come from the *Camoquins*. Exile Timothé, who had done an expert propaganda job for Paul Verna during the Cantave raids, disobeyed orders and went into one of the markets with his boots on. The footwear marked him as a *Camoquin*. Duvalierists executed him on the spot.

When the *Camoquins* moved on the little village of Mapou, they were greeted with cries of *Vive Fignolé*. They took over a store belonging to a man named Bernadotte who had fled, leaving his wife in charge. They distributed the goods and the cash in the store to the peasants, who insisted Bernadotte was a Tonton Macoute. A bundle of mortgage notes on peasant land was found in the store and, at a formal ceremony, the papers were destroyed in front of the people.

One *Camoquin* became over-zealous. He often told his fellow invaders how he once had to watch while the Tonton Macoutes dragged his mother from the house by the hair. Revenge got the better of him. He killed Madame Bernadotte before they could stop him. When the rebels moved off into the mountains, the peasants tore up the store of the Tonton Macoute and they took parts of it to their homes, which was later the only evidence Bernadotte and the revengeful troops of army and militia needed to execute them as collaborators. The man who killed Madame Bernadotte was one of two more deserters shot by the Dominican army as they recrossed the border.

A problem was to discourage recruits and hangers-on, for the rebels had neither food nor weapons to offer them. To overcome their lack of weapons, Baptiste pushed them on long, forced marches, kept them moving in a fashion that made it appear to the government troops that they were up against more than one band.

The *Camoquins* camped on virtually every peak in the La Selle range, often in the rain. Tonton Macoutes posing as innocent peasants were sent to spy on them. Two such men approached them pretending to be Protestant missionaries.

'Where is your Bible?' the *Camoquins* asked.

'It is where we are going,' one replied.

'Let us hear you preach.' The men said nothing.

They were searched and bayonets found hidden in their trouser legs. Villagers testified that the men were Tonton Macoutes. The *Camoquins* hanged them.

Baptiste's band found people in the region in a pitiful plight, some too poor to afford even the most elementary tools, like a five-*gourde* (one-dollar) machete. They planted their little crops of millet by scratching between rocks with their bare hands. It was not ideal guerrilla country. The people had little for themselves and almost nothing for sale. Water was another problem. For sixteen days across Morne La Selle and the other rocky mountains, dotted with a few scraggly pine trees and still recovering from the denuding of Hurricane Flora, there was little food or drink to be found. Their thirst became so great that they soaked up water caught in the rocks with rags and then chewed them for the moisture. One little peasant woman who joined them in the early days provided vital help by going into villages or markets, sometimes on two- or three-day treks, to bring back water or food. Among their medical supplies they found a chocolate-coated laxative which, together with other medicines, they ate for temporary relief of hunger.

The search for water sent them ranging far from the intended fields. Late in the month (21 July) one *Camoquin* patrol unexpectedly stumbled across the Dominican border and into the hands of a Dominican army patrol. In the mountainous border area small, nearly invisible markers indicated the boundary between the two countries. The rest of the *Camoquins,* sick and hungry, hid their weapons in Haiti and returned to the Dominican Republic.

Their return drew little public attention. The Santo Domingo newspaper, *Listin Diario,* noted that a group of Haitians crossed into the Dominican Republic but said they were believed to be searching for supplies to deliver to guerrillas fighting in the Haitian mountains.

The *Camoquins* were taken out of the hills and held at the Dominican army barracks in the town of Neyba. The Dominicans agreed to their release but first asked the US Central Intelligence Agency to determine the truth of the Communist charges made against them. The CIA was said to have checked and found among them one man who once had belonged to Haiti's Popular Socialist Party as a youth, but the report was that the group seemed to be driven by no other force than a desire to overthrow Duvalier.

In two weeks the *Camoquins* moved back into Haiti. The night of 5 August the Dominican army put them unarmed across the mountain border with a small rations supply provided by their friends in Santo Domingo. Baptiste and his men retrieved the weapons they had cached and resumed their operations. The number of original *Camoquins* had been reduced, but the fisherman-recruit from Saltrou stayed with them and four peasant recruits joined the ranks.

The *Camoquins* did not know it, but a second front was

opened the same day. A band of thirteen young men belonging to *Jeune Haiti,* and assisted by Father Georges, landed from the sea on 5 August on the tip of the south-west peninsula, near Dame-Marie. Of the thirteen, eight had received training the past fall at a Special Forces camp in North Carolina.

Later they had prepared themselves in New York on week-ends and at night, firing at rifle ranges, amassing equipment as best they could. They worked at part-time jobs and maintained an office at a nondescript midtown hotel. Their girl friends and wives assisted in hiding the weapons and transferring them from place to place as needed for training. One wife once carried her husband's carbine, taken apart, home on the subway beneath her 'sack' dress. Most of the young men had university training, including attendance at both New York University and Harvard.

At invasion time they slipped out of New York by various roundabout routes to Miami and boarded the same ferryboat Father Georges had supplied the *Camoquins* for the landing at Saltrou. The original plans called for the *Jeune Haiti* forces to be landed at Jérémie on the north side of the peninsula but they were put ashore at Petite Rivière de Dame-Marie a couple of days' march from Jérémie.

For two months and twenty days *Jeune Haiti*'s thirteen – fighting an unco-ordinated but complementary action with the *Camoquins* – kept Duvalier in a whirl.

First word of the new landing on 5 August sent Papa Doc crying Communism again to the American Embassy. He told the Americans that his intelligence reported that Haiti had been invaded by 200 Castro Cuban guerrillas, who had been brought near the shore by a large vessel, then ferried to land by three smaller landing craft. He said one boat remained ashore and important matériel had been found discarded including a Browning rifle and other made-in-U S A equipment.

Duvalier asked the United States to fly reconnaissance over the Windward Passage because he feared another vessel might be on the way, this time to Port-au-Prince. The U S Navy flew surveillance and reported it saw nothing.

From Petite Rivière the thirteen moved inland and Haiti's

south-west peninsula – sealed from the rest of the nation by Duvalier troops – became a war zone.

The *Camoquins* at the other end of the country operated well in August. This time they found a base near the border from which they could replenish their food and water with a half day's walk. They had handicaps as always, but functioned despite them. Their guns had been damaged by exposure while cached and they awaited better weapons – at least five automatic rifles they had been promised. The temperature in the mountains was bone-chilling and they had only light clothing.

They split into three sections, and on 11 August moved into Pine Forest. First, they sabotaged a sawmill belonging to Major Jean Tassy, one of Duvalier's Tonton Macoute chiefs. They hit the mill in the morning, burning a tractor and two trucks.

In the afternoon, on the road from Thiotte to Fonds Verrettes, they attacked a government truck loaded with militia, killing four but setting the driver and his bullet-scarred truck free to spread word of the attack. They blew up a section of the road. A Duvalier congressman escaped a *Camoquin* attack with his wounded son. The man later died from the shock.

That same August two columns of *Camoquins* attacked the military post of Savane Zombi at night. The militia chief, Jean Joachim, was killed and other Duvalierists fled. But a jeep the rebels had made no effort to attack the day before contained an even greater prize – Armed Forces Chief General Gérard Constant, as they learned from looking over seized documents at the Savane Zombi post. Peasants told the *Camoquins* that members of the militia were tearing up their identity cards so that in case of attack they could shout *A bas Duvalier* and join the rebels.

Duvalier set up a two-way radio in his palace office and devoted full time to the business of running the anti-guerrilla war on two fronts. All radio field messages had to be addressed to the Supreme Chief of the Armed Forces at the National Palace.

A favourite tale about the effect of *Camoquin* exploits on the army related how a military patrol solemnly reported to

Duvalier from the Pine Forest area that it had captured two cows, one mule, one horse, and two donkeys on the 'strategic Estimé Road'. It added significantly that one animal had the mark 'MW' on its side and concluded: 'We are awaiting instructions from our supreme chief.'

By the second week of August Duvalier decided to repay the Dominicans with a dose of what he thought they were giving him. He called together a group of twelve Dominican exiles, mostly people he had released from Haitian jails, and issued them olive-green uniforms and arms. According to the testimony of one of them, Duvalier called them to his office and outlined a special mission: 'attack and burn' the Dominican border post of El Aguacate and machine-gun its occupants. He told them a well-armed Haitian patrol would support them.

An exile, with the unlikely name of Termistocles Vicioso Abreu, testified that Duvalier gave each man $160 (in Haitian *gourdes*) and provided them with eight 7-millimetre rifles, two Thompson sub machine guns, two .45-calibre pistols, eight incendiary and fragmentation grenades, plus a quantity of gasoline and cotton to make Molotov cocktails. Vicioso Abreu identified all eleven men as former policemen or informers under Trujillo and said that Duvalier had housed them in a hotel for one month before the mission.

Their first try failed. They returned to a Haitian captain and claimed they had gotten lost. They were taken back to prison and the morning of 17 August hauled before Duvalier again. Vicioso Abreu described Duvalier as 'frantic' but said that the President gave them new weapons (five revolvers, two .45s, five Thompson sub machine guns, and one 7-millimetre rifle) and another chance. Two men refused to go.

The others were taken to a Haitian peasant house some three kilometres from the Aguacate post, where they rested, attacking just before midnight. The band threw grenades and opened up with the sub machine guns, but their hearts weren't in it. When the guards responded with rifle fire, they scattered. Among those captured was Vicioso Abreu. At a 21 August hearing in Santo Domingo he revealed what had happened.

But Duvalier had a second part to the plan. On 18 August he released to news services in Port-au-Prince the information that Dominican exiles had attacked and were holding a position on Dominican soil near Barahona and had declared a provisional government. In its reports United Press International properly attributed the tale to the Haitian government, quoting it as saying a 'great battle' had taken place either as a result of invasion or mutiny.

Outside Haiti the report was quickly proved untrue. Inside, where tight censorship was in force, it created confusion.

In releasing the Dominican story, the government also noted that an Air Force plane had dispersed a 'group of traitors and anti-patriots' who had camped near a rural school at Lesson. It said that the men had been posing as a medical team sent by Duvalier.

These were the *Jeune Haiti* forces. From Petite Rivière the thirteen had pushed inland to the rural school in Lesson. *Jeune Haiti* was led by twenty-four-year-old Guslé Villedrouin, a former US airman and son of Haitian Army Colonel Roger Villedrouin, beaten to death by Tonton Macoutes in April 1962. His chief lieutenant was Gérald Brièrre, thirty, an economics student who had lived in the United States and served in the US Army. Brièrre's brother, Eric, had been tortured to death by Duvalier's secret police as a plotter in 1960.

Most, though not all of the band, were mulattoes with families in Jérémie, the birthplace of Dumas Père and Audubon, the famous naturalist. This picturesque old provincial town, reflecting the decay into which Haiti, especially provincial Haiti, had fallen, was their first objective.

All details of the battle have not been revealed, but in the engagement near Jérémie it was known that *Jeune Haiti* ambushed a unit of the Haitian army's tactical battalion and inflicted severe losses. The invaders never reached Jérémie itself, however.

An army radio communiqué monitored at the time revealed Duvalier's mood. His voice was heard urging from the palace, 'Get me one prisoner, just one.' The army commander who survived the ambush replied by asking for transportation to remove his dead and wounded. The wounded were taken to Aux Cayes, on the sealed-off peninsula, rather than Port-au-Prince, in order to keep their number secret. During the Jérémie battle *Jeune Haiti* hit a Haitian Air Force plane (AT-6). Disabled, it made a forced landing at the Jérémie airport.

Villedrouin's intention was to land close to Jérémie and take the town by surprise, but this failed. His men encountered Duvalierist forces after they moved out of Lesson and, despite the successful ambush, the larger government forces drove them back. This upset a prearranged option – to be co-ordinated by radio – either for reinforcements to land from the sea or for *Jeune Haiti* to escape if things were not going well. In the retreat from the Jérémie area inland towards the town of Préville, Villedrouin's band lost their radio and were unable to arrange the possible landing of reinforcements.

At Préville one of the band, Yvan D. Laraque, tried to cover the retreat by throwing a barrage of grenades at the advancing Duvalierists. He was killed.

After the Jérémie episode Duvalier's revenge was typically morbid. Laraque's body was taken to Port-au-Prince. A police pick-up truck transferred it from the airport to the intersection of Grand'Rue and Somoza Avenue, where it was left as an exhibit. The bloated body was tied to a wooden garden chair with a ragged olive-green fatigue uniform coat thrown over one shoulder. It was set up facing a giant Coca-Cola sign saying 'Welcome to Haiti' across from the international airport.

This grisly scene took place just fifteen days after Duvalier ordered a new $40,000 campaign for tourism under Tourist Director Gérard de Catalogne.

Duvalier claimed that Laraque had led the rebel attack on Jérémie. A sign was hung on the body – 'chief of the traitors to his country killed at Grande-Anse' – and the putrid display remained there three days. The Liberian Ambassador complained to the foreign office that the exhibition was a disgrace to men of African descent.

The militia was ordered into Jérémie to kill the families of the invaders. Men, women, and children were tortured and executed, their homes looted and burned. Estimates place the victims at more than one hundred.

The Sansaricqs, a mulatto family, were unjustly and inaccurately accused of having a son among the rebels. They were stripped naked and made to walk through the streets of Jérémie before jeering Duvalierists. The father, Pierre Sansaricq, was told that the family would be released if he opened the store safe. He did, and the Sansaricqs were last seen being driven to the airport. Children were hacked to death in their mothers' arms and adults were shot.

It became a practice to shoot the women or children first to enrage the male members of the family, thus giving the Tonton Macoutes a little extra sport. Members of the Drouin, Villedrouin, Laforest, and Guilbaud families also were killed. Gérard Guilbaud and his wife, a Drouin, also store owners, were executed in the same way. First to go in the Villedrouin family was the father, Victor, and then the Tonton Macoutes went after the two children, Lisa, eighteen, and Frantz, sixteen, and their mother. They died singing a church hymn.

Meantime, the little *Jeune Haiti* forces were being whittled down in clashes with the army and finally were eliminated. According to the Haitian government's account, the *Jeune Haiti* forces moved south toward the lower coast of the peninsula after the Jérémie defeat and at Cahouanne 17 August fought briefly with the militia, both sides suffering casualties. They forged east through the mountains and ambushed a government patrol at Caliot on 29 August, wounding and capturing Haitian Army Lieutenant Léon Achille. *Jeune Haiti* gave him first aid and helped him find his way back to the coast with a group of peasants. Duvalier ordered Achille back to Port-au-Prince and came to his bedside to interrogate him.

Jeune Haiti had better luck with supplies than had the *Camoquins* on their Saltrou landing. They were able to buy food from peasants, carefully paying twice normal prices to show their good will. Water also was available.

In Port-au-Prince rumours of the two-front battle ballooned

and people began seeing rebels everywhere. Estimates of their strength climbed into the hundreds. Reports circulated that rebels masquerading as Tonton Macoutes had slipped into Port-au-Prince.

The capital appeared generally normal during the day, but at night the streets were empty, night clubs closed, and the usual long lines at movie theatres disappeared.

Paul Blanchet, as a proper propaganda chief should, discounted the whole thing. 'They are nothing,' he said of the rebels. 'They will not succeed. They do not have the support of the people.'

There was considerable unrest among officials, however, and many began sending their families to Europe on vacation. Some even went themselves – when Duvalier allowed them out of the country.

Late in August Hurricane Cleo struck across the southern peninsula, destroying many buildings in Les Cayes, killing at least 124 persons in the area, and leaving many homeless and without food. Les Cayes had hardly been touched by Hurricane Flora in 1963.

Fearing a long campaign, for which he was unprepared, Duvalier began a scramble for additional arms and ammunition. Father Jean-Baptiste Georges's Haitian Revolutionary Armed Forces or FARH was in the market, too, and urgently needed to get new matériel to the two invading groups.

The FARH cause suffered a serious setback on 1 September when Father Georges was arrested by customs agents in Miami and charged with 'conspiring to export munitions of war for revolutionary purposes'. Customs agents said that a trailer-load of arms transported from New York State was seized and that Father Georges had a key to the trailer. He was released on $1,000 bond and the charge was eventually dropped. Duvalier was elated at the news, and happily played up Georges's arrest in Haitian newspapers as US co-operation for his fight.

Duvalier had his own lines out for weapons, and it was not long before they also hit snags. He sent a delegation to Central America and Panama on an arms-buying mission and later tried his luck in the United States where the export of military equipment to Haiti had been banned after the May 1963 crisis.

Duvalier sought T-28 trainer planes, regarded as ideal for use against guerrilla forces, and at least two were shipped illegally to Haiti from the United States. Other attempted shipments were stopped by US authorities. Papa Doc ran into an additional problem when he discovered that his Air Force machine guns would not fit the mounts on his new T-28s. He could not find an armourer to do the job, and for this he also turned to the United States. The United States turned down Haitian requests to buy twenty-four Naval craft including torpedo (PT) boats.

Duvalier was furious when customs agents in southern Florida seized a huge arms shipment at the Fort Lauderdale airport as it was being loaded on a plane apparently bound for Haiti. Arrested and charged with arms smuggling was Dr Carlo Mevs, a Haitian dentist and businessman. Agents estimated that the arms, including 50,000 rounds of .30-calibre ammunition, were worth some one hundred thousand dollars in Haiti. Duvalier censored all news of the Mevs arrest.

Rudolph Baboun, Duvalier's Consul in Miami, Florida, was later charged with complicity in shipping arms, mostly pistols in small lots, to Haiti without an export licence. He was also implicated in the deal involving the two T-28 planes, purchased in Florida and flown to Haiti in violation of US laws. Baboun was given a choice of either leaving the country or facing trial in the United States. He left Miami, newspapers noted, one hour and three minutes ahead of the deadline on a Haiti-bound plane. A grateful Duvalier appointed Baboun first commercial attaché at the Embassy in Mexico City and then in 1967 elevated him to the post of Ambassador. Baboun is the first Haitian-born Lebanese to become an ambassador.

Political jockeying developed and eventually all charges were dropped at the request of the US State Department, apparently in an informal prisoner swap. Involved in the exchange were US citizens aboard the fifty-foot ketch *Fairwinds,* with five persons aboard. The *Fairwinds*, two and one half months out of the Virgin Islands, was on a combined cruise for pleasure, nautical chart, and historical exploration. Aboard were three US citizens, including the captain, Kit S. Kapp. The *Fairwinds* sailed from Jamaica to the port of Jacmel on the beleaguered Haitian southern peninsula, where Haitian authorities took them into custody. After nineteen days of unexplained detention they were taken to Port-au-Prince and released. Charges against Dr Mevs were dropped in Miami at the request of the State Department. Later, the charges against Father Georges were also withdrawn.

Duvalier kept the pressure on in Port-au-Prince. On 6 September a gang of men identified as police burst into a Catholic church service, locked the doors behind them, and beat up the persons inside, including priests. The men invaded the church after receiving a report that a 'black mass' was being held to bring evil upon President Duvalier.

One noon (30 August), as they anxiously awaited the arrival of new arms promised them, the *Camoquins* heard Spanish-speaking voices in the clear mountain air. They assumed there was a Dominican army patrol along the border. Not sure what to expect, a sentry fired a warning pistol shot into the air.

The Dominicans replied with a barrage of .30-calibre machine-gun fire, and the *Camoquins*, not wishing to fight Dominicans, scrambled in retreat. Fred Baptiste fell off a ledge during the chase and broke his leg in two places. Abandoning their camp, the young rebels took a circuitous route back across the border. Fred Baptiste's brother, Reneld, helped carry him.

A few days later, Dominican Armed Forces Minister General Victor Elby Viñas Roman announced that Haitian troops had attacked a post at Malpasse, wounding a Dominican sentry. He said that a Haitian plane had flown over Malpasse shortly before the attack. The border was reinforced and President Donald Reid Cabral later revealed that an army request for additional tanks at the border was denied by General Wessin y Wessin on the grounds that a Dominican *coup d'état* might be planned and he could not weaken his Santo Domingo forces.

Baptiste's men were captured and taken once more down from the hills to the little town of Neyba, where they were imprisoned, without rations and almost naked because they had sold other prisoners their clothes for scraps of food. The *Camoquins* subsisted in a semi-starved condition in Neyba until the President was informed of their plight, and they were released, once more to be housed in the dilapidated Insane Asylum of Nigua which had become home to Haitians returning from their little wars. Fred Baptiste, because of the lack of medical attention at Neyba, had a long battle in the hospital to save his foot from gangrene.

Under a loose guard at the Nigua Insane Asylum the *Camoquins* set to work to live off the surrounding land. They planted a garden, irrigated it with a home-made bamboo aqueduct, and set up an alphabetization school for the children of the neighbourhood and soldiers. For a living, they fished, made furniture, and were helped by such visitors as Graham Greene in purchasing baby chicks to start a chicken farm. Regular army discipline was never dropped, however.

The *Jeune Haiti*-ites, meanwhile, carried to the end their fight against Duvalier in the Southern Peninsula. The Haitian army report noted that from the Caliot skirmish on 29 August they moved across the Macaya Mountains to Dallest, where they encountered Duvalier's tactical battalion on 8 September. In this brief but ferocious exchange three rebels died: Brièrre, the second-in-command; Charles Henri Forbin, twenty-three, former US paratrooper and son of Colonel Alfred Forbin, arrested and executed in 1963; Jacques Wadestrand, twenty-nine, graduate of Harvard, survived by a wife and son in New York.

In the following days the rebels climbed to Pic Forman, second highest peak in the Macaya range, and lost two more men – the brothers Jacques, twenty-six, and Max, twenty-five, Armand. Their father, Benoit Armand, had been murdered by Tonton Macoutes in April 1963. Jacques, with a US wife and child, was an economics graduate of New York University. Max had a degree from the same school in electrical engineering.

To get supplies, *Jeune Haiti*'s Marcel Numa, twenty-one, dressed as a peasant and travelled south to the coastal village of Coteaux (27 September), where he was captured as he tried to make market purchases. Numa, a black, was the son of a Jérémie coffee planter, had studied diesel engineering at the Bronx Merchant Marine Academy, and worked for US shipping lines.

Duvalier gloated when Numa had told his interrogators that the rebels were running out of food and clothing and that their morale was low.

The pursuing Duvalierists engaged *Jeune Haiti* again (29 September) at Morne Sinai and their numbers dwindled to four as Mirko Chandler and Jean Gerdès were killed. Both had lived abroad as exiles and had lost members of their families to Tonton Macoute brutality.

The remaining four pushed east to Pic Tête Boeuf, where Roland Rigaud, thirty-two, was wounded in a militia battle 4 October. Some two weeks later the militia pinned them again (16 October), wounding Louis Drouin, twenty-eight, and capturing him three days later. Drouin, mulatto son of a Jérémie baker, also had served in the US armed forces and had studied finance and worked in banks in New York.

On 26 October 1964, Guslé Villedrouin, Roland Rigaud, and Réginal Jourdan fought their last battle at Ravine Roche, a few kilometres from L'Asile. Villedrouin, former US airman, was leader of the *Jeune Haiti* guerrillas. His father was an early Tonton Macoute victim. Rigaud was the son of Georges Rigaud, the dentist and one-time candidate of the PSP party who was jailed during the 1960 student strike and liquidated. Jourdan was one of the few remaining relatives of Hector Riobé, the young revolutionary who died in battle July 1963. Their ammunition gone and surrounded by a horde of militia and troops, they used stones in their last war effort. As usual, their heads were sent back to the palace in Port-au-Prince.

On 28 October the government issued a 'total victory' communiqué. Foreign Minister Chalmers furnished pictures to newspapers of the severed heads of Rigaud, Jourdan, and Villedrouin photographed on a white background and held by anonymous hands. Identity card pictures of the other nine also were published.

The same day Duvalier nationalized the properties of those killed during the Jérémie reprisals and said they were stripped of their Haitian nationality, and stricken with 'civil death'. Two days later Gérard de Catalogne, the tourism director, welcomed forty travel agents to Port-au-Prince. He told them all was quiet and peaceful in Haiti and that only sensation-seeking newsmen opposed to progress for the little Negro country said otherwise. 'We have no Harlem, Rochester, or Little Rock. Everyone is safe here,' he said.

There still remained a celebration – the execution of Numa and Drouin. Early on the morning of 12 November 1964, several thousand persons crowded before the high wall at the national cemetery. To ensure a large crowd, the government ordered businesses and schools closed. Government employees were allowed to report late to their jobs. Peasants were trucked in from the country. School children were urged to attend.

Duvalier had repeatedly said that his enemies were foreign whites, but the crowd saw only Numa, a tall black, and Drouin, a short mulatto, their hands tied behind them to pine poles. A nine-man firing squad, television cameras, and radio microphones faced them. The execution was broadcast like a football game and reshown over Tele-Haiti for a week. Blue leaflets, like programmes, were distributed to the crowd. They announced Duvalier's victory over the rebel thirteen, with this message:

> Dr François Duvalier will fulfil his sacrosanct mission. He has crushed and will always crush the attempts of the anti-patriots. Think well renegades. You will not enjoy the gold with which they filled your pockets. Here fate expects you and your kind. They will not pass. Duvalierism, leaning on the living forces of the nation, will crush any sacrilegious invasion of the sacred soil of the fatherland.... Thus will perish the anti-patriots who want to put again the Haiti of Jean-Jacques Dessalines under the whip of the colonials. No force will stop the invincible march of the Duvalierist

revolution. It carries the strength of a torrent.... The Duvalier revolution will triumph. It will trample the bodies of traitors and renegades and those who sell out....

When the two men were tied firmly to the stakes, a little French priest approached each in turn. Both Drouin and Numa, the negro and mulatto, declined his services and pronounced themselves anti-Duvalier and hurled insults with their last breath. Lieutenant Pierre Albert ordered the execution squad to fire. As the officer, carrying a book in one hand and a forty-five automatic in the other, delivered the *coup de grâce*, there was a great silence, as if the crowd were holding its breath.

Le Matin's account of the execution carried a vivid description:

And this morning one should have seen this huge crowd, this feverish crowd, communicating in a mutual patriotic exaltation; this crowd who had only one heart, one soul to curse adventurism and brigandage; this crowd, it was made up of people, they were workers, functionaries, and employees of the government, businessmen, all the forces of the nation standing, manifesting their total adhesion to the politics of peace of the Duvalier government....

There was no effort to disguise the suggestion that the United States had backed the gallant thirteen.

Before the month was over, Duvalier decorated 129 army personnel, civilians, militia, and police for their part in eliminating the thirteen rebels. Additional decorations went to Luc Désir and Elois Maître for 'exceptional bravery' on 14 July 1963, the day the Barbot brothers were killed.

Foreign Minister Chalmers had already said that Haiti was willing to negotiate, and with the invaders eliminated, Duvalier moved again to make peace with the Dominican Republic. Under the urging of the OAS, and with the United States agreeing behind the scenes, the two countries decided to expel their militant exiles. Duvalier submitted a long list of Haitians he wanted to see out of the Dominican Republic, and discovered only seven were there. These included Louis Déjoie and Pierre Rigaud. Déjoie protested in a letter to a Dominican official saying he had not been involved in any of the activities, as had Rigaud, Father Bajeux, and a number of others on Duvalier's list. He also wrote in the newspapers that he had as much right as the Dominicans to be on Dominican soil. This infuriated Dominicans. Rigaud, a smooth politician, graciously thanked the Dominican people for their courtesies, and departed.

The OAS persuaded Haiti to permit the exit of political asylees still in Haiti. Lieutenant François Benoit and other army officers who had been sentenced to death *in absentia* by a Haitian military court were finally allowed out of the country.

Visiting Haiti in December, Richard Eder of the *New York Times* noted that Haitian officials took every opportunity to express their satisfaction with US Ambassador Timmons. In a story (6 December) he summed up the US position in Haiti:

> A policy characterized as 'normal relations' with the government of President François Duvalier and the form in which it is carried out by the American Embassy appears to have placed American prestige here at its lowest point in many years.

Why did the guerrillas fail? There was no question of their dedication, perseverance, and faith in their mission. Their efforts failed because of the disunity among Haitian exiles; the persecution by Dominican authorities; the failure of so-called supporters to come through with material aid. Compounding all this was a fatal underestimation by the guerrillas of the bleak, hostile terrain they chose as a battlefield.

The small groups, ill-equipped, plagued by hunger and thirst and a lack of reinforcements, were doomed. In retrospect, it is surprising they lasted as long as they did. Their lack of planning and organization was underlined by the fact that the two groups, one led by Fred Baptiste and the other the *Jeune Haiti* thirteen, struck almost at the same time at opposite ends of the country with no signs of liaison or common objective either with one another or with opposition groups inside the country.

Of the two groups, the *Jeune Haiti*, operating in the south, appeared to be the best prepared materially and ideologically for the operation. They lasted nearly three months, fighting against numerically superior forces that later, in an official communiqué, unwittingly acknowledged their skill and determination. Except for two who were executed, the thirteen men all died fighting. They had gone into the campaign with a clear objective and faith in their concept of a future Haiti. Their formula of government had already been mapped, but even at this early stage it was infected with the curse of Haitian politics, sectarianism. Instead of joining up with the other guerrillas, they chose to strike out on their own.

The suicidal aspect of this mission aroused some of their Haitian supporters in the Dominican Republic to seek reinforcements in desperate haste. The wife of one of the *Jeune Haiti* guerrillas abandoned her home in a dramatic, if futile, effort to establish a training base for a support force. The camp, far removed from the Haitian border near the Dominican Republic's eastern shores, went well for a time – until the moment for the landing in Haiti arrived. Then the excuses began. Some of the leaders of this reinforcement group announced that they would refuse to sail until they had seen the guns promised them. They claimed that they did not trust their brothers in arms who, with the help of Cuban exiles, had obtained arms in Miami and were waiting to sail. They emphasized that they didn't want to incur the fate that overtook Baptiste's *Camoquins*.

Another fatal delay developed when the new expedition's leaders decided against a clandestine operation and sought permission from authorities for their landing craft, inbound from Miami, to use Dominican facilities for refuelling and loading operations. This permission was never granted, and before the painfully slow expedition could even get off the ground the Haitian government announced the defeat of the *Jeune Haiti* invasion.

The Baptiste operation in many ways was almost totally without formal planning and objectives. Vengeance was the primary fuel behind this expedition, made up largely of young men who had suffered directly or indirectly the brutal repressions of the tyranny. They were united by a desperation to rid Haiti not only of Duvalier but also of the contemporary Haitian politician whom they regarded as corrupt, opportunistic, and as bloodthirsty as Papa Doc himself. With only a primitive grounding in politics, there was no central idea to unify their thoughts, which seemed more anarchistic than anything else.

This group was continuously hounded by a fear of being betrayed and in this they were justified. They were victims of betrayal by both the far right and the left. First, a high-ranking Dominican military officer promised the guerrillas delivery of a consignment of weapons near the border which never took place. Trouble from the other extreme developed when Marxists intercepted a load of automatic rifles, smuggled into Santo Domingo from New York, consigned to the Baptiste forces. These weapons fell into the custody of Jacques Viau, a Haitian schoolteacher exiled in Santo Domingo since 1946 when his brother was lynched after killing a newspaper editor in Port-au-Prince. Unknown but to his closest friends were Viau's Marxist leanings. Viau later confided to intimates that he withheld the arms from Baptiste's group because they had failed to spell out a clear ideological position. A talented poet, Viau became a unit commander of the Castroite 14th of June Revolutionary Movement at the outbreak of the 1965 Dominican Civil War. On 15 June of that year a US bazooka shell shredded both his legs and after amputation he died in a hospital.

Other exiles who might have helped the Baptiste group sat safely but not quietly in Santo Domingo. They opposed Baptiste and happily predicted that his mission would end in failure. They wrote false stories about the guerrillas in the Dominican press, accusing them of being ruthless killers.

And then there is the peasant of the La Selle region. The poorest of the hemisphere's poor, he cannot feed his own family, let alone provide food, even in return for money, to guerrillas. He can be recruited, as the Baptiste group learned, but only if he is convinced that the rebels have a good chance for victory, since failure can mean execution for his entire family by the returning Duvalier forces.

When civil war broke out in the Dominican Republic in April 1965, Duvalier's spirits received another boost for, with the intervention of US troops, the country became too security-conscious to harbour much clandestine military activity no matter whom it might be directed against.

Haitian exiles found themselves supporting pro-Bosch constitutionalist forces. Fred Baptiste and his *Camoquins*, still living in the old Nigua Insane Asylum, sided with the deposed President out of fear of General Wessin y Wessin. (Wessin, it is worth noting, was the principal leader of the anti-Bosch forces in the early days of the civil war, and Baptiste said later that he had been warned that Wessin would have been only too delighted to kill every *Camoquin* he could lay his hands on.) The revolt began on Saturday, 24 April 1965.

The United States sent in the Marines and the 82nd Airborne Division. They hit Dominican soil on the evening of 28 April; and, the following month when the Organization of American States finally voted to use military measures to end the 'Dominican conflict', the American troops (23,000 of them) became part of the Inter-American Peace Force or IAPF.

The US intervention halted a victory by the constitutional forces, and when the US troops eventually departed seventeen months later the status quo was once again firmly entrenched in Dominican politics. Along into exile with the leading members of the constitutional forces, such as Colonel Francisco Caamaño, went the Baptiste brothers and several of their chief lieutenants. Their participation in the Civil War, together with the less than amicable overtures of neighbourly warmth by right-wing factions brought back to power with the election of Joaquin Balaguer on 1 June 1966, led the Baptistes to suspect that they and the vast majority of anti-Duvalier Haitians had overstayed their welcome and were about as safe in the Dominican Republic as exiles were under Dictator Trujillo, whom Balaguer had served loyally up until his assassination. They departed for Europe.

18

Seeking a New Image and the Press

In his 1 January 1965 Independence Day speech, Duvalier reviewed the bloody year that had passed, and assured his subjects that history would prove him right. 'I seek not violence. I seek not reprisals, but I do not fear to carry them out wherever called for,' he declared. Using a now familiar theme, he added, voice ringing with conviction, that 'we will take any action necessary for the fulfilment of the obligations we contracted as President for Life.'

But for the first time he showed both concern for his international image and a willingness to make concessions in an effort to change it. He said he was ready to resume relations with the Dominican Republic.

He criticized sharply 'a certain press' that presented Haiti as a country 'where you meet at every corner a thug, gun in hand, ready to grab the tourist's purse. We answer this corrupt press with our contempt and our work.' He invited all Haitians, again, to join in a national effort for the development of the country and cited the newly completed jet airport as an example of what Haitians could achieve working together.

The airport had been a long time coming, and was, as Duvalier had said, an example of what Haitians could do when they put their minds and bodies to work. But it was also an example of the ineptness of the Duvalier regime. If it had not been for greedy Duvalierists who sought kickbacks in return for securing the contract for foreign construction firms, jets could have been landing in Haiti five years before they did. On two separate occasions the United States came through with the airport loan Duvalier wanted, once after the blackmail at the Punta del Este OAS conference for Haiti's vote against Cuba. But even then the money-hungry Duvalierists invalidated the loan by signing a contract with a private American company which was soon found to be a phantom operation unable, indeed unequipped, to do the work.

Three expensive preliminary studies of the airport were made and at least four different contracts were signed with foreign firms for its construction, but each time the work was never started because the firms were undermined by Duvalierists pushing for their own companies, or because the firms turned out to be fly-by-night outfits. Taxes were collected for five years in the name of the jet airport and amounted to several times the final cost. The idea that Haiti should do the job independently was expressed in April 1960 by Haitian businessmen who suggested plans for Haitian financing, but they were ignored.

The airport dedication, on Duvalier's favourite date, 22 January 1964, was built into a major event which marked a new and serious effort to revive tourism. Streets in the city were swept and potholes filled. Some downtown buildings were painted and beggars were ordered out of town. Statistics showed 19,457 tourist arrivals in 1964, a staggering 58-per-cent drop from those who were still being lured by Haiti's many attractions during the hectic year of 1963. In its best years Haiti once had drawn over seventy-five thousand tourists.

Duvalier hired US public-relations firms, first Woody Kepner Associates, Inc., of Miami, later replaced by Newman-Schulte, Inc., also of Miami (at $2,500 per month according to figures listed when the firm registered as a foreign agent with the US Justice Department), and when he began to receive sound public-relations advice, he seemed, surprisingly, to listen.

Funds for the promotion of tourism, under the direction of Gérard de Catalogne, amounting to $1.9 million in 1964, were increased for 1965, and supplemented with $150 contributions solicited from local merchants. Some businessmen privately complained that capital driven out of the country each year by Duvalierism amounted to more than the tourism budget.

De Catalogne explained that the publicity campaign to attract US tourists would begin to show results only in 1966, if the country remained politically calm.

In all Haiti had 800 hotel rooms, but only one or two of the hotels had more than a half-dozen guests at the time. US cruise ships, which stopped weekly for a few hours, were providing the bulk of tourism. Before the jet airport dedication Richard Homan of the *Washington Post* visited Haiti and spoke of the empty hotels and resorts, the guns and the many reproductions of François Duvalier's face. He was struck by one jukebox that carried one selection which simply repeated over and over 'We all like him real good, we all like him real good, we all like him real good'. A waiter explained to Homan 'That's for our President.'

The inaugural flight for the new jet airport brought in a delegation of US travel writers and travel agents from New York.

They were entertained and told of Haiti's special attractions. Among the writers was Herbert Gold, an old hand in Haiti, who wrote knowledgeably of his trip for the *Saturday Evening Post*. He quoted one bitter resident of Port-au-Prince as saying that Duvalier had performed an economic miracle for Haiti – 'He has taught us to live without money and eat without food. No, that's not all. Duvalier has taught us to live without life.' But, Gold said, some of the visiting journalists went home with kinder impressions.

Duvalier decided to make a special pitch to US blacks. 'I think that perhaps because we are a Negro nation, the American Negro might be interested in coming,' said de Catalogne. The three black American journalists among the travel writers' group perhaps offered the most perceptive remarks of any. 'If the American Negro can ignore poverty, then he can have a good time for his buck,' said James Hicks, executive editor of the *Amsterdam News* in New York. Alex Poinsett of *Ebony* magazine and Phyllis Garland of the *Pittsburgh Courier* rejected the idea that American blacks would be drawn to Haiti simply because it was a black nation. Poinsett said: 'The color made me feel at home. But after a while you find prejudice. It is a subtle color and class prejudice and it sullies the first good feeling.' But all three recommended Haiti as a beautiful country to visit. 'If you've got money and want to get away, Haiti's the place. But if you're sensitive to poverty, you can get twisted down here. And most Negroes are sensitive to poverty. My advice is to stay put in your hotel and don't go to see the countryside.'

Early in 1965 Duvalier made his usual appeal for US aid. He asked President Johnson for financial aid and a word or two of public endorsement. That the United States had rejected five requests for aid within a year and no US President had spoken well of Duvalier in more than three years did not deter Papa Doc. But the United States was still trying to persuade Duvalier to clean up his debts to US private businesses, a campaign under way since 1962, and did not precisely rush to his assistance.

A murder that had stirred the population of Cap-Haïtien didn't help Duvalier in his image-seeking. An account of the death of Antoine Piquion, who had been a deputy during the Paul Magloire government, was published in the *New York Times* on 11 March under a Cap-Haïtien dateline by Edward G. Burks. The killing had taken place in the Rumba Club, a night spot heavily patronized by soldiers and Tonton Macoutes where the firing of guns 'was a frequent occurrence'. The orchestra leader at the club, regarded as a friend of Duvalier's, had complained to the President and asked him to stop the shooting. This enraged the local Tonton Macoutes, who went looking for him. They did not find him at the club, but killed Piquion instead with a wild burst of sub-machine-gun fire that also wounded two other persons present. The officer responsible for the incident was transferred back to Port-au-Prince.

Later in the year, when Duvalier decided that tourists did not have the proper atmosphere for fun, the Department of the Interior issued a communiqué advising Haitians to go out 'in the evening, enjoy themselves, and make the capital's night life more attractive'. It suggested that 'state employees and Duvalierists in general ... frequent bars, restaurants, and the international casino.'

De Catalogne's attempt to keep a happy mask over Haiti for the benefit of tourism was uncovered by *Time* magazine late in August. The magazine, commenting on Haitian conditions, said that some starving peasant mothers were trying to sell their babies for forty cents. Offended, De Catalogne wrote *Time* a letter calling the report 'a fantasy'. *Time* printed De Catalogne's letter, and underneath it carried another by a member of a Baptist Youth Mission which went to Haiti. It said: 'I can testify to the deplorable conditions you describe ...'

On 19 July, 1965, Radio New York Worldwide (WRUL shortwave) launched programmes competitive with the daily Communist offerings from Cuba. It began with a half hour each morning (six to six thirty), and an enterprising young exile named Raymond Alcide Joseph emerged as the primary commentator.

By September the criticism had become sharp enough to prompt a Duvalier protest. The *Miami Herald* commented:

> It is hoped that nobody in the State Department or the White House will waste any time or tears over the note of protest from Haitian President François Duvalier against a radio program being beamed to the Caribbean nation from New York. The head man in Haiti complains that many of his people believe that the US government is behind the anti-Duvalier broadcasts. If that were true, it would be one of the better ideas and better efforts of the State Department in dealing with the brutal dictator. If the United States supports radio broadcasts to the subjected people of Eastern Europe, then it would not have to apologize for beaming a message of truth and hope to the people of Haiti. ... It is certain that the people of Haiti do not know the US government has offered to donate $2 million worth of surplus food to be distributed by church groups to the starving peasants along the island's southern coast, and that Duvalier has refused to transport that food.

The reference was to a story by Louis Uchitelle of the Associated Press, who visited Les Cayes and reported thousands of persons starving because of drought. Hurricanes Flora and Cleo of the two previous years, which stripped the peninsula of much of its vegetation, were held partly responsible.

'The US government offered to make available $2 million worth of surplus food, to be distributed by Church World Service and CARE. The two agencies asked President François Duvalier's government to pay for transporting that food in Haiti, and were refused. The transportation bill would have been between $10,000 and $20,000,' Uchitelle wrote on 3 September.

De Catalogne, disturbed to see the new image slipping badly, fired off a letter of complaint to the *Miami Herald* saying he had read Uchitelle's article 'with stupefaction'. He denied it all. But Uchitelle, Church World Service, and the Associated Press reaffirmed the story. On 5 September Duvalier ordered three truckloads of food dispatched to the ravaged areas.

With his economy continuing to decline, Duvalier's bid for peace became more articulate. The pattern he chose to save Duvalierism was enunciated more clearly in his Independence Day speech of 1966.

'The time has arrived to put an end to the explosive phase of the Duvalier revolution,' he said, and called for an era of collaboration 'both national and international' to face the grave economic problems. He said that the country should not be burdened with 'explosion of distrust and incomprehension, fears, and terrors...

'To all Haitians, I repeat my patriotic call for reconciliation, agreement, concord, to valiantly face the battle for construction ... of a new Haiti.'

To implement his public-relations campaign, Duvalier relaxed his grip somewhat in 1966. Newsmen found him accessible and he saw a succession of them throughout the year. The message varied little – Haiti wanted peace, understanding, an end to the turmoil. But for the first time in several years the realities of the Duvalier dictatorship began to appear in a somewhat mellower light as newsmen, some strangers to Haiti and some Caribbean veterans, tried to present a balanced view of an unbalanced country. Robert H. Estabrook of the *Washington Post* wrote two stories in January which carried the intriguing headlines – 'Duvalier; Devil or Messiah?' and 'Haiti – It's Hell's Side of Paradise.' His observations:

> Duvalier is either the devil incarnate or something approaching a Messiah, depending on whom you talk to. Some compare his position to that of Stalin, with the addition of almost total corruption ... others regard him as a savior....
>
> In the Presidential Palace ... it is necessary to pass far more armed guards than in the Kremlin. Tanks sit in alcoves ... now the Tonton Macoutes ... are regarded as 'sentinels.' They have been upgraded from pistol-toting mobsters into a local version of the FBI, though guns are in evidence everywhere....

Reviewing his years in office, Duvalier told George Natanson of the *Los Angeles Times* that 'I have done most in the field of social legislation. My social legislation is the most advanced in the Western Hemisphere.' Natanson was told that the social programme, called the François Duvalier Code, guaranteed a one-dollar-a-day minimum wage among other rights. Current figures compiled by the Inter-American Development Bank put Haiti's per capita income at seventy-five dollars a year.

Robert Berrellez, the Associated Press's roving correspondent, described a telephone that sat on Duvalier's desk during his interview. It was an ivory-and-gold French cradle type with no numbers on the dial. It was just marked 'Doc'. While they talked, the telephone rang.

'Who are you calling?' Duvalier asked. 'No, this isn't the police. This is the President. [A pause.] Yes. Thank you, goodbye.' He then turned to Berrellez and explained, 'I get many calls like this. One day a soldier got the wrong number and rang me instead. We spoke a long time about some of his problems.'

Berrellez' reaction: 'The fact that the telephone rang is almost a news item in itself. The Port-au-Prince telephone system, like almost everything else in this impoverished but beautiful country, is run down and a satisfactory connection is like hitting a winning number in the lottery.'

Berrellez asked Duvalier if it were true, as exiles claimed, that he had killed all his political prisoners. 'No – all of them went abroad,' Duvalier replied. 'They went to Liberia, to the United States, Canada. Some are in Brazil in a place called

Island of Flowers.' He told Berrellez the now familiar story that there were no political prisoners in Haiti.

Berrellez pointed out that the fate of hundreds of political prisoners picked up during the crises of 1960, 1963, and 1964 was of deep concern to their relatives abroad. He noted that the Inter-American Human Rights Commission had been refused permission to come to Haiti and investigate. Duvalier, with a Gallic shrug and a cryptic smile, thanked him for the interview.

In the midst of the policy of sweetness and light a new crisis developed, apparently triggered by suspicion playing on the deep hatreds and bureaucratic jealousies built into the Duvalierist structure.

An anti-Duvalier plot was being pasted together in the United States by Haitian exile Henri Vixamar, who arrived from Africa with a vision of replacing Duvalier and set about the job with Cuban exile Rolando Masferrer. With minor variations, their plot was traditional: Cuban exiles would help Haitian exiles overthrow Duvalier, if they would then be allowed military bases from which they could attack Castro.

There was a variety of interpretations of what happened, but the most widely circulated story held that Duvalier, hearing that Vixamar was infiltrating men and matériel into North Haiti from the Bahamas, alerted his forces in Cap-Haïtien.

Raymond Joseph and his Haitian coalition radio broadcast quoted the Duvalier order: 'Eliminate physically any Haitian passenger from Nassau.' A half-dozen Haitians returning from Nassau in a small boat (March) were killed by the Tonton Macoutes on arrival in Cap-Haïtien.

Two other incidents in a matter of days, unrelated, heightened the feeling of unrest. A fire broke out in a two-block area of Cap-Haïtien, apparently started by a short circuit. It inspired rumours that it had been started by rebels or during government attempts to smoke out dissidents.

There was an equally obscure shooting in the area of the palace, but few facts leaked out as Duvalier sat on the happenings in an attempt to prevent tarnishing the new image he sought. Sifting the rumours, it finally was reported that eight members of the Presidential Guard, including a sergeant, were either discovered plotting or suspected of plotting. The incident revolved around weapons stolen from the palace, but there was suspicion that these might have been as much for sale as for revolt. Government employee salaries were being delayed because of lack of money. Interrogation and death for the eight followed. In the repercussion some army officers were shifted from Port-au-Prince and there were reports of other executions.

As news of these events leaked out of Haiti in various forms, it prompted a widespread belief that Duvalier was in such trouble that he could fall at any time. Most of these reports came late, after the incidents which prompted them had passed.

It was obvious, however, that the United States felt they had substance. Richard Reston, reporting from Washington for the *Los Angeles Times,* said, 'The administration has drawn in the last six weeks a new set of contingency plans to cope with a possible, perhaps sudden, collapse, of President François Duvalier's dictatorship.... Recent developments in Haiti suggest that Duvalier now faces internal pressures more serious than at any time since his last brush with political disaster in 1963.' Reston reported unrest in the military, arrests and executions, and 'corruption at a scandalous level'.

In March the International Commission of Jurists issued another bulletin condemning 'the flagrant disregard for the elementary notions of democracy in Haiti'. Duvalier was additionally angered because the British chose this period of unrest to withdraw their chargé d'affaires and close their embassy. The British reported that the move was for economy reasons and that it would be represented in Haiti by its Jamaican envoy. Additionally it was made clear, though, that the British found it hard to assist its citizens with difficulties before the Duvalier government.

The Inter-American Press Association, meeting in Caracas, gave Papa Doc another sock in the image when it commented in its report on press freedom in the hemisphere: 'Haiti is so far sunk in Duvalier's dictatorship that it can almost be said that it has lost contact with the rest of the Western Hemisphere. There is hardly a glimmer of hope for re-establishment in the foreseeable future of a free press there or other basic human rights.'

Papa Doc returned to the job of patching up his reputation. He announced that the Lion of Judah, Emperor Haile Selassie, would visit Haiti during a week's tour of the Caribbean. It was a rare event for any chief of state to visit Haiti, but Duvalier's second announcement caused greater surprise. Argentina invited all presidents in the Americas to attend its Independence Day celebrations in July and Duvalier, who never had left the country as President, said he would go. This set off a new wave of exile speculation. If Duvalier left the country, they said, he could never return. Before his plane cleared the airport, they predicted that Duvalierists would be scrambling to fill his chair.

Elaborate preparations were made for Emperor Selassie. A residence was prepared in Pétionville, and the streets over which the Emperor would drive were repaved. The palace was spruced up and whitewash liberally applied along the newly named Haile Selassie Avenue. Generous supplies of bunting, including 10,000 miniature flags, added to the festive air.

There was some disappointment when Emperor Selassie decided not to stay overnight, but Duvalier still made the most of the twelve hours he had. He insisted that only black, late-model cars transport the dignitaries. Since the government did not have enough of them, it simply 'borrowed' them from any Haitian residents who did.

There was a ceremony at the airport as Emperor Selassie arrived, and Duvalier, his wife, and children – surrounded by a ring of heavily armed Tonton Macoutes – were there in full dress. Papa Doc wore a top hat and tails; the Emperor was in uniform. They exchanged speeches, and Duvalier gave him the keys to the city and commented:

Your august presence exhorts my people, my government, and myself to continue to keep our sights riveted on those mountain peaks toward which we are walking, surely with pain, but with that faith which galvanizes, inspires heroism, and wins victories.

The Emperor commented that the world was a mixture of happiness and mischief and that it was necessary to have friends everywhere. The two chiefs lunched privately, exchanged decorations, spoke of international peace and co-operation. There was a formal reception at the palace before the Emperor left that night.

It was a banner day for Haiti, and Duvalier followed it up properly by throwing the palace open to visiting newsmen. He scoffed at reports of internal plotting against him, and reaffirmed his plans to visit Argentina.

Then he invited Haitian exiles to return and 'help put Haiti on its feet and forget the past. It is urgent for every Haitian', he said, 'to come home and work with the President and ministerial cabinet, and with every foreign investor that Haiti needs for its development.

'Everyone can come home because they are Haitians. The Haitian soil belongs to every Haitian.' He said they would be allowed to form opposition parties. 'In every democracy there should be opposition.'

The Haitian Coalition, expressing the sentiments of most exiles, replied over its daily radio broadcast from New York:

> It is evident that Duvalier is only trying to fool people by mouthing democratic slogans. What he really wants is money and any other aid, under whatever form, from the United States and the aid organizations, so that he may continue his iron grip on a populace that is showing signs of restiveness. Any help to the 'President for Life' of an 'American democracy', in any form, under any pretext, will be an affront to the hemisphere....

This and other exile comments, of course, received no reply.

Duvalier allowed himself to be interviewed on the Columbia Broadcasting System's *Face the Nation*. It was revealing. He led off with an explanation that contained the usual garble as his mind shifted gears: 'My doctrine is this, that in Haiti we have a democracy, Haitian democracy. Papa Doc ... is not a dictator. He is a democrat. His own people in the country consider him a democrat because he is a leader of the nation.'

When asked why he had a police state, Duvalier explained that there had been seven invasions of Haiti during his administration. One panellist asked why he had to resort to imprisonment and execution to protect the national territory. 'Nobody have been in prison or execution,' Duvalier replied in his fearless if grammatically leaky English. 'What ... what ... what ... what ... what ... what ... did you get that?'

He said he became President for Life thanks to 'the iron will of the Haitian people. The Haitian people is responsible because they want me because I tell you I am not only a President of Haiti but I am a leader of the Haitian people.'

One of the CBS men asked Duvalier if he thought he was the only man capable of being President of Haiti. 'Yes,' Duvalier said. 'I stress on that several times.'

There was an interesting exchange when a panellist asked why censors clipped out a story on Haiti from the *New York Times* before it was distributed in Haiti. Duvalier went into his act: 'What? ... No ... Your copy? Was cut out? Every Haitian get the *New York Times* here ... because it is the most popular newspaper in Haiti.' The panellist said 'Perhaps you don't understand.' Duvalier replied shortly 'I understand very well ... they cut out your article.... Cut out? ... What? ... With scissors? Where? From this copy? No ... no ... Everybody receive this issue of the *New York Times*.' Panellists tried to interject questions during this but made little headway. Duvalier told them that the question of United States aid was 'under way'.

Asked about voudou, he summed up: 'You do not understand me quite well. I am a scientist.'

But probably the classic description of a talk with Papa Doc was carried by *Newsweek* magazine 26 June, written by Milan J Kubic. Here is part of Kubic's report:

> When I asked a Presidential aide about reports that the peasants, who make up 90 per cent of Haiti's 4.7 million people, are suffering from malnutrition, he goggled with disbelief. 'Do you know how many mangoes they eat a year?' he countered – and then answered himself with a spur-of-the-moment statistic: '400 million....' Du-

valier himself impressed me as Big Brother masquerading as the Mad Hatter.

British novelist Graham Greene, using the real setting of Haiti and its exiles next door in the Dominican Republic, wrote a novel called *The Comedians*. It deals with the tragic and comic in Haiti, the happy and the sad masks, and the people who assume them. In the Introduction, Greene explained 'Poor Haiti itself and the character of Dr Duvalier's rule are not invented, the latter not even blackened for dramatic effect. Impossible to deepen that night.'

19

Communism Comes of Age

HAITIAN COMMUNISM

The parties and their publications[1]

PARTIES:

Haitian Communist Party (PCH). Formed 1934 by Jacques Roumain, outlawed same year. Roumain died 1944. The PCH re-emerged after the Second World War as a reorganized party which enjoyed, for a little more than a year, legal status. It dissolved itself in 1947 as a gesture of co-operation with Estimé.

Popular Socialist Party (PSP). Formed after the Second World War with some old members from the PCH. Outlawed 1948.

Popular Party of National Liberation (PPLN). Formed 1958 as 'Popular Democratic Party' but soon changed name to PPLN. Among its secret leadership was Professor Jean-Jacques Ambroise, murdered along with wife on Duvalier orders in 1966. PPLN shortly thereafter changed name to (Creole) 'Parti Unifié Démokrat Aisyin' (PUDA).

Party of Popular Accord (PEP). Formed 1959 by Jacques Alexis. Alexis executed on Duvalier orders 1961.

United Democratic Front for National Liberation (FDULN). Founded by congress of PEP and PPLN 4 July 1963 in Haiti as popular front of the two parties.

Exterior Organization of the FDULN (OREFH). Formed 1964 in Santiago, Chile, by FDULN and three exile affiliates.

United Party of Haitian Communists (PUCH) merged Haiti's

1. Acronyms are not translated from the French.

two communist parties, PEP and PUDA, in December 1968 after six months of unification talks.

PUBLICATIONS:

Liberation. Publication of the PPLN, began publishing in Creole in 1960. Changed name in 1966 to *Demokrasi*.

Voix du Peuple. Organ of the PEP, published in French.

Rassemblement. Began publishing in French, February 1964, for the FDULN.

Ralliement. Appeared in September 1962. Cover address in Switzerland. Adopted by OREFH. Ended publication in 1967 and was replaced by *Lambi*.

Avant-Garde. Theoretical and political journal of the PEP, began mimeographed circulation in Haiti in 1962. Internal party publication.

Cerf Volant. Publication of the Progressive Youth League, youth organization of the PEP.

Manchette. Two issues appeared in Belgium promoting Chinese Communist line of group of dissident Haitian Marxists.

Boukan. Organ of the PUCH, United Party of Haitian Communists, began publishing February 1969.

The indefinite, inconsistent pattern of Duvalier's governing methods – or lack of them – made him a handy target for anti-Communist zealots who regarded him as a Leftist extremist. In truth, Papa Doc is a Fascist of the same stripe as the late, unlamented Rafael Trujillo. He adopted a nationalist façade that had basic appeal to Haitians and which he then converted into a vehicle that wheedled him into the throne room of yet another hemispheric tyranny.

His early idealistic stances twisted under the strain of personal prejudices and the practical exigences of political survival. He squeezed every Haitian institution and level of society until the retrograde stamp of Duvalier was on everything.

Duvalier's youthful fascination for intellectuals who became Haiti's original Communists put him strongly to the left in political ideology, mostly unpractised. The bitterness of race, fierce anti-US feelings nurtured during the Marine occupation, the personality conflicts of a small, physically frail doctor who dreamed of being Dessalines, in conjunction with continuing danger to his regime, encouraged paranoia. He pictures himself as an embattled black genius.

Drifting into the more manageable mystic world, he became in his mind a messiah called to lead the people, his children, to reward and punish them as necessary. Like the king's subjects in the fable of the invisible clothes, no one in Haiti dared call him crazy. Nationalism, Communism, socialism, capitalism, and the men who represent them are his tools. He does not hesitate to drop one and pick up another.

Early in his Presidency, anti-Duvalierists assured the US State Department and CIA that Duvalier had slipped down to Mexico during his two-semester stay at the University of Michigan in 1944 to 1945 and signed a Communist manifesto. These and other charges were never proved, but what the opposition called tolerance of Communism by Duvalier has furnished a steady supply of propaganda material.

Duvalier welcomed back militant young leftists sent abroad by Estimé. He even invited some of those from the old intellectual crowd into his government. Well-known Marxists working for Duvalier included Lucien Daumec, a campaign speech writer and later his brother-in-law. He retained Jules Blanchet of the ex-PCH, one-time member of the French Communist party, as head of the Superior Court of Accounts. Duvalier picked him to advise one of his first economic missions to Washington; later appointed him Cabinet Minister Without Portfolio; eventually named him Haitian Ambassador to the European Common Market.

His brother, Paul Blanchet, was also close to Papa Doc. He, too, was accused of being a member of the French Communist party even though at the time the charges were made he had never been to France. Paul, Minister of Information and Co-ordination, is bitterly anti-American. Another former member of the French Communist party, Hervé Boyer, became Duvalier's Minister of Finance. These men represented the traditional European orientation of Haitian Communism.

They also illustrated why the party, up to the time of Duvalier, had little strength. They built luxurious homes, moved in the top circles of government, and had no contact with the people.

René Dépestre and Roger Gaillard were among the young militants who returned from Eastern Europe. Jacques Alexis, who had joined the PCH in 1938 at the age of sixteen, had returned from France with a medical degree in 1954. Dépestre and Gaillard followed in 1958. Dépestre's French-Rumanian wife went to work in the Department of Tourism. Gaillard worked on the newspaper *Le Matin*. Playwright Frank Fouché came back from Communist China and newspapers gave wide public attention to his lectures on the Chinese theatre.

Haiti was importing large quantities of textile goods from Eastern Europe when, in 1960, a hefty supply of old American flags gave these lively competition. The price was right and the print was colourful, but some American tourists were startled to see *marchandes* (market women) striding rhythmically down the streets with the Stars and Stripes covering their derrières. However, the flag operation was not some shady scheme of Balkan Communists, but legal enterprise by New York dealers who had to dispose of forty-eight-star flags, otherwise unsaleable because the fifty-star flags made them obsolete.

While Duvalier's enemies worked themselves into an uproar over these 'signs of Communism', the rising class of young Haitian Communists tended to sneer at them. In May 1965 the Communist publication *Ralliement* reported that Paul Blanchet had gone to Morocco to buy US-made arms for Duvalier and commented:

> Paul Blanchet, the jack-of-all-trades, was in charge of the delicate mission ... just as it was Jules Blanchet who was named Ambassador to the Common Market when Duvalier wanted to play up to De Gaulle. Oh, the Blanchet brothers! What a disgusting duet.... Yesterday they were saying they were Marxists; in reality they were – like many others – only small, ambitious intellectuals ... trying to exploit the prestige enjoyed by Marxism and popular thought....

The State Department's appraisals of Communism in Haiti have grown progressively cautious. In 1963 it issued a statement that said in part:

In the last year or two two clandestine Communist political organizations have become increasingly active: the Party of Popular Accord (PEP) and the People's National Liberation Party (PPLN). These entities, although relatively small in number, appear to be fairly well organized and growing. There is also increasing Communist influence in the country's weak labor movement.

Three years later, in 1966, the State Department said that Communist strength in Haiti was 'unknown' and repeated much of the 1963 summary:

The PPLN has suffered serious setbacks during the past year and is in considerable disarray. The PEP is small in number, but appears to be fairly well organized. Communist influence is apparent in the country's weak labor movement and also in sectors of the bureaucracy.

Clandestine Communist strength in any country is always hard to assess, but perhaps harder in Haiti than in most other places because of the difficult Creole language, clannish rural customs, the practice of voudou, and the undefined web of Duvalierism that offers a cloak to all willing to adopt it. Under Duvalier, Communism emerged from a salon game played by intellectuals to spread to the illiterate peasant and urban slum dweller as well.

The history of Communism in Haiti can be traced to a remarkable young mulatto writer from one of the old elite families, Jacques Roumain, whose poetry and other works must rank among the best produced in Haïti.

Roumain was born in 1907, attended a Catholic school in Port-au-Prince, and studied agriculture at a Belgian university. He returned to Haiti in 1927 and joined the literary set which, during the Marine occupation, expressed its nationalism in *La Revue Indigène*. He lived in his family's big two-storey house in fashionable Bois Verna.

Roumain accepted a department head's job in the Ministry

of Interior under the 1930 interim government of Louis E. Roy, but resigned after less than a week.

In 1934 he published a manifesto called *Schematic Analysis 32, 34,* a study of the Haitian social, political, and economic situation from the Marxist point of view. With it he announced the founding of the Haitian Communist party (PCH). Many of his literary associates joined, though not all. The party had little activity within the masses.

Roumain also edited with Georges Petit and Roger Cauvin *Le Petit Impartial.* President Sténio Vincent arrested all three and charged them with printing subversive literature. The trial was sensational. It degenerated into a courtroom brawl when the prosecuting attorney accused Roumain of springing from a family of murderers. (The reference was to Roumain's grandfather, President Tancrède Auguste, who had been suspected by some of blowing up the old palace in 1911.) Roumain hit the prosecutor and then fought courtroom attendants. President Vincent shipped him off to European exile after his release. A decree issued on 19 November 1936 outlawed the Communist party.

In Paris Roumain became a habitué of the Museum of Man and a close friend of the Communist poet Louis Aragon and a variety of other Leftist intellectuals. In Port-au-Prince C. Beaulieu took over the leadership of the party despite his failing health and constant police surveillance. When the Second World War broke out, Roumain returned to Haiti, and in 1941 founded the Bureau of Ethnology, whose principles attracted Duvalier.

Because Moscow backed all governments fighting Hitler, including Elie Lescot's, Roumain accepted an appointment as chargé d'affaires of the Haitian Embassy in Mexico City. He was criticized and called a pseudo-Marxist for collaborating with Lescot. Roumain defended himself, saying, after all, Lescot was an ally and a member of the anti-Fascist coalition. Although the Haitian Communists had no formal ties with Moscow at the time, Roumain was instinctively doing what Moscow would have wanted him to.

He drank excessively, became sick, and returned to Haiti

on 18 August 1944, where he died. His best-known work, the novel *Masters of the Dew*, was published posthumously. There were rumours that he had been poisoned, but the only poison he took was self-administered. He died of cirrhosis of the liver.

With the departure of Roumain the party lost impetus. Many of his old friends broke away and again confined themselves to what they called 'intellectual Marxism'.

At the close of the Second World War a group of young students organized a newspaper called *La Ruche* (The Beehive). These included Dépestre, Alexis, Gaillard, Daumec, Gérard Dominique, Jean and Gérard Chenet. When President Lescot closed *La Ruche*, it triggered a student strike which led to his downfall in January 1946.

After the fall of Lescot a new Haitian Communist party (PCH) surfaced anew. The thesis of the PCH of 1946 to 1947 was that the democratic revolution of 1946 should be turned into a socialist revolution and that the public enemy number one therefore was the Haitian bourgeoisie. The Cuban PSP denounced this thesis as 'infantile'.

Plagued by colour prejudice, a crucial issue of the 1946 revolution, the Communists split into two parties. Most of the mulatto Marxists formed the *Parti Socialiste Populaire*, while the youth of *La Ruche* gathered around Felix d'Orléans Juste Constant, a Protestant minister who once worked with Roumain. He became secretary-general of the PCH. The new PCH published a newspaper called *Combat*. Numerically it was weak, and did not bother to back a candidate in the 1946 elections.

PSP was formed with chicken farmer Anthony Léspès and Etienne Charlier, both mulattoes, as its leaders. Léspès was secretary-general. The PSP supported Georges Rigaud as their candidate. When he was eliminated in a sensational race, the PSP switched its support to Edgar Néré Numas, a black intellectual and former deputy who was also backed by the American Embassy, Trujillo, and senate-candidate Louis Déjoie.

Estimé won, elected by the Assembly, since there was no popular vote for the Presidency at the time. The PSP had a measure of success when one of its members, Max Hudicourt, was elected to the senate. Rossini Pierre-Louis, elected a deputy, joined the PSP after his victory. Hudicourt and Georges Petit were publishing the newspaper *La Nation*, and Hudicourt handed it over to the PSP.

Estimé began with a coalition cabinet with Rigaud as Minister of Commerce and Daniel Fignolé as Minister of Education. Rigaud launched a campaign that could have forced some foreign businessmen out of the country. To eliminate black-marketing, which had become widespread, especially among foreign merchants in Haiti during the war, he fixed prices by decree and threatened severe punishment for violators. Store owners caught selling goods above ceiling prices were under the threat of having their businesses seized, their stocks inventoried and sold. The money was to be given to the owner after expenses were deducted and his business licence withdrawn.

The volatile Fignolé took to the radio to attack his fellow cabinet minister. In protest, Rigaud resigned. This precipitated a cabinet crisis and Fignolé also quit the government. Estimé was easily rid of his coalition government.

Rigaud led the PSP into the Estimé opposition, but the PCH continued to support the President. In April 1947 the PCH published a communiqué stating that to avoid embarrassing Estimé and complicating his relations with the United States, which had been showing signs of nervousness over his policies, it was dissolving. PCH members who did not agree with this tactic turned to the PSP.

It was the capital mistake of the PCH to dissolve itself. They said it was in the 'national interest' but, in fact, it was condemned by the French Communist party as a 'capitulation to American imperialism'.[2] But the PCH was strongly influenced by 'Browderism', a postwar co-existence thesis promulgated by the American Communist party under the leadership of Earl Browder.

2. *PPLN – Analysis of the Haitian Situation*, p. 25.

The thesis of the PSP at the time was also far from extreme:

> Haiti being a semi-feudal, semi-colonial country dominated by imperialism, the Haitian Socialist movement is at the stage of the anti-imperialist struggle for democracy and national independence, for the creation of national agricultural and industrial enterprises; it must therefore ally itself to the fringe of the national bourgeoisie, opposed to foreign monopolistic interests, since the principal enemy is American imperialism.... However, by its constitution and the social origin of its members, generally from the bourgeoisie and middle classes, the PSP had no popular roots and could not effectively penetrate the masses. Finally it was internally undermined by the colour question.[3]

The existence of two parties (PSP and PCH) shows the internal division, from the start, within the Haitian socialist movement.

On 20 February 1948 Estimé officially outlawed Communist activity under any party name and banned manifestations subversive of public order and peace. It was partially repetitious of the 1936 decree.

Estimé handled the young firebrands of *La Ruche* by sending them to study in France. Three of the ten who went abroad, Dépestre, Alexis, and Gaillard, expanded their travel to include study time behind the Iron Curtain.

When the military strong man Colonel Paul Magloire ousted Estimé in 1950 and then became President, a major point of his platform was the anti-Communist issue. Communism for a while seemed to fade from the Haitian scene. Leftist students seeking an outlet formed Progressive Youth Associations in several towns.

Analysing the 1957 period, five years later, the Communists noted:

> Magloire had not really been a puppet; however, he served as a cover for the bourgeoisie awaiting the opportune time to take over the power it had lost in 1946. If, under the disguise of national union, there was a relative pause in the class struggle in Haiti, there was, however, no effective basis of understanding between the

3. op. cit., p. 26.

different social strata and his fictitious harmony had to break down against the rock of reality.

The dissolution of political parties and the domestication of unions by Magloire had as a consequence the deprivation of the country of any democratic institution capable, during the events that followed Magloire's downfall, of projecting the economic and social aspirations of the masses rationally and efficiently. Besides, clandestine action aiming at taking power and transforming the social structure requires an organization, cadres, a popular basis, and an experience of revolutionary struggle which the Haitian socialist movement generally lacked. Since they had been unable to agree and organize – without contact with the masses – the elements of the left spread, in the majority of cases, according to their sympathies or interests. The 'Democratic Alliance', headed by dentist Georges Rigaud, was a tentative gathering of democratic forces but it did not succeed in constituting a political front above all factions. Without popular roots, without revolutionary organization, playing the liberal game at a time of national crisis, abandoned by the Duvalierists, it was finally suspected of pro-Déjoie tendencies and had no decisive influence on the march of events. However, some Marxist militants, determined to pursue the revolutionary activities of the socialist movement in Haiti, had succeeded in grouping and forming a homogeneous nucleus. Because of the political conjuncture and the social forces in presence, this group backed the candidacy of Professor Fignolé, the leader who was then closest to the masses and whose platform took into account, in a certain measure, the interests of the workers and labourers. Its members, therefore, did not act on their personal behalf but within the line of the group which, in fact, never melted into the Fignolist movement. In spite of the negative aspects owing to the lack of cohesion of the left, the positive aspect was that this socialist nucleus – safeguarding unity and discipline – was able, through methodic daily action, to grow roots in the masses and better organize its cadres.[4]

As a campaign contribution in 1957 leftist intellectuals used their writing ability and know-how in preparing radio programmes and campaign speeches for their non-Communist candidates.

During the brief Duvalier–Déjoie alliance to overthrow

4. op. cit., p. 27.

Magloire, former PSP members Etienne Charlier and Michel Roumain prepared a speech that Duvalier delivered at Saint Gérard in September 1956, three months before Magloire's fall.

Lucien Daumec, member of the former PCH, was a close Duvalier adviser and main speech writer all through the campaign and followed him into the National Palace, while poet Jacques Alexis is said to have written one of Déjoie's most sensational speeches, his eleventh-hour warning that elections should be honest.

The 1956 to 1957 crisis found the Communists an unprepared, unorganized array of leftists who did not have the slightest chance of taking advantage of the turmoil. It took the Duvalier dictatorship to bring the Communists together and consolidate their organization.

The 'Popular Democratic Party' was founded in 1958 and soon changed its name to PPLN, the 'Popular Party of National Liberation'. The founders of this party managed to stay unknown even to many party members. The return of poet Dépestre, an international Communist, gave impetus to the budding new leftist movement. The SNAD, National Society of Dramatic Art, helped also in fostering the birth of a new left-wing intellectual movement. But the contempt and animosity Dépestre and Alexis had for each other soon spilled over into a newspaper polemic that displayed their antagonism to readers of *Le Nouvelliste* and *Le Matin* and did not help the leftist cause.

The PPLN's 'fundamental principles' are:

non-intervention in the internal affairs of other countries; the respect of auto-determination of peoples; the free choice by our people, and by it only, of the way most appropriate for the economic development of the nation as a basis for the social and spiritual evolution of the Haitian man, and finally the freedom to establish economic, commercial, diplomatic, and cultural relations with all the countries of the world who want to help us on the basis of reciprocal advantages and the respect of our sovereignty. This democratic, popular, national and anti-imperialist movement is opened to parties, groups, and citizens of diverse political tendencies but tied by common goals. Its first objectives are: a) the overthrow of the neo-Fascist dictatorship of Duvalier; b) the demolition of the terrorist state; c) the taking of power by a government of national coalition.[5]

In 1959 Jacques Alexis founded his 'Party of Popular Accord', PEP. In 1960 the PEP manifesto programme was published. PPLN criticized it:

In this document it is stated that one of the aims of the democratic, anti-feudal, and anti-imperialist struggle is 'to respect the strategic interests' of the greatest continental power, that is the greatest imperialist power in the world, the United States. But how can one conciliate the interests of the struggle for the anti-imperialist revolution and the strategic interests of the greatest world imperialist power which is at the same time the principal force of aggression and war in the world? The contradictory character of such a declaration – cardinal thesis of the PEP – is obvious. This opportunism is bound to mislead the masses and to deviate the sense of the revolutionary struggle. In fact, it is a new capitulation to imperialism as in the case of the PCH. . . .[6]

This definition of the PEP was made by the PPLN at a time of violent polemic between the two parties, and the PEP continued to reproach the PPLN with having taken one sentence out of context from its manifesto and magnified it into its 'cardinal thesis'.

The PPLN analysis of the PEP goes on to state that the consequences of such a position are

the condemnation of the democratic and nationalist struggle since the two aspects of this struggle (anti-feudal and anti-imperialist) are irremediably tied. The protagonists of the thesis 'of respect' – in this case the leaders of the PEP – have been denounced to the people as new representatives of the traditional policy of abdication of the fundamental interests of our motherland and as saboteurs. . . .

In 1960 Dépestre, harassed by the police, left Haiti for Cuba and began to write regularly for the Havana newspaper *Revolución,* the official voice of Castro's '26 July movement'. Dépestre complained on leaving Haiti of the strange press of his homeland. Instead of paying contributors for articles published in Haiti's dailies, it was the custom for the writer to pay

5. op. cit., p. 44.

6. op. cit., p. 42.

for publication, a fact that Dépestre found both sad and disconcerting. In 1962 he began Creole broadcasts to Haiti over Radio Havana. In his quiet nasal voice, sometimes the only one Haitians could hear raised against Duvalier, he gave a Marxist view of current news, and broadcast long, historical pieces on the Marine occupation, recalling the *Caco* wars, and dwelled on what he called US abuses of Haiti's sovereignty. While not a member of either of Haiti's two Communist parties, Dépestre is one of Haiti's main voices in the Marxist-Leninist world.

In the early sixties some Haitian students found the only road to higher education open to them led across the short span of sea to Cuba. It did not cost much. They could simply steal a small boat and sail the Windward Passage.

Alexis left Haiti clandestinely, in August 1960, to visit Moscow, and signed the Declaration of the Eighty-one[7]. He returned via Peking and Cuba. He was away during the student strike that began in November, and when Duvalier used a PEP letter to help call off the strike. His attempt to return to Haiti in April 1961 provided the PEP with a martyr. It was just as if his enemies were following the words uttered by Hilarius Hilarion, the hero in Alexis's novel *Compère Général Soleil*. 'When one gets to a one-eyed people's country, one closes one eye,' said Hilarion. Alexis had an eye stoned out after his capture. He had landed near Môle Saint Nicolas on 22 April 1961, his thirty-ninth birthday. Bound with rough sisal cords, Alexis and his companions were stoned in the public plaza of Môle Saint Nicolas like the lepers of the Scriptures. Within twenty-four hours after their capture they had been tortured and joined ... the missing legions of anti-Duvalierists.

Alexis was an intellectual in the Roumain tradition. His books were published in Paris along with a collection of his short stories. The PEP borrowed the closing passages of his second book as his epitaph: 'The trees fall from time to time but the voice of the forest never loses its power. Life begins.'

During the summer of 1963, including the time of Papa

7. A declaration signed by eighty-one Communist parties which had gathered for a congress. Alexis signed for Haiti.

Doc's world-shaking crisis involving the Dominican Republic and the United States, the Party of Popular Accord (PEP) and the Popular Party of National Liberation (PPLN) held a joint congress for the purpose of uniting. Significantly, while strict security measures were in force, they were able to meet and arbitrate their differences at a congress in Port-au-Prince. After several weeks of discussion, the delegates agreed, on 4 July, to unite their efforts under a new banner, the United Democratic Front for National Liberation (FDULN). The idea was to put aside friction among the leadership and ideological conflicts to forge a 'popular front' against Duvalier. They reached general agreement to forget the past, but failed to achieve full agreement on the future. In time this served to dredge up the old problems again.

A year later Communist publications revealed that the FDULN had met in Santiago, Chile, with three other Haitian political organizations, unidentified, to found a foreign branch – the Exterior Organizations of the United Front for National Liberation of Haiti (known by the French acronym of OREFH). *Ralliement* (published from 1962 to 1967) was its newspaper; it circulated around the world as well as inside Haiti. It listed its address as Switzerland. In 1968 *Ralliement* was replaced by *Lambi*

The emergence of the FDULN and the OREFH, however impressive their propaganda, did not produce a homogeneous party as hoped. Originally, there had been the antagonism of Alexis and Dépestre. Now there were contrasting views of Haitian reality and organizing tactics.

Nonetheless, they agreed on the necessity of working within the peasantry. The PPLN made tactical efforts in the student movements while the PEP concentrated its effort in the labour movement. The PPLN was first to recognize theoretically the necessity of armed struggle, while the PEP kept active with militant work along the traditional lines of numerically small Communist parties operating in an antithetical milieu: education, propaganda, and organization.

The Sino-Soviet split was of little importance to the two

Haitian Communist parties because they were plagued with their own differences and problems peculiar to the Haitian situation.

Following their alliance, both the PPLN and the PEP shifted their sights to propagandize against the forces which victimize the rural landowner and result in taking or reducing the size of his holdings. They attacked middlemen speculators who lived off peasant production and a government structure which gave the rural chieftain near absolute powers over their lives and property.

To organize in the country, the PPLN began to work in crowded urban areas where its roots already were strong, recruiting recent arrivals from the country to train as future cadres. These would be sent back to their own villages as organizers.

Cuba became an influence toward unity. As Castro, out of economic necessity, shifted toward a distinct Soviet line, the PPLN position also was modified.

The internal dialogue continued. *Rassemblement* criticized the PPLN and exposed the problems of the 'popular front' in June 1965. 'It is evident to all that the PPLN from its foundation ... has never walked the path of Marxism-Leninism. ... It has preserved the imperfections of its predecessors....'

Rassemblement complained that the PPLN had called the creation of PEP by Alexis a 'divisionist manoeuvre'.

Some wondered whether enough Haitians owned radios to make the Dépestre Cuban broadcasts important, but transistors had spread the number of receivers, and those who could not afford one could attend small, often secret, radio-listening clubs. Others benefited from exaggerated versions on the *Télédiol,* Haiti's word for the swift dissemination of gossip. Dépestre's broadcasts had begun with one hour daily and then increased to two, one early each morning (six to seven) and another at night (nine to ten). In some areas of Haiti, especially in the north and south-west, Cuban stations were the only ones that could be heard. The mountains are too much of a barrier for weak Port-au-Prince or Cap-Haïtien stations. Until the exile organization, Haitian Coalition, began daily Creole broadcasts from Radio New York in July 1965, it was the only opposition voice available to Haitians. Both the Voice of America and Radio Santo Domingo offered foreign views of the news, but their broadcasts were in Spanish and consequently most of their value was lost in Haiti.

Foreign broadcasts and leftist mimeographed clandestine publications assumed greater importance than might normally be expected because of strict censorship within the country. Haitian newspapers and radio stations, rather than risk retaliation from the government, quit airing news except that which the government released or which was too innocuous for anyone to care. Foreign publications are censored. It is not unusual to buy a US magazine or newspaper and find huge holes in it where articles about Haiti have been clipped out. Stores were warned that if they sold any foreign publication that included an offensive article which might have escaped the censor's eye they personally would be held responsible. After President Kennedy's death the government went to the extreme of severely reprimanding literary figures who paid homage to him in a booklet published by the Haitian-American Institute.

Periodically Duvalier ordered a ban on the sale of Communist literature to impress the American Embassy. However, store owners were told privately that this meant Communist propaganda only and not doctrinal works. The latter, some printed in Moscow, were available and inexpensive. Marxist books could even be purchased on an easy-payment plan if necessary. During turbulent 1963 one bookstand received forty-eight copies of a giant (three and one half inches thick) book on Marxist-Leninist theory and sold out within a week.

The hard-line Chinese Communist position attracted a new group in 1966. This small group of dissident Marxists living in Europe, in a publication called *Manchette*, complained that the PEP and PPLN and their 'popular front' had been captured and charmed by 'Khrushchevian revisionists'.

The May issue of *Manchette*, which listed its address as Belgium, commented:

They are becoming dangerous for they are trying to patch up their false theses with certain of the revolutionary theses. They are feeling their way haphazardly. Haven't we seen the PPLN, while it recognized through lip service armed struggle as the principal form, accuse the Chinese comrades of favouring Duvalier? Haven't we seen the PEP, the chameleon of the revolution, publish semi-private texts of alignment with revisionism?

In June *Manchette* added:

These two groups are only following step by step the opportunistic tradition of the old Haitian Leftist leaders. They are staffs without an army, intellectuals in quest of honours, devouring themselves for the favours of Moscow.... Without ceasing to pay lip service to armed struggle ... they are only organizing the economic struggle of the working class; for them a spontaneous *prise de conscience* of the working class must be awaited to launch the revolutionary struggle.... Nowadays they are not even talked about except in certain capitals, apparently Havana and Paris, where their leaders took refuge, not to organize the revolution but to sing it. Is this why these leaders are called the 'Troubadours of the Haitian Revolution'? These gentlemen patiently await the arrival on our shores of the beneficial effects of pacific co-existence....

It is with great joy that the diverse Haitian democratic milieux have welcomed the birth of a true revolutionary Haitian Marxist-Leninist movement.... One of its tasks necessarily will be ... the construction of a popular army.

Manchette ridiculed what it called a 'messianic complex' through which the PEP and PPLN waited for Fidel Castro or Che Guevara to make the revolution for them.

On 27 July 1966 an explosion in a house in Pétionville caused important changes in the Communist leadership in Haiti. The PPLN, which had decided to prepare for armed action against Duvalier, had one of their training schools and storage houses accidentally revealed by this explosion. In the panic and round-up that followed, PPLN leader Professor Jean-Jacques Ambroise and his wife were arrested and tortured to death, as was Professor Mario Rameau. Ambroise was a rare Haitian Communist who lived according to his beliefs and was not just paying lip service to his cause. Other important leaders escaped into exile. In the following months the decapitated PPLN changed its name to PUDA, Creole initials for Party of the Union of Haiti Democrats. The PEP took the decision at the end of 1966 also to adopt the armed fight.

The PEP claims credit for the April 1967 bombs that exploded in Port-au-Prince. In May 1967 the central committee of the PEP of Haiti issued a booklet entitled *Tactical Means toward the New Independence of Haiti* in which they define clearly the tactical and strategic aims of the forces of the left in Haiti.

In this report the PEP stated that 'No political opposition force has been able to channel the popular discontent in Haiti today into action. Some sectors of the population openly call for North American or Dominican intervention to liberate them from the Duvalier yoke. The Dictator has provoked a paralising fear in large sectors of the people and only intervention from outside or voluntary exile would be feasible exits for these important sectors.' The PEP noted that meanwhile the Duvalier regime is looking for new means of relieving the existing tension. The PEP considers that there exist favourable conditions to launch the fight soon. In the meantime the extreme left will have to face the alternatives of traditional opposition which, up to now, has only carried out periodic actions. In the document the PEP considers that the Haitian Coalition, considered as the major and most influential opposition group, has the official backing of the North American spying services.

> Some of their leaders are paid agents on the budget of the CIA and have acted as North American spies in some African countries and in Guyana. This Coalition is trying to regroup different anti-Duvalierist reactionary sectors. The game consists of making at the same time a vigorous campaign against the Dictator, closely tying it with a vulgar anti-communism which would identify Duvalierism with communism.

The PEP also sees as an element of discord the North American sectors which do not want to be totally identified with the Duvalierist dictatorship to avoid being included in a popular judgement.

Its official backing of the coalition, so-called Haitian, constitutes an important step in this policy of double play. This aid is moulding the first pieces of the mechanism capable of eventually insuring the passage from Duvalierism to post-Duvalierism without popular upheaval.

'The United States are actively preparing for the invasion of Haiti when they find it necessary,' says the PEP, which adds 'good proof of it is that the Marines are learning Creole at the University of Indiana.'

The PEP stresses the political backwardness of the population, which they say is expecting a 'saviour'. 'The national situation is such that the realization of the revolution essentially depends on the work of the revolutionaries.' In this they are in agreement with leftist groups dissident from the traditional Communist parties.

The PEP foresees the necessity of the formation of a popular army for a popular war. Their main theatre of operation, they say, will be the country, without excluding, however, armed action in the rural towns, *marronage,* and creation of guerrilla fronts. They point out that this *marronage* is a form of struggle peculiar to the Haitian situation:

it corresponds to a political reality, to the degree of revolutionary conscience and to the disposition to action of the Haitian peasants right now. In addition, it is a tradition of fight in our country. Our peasants, who live under the influence of the ideology and of the paternalism of the feudal landowners, to whom is transmitted from generation to generation the spirit of obedience to the exploiters and to the power, who are strongly influenced by the religious ideologies and their propaganda of resignation, who for a long time have lost the practice of handling arms, do not keep from the multiple past insurrections more than an imprecise recollection, based on the stories of the old people, on the legends or on the nostalgia of heroic times.

The *marron* was Haiti's – and perhaps the Western Hemisphere's – first guerrilla. He was a runaway slave who later became the basic fighting unit for the war of independence against the French

Politically and ideologically modern *'marronage'* differs from the one which created the conditions for our first independence war, because it is directed against Haitian exploiters, accomplices of the foreigner and of their power, because it must be directed according to the sector of the socialist ideology and the artisans of the workers–peasants alliance. Modern *marronage* pretends to destroy the feudal state apparatus and establish a workers–peasants' government. Militarily this *marronage* must also be modern because of the quality of the armament and the means of exercising popular violence, as well as owing to the huge technical resources which the reactionary power has at its disposal.

The PEP says that all the other forms of opposition will have to be subordinated to the armed fight to form a popular front.

The *marronage* idea set forth by the PEP is to inculcate 'a spirit of rebellion, disobedience, and hate'. This would be 'a violent revolutionary action whose perspective would be more political than military.' Their contribution to the struggle would be the job of 'armed propaganda'.

'The modern *marrons* would have to convince the peasant of the possibility of vanquishing Duvalier; further, they would militarily organize the rural populations first on a local scale, then grouping them into bands.' In other words, it is 'guerrilla in the egg', the main link of the chain which will finally form the guerrilla pockets and the popular army.

Ironically, after the PEP came out with these plans to bring about a rebirth of the spirit of revolt of the *marron* slaves, in preparation for guerrilla war, Duvalier ordered a quarter-of-a-million-dollar statue to be made and erected to the *marron*.

Speaking at the July to August 1967 meeting of delegates to the Organization of Latin-American Solidarity (OLAS), René Dépestre declared that the PEP and PUDA had reached agreement for the Haitian revolution and noted that the two parties had decided that 'the armed struggle constitutes the principal, fundamental way towards the triumph of the revolution.'

Haitian delegate André Faray, speaking on 5 August 1967, said: 'We are accelerating the conditions for the armed struggle in Haiti. All the objective conditions for the Haitian revolution are ripe and it will not be a long process.'

Ten years of Papa Doc finally succeeded in eliminating the differences that gave Haiti two Communist parties. After six months of talks the PEP and PUDA finally merged into a single party, the PUCH, United Party of Haitian Communists, in December 1968. The fusion of these two parties ended the publication of their respective party organs and replaced them with *Boukan* (bonfire), now recognized by all Haitian Communists as the voice of PUCH. *Boukan*, publishing the principles of PUCH, stated:

> the essential political tasks of the democratic and national revolution are to overthrow the Duvalierist Dictatorship and to take power in the name of the united front of all the anti-feudal and anti-imperialist forces led by the working class, to destroy the present economic and social regime and bring about the essential transformation of the revolution of national liberation on the social, economic, political, and cultural fields.

As a means to their goal, the Communists declare they have chosen 'the armed struggle' (*marronage*).

20

Voudou Is His Arm

Even if he could control his own avarice and that of his followers, Papa Doc truly does not have the wherewithal to put over the public-works and prestige programmes used so often in the hemisphere to justify dictatorships. But the little doctor knows his people and makes them respond to him, to his cult of blackness, to the prestige of his intellectual ties and his medical degree. He has another asset, which he exploits to enhance his stature, particularly among the lower classes: voudou.

When the occasion demands, he is able to enswathe himself in an air of virtual preternaturalism. Dressed in his favourite colour, black, his smooth, round face assumes a special sheen. He moves hyperslowly, speaks in a whisper. His eyelids droop. Wearing a slightly bemused, unshakeable half-smile, he does nothing for disconcertingly long periods of time, and Haitians, receptive to the unusual, are awed. The man appears to be as calm as death.

When they first beheld this sombre little figure they immediately made the connection – he was *like* Papa Guédé Nimbo of the powerful Guédé *loa* family, masters of the cemetery. In time the likeness gave way to kinship.

In 1944 a booklet he co-authored (with Lorimer Denis), *The Gradual Evolution of Voudou.* had earned him a reputation for expertise. His close links with voudou folklore took on a new significance in the minds of the people when he assumed office. On one occasion, when a question concerning voudou arose during his Presidential campaign, he told reporters:

Every country has its own folklore. It's part of the patrimony. It's so in England, Japan, and Central Europe. Grieg took his music themes from Norwegian folk culture. Similarly we should point out our folklore to permit intellectuals of Haiti to exploit this richness for national literature. As the most beautiful manifestation is popular religion, we have studied this to furnish material to men of letters. There is an aspect of voudou that is like the vulgar and primitive side to all religions. I have been able to study the mental and material culture of the peasants. I am a candidate to save the peasant from the superstitions of his ancestors.

A few years after he became President, disenchanted former associates told of strange rites that took place in the palace's Salon Jaune. They claimed that Duvalier studied goat's entrails for guidance, that he sought counsel from the gods by sitting in a bathtub wearing a top hat, that he slept one night a year on the tomb of Dessalines, with whom he claimed to be in spiritual communication. Palace gossip had it that one army chief of staff's wife and his own daughter Marie-Denise acted as his mediums.

There is no question about Duvalier's involvement in the strange rites of voudou; how deeply is a matter of controversy. Loyal Duvalierists insist that Papa Doc is a gifted individual, an expert in many fields, especially in the folklore of his country, a skilled politician who capitalizes on this knowledge. On the other hand, ex-Duvalierists feel that Papa Doc suffers from a delusion that he is in contact with voudou gods and that he feels he can cross into their world. He calls in *houngans*[1] and *bocors*[2] for help in peering into the future, and has developed his own methods of clairvoyance. According to them, he has gone from voudou to black magic – rites designed to bring good to self and harm to enemies. Reputable *houngans* reject *magie noire* and believe that to practise it one must make a bargain with evil spirits that one day will destroy one.

In the pre-election campaign of 1957, Duvalier had rallied some *houngans* and *bocors* to his side, while others supported former President Paul Magloire and Louis Déjoie. Others still, particularly those from Port-au-Prince, backed Daniel Fignolé.

1. Voudou priests.
2. Sorcerers.

As President, Duvalier appointed Zacharie Delva, a *bocor* from Gonaïves with an unsavoury reputation, as head of the nationwide militia force. Zacharie had a siren installed in his large black limousine. During formal inspection visits to rural villages he was greeted by local bands who played the special Presidential hymn ordinarily reserved solely for the Chief of State. The appointment of a voudou priest as his personal representative bestowed upon Duvalier the aura of commander in chief of the voudou legions.

Every *houmfort* or temple is autonomous. The *houngan* and the *bocor* each runs his own show and sometimes adds the personal touches and frills to his ceremonies and services. The priest takes orders from the *loas*.[3]

From the very beginning Duvalier set out to bring to his side the thousands of priests from the most isolated villages – from Bombardopolis to Anse d'Hainault – in the desire to have them regard him as their supreme master.

He hired a knowledgeable Haitian for the sole task of arranging visits to the National Palace of notable priests and *bocors* from the most isolated areas of Haiti. No other President until Duvalier had taken such pains to dominate this influential group.

One such visit in 1962, designed to impress a *bocor* and his community that the 'supreme being' was Papa Doc, ended disastrously. The ancient *bocor* from Aquin in south-west Haiti became so terrified at the sight of all the armed soldiers and militiamen in the halls of the palace that he was seized by a sudden attack of diarrhoea. He never did get his audience. Instead, he was given medical treatment and a new pair of pants and permitted to return home.

These visits have their effect not only on the *bocors* but on their communities. Rural Haitians have always taken the state for granted and expect nothing from it but a hard time. They accept the white Catholic priest, *monpère*; but they reserve their reverence for his voudou counterpart. Duvalier has managed to supercharge that reverence. *Houngans* and *bocors* fear him; their flocks see in him a kind of super-*bocor*.

3. Voudou gods or spirits.

It is not unlikely that Duvalier himself began circulating the stories of strange practices going on at a calvary in the Bel Air section which he ordered rebuilt shortly after taking power. Port-au-Prince, Fignolé's traditional stronghold, needed to be impressed. Stories of Papa Doc burying people alive at the base of the giant cross took care of that. And when his adversaries disinterred his father's corpse and took to smearing excrement on the calvary, Papa Doc was made.

After the 1963 rebel attack on the village of Ouanaminthe was beaten back, Duvalier ordered that former Army Captain Blucher Philogènes's head to be cut off, packed in ice, and brought to the palace in an Air Force plane. News spread around Port-au-Prince that Papa Doc was having long sessions with the head; that he had induced it to disclose the exiles' plans.

During this Ouanaminthe period mere mention of Duvalier's envoy – Zacharie Delva – was enough to send whole families into a trembling silence. At rumours of the approach of Delva's big black limousine, entire villages shut down.

Delva let it be known that he was holding ceremonies to combat his chief's enemies and, in some areas of northern Haiti, peasants claim that human babies were sacrificed. Indeed, some can even tell you exactly how many, where, and when; who attended and what the *loas* told Delva.

As Duvalier survived international crises, natural disasters, hurricanes, heart attacks, explosions, gunshots, and succeeded in reducing both the army and the Church to vassalage, besides destroying the influence of the American Embassy, it is not surprising that he succeeded in persuading those around him that he was chosen by fate, the gods, and history. 'Only the gods can take power from me,' he once said.

It is a matter of speculation whether voudou will become discredited after Papa Doc is gone, however, since he has made virtual pawns out of so many witch doctors and closed those *houmforts* which refused to sell out. Voudou, like every Haitian business, has been heavily taxed. In 1960 Duvalier had increased taxes on voudou rites to the point that at Easter many *houmforts* in Port-au-Prince could not afford to hold their traditional Guédé ceremonies.

The year Duvalier came to power his men stencilled on the walls of the old Finance Ministry: 'Man talks without acting. God acts without talking. Duvalier is a god.' In a series of speeches in 1963, when he was battling enemies on every front, he cheered his followers on with: 'They cannot get me, I am immaterial.' One could sense that among the little people, repeatedly subjected to these displays of power, there was respect, fear, even admiration; only a *gros nég*, one protected by the gods, could wield such power. To many, the relationship of the gods to Duvalier was quite palpable. Was not Duvalier a member of the greatest centre of voudou, Souvenance, and was not one of its highest priests, Zacharie Delva, a top official of the Duvalier government? It is tempting to dismiss such views as foolishness and think that grown people could not possibly be influenced by such thin fare. But past presidents did nothing – not even offer voudou as a distraction – to lighten the burden of the poor. In addition, Papa Doc has publicly proclaimed his allegiance to the *dieux tutélaires*, the lesser *loas* or tutelary gods, which no one since Boukman, and that includes Dessalines, had done.

To be sure most Haitian presidents have furtively gone to the *houngans* – some as believers; some as a shrewd public-relations move – but the little doctor is the first chief of state to proclaim publicly that voudou is legitimate. In fact, it comes close to being the official state religion.

Voudou – or vodun, a word derived from the Dahomean (West African) term meaning 'spirit' – represents a real link between the Black Continent and Haiti, and under Duvalier has attained perhaps its greatest notoriety since the nineteenth century. Nothing else has reached into the country in any sort of organized fashion except the rural police (representing the government) and the Catholic Church.

Voudou is the spiritual blood of Haiti, a rebellious reaction against French Catholicism vying with the African beliefs imported by the slaves. It is a religion tailored for the Haitian, geared to his life and spirit. It provides a structure of beliefs that explain the mysteries of life and death; rituals of thanksgiving, consolation, healing, and protection; sanction for social acts, such as marriage; a sense of communion; a spiritual identification. It channels pleasures rather than curbs them. In it there is a primitive release and purgative for heavy hearts rather than the accumulation of sin-inspired guilt. It has survived and grown as a working belief that acknowledges and deals liberally with the practicalities of a harsh life – food, shelter, sex, disease. It is a changing, flexible faith, transmitted by word of mouth from generation to generation, in which services and beliefs differ from *houngan* to *houngan* and village to village.

God is regarded as an impersonal power. *Le Bon Dieu* or *Le Grand Maître* represents a vague image of good. Voudou deals with the lesser spirits, *loas*, who are believed more accessible, more comfortable. The pantheon of *loas* is as elastic as the human imagination, but there are two main categories – Rada and Petro. Rada is of African origin. Petro is Haitian, and considered the more violent and fierce of the two. It was in a Petro ceremony that Boukman, the slave *bocor*, incited revolt one 'red night' against the French in 1791 as he swore in the blood of a sacrificial pig to 'live free or die'. *Loas* may spring from historical heroes, pirates, *houngans*, or any of the distinguished dead. In general, the greater gods are those of African descent, and lesser ones those who have since joined the ranks. Through voudou the spirits of the dead may be called upon for advice and help when human resources prove inadequate. Because the spirits of the dead may become *loas*, great care is taken at funerals to release the dead properly so that their spirits may have the opportunity of joining the great cosmic family. *Loas* are expected to provide for the faithful, and, in turn, must be served by them. The formula is practical and satisfying. Since the *houngans* or *mambos* (priestesses) hold the important positions of intermediaries with the other world, they are powerful figures. Their influence is a considerable factor in shaping the community's *Weltanschauung*.

The trappings of voudou borrow heavily from Catholicism. Voudou altars often are decorated with cheap prints of saints. Some of these services require recitations of the Apostles' Creed and the Hail Mary. The Virgin Mary is used to represent the feminine god, Grande Erzulie, the goddess of fertility, forgiving, motherly, but also unabashedly erotic. Men dance to Erzulie, pray to her, worship her, fall in love with her. The cross of Christ is the sign of Baron Samedi.

Some of the other gods are Papa Iegba, a sort of voudou Saint Peter who guards the gates to the spiritual world and presides over journeys and is represented by pictures of Saint Christopher; Agwé Awoyo and La Sirène, gods of the sea; Loco Attiso, major healer and protector against black magic; Damballah Ouedo, the snake god, represented by Saint Patrick; Papa Zaca, god of agriculture. There are saints, angels, and demons. Ro Ra is Lent; the Holy Trinity is Les Mystères, Les Morts, Les Marassas (the spirits, the dead, the twins). Les Marassas are believed to have special powers, and are shown special favours even when alive. Dead twins will cause trouble if not properly appeased by special services. This applies not only to twins of the immediate family but to twins in general, and all families fear them.

The *loas* are believed to be more at ease in a hut than a palace, happier using the back entrance and hard benches; comfortable in the company of illiterates.

Periodically the Church has launched crusades against voudou, but these rarely have great effect. The entwining of the two is so great that the target is elusive. Typically, when it issued 'Carte Rejeté' as proof of a sworn oath to reject voudou, some practical-minded *houngans* required their followers to get the cards. They were not at all disturbed by the contradiction. Even baptism in Haiti has its origins more in Africa than in the Apostles' Creed.

The voudou service itself is the act through which contact is made with *loas*. The temple has one or more rooms and an adjoining court called the *peristyle,* which has a thatched roof supported by poles. There are benches and chairs. A centre pole, called the *poteau-mitan*, is the entrance and the exit for the *loas*. It is often fixed to look like a snake, and sports voudou designs which encourage the *loas*. Today, the photograph of Duvalier hangs on the *poteau-mitan* place of honour.

Within the temple is an inner chamber called the *houmfort*. In this the *houngan* displays all his symbols. The basic elements are the drums, made of hollowed-out logs with goatskin stretched tightly across the top; the *asson*, or holy gourd, decorated with snake vertebrae, a bell, and beads; the altar; earthenware jars called *jovis* or stones (*pierres loas*) which contain the ancestral spirits; the flags of the société. There also may be the fiery native rum, clairin; herb mixtures to drink; live chicken, goat, pig, or even bull sacrifices. These are to provide the *loas* with food, to give them more strength. The sacrificial animal usually is washed, dried, perfumed, and sometimes even powdered. Bulls or goats may additionally be clothed in silk or velvet and wear a headdress. The animal must partake of a sacred liquid or consecrated food in order to be approved by the *loa* whose agent, when 'possessed', will sacrifice it. Those participating in the ceremony try to attain as close contact with the animal as is physically possible – they pet it, rub it, ride it. In the course of elaborate rituals the animal's throat is slashed and its blood drunk.

A typical ceremony begins with a salute to Papa Legba, god of all gods, who, if not flattered, might become angry and abort the entire ritual. The *houngan* then lights a candle and, in a method that closely resembles the late Jackson Pollock's technique of action painting, dribbles a *vévé* or design on the ground with flour or ashes. His assistants, dressed in white, perform introductory gestures and recite prayers in answer to the particular needs of those present. Then drums begin to beat and the hours of dancing start.

The dancing, accompanied by chants repeated to the point of autohypnosis, reaches frenzy. The effect is contagious. The *loa* deigns to enter the body of one of the participants, who is said to be possessed. The god rides him like a horse. Speaking with the god's voice, sometimes he convulses in a state of *exaltation mystique*. Orgasms are not infrequent, nor are syncopes. The sacrifice usually brings one or the other on, for when an animal's throat is suddenly slashed and a hot jet of blood spurts forth after hours of rhythmic monotony, the impact can be startling. After the possession and the gibbering in an unknown tongue, the participant is left in a state of satisfied weariness sometimes accompanied by amnesia. It has been argued that this process, by permitting persons to act out inhibited desires without fear of personal embarrassment, provides a sort of national safety valve. The braggart can become the 'horse' of Ogoun Feraille, the noisy god of war; the effeminate can be possessed by a female *loa* and act the part of an amorous woman. Some Haitians argue that when such repressed needs are given spiritual explanations, guilt is purged and problems lessened.

All these are powerful stimulants to artistic expression. The painting of *vévés*, the drama of spiritual confrontations, the colourful and weird trappings and the priestly powers are rich fields for the imagination. Voudou is as real a Haitian expression as the earthy Creole language. Poet Felix Morisseau-Leroy adapted *Antigone* into Creole, making Creon a repressive rural policeman and Tiresias a *houngan*.

There are a variety of services and different stages of initiation. A participant most frequently joins in the baptismal ceremonies, but there are higher levels such as *kanzo*. This requires endurance, courage, time, patience, and sometimes financial sacrifice. Once achieved, it means that the participant is under the immediate care of a *loa* and therefore has greater protection from demons and additional status in society. The *houngan* also accepts greater responsibility for the care and comfort of the initiate. Part of Kanzo is a fire ritual in which the initiate places his hands in a fire or perhaps moulds meat balls in a pot of boiling oil. A more advanced fire ritual, *bulézin*, might require walking over hot coals. Voudou experts explain the unnatural physical tolerances required in such initiation ceremony in terms of self-hypnotism, or of application of ancient and practical native immunities that permit practices which seem miraculous to the uninitiated.

The voudou rites have been exploited as a tourist attraction. Travel brochures suggest that you can see the 'real thing' by venturing off the regular tourist paths. The man to take you there, of course, is the taxi driver or tourist guide. To accommodate interested and sometimes gullible tourists, voudou at times becomes a sideshow-type affair. Charlatans set themselves up in *peristyles* and put on 'specials' for tourists. One favourite spot for such exhibitions was La Saline, that stinking section of mud flats and wooden hovels along the waterfront in Port-au-Prince. One distracting factor to the purist, however, was a sign posted outside in English advising that the price of admission was one dollar. The bloodier, sexier, and louder it was, the more it pleased the customers. Sometimes real flavour was added when participants, bored with the show, would wring the neck of a chicken and drink down its blood while the drums pounded and the *hounsi* (assistants) danced. The blood would be washed down with clairin. What the tourist did not always realize was that often peering through the cracks, wide-eyed and amused, were dozens of Haitians – enjoying the show the tourists themselves offered.

The *houngan* demonstrates his leadership and superior wisdom by curing illness or preventing it. In this he must combine knowledge with a flair for the dramatic. Many of his cures are believed to be the result of deftly applied psychology, but some also have simpler explanations. Most *houngans* also qualify as herb doctors, and their medicines sometimes are home-type remedies. They apply garlic to infections, use spiderwebs to stop bleeding, and treat shock with salt. Because of his supposed ability to command spiritual power, the *houngan* has one advantage over the medical doctor. He can virtually assure a patient's proper mental attitude by insisting that he appease offended *loas* before the healing process starts. In Haiti this is particularly valuable, and perhaps may help explain Duvalier's early interest in voudou, because the peasant sees supernatural causes for all illnesses and misfortunes – especially if they come on suddenly. Generally, it is felt that such problems are caused by a sacrilegious act, or that the failure to perform some ceremony has offended the spirits and therefore brought on punishment.

The *houngans* combat weird forces with weird formulas. Because so many Haitian babies die, there is a belief that *loup-garous* are the cause. They fly about at night and suck the blood from unprotected babies. They cannot, however, harm the child without the permission of the mother, and, therefore, they try to trick and deceive the mother into granting permission. To combat this problem or others similar to it, a *houngan* must dig into his own repertoire of tricks. By divination, invoking the spirits, he finds out the supernatural cause of an illness. After this diagnosis there is a long and costly treatment which includes offerings to the gods, magical practices, perhaps an old-fashioned remedy, or maybe even a call on the Catholic saints for special help.

The most dreaded disease probably is caused by an unfriendly *bocor* sending the spirit of the dead against a victim. This calls for a treatment in which the patient is regarded as already dead. Chickens are put close to his body and then they are taken away and buried alive. Sometimes the patient is given a rub-down with burning alcohol. The *houngan* may throw a handful of gunpowder into a nearby fire hoping that the flash will scare away the bad spirits. This is also frequently recommended as a cure of a childhood disease, the evil eye. Most Haitian mothers combat this by hanging an amulet or charm around the baby's neck. A child sick from the evil eye requires extensive treatment.

Tuberculosis is one of the peasant's most feared diseases. It is one of those believed to have descended from *l'envoi d'un mort* (messenger from the dead), and the afflicted despair of cure. Elephantiasis is believed to be caused by the victim stepping on a strong magic powder put in his path by the *bocor*. When the blood shoots rapidy to the head, it causes conjunctivitis and then the head must be cleared by blood-letting, with leeches, around the neck. 'Maling', or tropical ulcers, is attributed to the anger of a supernatural being, and only the *houngan* can help. A problem called *bisket tombé*, depression of the sternum, is treated by having the patient sit with legs stretched out while his back and abdomen are massaged and his thumbs are pulled. Another treatment calls for infusions with three leaf buds of coffee and the stem of a special flower. This should be accompanied by a prayer repeated five times in front of the patient, four times in back, and three times while he lies on his stomach. Some cases of sexual impotence are believed to be caused by a mother carelessly letting a drop of breast milk fall on the son's genital organ. Some skin irritations are treated by having the patient sit on cold stones.

Death also brings duties to the *houngan*. This is the peasant's greatest moment and calls for the fanciest wake that begging or borrowing can buy. The spirit of the deceased is ceremoniously removed by the *houngan* and allowed to lodge in a surviving member of the family or a close friend. Always suspicious, the peasant believes that the dead need special protection. Before burial the white powder of an arsenic herb is slipped between the stiffened lips to guarantee a peaceful sleep. If an unknown enemy makes a nocturnal visit to the grave, calling out the dead man's name thirteen consecutive times and commanding him to rise, the arsenic will keep him quiet and save him from becoming the zombie slave of his enemy.

The fear of zombies and of becoming one is a very real one. The zombie is believed to be a person who has been buried and raised from the dead by some mystical formula which makes him a total slave to a sorcerer. Because *houngans* are so skilled in the use of native herbs and drugs, it is said that some zombie cases are the result of a drug-induced catalepsy. In such a state, a person is pronounced dead, buried, and then dug up. The theory is that regular doses of narcotics keep the enslaved person in a state of mental apathy. The Haitian criminal code specifies that anyone practising this shall be guilty of murder even if the victim does not die. Since most burials take place shortly after death, it is possible for a *bocor* to drug his victim, bury him, and then dig him up before he smothers. One native plant whose leaves cause such sleep is called the *tuer-lever*, 'kill and heal' (literally, 'kill and rise').

In the black-magic realm of the zombies are the *ouangas*, or symbols which cause harm to a person. Peasants believe that a *bocor* can cause sickness or even death with the *ouanga*. The seriousness of this attitude is reflected in an old Haitian law which strictly forbids their use under any circumstances. Numerous specific tales of the effectiveness of *ouangas* have been dismissed as products of self-hypnosis. Some zombie or *ouanga* stories, however, are not so easily explained.

The most outstanding job of zombifying people, it has been pointed out repeatedly, is the job Duvalier has done on Haiti. His method of total domination of rural Haitians has been accomplished by superstition and fear.

In bringing the masses under iron-fist control Duvalier was careful not to disturb their political somnolence that has continued almost uninterrupted since 1804 revolutionary times. He chose their natural community leaders, the voudou priest and *bocors*, to implement his will. In the process voudou gained martyrs. Those *houngans* who failed to co-operate with the Supreme Chief were liquidated.

Dessalines angered his ancestors' spirits by using his hard hand against voudou. Like the other revolutionary heroes, he knew the conspiratorial nature of voudou and feared it. Yet after his assassination in 1806, he entered the voudou pantheon as a *loa*.

No such honour is expected for Duvalier because voudouists see it as already conferred. He has mounted Haiti as the *loa* does his 'horse'. The ride has been disastrous, even for voudou.

21
The Year Ten

The Year Ten of Duvalier's reign was marked by commemoration ceremonies, a number of bizarre conspiracies – one dividing his own family – and at least nineteen summary executions of once-trusted aides. Looking back to 1957, the pattern was familiar.

Although Papa Doc lavished upon his family all that money could buy, it did not hold them together. The power that rested uncertainly in the palace produced the ancient pattern of ambition, jealousy, and suspicion. The Duvaliers had expensive clothes, flashy cars, made frequent trips to Europe and the United States, enjoyed their own movie projection room in the palace (with films commandeered from local theatres). When the daughters took husbands, it inevitably caused the family to reappraise the future.

Duvalier's favourite daughter, Marie-Denise, the eldest, chose six-foot-three palace guard Captain Max Dominique for her husband. Plump Nicole followed her sister to the altar with a green-eyed mulatto, Luc Albert Foucard, an agronomist from Port-de-Paix. He is the brother of Mme France Foucard Saint-Victor, Duvalier's private secretary.

Soon rumours of rivalry between the two brothers-in-law began to circulate. Ever-suspicious, Duvalier had doubts about his military son-in-law, who was influential in the palace guard and security forces in his home town, Cap-Haïtien. Max Dominique, thirty-four, had been a married man with a family when twenty-six-year-old, strong-willed Marie-Denise decided she wanted him. Max divorced his wife to marry her. One immediate reward was promotion to colonel. He commanded the military district of Port-au-Prince. Duvalier preferred the more sophisticated Foucard and in this was encouraged by Madame Saint-Victor. The jockeying for Papa Doc's favour sharpened as the Year Ten progressed. Madame Duvalier sided with the Dominiques. Some said she was jealous of Madame Saint-Victor, whom she regarded as more than just a secretary.

On 15 April two bombs exploded close to the palace fence during Duvalier's sixtieth birthday anniversary celebration, decreed 12 to 16 April (the birthday was 14 April). One bomb went off inside an ice-cream cart, killing the vendor. Duvalier suspected that Colonel Dominique was trying to embarrass Foucard, newly appointed Minister of Tourism, who had organized the celebrations.

A third bomb exploded at the International Casino. It was said to be Foucard's answer to Dominique. Communists claimed credit for all three bombs, but few took notice. The palace feud was more interesting conversation.

Papa Doc, as usual, wasted no time. With the Foucard faction's help, he began to clean house. Late in the evening of 24 April 1967, Duvalier ordered the immediate transfer of some of his most trusted young Presidential Guard officers to remote rural areas. Two weeks later he ordered them demoted. Another three weeks and he ordered them to return to the capital. Some came back smiling, sure of reinstatement for years of devoted service. On arrival, they were disarmed and placed incommunicado in Fort Dimanche.

Papa Doc decided that his purge should include the top Tonton Macoutes and militia chiefs of Cap-Haïtien, Dominique's home town. They were fired and, with official sanction, their homes pillaged. Some escaped by hiding in the trunks of automobiles or with bribes. The second week in May Duvalier also struck down Tonton Macoute chiefs in Port-au-Prince and nearby Pétionville.

Before the month was over another Duvalierist, Trujillo's former spy chief and exterminator, Johnny Abbes Garcia, disappeared. He had arrived in Haiti the year before on a false passport with his Mexican wife and two children. All four vanished. Johnny Abbes had offered his services to Papa Doc, and lived in a Pétionville residence Duvalier placed at his disposal.

In all, Duvalier imprisoned nineteen army officers, ten of

whom had been top men in the Presidential Guard. A scramble for asylum in Latin-American embassies began among others. On 2 June Lieutenant-Colonel Jean Tassy, sent to Cap-Haïtien from his post as criminal research chief of the police department, ran instead to the Brazilian Embassy with his wife and four members of his family. Even Haitians, who had suffered under the brutal Tassy and others, were shocked. Father Luc Hilaire, Duvalierist palace chaplain, went into asylum in the Chilean Embassy after he tried and failed to get Duvalier to release his brother, Lieutenant Serge Hilaire. The number of those fleeing to asylum reached 108.

Then Duvalier put on a ceremony fitting for his Year Ten. Late in the night of 8 June he called a surprise meeting of the army general staff, including General Gérard Constant and Colonel Dominique. As the staff entered the palace they were joined by heavily armed militiamen. For two nervous hours Duvalier kept them waiting in the humid summer night. When he appeared, in uniform, he instructed them to follow. They drove through the deserted streets to Fort Dimanche on the outskirts of town. Other militiamen, armed with sub-machine guns, stood guarding the gate. Duvalier and the trailing officers alighted on the rifle range. At the end of the range, under the guns of militiamen, stood the nineteen officers. All were Dominique's friends.

There had been a secret trial of the nineteen, who, six weeks before, had been loyal Duvalierists. Included in the line-up were Major José (Sonny) Borges who had led Duvalier's anti-guerrilla campaign and had, until a week before, been in charge of the Radio 'Voice of the Duvalierist Revolution'; Captain Harry Tassy, a long-time Duvalierist whose major crime was that he had been too close to the President's eighteen-year-old daughter, Simone; Lieutenant Joseph Laroche, aide-de-camp of the President's wife who accompanied her on visits to Max Dominique's home; Lieutenant-Colonel Joseph C. Lemoine, a tough and loyal Duvalierist, commander of the north of Haiti; three Monestime brothers, two of whom had been in the Presidential Guard; Major Pierre Thomas, chief of the immigration service of the police department, accused of being a CIA agent because his work brought him in daily contact with the American Embassy.

The nineteen were tied to stakes, hands behind their backs. Duvalier ordered his staff officers be issued rifles, and they formed a firing squad. At Duvalier's command they shot the nineteen. Few except their families mourned their end. A decade of zealous service to the Dictator had not endeared them to the public.

Dominique's turn was still to come.

Duvalier had a horde of peasants trucked into the city on 22 June and put on a show for them. Papa Doc spoke, in his own inimitable manner, from the palace: 'Duvalier is going to do something. He is going to make a roll call. I do not know whether you will be able to answer this roll call that I am taking so that I may be able to defend you. Here is the call: Major Harry Tassy, where are you? Come to your benefactor ... Absent.'

In this theatrical manner he called the names of the nineteen executed officers, then commented, with a cunning smile: 'All of them have been shot.'

Next came another roll call, this time of officers who had taken Embassy asylum. These were 'trusted ones', he said. 'Honorary Lieutenant-Colonel Jean Tassy, where are you? Come.' The same call went to each, including the Corsican Pierre Giordani, who rose through the ranks of the Tonton Macoutes to become a chieftain, a Haitian citizen, and deputy of the Republic. 'These have run away after having benefited from the favour of Caesar,' Duvalier continued. 'They are no longer Haitians. Beginning tomorrow the general court-martial will receive orders to work on their trial. They will be tried according to the law, for we are the civilized.'

Duvalier concluded:

Now that we have made the roll call of the traitors, we are going to address the valiant populations of the nine geographic departments of the country. I am an arm of steel, hitting inexorably ... hitting inexorably ... hitting inexorably. I have shot these ... officers in order to project the revolution and those serving it ... I

align . . . myself with the great leaders of peoples as Kemal Ataturk, Lenin, Kwame Nkrumah, Patrice Lumumba, Azikwe, Mao Tse-tung.

The next day Papa Doc and his wife went to the airport to wave a 'fond' farewell to daughters Marie-Denise and Simone and son-in-law Dominique who, had it not been for the protection of his wife, would have been just another corpse in the communal burial ground at Fort Dimanche. Upon the insistence of his wife and mother-in-law, Dominique had been named Haitian Ambassador to Spain. The two girls left with all the cash and jewellery they could muster. As the plane took off, the Tonton Macoutes seized Dominique's chauffeur and two bodyguards. Several shots rang out. Reports spread that there had been an attempt on Papa Doc's life, but it was only the simple thoroughness of eliminating those who had been close to Dominique.

Formal charges of treason against Dominique were published on 1 August under the signature of Colonel Jacques Laroche. Dominique was dismissed from the army 'for the good of the service', ordered to return to Haiti within thirty days to stand trial before a grand tribunal of the armed forces. He was accused of launching an insurrection with the executed nineteen, planning to assassinate Duvalier on 24 April, and promoting a situation of panic throughout the country. The April bombing incidents were also laid at his doorstep.

Duvalier, in an ugly mood, berated his wife in their palace apartment for intervening on behalf of Dominique so that he and their daughters could leave the country. He demanded that they return to Haiti, and received a curt no as answer. Wife Simone even dared to suggest she would join the Dominiques abroad. As Papa Doc's rage built up, he began to hit her. Pudgy son Jean-Claude, fifteen, shoved his father into an adjoining room and locked the door. For three hours the old man fumed, then he pulled an emergency alarm that not only brought palace guards running but set off the palace siren. Papa Doc justified the alarm by proclaiming a curfew and a general alert.

Duvalier told the hastily mustered militia that he was most unhappy with his wife, who had stopped him from keeping

Dominique in the country to face his fate. To the wide-eyed militiamen Duvalier rambled on against his wife and at one point reproached her for not being as helpful as Eva Perón had been to Dictator Juan Perón in Argentina.[1]

While Haiti boiled internally with family intrigue and the Dominique ouster, exiles in southern Florida decided to make another try. The persistent Father Jean-Baptiste Georges, former Duvalierist who became obsessed with overthrowing Papa Doc, in desperation sought the aid of The Tiger, Cuban exile Rolando Masferrer. In the process, he became caught in a quagmire of Cuban exile plots and counterplots around Miami. He moved into a circle of people who made revolutions for a price, who would sell anything from pistols to torpedoes.

Father Georges's association with Masferrer, allegedly a notorious hatchet man in the days of the Cuban dictatorship of Fulgencio Batista, had begun to take form in the summer of 1966. An invasion plan sputtered and backfired for months, but eventually produced shock waves that rolled across the Caribbean and were felt in Haiti during the Dominique affair.

Father Georges had become quite an expert at raising funds. A sympathetic movie director donated $50,000. Strangely enough, the Columbia Broadcasting System got involved by buying exclusive rights to filming the proposed expedition. It began as the plotters met in a New York basement and was supposed to climax with the overthrow of Duvalier through an invasion from Florida. CBS got only half the film expected, at an estimated cost of $100,000.

The invasion was the talk of Miami. Not since the Bay of Pigs invasion of Cuba had there been a 'secret' operation so well known to the general public. It became known as 'Operation Bay of Piglets', and never left Florida.

The would-be invaders, at one point, held a strategy session

1. On 18 March 1969 Colonel Dominique, his wife and son returned to the bosom of Haiti's First Family. Public embraces were exchanged at the François Duvalier International Airport, then the motorcade made its way to the palace, recently vacated by Madame Saint-Victor who, for the time being at least, appears to be out of favour. (See the Epilogue.)

on the lawn of a home in Coral Gables, using a megaphone to make themselves heard. One enthusiast test-fired his machine pistol in his front yard, later hung it on a clothesline, and painted it. Miami police interrupted another meeting. They had been tipped off that something strange was going on, and knocked on the door of the house in question. A well-muscled, bearded invader answered. 'What's going on in here?' the policeman asked, explaining that there had been a complaint. The invader apologized and told the officer it was a meeting of 'senior Boy Scouts' preparing for a field exercise. The police took a quick look, left, and as they drove away thought better of it. But they were too late. The senior Scouts had cleared out.

By November 1966, the CBS team packed up its Miami gear and returned to New York (at one point CBS mistakenly reported that the invasion force had actually landed in Haiti). The first attempt at invasion had blown up when a Cuban exile designated as military chief quit and charged that the operation was phony. Napoleon Vilaboa, one-time captain in Castro's Cuban rebel army, said that the weapons for the invasion were inadequate and the mini-navy and mini-air force promised by Masferrer existed only in his imagination. The invasion appeared to have dissolved in a sea of charges and counter-charges.

There was even a case of James-Bond-style dealings that involved the Haitian Consul in Miami, Eugene Maximilien. He claimed that Masferrer offered to call off the invasion for $200,000. Masferrer denied this, and countered with the claim that Maximilien had volunteered to support the invasion in return for a diplomatic post in Europe if it succeeded. Neither could prove his case, but a sometime contract CIA agent who bugged a 'business' conversation with Maximilien decided not to use the evidence against the Consul.

Although the 'invasion' was under constant US surveillance, Father Georges and Masferrer did not give up until early in 1967. US customs agents broke it all up then. They seized seventy men and a load of war equipment which had been installed in a two-storey concrete blockhouse on Coco Plum Beach in the Florida Keys. The invaders had a .50-calibre machine gun sitting on a doorstep.

When arraigned and charged with conspiring to violate the Munitions and Control Act, both Masferrer and Father Georges pleaded guilty. Their November 1967 trial revealed two plans. One called for the aid of Dominican General Antonio Imbert, the sole survivor of the group who assassinated Dictator Trujillo. Imbert was to assist them with men, arms, and money, and use his influence to get them a base in the Central American Republic of Honduras. The other called for the invasion to take off from the Florida Keys and capture the two Haitian islands, Gonave and Tortue, one on the bay fronting Port-au-Prince and the other off the northern coast. The jury found them guilty. The fifty-year-old Cuban 'Tiger', Masferrer, was sentenced on 28 February 1968 to four years in prison by Federal Judge Ted Cabot. Father Georges, forty-eight, was sentenced to two years, but Judge Cabot suspended all but sixty days and put him on three years' probation. Haitian former Colonel René Léon, forty-three, was also given sixty days. Martin Francis Xavier Casey, twenty-nine, described as an American soldier of fortune, was sentenced to nine months.

Whether the would-be invaders had links inside Haiti is unknown, but it was suggested that Father Georges had collaborators in the army. At the 18 November 1966 Army Day parade, eleven top officers were absent. They had fled with their families into asylum in the Brazilian Embassy.

The Year Ten, like each of those before it, was full of pomp and pretension. Much of it masked failure, but survival alone was a measure of progress for Papa Doc. And, here and there, in this land of misery, a glimmer of hope sometimes appeared. It was hard to detect, however.

The government issued postage stamps with a golden Duvalier profile and his personal emblem, the guinea hen on a conch shell. They were inscribed: 'Year X of the Duvalierist Revolution.' A law authorizing the minting abroad of $1,850,000 worth of gold coins bearing Duvalier's likeness was voted by Congress. The issue was described as 'an element of prestige and propaganda capable of reinforcing the credit and renown of Haiti abroad.' But the gold coins, to have been issued in midyear, were not seen during the Year Ten. It was explained that they were such collectors' items that speculators were holding them off the market.

To honour *Le leader* youthful writer Gérard Daumec, a court favourite, published a flattering little treatise that aped Mao Tse-tung's *Little Red Book of Thoughts.* The Duvalier book, originally in white, was reissued in red, and contained Papa Doc's 'thoughts' from his early days on. It was entitled *Forty Years of Doctrine – 10 Years of Revolution – Breviary of a Revolution.* Extracts of Papa Doc's writing during the late twenties and early thirties and maxims from his Presidential campaign speeches were set forth in prayer-book style. Example: 'God prevent me from considering this cause as being my cause. No, it is *yours*! I have entered the struggle only because of YOU.'

Another tenth-anniversary publication was an opus entitled *A Guide to Duvalier's Essential Works,* also offering excerpts from the wit and wisdom of his early writings. And yet another book on the Messiah's accomplishments was ordered in August from the Henri Deschamps publishing house, which had produced a similar work for Magloire. Duvalier's big red book (not to be confused with his book of thoughts) was supposed to be ready for the tenth anniversary of his 1957 election but was delayed because of production problems, one being the difficulty of finding pictures of the little doctor which did not also include the faces of purged aides. These photos had to be drastically retouched and, for the most part, were discarded.

(And more may well have to be.) Still another conspiracy appears to be dividing the devoted members of the Duvalier clan, but, this time, the forces of nature are more to blame than mere human ambition.

On the morning of 18 October 1968 FBI, State Department and CIA agents were summoned to the North Dade County sheriff's office where Duvalier's son-in-law and current front man, Luc Albert Foucard, was begging the Miami police for 'protection'. The Old Man's agents were after him, he claimed. It was the classic case of a suspected Other Woman, complicated by the fact that Madame Foucard, a chip off the old Doc, never travels anywhere (not even to Miami on a shopping trip, as in this instance) without several very tough Tonton Macoutes in tow. Suspicious of her husband's prolonged absences on 'business', she ordered her personal bodyguard to trail him; which they did, to a hotel.

However, Foucard spotted them and, being in a position to know better than anyone what the TTMs were capable of doing, he called the police and demanded to be taken into protective custody.

The next morning, Nicole told the Haitian Consul to spring Luc and deliver him to her – which was the last thing Luc wanted. Well aware that Luc's sister, Madame Saint-Victor, was the woman behind Papa Doc and the person most often mentioned as his successor, the Consul refused to embroil himself in this phase of Haitian political science. He promptly went into hiding and Luc remained thankfully behind bars. Unable to obtain justice, Nicôle booked passage home for herself and her retinue. Negotiations began.

After more than two weeks of bargaining, Luc was convinced that he could return to his posts (Chief Planner, Head of the Department of Tourism), his family (he and Nicole have presented Duvalier with his first grandchild), and to the sober delights of holy matrimony without undergoing reprisals. Nicole flew to Miami to fetch him and the happy couple returned to Port-au-Prince on 2 November.

Truly, as a script for a travelogue might read, Haiti is A Land of Contradictions. In the middle of all the poverty, supermarkets financed by the oil companies mushroom in the capital, and compete fiercely for customers. And there was a climate of *détente* at the end of the Year Ten. Duvalier increased his efforts to promote tourism, and there was a response. The beauty of Haiti and its attractions managed to lure even visitors appalled at the Duvalier government and the poverty to which it condemns the island. Seemingly overnight the water-front International Casino changed hands. Without explanation the Canadian management left and was soon replaced by the Cohen family from Woodridge, New York – father Louis, sons

Solomon and Matthew. With a ten-year lease, agreeing to pay Duvalier a fixed sum plus a percentage, the Cohens have put new life into the casino. They previously had been known as restaurant operators in the Catskills. Their formula is to arrange junkets for high-rolling US gamblers, who are given their basic expenses back in gambling chips. Some estimates say that Duvalier's share of the casino take runs as high as $100,000 a week, which gives it high priority in Haiti.

Duvalier even co-operates with his old enemy, the elite. He leans on them, and they lean on him. The business community is starting to forget, for convenience, how the government once cut into its receipts by handing out monopolies to trusted aides as bonuses. Many of the old rancours of the 1957 election period have healed.

It is difficult, too, for the visitor to understand how the social life of the elite can be as active and full as ever. Despite a shortage of dollars, stores are full of jewels, perfumes, clothing, toys, at year's end. Only the wealthy or the Duvalierists could afford them.

In sad contrast, school standards have lowered. More and more children in rural areas cannot go to school because their parents can hardly afford food, let alone clothing.

When the United States cautiously began to dribble aid back into Haiti in small amounts in 1966, after most had been cut off since 1962, it tried to funnel it towards areas which would benefit Haitians and not just government officials with big pockets. Malaria eradication (which was a United Nations project) and US surplus food (amounting to $1 million a year) were two US aid programmes not discontinued. In addition, the Agency for International Development in 1966 gave some $500,000 in funds for a pilot project in community development. These were administered by CARE.

Surveys on nutrition indicate pitiful conditions. Eighty per cent of pre-school and school children suffer from malnutrition. Doctors pointed out in dismay that severe malnutrition in pre-school years can cause permanent brain damage and leave the children more vulnerable to crippling diseases. A survey at the village of Fonds Parisien, some thirty-five miles from Port-au-Prince, found that the average villager spent eight cents a day on food, consumed 1,359 calories, and 32 grams of proteins daily. Minimum daily requirement is considered 2,590 calories and 40 grams of proteins. The US average is 3,100 and 91.6.

In 1958 Duvalier had set up a nutrition bureau, but it did not begin to operate until 1962, and not until 1966 did the government begin giving it $300 a month. Under the system, four centres offered four-month nutritional rehabilitation programmes which could take thirty children each. The US surplus food was a major contribution but of course was not enough. One of every five Haitian babies dies before it reaches the age of three months; life expectancy is forty; 95 per cent of children receive less than a sixth-grade education; agricultural production continues to fall. Statistical surveys make estimates and do not pretend to be complete. There is simply no organized method of gathering reliable figures on the country as a whole.

At the close of 1967 the Inter-American Development Bank (IDB), in operation since 1961, could point to three loans to Haiti – $3.5 million in 1961 for agriculture and industry; $2.4 million for potable water in Port-au-Prince in 1964; $1.3 million for education in 1966. In addition, $615,000 was granted Haiti in the form of technical assistance in connection with the loans. As with other financial assistance, few results showed.

A major jolt to the economy came at the end of 1967 when the International Monetary Fund (IMF) did not renew the agreement providing a stand-by fund which served to keep the *gourde* stable. The agreement had been renewed each year since 1958. As a result, the *gourde* went on the black market for a time for as little as half its previous value (twenty cents).

All three agencies, Agency for International Development, the IDB, and the IMF, in 1967 reports to the Inter-American Committee on the Alliance for Progress, noted where improvements could be made. The bank suggested 'improvement of the country's institutional capacity'; AID recommended 'proper political and administrative climate'; the IMF said that 'the administration and control of tax collections should be improved.' All used the polite language of international institutions to indicate that what Haiti basically needed was efficient government.

This was another clear answer to Duvalier apologists who liked to compare him to Trujillo (!), whose brutality achieved something resembling efficiency and which left physical evidence of progress of a sort in roads and buildings. Ten years of Duvalier have built a contrary case: the country remains in general decline, and the apologist can point only to partially completed Duvalierville, a monument to corruption, or the new jet airport, which once had been a semi-permanent fund-raising gimmick.

Coffee and tourism, Haiti's major sources of income, are not enough to keep the country out of the red on balance of payments. For the three years ending in 1967 the deficit – in a country where the annual budget was about $28 million – was $5 million to $6 million. Coffee had the traditional alternately good years, but poor weather made even this an unreliable cycle. Tourism, at its peak under Magloire and its depth during the 1963 crisis, picked up, but not enough. The new airport and improved airlines service to Port-au-Prince have helped, but Duvalier's uncanny knack for scaring off vacationers by issuing blood-curdling statements and provoking scary 'happenings' continues to hurt.

One thing that impressed observer after observer was that many of Haiti's skilled and professional men abandoned the country, often for Africa. These included lawyers, judges, physicians, linguists, professors, secondary school-teachers, doctors of philosophy, engineers, financiers, and journalists – all educated men and women desperately needed to develop Haiti. Some found middle-level administrative jobs in the governments of emerging nations. Others rose to influential posts. For example, Dr Joseph Déjean, a Haitian exile, became counsellor to the Department of Foreign Affairs – the State Department – of Guinea. One Haitian estimated that the number occupying official posts in the Congo alone was nearly one thousand. Colonel Paul Corvington, formerly of the Haitian army (one of those in asylum in the Dominican Embassy in 1963), won a high post in the Congo security forces. M. Rigaud Magloire became a top Congo financial adviser. The United Nations appointed a Haitian exile, Ambassador Jacques Léger, to be its regional representative for technical assistance on the Ivory Coast.

A mission from the Congo, with official permission to recruit Haitian teachers, once came to Port-au-Prince, and more than half the graduating class of the teachers' training school at the National University applied. Haiti, 90-per-cent illiterate, contributed more than half its new teacher crop.

Of 264 Haitian medical graduates in the past ten years, only three remained in Haiti. There are more Haitian doctors (250) in Canada than in Haiti.

Hurricanes that struck across Haiti's south-west peninsula in 1963 (Flora), 1964 (Cleo), and 1966 (Inez) did lasting damage to the economy. The heaviest destruction was in the south-west, but heavy winds and rains damaged crops over large parts of the country. Duvalier could not negotiate with nature as he could negotiate with diplomats. Flora killed thousands, laid waste scores of villages, and ruined a large part of the coffee crop. When the United States quickly offered help, Duvalier refused on the grounds that the help might be used as a cover for subversive purposes. This was during the period of the invasions. He allowed only a trickle of help for a week, until reports began to snowball, raising death estimates as high as 5,000 and the number of homeless and starving to 125,000. Duvalier cautiously kept his 5,000-man army and his 500-man Presidential Guard on the job while the United States gave $25,000 for hurricane relief, shipped in 25 million pounds of food in four months, and the US Navy helped transport it. Again typically, Duvalier showed no gratitude but resentment for not having received more.

When President Kennedy less than two weeks after Flora announced the appointment of Benson E. L. Timmons as the new US Ambassador, succeeding Raymond Thurston whom

Duvalier had booted out, Duvalier would not receive him for several weeks. When the audience came, Duvalier gave Timmons a lecture on behaviour. Less than a month later, when President Kennedy was assassinated, Duvalier's Tonton Macoutes drank a grisly toast of congratulations that a Duvalier enemy had fallen. Duvalier, who called Kennedy 'that evil genius', had convinced them that both Thurston and Kennedy were removed by his mystic will.

One economic vehicle that always dismayed the United States (a factor in cutting off aid in 1962) and the international agencies which tried to assist Haiti in putting order into its financial affairs was the Régie du Tabac, or tobacco monopoly. It was an authority with retail distribution items such as cigarettes, soap, and others. Under Duvalier, the monopoly items grew to include cement, flour, milk, and many more. In some cases taxes averaged 10 per cent of the cost. The Régie funds are unbudgeted, and are spent as Duvalier chooses. International agencies felt that these funds should be used to alleviate budget problems, but Duvalier regarded this as infringement on sovereignty. The funds were deposited in Clémard Joseph Charles's Banque Commercial, a private bank.

Duvalier added another vehicle for unbudgeted money in 1966 when he introduced an old-age-pension system to which Haiti's 30,000 salaried employees had to pay 3 per cent of their earnings. After contributing for at least twenty years, an employee could collect the benefits if he were sixty-five years old and had a medical certificate that he no longer could work. As has been noted, life expectancy in Haiti is forty.

Duvalier in his efforts to attract foreign capital granted exclusive operating concessions. Few paid off. Foreign businessmen had become reluctant to invest in Haiti because of the uncertain conditions. Neither did Haiti want to be dominated by US investment. Inevitably, speculators were attracted.

One government business gambit, perhaps one of the most spectacular, involved a twenty-five-year-old Egyptian-born businessman, Mohammed Fayed, who arrived in June 1964. Fayed called himself a sheik and distributed a calling card that associated him with a Kuwait oil company. Haitians described him as a man of considerable charm, and his investment proposals won major government concessions.

Fayed received exclusive contracts which gave him control of the oil industry, shipping, and the port. He agreed to invest $1 million within two years in an oil refinery and $5 million within four years on a variety of harbour-improvement programmes. In addition to his oil concession he was named sole shipping agent for twelve steamship companies serving Haiti. Besides these agent fees he collected wharfage fees that previously went to the government, and he quickly increased these fees. Among his other accomplishments he became a Haitian citizen in a matter of months although normally a ten-year residency is required. To improve the harbour, Fayed set out buoy markers, hired a British harbour master, and put lights on the pier.

He ran into opposition from the West India Trans-Atlantic Conference and the United States-Gulf-Haitian conference of shippers, who protested to Duvalier. At a meeting of the conference Fayed did not show up and Duvalier admitted that there was trouble. Duvalier said he was searching world capitals for Fayed and acknowledged that a large sum of money had left Haiti with him. Fayed's bank accounts were frozen too late. The local manager of a bank where he did business was ousted from the country on the excuse that he had expressed anti-government views.

The arrival of Fayed and other foreign investors in Haiti prompted Richard Eder of the *New York Times* to write:

> Both business and diplomatic circles have been paying close attention to the arrival over the past year of a series of visitors who let it be known that they plan to invest large amounts of money here. These visitors have in common a lack of much conventionally traceable business background and a close connection with one [Haitian] government official or another.

Fayed's connection was Clémard Charles, Duvalier's banker. Charles received a government concession on automobile insurance and Fayed assisted him with it. The concession, by government decree, required every motorist in Haiti to purchase liability insurance from Charles's private bank. The premium was sixty-seven dollars annually and maximum benefits $1,000 property damage and $2,000 bodily injury per accident. Charles's bank also had an interest in an exclusive government franchise granted a Canadian to handle all public transportation of merchandise and passengers in the country.

Fayed's oil concession went to him only after an American company, the Valentine Petroleum and Chemical Corporation, had its representative expelled from the country and its contract to build a refinery cancelled. Valentine had an investment guarantee from the US Agency for International Development, and tried to sue the United States to collect $817,000 in damages. (The president of the company said that the United States offered him a settlement 'so small it's ridiculous.')

Duvalier once made a deal with an Iranian prince who agreed to construct a road in return for exclusive right to build tourist hotels along most of Haiti's south shore; another with an American geologist who, in return for mineral prospecting, was given a share in the government's sisal operation.

An interesting arrangement with the government came up during a 1963 US Senate investigation of the affairs of Robert G. ('Bobby') Baker, one-time secretary to the former Senate Majority Leader Lyndon Baines Johnson. The Senate Rules Committee produced testimony that the Haitian-American Meat Packing Company, S.A., was exporting meat from nutrition-starved Haiti to the United States and Puerto Rico and paying Baker a cent-a-pound commission. It was said that Baker helped the company get a US export licence, which required approval from the US Department of Agriculture that the plant's sanitary conditions and inspection procedures met US standards. An American Embassy official had inspected the plant in 1961 and denied the certificate because of 'certain deficiencies'. This time it was granted.

The committee revealed that members of the family of Texas plutocrat Clinton W. Murchison, Jr, owner of a Haitian flour mill, were the 'money partners' in the meat company. From 1 July 1961 to 30 September, the company had exported

5,237,242 pounds of meat, mostly to Puerto Rico. The meat-packing plant, set up near Damiens, had seemed a good thing for Haiti. It replaced an unsightly nineteenth-century abattoir at La Saline that had added to the water-front stench. Then the plant began to have problems. Dressed, packaged meat proved too expensive for most Haitians, who frequently bought it in five-cent balls. The government gave the plant a monopoly but had trouble enforcing it. The butchers who had been put out of business began slaughtering their beef illegally under bridges, in back alleys, where there could be no sanitation or inspection. To save its investment, the plant turned toward Puerto Rico as a market, and Robert G. Baker apparently was a big help in cutting down red tape.

Duvalier always turned to whatever resources he had at home. One of these was O. J. Brandt, a Jamaican who came to Haiti fifty years earlier as a bank clerk and made millions in coffee and textiles. Brandt, still a British subject, once went to Jamaica and found himself barred from returning to Haiti. After he purchased $2 million worth of government bonds, his problem disappeared. To retire Brandt's bonds (he had made similar purchases before) Duvalier devoted a five-cents-a-gallon gasoline tax exclusively to Brandt.

Nevertheless, Duvalier was not a happy dictator in the Year Ten. His wrath seemed to have no bounds. He was tired of fighting the old demons, and now he was consumed with the desire to strike down some of the cocksure partisans whom he had permitted to amass enormous wealth. Duvalier enjoyed humiliating those who thought they had a right to deference because of official positions. At a rare cabinet meeting attended by several foreign businessmen a cabinet Minister complained to Duvalier that a militiaman guarding the door had been rude to him. Duvalier became furious and slapped the minister. 'I can find a new Minister on any street corner, but a man like that guard is very hard to find. He has fought for me, and protects me at the peril of his own life,' he said.

Following the April (Max Dominique) purge, Duvalier fired

his Interior and National Defence Minister Jean Julmé and Public Works Minister Luckner Cambronne. Duvalier gave Julmé and Justice Minister Rameau Estimé a short run before they fell. Newly appointed Interior Minister Morille P. Figaro, Duvalier's personal secretary for twelve years, went before the Assembly on 27 June and declared that Julmé and Estimé (also deputies) were traitors. Figaro told the Assembly that the people

> demand vengeance.... The people adore their Chief and the Chief loves the people.... Bread does not reach the people, because invisible hands are stealing the bread.... As long as there is a hand stealing the bread that Duvalier hands down to his people there will be a head to chop...

Figaro's oratory was prophetic. In October he, too, disappeared and a new Minister, Dr Aurèle Joseph, was named. Dr Joseph, who had held the job once before, had worked with young Dr Duvalier in the yaws campaign.

Another law Figaro introduced before his disappearance made it a crime to seek asylum in a foreign embassy and said that those who granted the asylum (the foreign embassies) would be considered accomplices. It deprived the refugees of citizenship and confiscated their properties. The vote was unanimous. The Assembly passed decrees in August repudiating four conventions governing political asylum in Latin America.

Duvalier received a blow from an unexpected quarter when Dr Jean Price Mars, acknowledged father of *Négritude*, wrote a booklet, *Open Letter to Dr René Piquion* (who had been an early adherent of the doctrine), in answer to Piquion's 'Manual of *Négritude*'. The Haitian sociologist and historian, now in his nineties, declared that the problem of colour was distinct from the problem of class. 'Indeed, from the very beginning, Toussaint Louverture's reform divided Saint Domingue's population into two distinct categories – the ruling class, and the majority class of the *asservis* on whom sat the economic scaffolding of the new society.' And Dessalines's law maintained the same pattern. Price Mars emphasized that in both cases the ruling class was composed of black and mulatto. He felt that the base of Haiti's problems was this social question and not colour. His booklet thus refuted the thesis of Duvalier and Lorimer Denis, which became Duvalier's political doctrine, that class problem is a problem of colour. But to some extent, even before Price Mars's book appeared, Duvalier had disproved his own theory by surrounding himself with mulattoes as well as blacks. His most trusted aid was a mulatto woman, Madame Saint-Victor, and he gave preference to his mulatto son-in-law, Luc Foucard, over Max Dominique, the black. The Price Mars booklet disturbed Duvalier, and he suppressed its printing. Copies, even those Dr Price Mars possessed, were confiscated.

While the Dominique affair was at its height, Ecuador severed diplomatic relations. Foreign Minister Julio Prado said that the action was taken because of the 'obstinate attitude of the government ... against the humanitarian institution of political asylum', and its lack of respect for 'essential human rights'. The Inter-American Commission on Human Rights tried to investigate and Haiti refused it any information or permission for a visit.

The International Commission of Jurists, long critical of the Duvalier regime, summarized the latest developments in the harshest possible terms. The jurists charged that Haiti had 'become the poorest country in Latin America as a result of the incompetence, inertia, and corruption of its government.' The Inter-American Press Association refused the application of two Haitian newspapers for membership on the grounds that newspapers must be free from government control to be eligible.

The Year Ten ended in a fitting manner. There were open demonstrations against the government in Cap-Haïtien in September. People went into the streets yelling 'Down with misery; down with hunger.' Someone painted on the wall of the Haitian-American Institute *Vive l'occupation*, which was a way of saying that he preferred US occupation to continued misery and poverty. The reaction of the government was to send in Macoutes. Duvalier ordered the Haitian-American Institute, which taught English and carried out the functions of the US Information Service, to be closed and its American director recalled.

An act on 8 November was an apt footnote to much that had happened in ten years: Haiti had become civilized in the Duvalierist sense, and the country had a bank robbery that was pure Jesse James. The newspaper *Le Matin* carried the following account: 'Four armed men made off with $77,800. It occurred at eight a.m. It was a big operation, carried out with perplexing boldness and speed.' *Le Matin* quoted the manager of the bank as saying that he witnessed the hold-up from his office window. Three of the men 'did not even bother to wear a mask or disguise themselves.' The bank robbers had stolen a small bus from the Turian Kindergarten the night before, painted on two red crosses, and installed a siren. With a safe from the bank hoisted into the van at machine-gun point they made their way across town with siren wailing. On a back road they dumped an empty safe and disappeared. Who were the robbers? It remained a mystery. Many Haitians decided that it was a new, dramatic manner for Papa Doc and his henchmen to collect revenue. Others speculated that the job was done by Tonton Macoutes without Duvalier's okay. Orders were passed for all vehicles to be searched leaving the city and even passengers departing by plane were searched; perhaps related was the shooting and serious wounding of spy chief Elois Maître at the International Airport on 7 December. This was followed by the unexplained death of Captain Jacques Delva, who had replaced Mme Max Adolphe as warden of the infamous Fort Dimanche. Who had ordered the shootings? Who had the power – besides Papa Doc?

Despite an occasional mystery or two, Duvalier's terror machine runs smoothly, however. It works quietly in order not to disturb tourism, and few tourists ever would be aware that it existed.

To clean up the town for them, Duvalier issued a decree

early in December making it mandatory to paint houses. Even those living in workers' cities had to paint their houses. One communiqué dated 7 December gave workers living in Cité Saint Martin until 15 December to paint their houses, warning that sanctions would be taken against those who did not conform. Another communiqué dated 15 December gathered all painters at city hall to decide on the sanctions to be applied.

Another major measure came on 23 December. La Saline, the water-front slum, was burned and bulldozed. People living there were not warned and relocated. Some went to vacant lots in Déprez, a residential area in Port-au-Prince foothills, and set up a shanty town. These were again chased away and their shacks burned. After La Saline was razed, people could be seen squatting on the sites of their former homes with small bundles containing all they owned.

A ten-year review of the Duvalier record drips blood. He has killed or driven his enemies or suspected enemies into exile with a ruthlessness perhaps surpassed only by the revolutionary Dessalines, who at least had the excuse of having felt the sting of the slave whip. Duvalier has consolidated his power politically and economically. He has even gained a goodly amount of prestige by defying the United States and getting away with it. Time and again he has purged the army, that traditional bugbear of all Haitian strong men. He has managed not only to resume relations with the neighbouring Dominican Republic, but he has received pledges of peaceful co-existence as in the palmiest Trujillo days. Many of his accomplices with long memories are dead (Clément Barbot); in exile (Jean Tassy, Brazil); or in disgrace (Luckner Cambronne has quietly entered the coffee business; under constant surveillance, he appears almost magically transformed into someone mild, shy, and retiring). All in all, considering the facilities at his disposal and the forces which, at one time or another, have been arrayed against him, Duvalier has turned in a truly remarkable display of political acrobatics.

Of course – credit where it is due – the authors must admit that the quasi-sublime ineptitude of his foes has played a major part in Papa Doc's tenure. On the limpid azure morning of 20 May 1968 yet another off-key aria in the comic opera was sung.

A B-25, flying over the Presidential Palace, released a cylindrical object which, upon striking the ground, added one more pothole to the Port-au-Prince street system. Closer to the mark (indeed, it is said to have dealt the palace a glancing blow) was a square package probably containing anti-Duvalier leaflets. Port-au-Prince never found out because the bombardier had forgotten to untie the package and so its contents failed to scatter. The plane banked slowly and made another pass over the *Président à Vie*'s residence. One more cylinder was dropped. This one failed to go off at all.

Four uneventful hours later, a single-engine Cessna sky-bus, modified to carry cargo, requested permission to land at the Cap-Haïtien airport. Immediately upon disembarking, its passengers began blazing away with the Tommy guns they were carrying. They raked the control tower, the only building of military or architectural significance within a mile-and-one-half radius. There was no answering fire. It was siesta time.

In a closely co-ordinated military action, the Cessna was followed by the B-25 which, after bombing Port-au-Prince to its knees, had returned to base, a Bahama in the Inagua cluster, where it had picked up some twenty battle-hardened, leather-tough invaders who were dressed in camouflaged uniforms bearing the label *Big Game – Styled by Broadway*. Someone must have been sufficiently awake to sound an alarm, for, in a very brief time, the invaders became big game for the Duvalier forces.

On the fateful day of 22 May (by the technique of what in Haiti is called *Onomancie* and what is supposed to mean 'divination by numbers', Duvalier has determined that 22 is 'equal to himself'), the prisoners were flown to Port-au-Prince, where they were personally interrogated by The Chief of the Revolution and Grand Protector of Commerce and Industry. They have disappeared, but their B-25 was, for a long while, on display at François Duvalier International Airport. (It has subsequently become part of the Haitian Air Corps's *force de frappe*.)

Initially, Papa Doc's ministers followed the by now well-engrained ritual of blaming the affair on Castro in an attempt to play on the manic Communist fears of the United States, and Duvalier routinely complained to the Organization of American States and to the United Nations. The complaints were duly registered. So much for Invasion Attempt Number Eight.

At time of writing, almost certainly a ninth invasion is being planned somewhere – and probably a tenth by anti-Duvalierists opposed to the instigators of number nine. What will happen if one should ever succeed is open to conjecture. The persistent hope – which is about all that nourishes Haiti today – is that tyranny will be buried alongside Papa Doc, and that the gorgeous, impoverished land will at long last begin to make its way into the twentieth century under the leadership of responsible human beings. Certainly, the outlines for eventual rehabilitation plans are numerous.

But there is one factor that ensures Haiti's continuance along traditional lines, one independent variable which no equation for progress can either assimilate or ignore.... Day by day, month by month, year after year, old Number Twenty-Two sits behind his heavy mahogany desk with the loaded .45 (poetically, if not onomantologically, equal to him) in his top drawer and complains about being misunderstood – by the United States, by 'trusted' associates, by the world. Nearby is a balcony to which he often repairs – now to address a throng in the high-pitched nasal gibberish that is the hallmark of those possessed by the Guédé Loa, now to watch a spectacular tropical sunset, now to gaze down on his current obsession, a giant bronze statue of the *Nègre Marron* which has replaced the statue commemorating Toussaint Louverture.

In addition, the balcony offers the creature on it the best view in town of two other monuments to his reign: the tall, proud, new tax office and, just across the street, the long, dingy yellow-drab police station presently called Casernes François Duvalier.

Epilogue (August 1971)

Despite all the praise and rhetoric heaped upon Duvalier and his 'revolution' by his clique during thirteen and a half years in power, at his death the country had come a full circle; the rich were getting richer, the poor poorer and more numerous; the old elite (oligarchy) was more secure in its privileged position as a class and still held economic power; and on Duvalier's death bed, the American Embassy regained the political dominance it had lost during his 'reign'.

What was even more significant, in the early post-Duvalier period, was the army regaining its former role of keeper of public order, and once again a major force in the political life of the country. Duvalier had maintained power by neutralizing the army through the Tonton Macoutes. Duvalier's heirs found it expedient and safer to curb the power of the warlord Tonton Macoute chieftains. It meant the balance of power and influence had shifted back in favour of the army.

Duvalier's political 'genius', writes Haitian social scientist Leslie Manigat in a paper following his death, was mainly the art of using to his profit the structural ills of the Haitian system. He also exploited – being careful not to remedy them – the psychological and objective consequences of the injustices of which the popular and mainly rural masses were victims, to the benefit of less than 10 per cent of the population.

The Haitian crisis, Manigat notes, goes back to the beginning of this century, and the issue was postponed by the American occupation of 1915–34. This is why Duvalier combined nineteenth-century Haiti, and a contemporary ruler, with the pressures of twentieth-century progress.

So upon Papa Doc's death all the pieces were once again in

their traditional position on the old Haitian political chess board.

With a certain clairvoyance, Duvalier began the difficult task of reuniting his family in 1968. Upon his death three years later, this united family smoothly assumed the reins of government.

In a press conference in mid-1968, Duvalier divulged that he wanted his daughter and her family back from exile in Europe, and that his son-in-law, Lieutenant-Colonel Max Dominique, condemned to death *in absentia*, was now free to come home. Charles de Gaulle, he added, had increased his prestige by pardoning his enemies. He would follow that same course. But this amnesty was extended only to his family, and not to the thousands who had disappeared into his prisons.

In a sudden flash of candour he announced that his government no longer ruled by terror. 'I hope', he told American reporters, lecturing the US on government, 'the evolution of democracy you've observed in Haiti will be an example for the people of the world, in particular in the United States, in relation to the civil and political rights of Negroes.'

Marie-Denise had given birth to a son in exile. Out of spite, she had named him Alexandre after her father-in-law imprisoned in Haiti on Duvalier's orders. Papa Doc's determination to get his daughter back was obvious as he began harassing those who had shown too much initiative in the anti-Dominique drive. Morille P. Figaro, who wrote in support of Papa Doc's move in a Port-au-Prince newspaper, 'There is no room for two Caesars', ended the briefest term on record as Minister of Interior, purged by Papa Doc.

Talk of the Dominiques' return revived speculation as to who would succeed Papa Doc. Who was his favourite, and most likely to be chosen as his successor?

Son-in-law Luc Albert Foucard, who married daughter Nicole and delivered to Papa Doc Natasha, his first grandchild, appeared to have a clear lead after the ouster of the Dominiques. A capable front man for the government, his position of son-in-law and head of tourism drove him to drink in excess.

Foucard's trump card was his sister, Madame Francesca (France) Saint-Victor, the powerful private secretary of Papa Doc – the *éminence grise*. For eleven years Papa Doc's government held no secrets from Madame Saint-Victor. Her power and influence could only compare with that of Papa Doc.

Shortly before Christmas 1968, Marie-Denise came home to arrange the terms of her family's return. Papa Doc melted before her. Nineteen months previously her husband had been accused of plotting the overthrow of Papa Doc, but had escaped execution; now it was Marie-Denise who actually delivered. With a thoroughness worthy of a younger Papa Doc, Marie-Denise carried out her *coup d'état*. She swept the palace clean of her enemies. It was the end of Madame Saint-Victor's reign. She was the major object of Marie-Denise's palace *coup*. Into Madame Saint-Victor's job and title slipped Marie-Denise, a position of influence she held up until her father died. Whether she knew it or not at the time, Marie-Denise was then setting the stage for the peaceful transition of power after Papa Doc had gone.

To render her *coup* irreversible and prevent Papa Doc from intervening, Marie-Denise had left her child, sister Simone, and husband in France, making their return conditional on the complete success of her palace spring cleaning. It was a way of blackmailing her father, and it worked. Duvalier was impotent before his daughter's brisk action, and she had the full support of her mother. Among the scores of opponents she swept from the palace was Pierre Novembre, her father's faithful food-taster and *houngan*-in-residence.

Papa Doc was berated for his social life and friends. Many were faithful, semi-literate Tonton Macoutes from the lowest rung of the social ladder. Along with new friends acquired in Paris, Marie-Denise had picked up new social values, and tried to impose them on her father, who noted that his mentor Machiavelli had made no provision for such strange family contingencies, alas!

The second phase of Marie-Denise's plan was executed on 16 March 1969, when Simone, whose lover had been executed by father, returned with baby Alexandre and his French nurse.

A proud and doting grandfather was at the François Duvalier jet airport to greet them. As one Duvalierist was later to remark, Alexandre was the only object of his affection that he could not bestow his name on.

Two days later, in time for Madame Duvalier's birthday (19 March), Marie-Denise, who had flown to Paris to fetch him, returned with her tall and handsome husband. 'The cream of Duvalierism' was on hand to greet them, *Le Nouvelliste* noted, describing the 'great moment' when Papa Doc embraced his son-in-law. But many of the high-ranking army officers who had, on instructions from Duvalier, tried and condemned Lieutenant-Colonel Max Dominique to death were less than comfortable at Papa Doc's change of heart.

Taking advantage of Marie-Denise's brief trip to Paris to fetch Max, Papa Doc arranged for Madame Saint-Victor to escape into exile in Florida. With the Dominiques back in power, the Saint-Victor clique and all those who had tied their fortunes to it were now out in the cold, for good. Nicole soon divorced Luc Albert Foucard, who went to the United States for specialized medical treatment. Haitians followed the Byzantine court intrigues with undisguised relish, and paid little attention to the antics of a group of dedicated Communist youths who had decided to widen their two-year-old hit-and-run terrorist war against the Duvalier regime.

Members of the PUCH (Parti Unifié des Communistes Haitiens) on 26 March 1969 led an uprising in the village of Casale, in the Chaine des Matheux, some thirty miles north of Port-au-Prince. For six hours the Communists held the village after chasing both the Tonton Macoutes and the soldiers away. The Communists explained their cause and war to liberate Haiti at a mass rally, and signs of support were scrawled over the mud and wattle walls of the humble village dwellings.

Led by an ex-army sergeant who was said to have served in the crack Palace Guard, the Communists slipped away into the hills with the army in pursuit.

In early April, Communist publications and press releases told the world of Casale. Duvalier had suppressed mention of his Communist enemy until then. The Communists stated that Casale 'is a classic action in the beginning of a revolutionary struggle. It is an obtrusive act which has historical significance. It was, in fact, the first time that true revolutionaries sought the support of peasants in the mountains, and, at the same time, explained to them that the PUCH struggled for all the people, and that the time has come for the people to join the action.' They went on to stress 'the time has come for all Haitians to rise, help the revolutionaries, and continue the operation that has begun in Casale, and which might very well make the starting point of a glorious struggle of National Liberation ...'

But Casale proved a turning point in Duvalier's favour. His usual harsh message, liquidation of the inhabitants of Casale tainted by Communism, soon spread through the mountains, and the Communists did not receive the material or recruits they hoped for. Spotlighted by publicity throughout the world after the Casale uprising, the young men who had so cleverly infiltrated into Haiti from their studies in Europe, and kept their identities secret while carrying out acts of terrorism against the government, were on the run by April. They discovered too late that their Central Committee had been infiltrated since 1961 by a government agent whom they later identified as Frank Eysalene. Throughout that spring Papa Doc's troops rolled up to Communist hide-outs, usually early in the morning, with the precision of the returning swallows.

The final blow came on Monday, 2 June. When the army announced that twenty-two Communists had been engaged and killed in a house on Martin Luther King street in Port-au-Prince, it was no idle boast. Some of the twenty-two had been removed from prison and executed to swell the numbers of dead in the house, but important members of the PUCH Central Committee had fought to the death in this early morning engagement against a superior force of well armed soldiers. A month later, Raymond Jean-François, twenty-nine, a student leader and member of the PUCH leadership, was recognized in a Cap-Haïtien street, and shot dead. Jean-François, jailed and tortured in the early 1960s, had escaped into exile only to return in 1964 to carry on the secret war against Duvalier.

When New York Governor Nelson A. Rockefeller arrived in Haiti on 1 July on his presidential fact-finding mission throughout Latin America, Duvalier could boast that he had indeed wiped out the Central Committee of the Unified Party of Haitian Communists, and proven himself a staunchly anti-Communist American ally deserving substantial financial aid.

Some New York exiles, who had access to the news media, contradicted Duvalier's claims of wiping out the Communists. They would, up until the end, try to align Duvalier with Communism in the vain hope that the United States would support their efforts to overthrow the tyrant.

Among the dead Central Committee members were Adrien and Daniel Sansaricq, whose entire family had been massacred in Jérémie on Duvalier's orders in 1964. Adrien studied medicine in Mexico, and went to Cuba to work. He accompanied Che Guevara to Africa on his Congo episode. Gérald Brisson, thirty-two, had been converted into a legend long before his death. An anti-Duvalierist youth, he was on the point of being executed and buried when his father bought his freedom. In exile, he and his wife attended Lumumba University in Moscow, and returned clandestinely to Haiti to fight. He wrote an economic study of Haiti's need for a real agrarian reform. It was the New-York-based Coalition Haitienne that first alerted Haiti and its government to the return of this Communist.

The Communists gave Haiti its first bank hold-up, made lightning attacks on isolated army posts, and liquidated a number of small Tonton Macoute chieftains. If they had continued their terrorist attacks, and not involved themselves in a village uprising, they might have lasted until Duvalier died of natural causes. Then they might have written a new page in Haitian history.

Those New York exiles, who continued to play on America's Communist phobia, declared that Fidel Castro had armed Haitian cane cutters who were prepared to invade Haiti. But this was a belated obituary from those exiles to the dead Haitian PUCH members. They were admitting at last that Duvalier had indeed liquidated the Communists. The Communist death toll had been given as 204 activists and cadres killed in the spring

1969 bloodbath. The Communists also confess that years of carefully built infrastructural work had collapsed. Their verbose, clandestine press dried up.

While Duvalier was successful in warding off the Communists, exiles and internal plotters, the strain of living and working in his big white fortress, the national palace, was taking its toll: his health deteriorated. The absolute master of all Haiti and Haitians, cooped up in his office and adjoining bedroom, dressed most of the time in dressing gown and slippers, shuffled back and forth the few steps from bed to office and family table, with one leg giving him more and more trouble because of the bad state of the blood vessels. Thirty years of diabetes began to tell.

Then on 8 May, ten years after his first coronary occlusion, Duvalier suffered a second heart attack. Marie-Denise quietly assumed the reins of power, and issued orders like a true Mama Doc.

The news of Papa Doc's illness soon spread (although, as usual, it was never confirmed officially), and a group led by exiled Lieutenant-Colonel René Léon tried to deliver the *coup de grâce* to his weak heart by dropping giant molotov cocktails on the palace from an aircraft. But this raid on Port-au-Prince on 4 June caused only panic, and, according to a government communiqué, the death of three persons. Of the six 55-gallon drums of gasoline that were tumbled out of the belly of a four-engined Lockheed Constellation, only one exploded. No damage was inflicted on the palace, although the raid drew the usual response from Duvalier: he informed the United States that Cuba was bombing him.

But a real tonic for Papa Doc's skipping heart was the visit of Governor Rockefeller on his fact-finding tour. Duvalier had made it known that he was encouraged by the election of Richard Nixon. In his telegram of congratulations he expressly wished that Nixon would follow in the path of his 'illustrious predecessor, Dwight Eisenhower ...'

When Rockefeller's mission arrived in Haiti on 1 July, it had run into a series of anti-American demonstrations that turned it into a circus. Three countries, Peru, Chile, and Venezuela, even declined to accept the visit. Upon Rockefeller's arrival in Port-au-Prince, Duvalier added more colour to the circus. The Haitian masses, who enjoy playing the clown, were ordered out into the streets with masks of happiness to welcome the visitor, whose presence, some hinted, meant money in the bank for Haiti.

Duvalier, recovering from his heart attack, refused to see anyone or show himself, protesting that he was busy working on the Rockefeller tour. With a touch of his old genius, Duvalier made it a personal triumph. He outmanoeuvred the governor with admirable finesse.

The governor, smiling at the happy, hospitable crowd, climbed the palace steps to Duvalier's second-floor office over a brand-new red carpet. First the governor and dictator exchanged a few words in French. Then Rockefeller handed Duvalier a letter from President Nixon. Papa Doc sat at his desk in a relaxed manner, read the letter, and smiled. He rose feebly, as one might expect from a man recovering from a heart attack, and asked Rockefeller to join him on the balcony of his office, a few feet away. To Rockefeller, it apparently seemed almost a request for physical assistance. Outside on the palace lawn and street, the usual carnival crowd waited. Newsmen estimated it at 35,000.

Rockefeller joined Papa Doc, and, arm in arm and smiling, the two of them stood on the little balcony, and waved to the crowd. To the Haitians below, Papa Doc was confirming he was alive and well. To his enemies and for worldwide consumption, the photo of President Nixon's envoy holding his arm, and joining him in waving to the people carried an even more important message: they were bosom buddies. Duvalier could not have staged it more masterfully for propaganda effect had he written the script.

Nothing Rockefeller did on the entire controversial mission drew more criticism internationally. Back in Washington, a few months later, Rockefeller testified about his tour before a congressional subcommitte. US Representative Jonathan Bingham, a Democrat also from New York, told Rockefeller it was 'most unfortunate' that he had been photographed 'in a very happy pose with Duvalier ... a dictator of the worst sort.' Rockefeller: 'What would you say if he says "Will you step out on the balcony?"' Bingham: 'If I had presence of mind, I would not have waved and smiled.' Rockefeller: 'There were 300,000 people out front. If you're a politician, your natural instinct is to respond.'

Whatever the crowd, whether it was as high as the governor said or as low as the newsmen estimated, and the extenuating circumstances, Duvalier had his way. Rockefeller recommended aid be resumed to Haiti.

When sixty-one-year-old Clinton E. Knox, a Negro, arrived in late 1969 to replace Claude G. Ross as the US Ambassador, there was fresh evidence that Duvalier had been able to draw the United States closer. Knox had good credentials, including a Ph.D. from Harvard (1939). He was a career foreign service officer, born in Massachusetts, and had served in European posts from 1945 to 1963. After a brief stretch in Honduras, he had been named ambassador to Dahomey in 1964, his last post before coming to Haiti.

The trickle of US aid, cut to a minimum the past seven years, soon began to grow. Because public opinion in the United States might erupt against open resumption of aid, it was ladled out in small, quiet doses that did not attract attention. One of the first examples was financial aid out of the Ambassador's 'special fund' that went for fifty small-impact projects.

Ambassador Knox said he felt the US's 'cool and correct' attitude towards Haiti was a mistake. Later, he expanded that to state that American policy had been discriminatory towards a small, black country, and he openly advocated resumption of aid. Papa Doc liked the man.

Duvalier's complaint that his government was ostracized because of its blackness rather than its repression was an old theme he repeatedly drummed out to visitors and newcomers. He could upbraid the world on matters of conscience. But had the lament come from anyone else, it might have been effective. From Duvalier it was recognized not as a plea for the mass of the Haitian people, whom he preserved in a state of misery, but for the deification of Papa Doc. The Black world knew this and did not respond. It did not seek new liabilities. Yet Ambassador Knox listened, and in a very short time was echoing many of the hollow themes.

Duvalier, he repeatedly told newsmen, had lifted the blackman up while chastising the mulatto elite. Nothing was further from the truth. A roll call of Duvalier's casualties shows clearly that the blackman was his number one victim.

'... The traditional oligarchy, in the person of its members who had not fled before the storm, or who have returned to the country after it, kept, and even consolidated, the essential of its economic power as a class which remained untouched, and [it also kept] its social command, in exchange for the acceptance of being kept away from positions of political leadership, held now by the new "consumer style bourgeois",' writes Leslie Manigat.

During Duvalier's reign, Port-au-Prince had grown from a city of 200,000 to over half a million. It has always been the last refuge of the peasant chased from his lands by misery and disease. Under the 'country doctor', tuberculosis had become endemic in many areas of rural Haiti, and the peasant migration to Port-au-Prince became more pronounced. La Saline, the largest of Port-au-Prince's slums, spreading its misery in the port area, was levelled because, besides being an eyesore, it was politically unsafe for the government, offering an unexpugnable hideaway to popular leaders of the opposition. The inhabitants moved a couple of miles away to rebuild their tin and cardboard town. With the desperate humour which is the only means of surviving misery, they called this new slum Brooklyn, after that Eldorado in the United States where hundreds of thousands of Haitians have migrated during the past decade of Duvalier's rule.

'Our revolution has given rise to all sorts of hopes for the rural and urban masses as well as the middle classes,' Duvalier solemnly announced to poor Haiti in his annual Ancestors' Day speech on 2 January 1970. 'I want to continue to organize the revolution. The great awakening is continuing and is accompanied by the will for change and development.'

He was still peddling hope, though he also made note of reality. 'I have noted with satisfaction the awareness and the determination of the Haitian people to survive amid conditions that are totally different and contrary to those that bring development,' he stated.

The same month, two youthful and determined opponents of Papa Doc, Fred and Reneld Baptiste, after nearly five years of travelling in Europe and Africa, crossed into Haiti once again with five companions to set up a guerrilla nucleus. The Baptiste brothers, the persistent guerrilla fighters of 1963–4 and combatants on the Constitutionalist side during the Dominican Civil War, had returned clandestinely to Santo Domingo (Fred was jailed and released). With an odd assortment of arms borrowed from Maximiliano Gomez, the Dominican rebel, the group crossed into their old familiar guerrilla ground only to be captured near the village of Thiotte where Duvalier's troops, alerted to their coming by the Dominican government, were waiting. During the engagement one was killed on each side, and the captured were taken off to imprisonment.[1]

The Baptiste guerrillas of 1964 were the inspiration for the guerrillas in Graham Greene's *The Comedians*. Reneld, the younger brother, later in Dahomey where the movie version of the book was made, played the part of a Tonton Macoute in the film. Ambassador Clinton Knox then represented his country in Dahomey and offered a reception for the cast.

Early in April 1970, Duvalier heard whispers of a new plot against him. An investigation followed that implicated, at least by Papa Doc's standards of evidence, a number of prominent Duvalierists, including army Colonel Kesner Blain, Quartermaster. A spate of rumours followed, and uncertainty ruled the Duvalierist camp.

On the night of 23 April, Duvalier called the commander of the Coast Guard, Colonel Octave Cayard. He asked the Colonel to bring several of his Coast Guard officers to the Dessalines barracks the next morning for questioning. A friend in the palace warned Cayard not to go.

1. The Baptiste were reliably reported to be alive in Fort Dimanche after the death of Papa Doc.

Cayard, forty-eight, had been for three years (1960–63) the commander of the Dessalines Battalion, the Marine-trained tactical force. The events of 1963, in particular the brutal killing of accused conspirator Colonel Charles Turnier, convinced him that he would prefer a quieter life, away from the palace. He asked for the Coast Guard command, which would put his headquarters at Bizoton, away from the political mainstream. Since then he had tried to stay out of politics, and lived quietly, applying off-hours to his poultry farm and cattle ranch.

Cayard refused to appear at the barracks. Instead, he and 118 other members of the Coast Guard (out of 325) took over Haiti's entire navy – the three patrol ships *Dessalines, La Crête à Pierrot,* and the *Vertières*. They pulled out into the bay, and radioed an ultimatum for Duvalier to surrender his government.

When there was no response, Cayard and his men levelled the ships' three-inch guns on the palace and fired. All told, some fifty shells struck the palace and around it, but there was no heavy damage. The second floor of the west wing was hit at a time when Duvalier was on the first floor. The government reported two killed and thirty-four injured.

A Haitian Air Force P-51 strafed the ships, and gun batteries were set up along the shore to repel possible landing parties, but none of these stopped the rebellion. The ships simply ran low on fuel, and had to quit. Cayard broadcast an appeal to the free world for supplies, particularly fuel, and got no response. On 25 April, the ships moved out of the harbour, and made their way towards the American naval base at Guantánamo Bay, Cuba, seeking aid.

The US Navy stripped their guns, and referred them to its Roosevelt Roads Base in Puerto Rico. The *Dessalines* made it under its own power, but the other two, barely seaworthy, had to be towed in. All but one of the coastguardsmen chose asylum in the United States, and the ships, after repair, were returned to Duvalier, who rechristened them La Marine Haïtienne. The Haitian who chose to return to Port-au-Prince was Lt Fritz Tippenhauer, member of a wealthy elite family.

Duvalier went on the radio on 26 April, while the rebel ships were still at sea, to tell Haitians of his latest victory. 'Our great social revolution, the undefeatable forces of 22 September 1957, are triumphing and will always triumph over any conspiracy and any obstacle,' he said. 'The nation continues, under my leadership, on the ascending march of the great infrastructural works of the second decade of ethnology, and will continue to be able to race disaster.... Always follow the star of the chief of the revolution, and have full confidence in his destiny. He was chosen by the gods to fulfil a great task. His strong arm will never give way.'

Papa Doc once again moved against his real and suspected enemies. Among those arrested were seven congressmen, including Colonel Caynard's brother, Volvic, and Léonce Bordes, a prominent business supporter of President Estimé, and later a Duvalierist. Bordes died of a heart attack in prison, but because of his ties, he was accorded a public funeral.

Again, Duvalier slipped noticeably after a crisis. His 'strong arm' did begin to give way. His body simply could not keep pace with the demands of his mind. Age and the pressure of being constantly on the alert against conspiracies, as well as the periodic frontal assaults, were taking their toll. Playing out the script of Machiavelli's *The Prince* was an energy-consuming role. On 12 November he suffered a mild stroke due to the thorough deterioration of his vascular system.

Marie-Denise and Ambassador Max Dominique were in France at the time, and they rushed home with three medical specialists. But not until Armed Forces Day, 18 November, did the seriousness of Papa Doc's state of health become apparent.

On that day, the 300-pound Buddhaesque Jean-Claude, nineteen, took his father's place on the reviewing stand before the troops. The sight of the huge, moon-faced boy playing Papa Doc highly amused Haitians in the days that followed. But Jean-Claude went through his first official duties with cool aloofness, not unlike the parade ground mummy-like stance his father affected. When he retired to the palace after decorating members of the Armed Forces, he bestowed medals on the foreign specialists attending his father. This was the first time in thirteen years anyone had been permitted to stand in for the dictator.

But the doctors' prognosis was not encouraging. Papa Doc, the family was told, could last two to five years, or he could die any time. He could prolong his life by quitting the national palace, and taking a rest away from the rigours of power. This Papa Doc could not do. For thirteen years, he had been a prisoner of the palace. It was his power base, and he had, time and again, told the world he would leave it only 'to the roar of the cannon' when life had left him.

It was the tall, brooding Madame Duvalier who forced Papa Doc's hand into providing for a successor, something his custom-made 1964 constitution made no provision for. It was no easy matter for Papa Doc to admit he was mortal, especially to poor Haitians to whom he had so often declared himself immortal and an immaterial being, striking chords of fear, and causing them to hold him in awe.

Madame Duvalier arranged for *Le Nouveau Monde* to disclose in its 23 November edition that Jean-Claude, their only son, who had had no time to make enemies, would be the successor of his father. The front-page editorial, discussing the future of Duvalierism, stated: 'It is in this *optique* that the Hon. President Duvalier chose his son Jean-Claude for the continuity of his task of repair. Thus, he insisted that the projection of the future be around this youth, and in all the manifestations of national life.' This edition with the premature disclosure was recalled, but the astounding message was now public.

To give the transfer of power a semblance of legality in the eyes of the world, and introduce the new Caesar to Haitians, the window-dressing machinery was wound up.

First the Armed Forces command was restructured, with Colonel Claude Raymond, forty, a graduate of Mexico's tough Military Academy, brought back to the palace to replace General Gérard Constant. Raymond, a godson of Papa Doc, and a distant relative, had held the command of the Presidential Guard during the early crisis-racked days of the dictatorship. He had at that time also commanded the militia. Upon Raymond's shoulders were placed a general's star, and the responsibility of seeing that Jean-Claude became the eighth president for life of Haiti.

In his annual Ancestors' Day message on 2 January 1971, Duvalier revealed that his inner circle of power had been wrought by some spectacular in-fighting over the succession. Because of Duvalier's divide-and-rule technique, there was not one Duvalierist who could command the loyalty of the whole clique except Jean-Claude.

> ... The time has come to clear up a certain confusion which has marked our political life at the end of last year. During my few days of illness, capitalizing upon my delegation of some authority to my son Jean-Claude, a thousand plans seem to have been hatched by politicians hoping for a government crisis and a vacancy of the presidential chair. Like angry ants, those who profess to be my friends – as for my enemies we all know what they are dreaming of – ran all over the place in search of a plank of salvation to assure them a cosy position. However, for almost six years, I have ceaselessly repeated that when the time came I would hand the government over to the youth ...

This was news even to high-ranking Duvalierists.
He continued:

> If we want to assure the survival of our revolution, blow new vigour into it, it is towards Haitian youth we must turn.... We all know that Caesar Augustus was nineteen when he took into his hands Rome's destinies, and that his reign remains 'the century of Augustus' ...

Papa Doc and his speech writers reached back into Roman times to justify the choice of his nineteen-year-old son as successor. There was nothing like it in Haitian history.

On 13 January Deputy Luckner Cambronne, son of an Arcahaie Justice of the Peace turned preacher, who had returned to favour after a period of disgrace, set the machinery in motion to give the succession of power 'legality'. In a stirring speech to the rubber-stamp congress, he called for the necessary constitutional amendments to name Jean-Claude the next president for life with: 'The revolution will pursue its course, for Duvalier will be succeeded by Duvalier.' Twelve other laudatory speeches followed, and the amendments were passed by acclamation. The official gazette, *Le Moniteur*, on 22 January, carried the amendments, which included lowering the age for the presidency from forty to eighteen.

The 30 January letter of acceptance that carried Jean-Claude's signature touched a truthful note: 'I believe I understand that you want the nation to avoid fratricidal fights, mortal for the future of the country.... I believe I also understand that you want to assure the perennity of the revolution, giving it time – such a precious factor – to anchor itself in the conscience of the people.'

Papa Doc, in recognizing he was mortal despite all his past rhetoric to the contrary, took care of the most minute details to ensure the peaceful transition of power, cheating his opponents to the last. By settling his son in the palace as his successor, he intended to deprive opponents, and even some followers, of that great moment they awaited – when a power vacuum would bring about a struggle that would surely upset the fourteen-year-old dictatorship.

A farcical national referendum, pure papadocracy, was held on 31 January. The ballot simply said Jean-Claude had been chosen to succeed his father, and carried two questions, plus the answer:

> Does this choice answer your aspirations?
> Do you ratify it?
> Answer: Yes.

By official count published in Port-au-Prince newspapers, the vote was 2,391,916 in favour, and not a single Haitian opposed.

But this pantomime referendum was important for Papa Doc to seal Jean-Claude's future in the eyes of the world, and in keeping with international commitments, as 'eighth president for life of Haiti'.

A campaign to glorify the boy heir of the presidency for life was launched with a giant poster showing a feeble, white-headed Papa Doc standing behind his seated son. One hand rested on his enormous shoulder. (It was a replica of another poster that appeared in the early 1960s with Jesus Christ standing in the same position but with a hand on Papa Doc's shoulder.) The caption read: 'I have chosen him.'

Whenever Jean-Claude appeared, it seemed that the buttons on his expensive suits were about to fly off from the pressure of his enormous torso.

The prospects of being ruled by a boy dictator did not seem to perturb most Haitians. Deep down they felt Jean-Claude would never get to govern them. They dismissed him as stupid, a dull student with little chance to get to power. 'He has as much political depth as an oil slick', 'he is stupid', were a sample of some of the remarks from businessmen. But when Duvalier died, these same members of the business community, fearful of the unknown, were very happy to have been bequeathed a boy figurehead leader, no matter what.

As is customary, a thousand jokes and tales grew up around the new leader. Some depicted him as mentally retarded, fat, preoccupied by food, girls, and fast cars. The government, to the contrary, described him as a serious boy, a genius, expert in judo and karate, and a crack rifle shot. The truth lies somewhere between the two. Jean-Claude is a youth of average intelligence, spoilt by having grown up the only son of a megalomaniac dictator who catered to his every whim. He had a special love for fast cars which provided an ideal means of escape from the national palace, where he lived cooped up for most of the fourteen years of his father's reign. He had recently become a first-year law student at the Port-au-Prince faculty, and his loyalty to his friends had gained him some admirers in the student body.

Sister Marie-Denise had arranged his only trip abroad, a summer in Europe, and for her and her husband Max he had a discernible fondness. As he was to be the family figurehead dictator, he appeared prepared to take instructions from Marie-Denise and his mother.

Haitian masses take French leave of their misery during carnival time in February with clairin (raw rum) and revelry to achieve release of body and soul. Carnival 1971 was especially merry because of the free rum and the money handed out for praise to 'Jean-Claude, the successor designated for life'. A thousand dollars was the offer to the best *méringue* composed in Jean-Claude's praise. The dusty streets of Port-au-Prince exploded into snake-dancing by thousands of sweaty bodies and sandalled feet. They sang lusty *méringues* to the accompaniment of little jazz bands of tambours and trumpets, and a generalized unleashing of the pelvis.

In early March, news that Papa Doc's condition was critical caused a new wave of concern among those, particularly the old elite and the new political establishment, who over the years had learned to adjust to Duvalier and prosper personally by his rule. What, asked the mulatto elite, if Papa Doc died? If there were a new government, would they not again have the painful task of going through the adjustment to power? The elite, even some who were old-time Déjoists, preferred the safety of Duvalierism, where they already had burrowed out the treasure and privilege that traditionally had been theirs. For the poor Haitian, it did not matter. He too still had his traditional position, and it amounted to bondage.

The business upturn in the last couple of Duvalier years strengthened both the influence and the degree of this concern. The flow of tourists was better than ever. The American ambassador was calling for renewed aid, and it had been announced that a new US Agency for International Development (AID) man was on the way. He arrived on 15 April, eight years to the month after the AID mission had left Haiti. The Péligre dam hydroelectric project was becoming a reality at last. The Inter-American Development Bank had loaned another $5.1 million to improve the capital's water system, and the International Monetary Fund approved a new stand-by credit. The cheap, abundant labour supply (paid about seventy cents a day) had lured a series of small assembly plants employing mostly women. They imported components, assembled them, and shipped the product back to the United States for sale. They made such items as shoes, baseballs, brassieres, etc.... Canadians had revamped the telephone company, and made it work.

The list did not end there, either. Mike McLaney, an American famed for his work in the gambling casinos of pre-Castro Cuba, took over and revived the National Casino. The United States was still issuing some 7,000 visas a year, but to get one a Haitian had to go through one of the government-authorized tourist agencies, which charged up to $500. Haitians who had fled abroad for economic reasons during the past fourteen years numbered hundreds of thousands, and were now a major source of foreign exchange for the country. It is estimated that their annual remittance to Haiti amounts to 14 million dollars.

Duvalier, who had entered the 1957 electoral campaign as a Nationalist, made his last actions, like his first, anti-national. No matter how corrupt they were, few Haitians, presidents or politicians, would hand over any part of Haitian soil to foreigners. Duvalier had no such sentiment. Time and again he offered foreign leases on large tracts of land for their exploitation. His last such act was to lease La Tortue island to a group of Americans for ninety-nine years. This group intends to turn La Tortue into another Freeport (Bahamas), with tourist resorts, gambling, and freedom from taxes and customs duties. La Tortue, lying off the north coast, was the first base from which Saint Domingue was settled.

Mexico, worried about her image, decided to do away for good with the divorce mills on the border at such towns as Ciudad Juarez. Duvalier, who was unconcerned about his country's image, and in the end more interested in the cash it would bring in, authorized a new divorce law that made 'quickie divorces' possible in Port-au-Prince. Cambronne, a gambler, also operated a new tourist agency, 'Ibo Tours', and it was to Ibo Tours that direct benefit from the new divorce law went. A percentage of the judicial profits were authorized for the defence fund. Before Duvalier was laid to rest in a small mausoleum in the national cemetery, there was talk among Duvalierist politician-cum-businessmen of a new export. Plans were put forth for the sale of unclaimed cadavers from the Haitian morgues to American hospitals and medical schools.

When Papa Doc failed to appear, as advertised by *Le Nouveau Monde*, for his 14 April birthday celebration, the seriousness of his illness dawned on Haitians. Many suspected he had been playing sick to ferret out new enemies. Despite continual denials by palace spokesman Gérard de Catalogne, they now knew he was ill and dying.

Marie-Denise was ruling in her father's stead, and was continually by his sick bed with Haitian doctors Alix Théard, Gérard Désir and Fritz Médard.

On Wednesday, 21 April, Duvalier had told them he was feeling much better, and his family gathered around him for dinner. At 8.15 p.m. he lifted a forkful of meat to his mouth and collapsed. The doctors were called in, and upon arrival pronounced him dead of a myocardial infarctus.

Madame Duvalier had the names of Jean-Claude's first cabinet. The first move was to swear Jean-Claude in as president for life, leaving no vacuum. American ambassador Clinton Knox was sent for, and shown the body. He presented his condolences to the family, and asked the new president what he could do to help. This act reinstated the American Embassy to its pre-Duvalier dominance in Haitian politics, which meant the Embassy would be once again consulted on important domestic issues. The Duvaliers requested that Knox ask his government to set up a watch over the Haitian coast to prevent any attempted landing by exiles. While the subject for alarm supposedly was traffic from Cuba, any exiles with plans – wherever they came from – were also effectively cut off.

At the funeral, on 24 April, Knox wore a Duvalier and Jean-Claude lapel button, and in subsequent press conferences he left no doubts as to where his sympathies lay – with the Duvalier family.

Jean-Claude was installed on 22 April as his father's successor. It appeared that Duvalier had controlled his death so that his son would assume the presidency on his favourite 22. The boy dictator promised his subjects in his first speech that the Duvalierist 'revolution' would be continued by him with 'the same fierce energy and intransigence'.

Haitians who had been held in awe by Duvalier and some of his almost supernatural doings could not comprehend that he had actually died.

Wearing spectacles, he lay in state in a refrigerated casket on 23 April. A gold cross rested on a pillow near his left ear, and, propped against his left side, was a copy of his book *Memoirs of a Third World Leader*. Before the bier stood an honour guard of twenty-two soldiers and twenty-two militiamen.

The following day, 24 April, the funeral service began at 8.30 a.m., and lasted six hours, punctuated by 101 rounds of cannon fire and the tolling of church bells. Duvalier had promised in 1963, during the April crisis, that he would leave the palace only to be laid to rest to the thundering of cannon fire.

Haitian singer Guy Durosier sang his composition 'François, we thank you for loving us. Your star will be shining in the night.' The service was piped to the crowd outside. Among the family, only the two yougest daughters, Nicole and Simone, along with Madame Duvalier showed signs of weeping. Jean-Claude, wearing his father's stolidness, masked his feelings from all from a high-backed wooden chair.

When Papa Doc finally left the palace for the last time, a strong gust of wind raised a column of dust on the nearby Champ de Mars. Humble Haitians watching found it eerily significant. To them, this was the sign that the spirit was leaving the casket to stand by Jean-Claude, and guide him in the National Palace, which he did not leave for the burial. In Haiti, where the cult of the dead is very much alive, it also means that the humble Haitians, reduced almost to a zombie state by Duvalier, will need time to overcome their fear of him.

There were two instances of panic during the funeral which came close to touching off the chaos Haitians all feared so much. So high was the tension that for no apparent reason, people, militiamen, and children dived for shelter, even into culverts, to escape. But the expected blow up did not come.

In a statement to the foreign press that had converged on Haiti to cover Papa Doc's death, Jean-Claude pronounced an amnesty for all exiles 'except Communists and trouble makers', which in effect barred all political exiles from returning. One exile who replied to the hollow invitation was ex-Father Jean-Claude Bajeux, teaching at the University of Puerto Rico. Bajeux wrote to Jean-Claude requesting permission to return and give a Christian burial to his mother, who in 1964, at the age of sixty and ill, had been arrested along with two sons and two daughters. He asked the same for all the exiles: the right to return and give Christian burials to their loved ones buried in unknown graves under Duvalier. There was no reply. But not only was the regime against the return of political exiles; they did not want the 'economic' exiles back either, because of the 14 million dollars in hard currency they channelled into Haiti yearly.

Deputy Luckner Cambronne, in the powerful position of Minister of Interior, National Defence and Police, took an early lead as one of the prop men in the post-Papa Doc regime. In response to a question about liberalizing the government, Cambronne barked at reporters 'There has been no change. President Duvalier's mission was to allow the black people to raise up their faces to the sun. That was the aim of his revolution, and we will continue his path. We are Duvalierists.' In a later interview he noted 'Duvalier left no money, no sound economy, but he left us something – his revolution. We believe in it, and we are willing to defend it with our lives and the lives of our families.'

Cambronne declared that a new 509-man elite unit to be known as 'The Leopards' was to be established immediately. Their job would be to protect the new president and fight 'Communism'.

The United States had decided the perpetuation of the tyranny would not in any manner affect American interests. While Ambassador Knox openly promoted a continuation of Duvalierism and American financial assistance, the American government applied the same rationale to the situation as it had applied in the days following the assassination of Dictator Rafael Trujillo in the neighbouring Dominican Republic, with disastrous results. Then, in 1961, President Kennedy summed up the situation, and found three possibilities: a decent democratic government; continuation of Trujillism; or Castro Communism. Now in Haiti, it gave up the first as impossible, and held to the second because it feared the third.

While the bogeyman of Communism was no longer present

in Haiti, Duvalier had managed to bait the United States in his last interview with Ambassador Knox, on 4 March. He told Knox that he feared an invasion from Cuba by trained Haitian cane cutters. It was a bogus story that helped justify the immediate post-Papa Doc embargo on the movement of exiles throughout the world.

With Duvalier's death, the first really united exile movement was born. Called 'Résistance Haïtienne', it grouped together as a united opposition exiles whose activities had been remarkable only in the amount of dissension they created among themselves and their chauvinistic action groups. It was the climax of two years of hard work, and despite the growing odds against them, they declared their intention to continue the war against the Duvalier clan in Haiti.

As many of the old political props fell neatly back into place, with Papa Doc, the epitome of one-man rule, laid to rest, Haitians pondered how long it would be before the traditional cannibalistic palace politics devoured the many-headed ruling family.

Index

Breinigsville, PA USA
12 January 2010

230617BV00001B/3/P

9 781558 76290